Humphrey Prideaux

The Old and New Testament Connected, in History if the Jews and

Neigbouring Nations

Part 1, Vol. 1

Humphrey Prideaux

The Old and New Testament Connected, in History if the Jews and Neigbouring Nations
Part 1, Vol. 1

ISBN/EAN: 9783744733625

Printed in Europe, USA, Canada, Australia, Japan

Cover: Foto ©Lupo / pixelio.de

More available books at **www.hansebooks.com**

THE
OLD AND NEW TESTAMENT
CONNECTED,

IN

THE HISTORY

OF

THE JEWS AND NEIGHBOURING NATIONS,

FROM

The Declenſion of the Kingdoms of Iſrael *and* Judah, *to the Time of* CHRIST.

BY HUMPHREY PRIDEAUX, D.D.
DEAN OF NORWICH.

PART I. VOL. I.

𝕰𝖉𝖎𝖓𝖇𝖚𝖗𝖌𝖍:

PRINTED BY D. SCHAW AND CO. LAWN-MARKET:
FOR JAMES AND ANDREW DUNCAN,
BOOKSELLERS, GLASGOW.

1799.

TO THE RIGHT HONOURABLE

DANIEL,

EARL OF NOTTINGHAM,

PRESIDENT OF HIS MAJESTY'S MOST HONOURABLE PRIVY COUNCIL.

My Lord,

IT being by your recommendation to your noble father, that I was by him made prebendary of the cathedral church of Norwich, while he was Lord Chancellor of England, and it being also by your Lordship's like favourable recommendation of me to her late Majesty Queen Anne, that I was promoted to be dean of the same church, I humbly offer unto your Lordship this product of my studies, in a grateful acknowledgement of the favours I have received from you. And, if the Public receive any benefit from it (as I hope some may), nothing is more just and reasonable, than that they should receive it through your Lordship's hands, who, in having been so much a patron to the author, have acquired thereby the best title to all the fruits of my labours.

labours. What I now offer unto
ſhip is only the firſt part of what
If God gives life, the ſecond ſhall
beg its paſſage into the world und
patronage. The only additional
now capable of receiving, is you
kind acceptance of this expreſſion
titude; which I humbly pray from
and I am,

My Lord,

Your moſt obedient, and

Moſt obliged humble

Humphrey

THE PREFACE.

THE calamitous distemper of the stone, and the unfortunate management I fell under, after being cut for it, having driven me out of the pulpit, in wholly disabling me for that duty of my profession, that I might not be altogether useless, I undertook this work, hoping, that the clearing of the sacred history by the profane, the connecting of the Old Testament with the New, by an account of the times intervening, and the explaining of the prophecies that were fulfilled in them, might be of great use to many. What is now published is only the first part of my design. If God gives life, the other will soon after follow; but if it should please him, who is the Disposer of all things, that it happen otherwise, yet this history being brought down to the times, when the canon of the Hebrew scriptures was finished, it may of itself be reckoned a complete work: for it may serve as an epilogue to the Old Testament, in the same manner, as what after is to follow, will be a prologue to the New.

Chronology and geography being necessary helps to history, and good chronological tables being most useful for the one, as good maps are for the other; I have taken full care of the former, not only by adding such tables in the conclusion of the work, as may answer this end, but also by digesting the whole into the form of annals under the years before Christ, and the years of the kings that then reigned over Judea; both which are added in the margin at the beginning of every year, in which the actions happened that are related. And as to the latter, since Dr Wells, Cellarius, and Reland have sufficiently provided for it, both by good maps of the countries this history relates to, and also by accurate descriptions of them, I need do no more than refer the reader to what they have already done in this matter. What Dr Wells hath done herein, being written in English, will best serve the English reader; but they that are also skilled in the Latin tongue may moreover consult the other two.

In the annals, I have made use of no other æra, but that of the years before Christ, reckoning it backward from the vulgar æra of Christ's incarnation, and not from the true time of it. For learned men are not all agreed in the fixing of the true time of Christ's incarnation, some placing it two years, and some four years, before the vulgar æra. But where the vulgar æra begins, all know that use it; and therefore the reckoning of the years before Christ backward from thence, makes it a fixed and certain æra. The difference that is between the true year of our Saviour's incarnation, and that of the vulgar æra of it, proceeded from hence, that it was not till the 527th year of that æra, that it was first brought into use. [*] Dionysius Exiguus, a Scythian by birth, and then a Roman abbot, was the first author of it; and Beda our countryman, taking it from him, used it in all his writings; and the recommendation which he gave it thereby, hath made it of common use among Christians ever since, especially in these western parts. Had all Christians calculated their time by it from the beginning of the church of Christ (as it could be wished they had), there could then have been no mistake in it. But it being 527 years after Christ's incarnation, before this æra of it was ever used, no wonder, that, after so great a distance of time, a mistake was made in the fixing of the first year of it.

The æra from the creation of the world is of very common use in chronology; but this I have rejected, because of the uncertainty of it, most chronologers following different opinions herein, some reckoning the time of the creation sooner, and some later, and scarce any two agreeing in the same year for it.

The Julian period is indeed a certain measure of time, but its certainty depends upon a reckoning backward, in the same manner as that of the æra before Christ. For it being a period of 7980 Julian years, made out of the three cycles of the sun, moon, and indiction, multiplied into each other; and the first year of it being that in which all these three cycles begin together, this first year can be no otherwise fixed, than by computing backward from the present numbers of those cycles through all the different combinations of them, till we come to that year, in which the first year of every one of them meet together; which carries up the reckoning several hundred years before the creation, and fixeth the beginning of the period in an imaginary point of time before time was. And therefore, although from that beginning it computes downward, yet the whole of its certainty is by a backward reckoning from the present years of those cycles: for, according as they are, all must be reckoned upward even to the beginning of the period. So that, although in appearance it reckons downward, yet in reality it is only a backward computation, to tell us how many years since any thing was done from the present year. For in the numbers of the three cycles of the present year, it hath a real and fixed foundation for an upward reckoning, and so in any other year, in which the said numbers are known; whereas it hath none at all for a downward reckoning, but what is in the imagination only. And therefore, this being the true and real use of the Julian period, the æra before Christ for the times I treat of, serves all the purposes of chronology altogether as well, if not much better. For, adding the years before Christ, to those since Christ, according to the vulgar

---

[*] See Scaliger, Calvisius, and other Chronologers, in those parts of their works, where they write of the vulgar æra of Christ. And see also Du Pin's History of Ecclesiastical writers, cent. 6. p. 42. and Dr Cave's Historia Literaria, p. 405.

gar æra, it immediately tells us, how many years since any action before the time of Christ was done, and the Julian period can do no more; and indeed it cannot do thus much but by reduction, whereas it is done the other way directly, immediately, and at first sight. However, in the tables I have put the Julian period, and have reduced to it not only the years before Christ, but also the years of the princes reigning in Judea, and the neighbouring countries, and all things else that are treated of in this History; and hereby the Synchronisms, or coincident times and transactions of other nations may easily be known.

The year I compute by in the annals is the Julian year, which begins from the first of January; and to this I reduce all the actions I treat of, though they were originally reckoned by other forms. The [a] Greeks, before the time of Meto, began their year from the winter solstice, and after from that of the summer. The Egyptians, Chaldeans, and ancient Persians, reckoned the first of the month Thoth to be always the first day of their year, which, consisting of 365 days, without a leap year [b], it begun every fourth year one day sooner than it did before; and so, in the space of 1460 years, its beginning was carried backward through the whole solar year. The Syrians and the Phoenicians begun their year from the autumnal equinox; and so did also the Hebrews, till their coming up out of the land of Egypt. But that happening in the month of Nisan, in commemoration of this deliverance, they afterwards begun their year from [c] the beginning of that month, which usually happened about the time of the vernal equinox: and this form they ever after made use of in the calculating of the times of their fasts and festivals, and all other ecclesiastical times and concerns; but, in all civil matters, as contracts, obligations, and such other affairs, which were of a secular nature, they still made use of the old form, and begun their year as formerly, from the first of Tisri, which happened about the time of the autumnal equinox: and from hence they began [d] all their jubilees and sabbatical years, and all other their computations of civil matters, as they still do the years of the creation of the world, and the years of their æra of contracts; which are the only epochas they now compute past times by. Anciently [e] the form of the year which they made use of was wholly inartificial: for it was not settled by any astronomical rules or calculations, but was made up of lunar months set out by the phasis or appearance of the moon. When they saw the new moon, then they began their months, which sometimes consisted of

a 2   29 days,

---

[a] *Vide Scaligerum, Petavium, aliosque chronologos, in eis locis ubi de anno Græcorum agunt.*

[b] So it was in the time of the last Darius; but afterwards the Persians compensated for the loss of the leap year, by adding an intercalary month of 30 days every 13th year.

[c] Exod. xii. 2.

[d] Levit. xxv. 9. 10.

[e] Talmud in Tract. Rosh Hasshanah, Maimonides in Kiddush Hachodesh, Selden de Anno Civili veterum Judæorum.

29 days, and sometimes of 30, according as the new moon did sooner or later appear. The reason of this was, because the synodical course of the moon (that is, from new moon to new moon) being 29 days and an half, the half day, which a month of 29 days fell short of, was made up by adding it to the next month, which made it consist of 30 days; so that their months consisted of 29 days and 30 days alternatively. None of them had fewer than 29 days, and therefore they never looked for the new moon before the night following the 29th day; and, if they then saw it, the next day was the first day of the following month. Neither had any of their months more than 30 days, and therefore they never looked for the new moon after the night following the thirtieth day; but then, if they saw it not, they concluded, that the appearance was obstructed by the clouds, and made the next day the first of the following month, without expecting any longer; and of twelve of these months their common year consisted. But twelve lunar months falling eleven days short of a solar year, every one of those common years began eleven days sooner than the former; which, in thirty-three years time, would carry back the beginning of the year through all the four seasons to the same point again, and get a whole year from the solar reckoning (as is now done in Turkey, where this sort of year is in use); for the remedying of which, their usage was sometimes in the third year, and sometimes in the second, to cast in another month, and make their year then consist of thirteen months; whereby they constantly reduced their lunar year, as far as such an intercalation could effect it, to that of the sun, and never suffered the one, for any more than a month, at any time to vary from the other. And this they were forced to do for the sake of their festivals: for their feast of the passover (the first day of which [a] was always fixed to the middle of their month Nisan) being to be celebrated by their eating of the Paschal lamb, and the offering up of the wave-sheaf, as the first fruits of their barley harvest; and their feast of Pentecost, which was [b] kept the fiftieth day after the sixteenth of Nisan (which was the day in which the wave-sheaf was offered) being to be celebrated by the offering of the two wave-loaves, as the first fruits of their [c] wheat-harvest; and their feast of tabernacles, which was always begun [d] on the fifteenth of Tisri, being fixed to the time [e] of their ingathering of all the fruits of the earth: the passover could not be observed, till the lambs were grown fit to be eaten, and the barley fit to be reaped; nor the Pentecost, till the wheat was ripe; nor the feast of tabernacles, till the ingatherings of the vineyard and oliveyard were over: and therefore these festivals being fixed to these set seasons of the year, the

the making of the intercalation above mentioned was neceſſary, for the keeping them within a month ſooner or later always to them. Their rule for the doing of this was; [a] whenever, according to the courſe of the common year, the fifteenth day of Niſan (which was the firſt day of unleavened bread, and the firſt day of their Paſchal ſolemnity) happened to fall before the day of their vernal equinox, then they intercalated a month, and the Paſchal ſolemnity was thereby carried on a month farther into the year, and all the other feſtivals with it: for, according as the Paſchal feſtival was fixed, ſo were all the reſt; that is, the Pentecoſt fifty days after the ſecond day of the Paſchal feaſt (*i. e.* the 16th of Niſan), on which the wave-ſheaf was offered; and the feaſt of tabernacles ſix months after the beginning of the ſaid Paſchal feaſt. For as the firſt day of the Paſchal feaſt was the fifteenth of Niſan (the fourteenth, on the evening of which the ſolemnity began in the ſlaying of the Paſchal lambs, being but the eve of the paſſover), ſo the firſt day of the feaſt of tabernacles was on the 15th of Tiſri, juſt ſix months after. To make this the more clear, let it be obſerved, that the Hebrew months were as followeth, 1. Niſan, 2. Iyar, 3. Sivan, 4. Tamuz, 5. Ab, 6. Elul, 7. Tiſri, 8. Marcheſvan, 9. Ciſleu, 10. Tebeth, 11. Shebat, 12. Adar. And theſe twelve made their common year: but in their intercalated years there was another month added after Adar, which they called Veadar, or the ſecond Adar; and then their year conſiſted of 13 months. Suppoſing, therefore, their vernal equinox ſhould have been on the 10th of March (whereabout now it is), and that the 15th of Niſan, the firſt day of their paſſover, ſhould, in the common courſe of their year, happen to fall on the 9th of March, the day before the equinox; then, on their foreſeeing of this, they intercalated a month, and after their Adar added their Veadar, which ſometimes conſiſted of 29 days, and ſometimes of 30, according as it happened; at preſent we will ſuppoſe it to be of 30 days, and then the firſt of Niſan, which is to begin this year, inſtead of being on the 23d of February (as otherwiſe it would), muſt be carried on 30 days forward to the 25th of March, and their paſſover to the 8th of April following. But the next year after beginning eleven days ſooner, for the reaſon I have mentioned, the 1ſt of Niſan muſt then have happened on the 14th of March, and the firſt day of the paſſover on the 28th of the ſame month; and, the next year after that, the firſt of Niſan, muſt for the ſame reaſon have happened on the 3d of March, and the firſt day of the paſſover on the 17th of March; and, the next year after that, according to this calculation, the 1ſt of Niſan would have happened on the 20th of February, and the firſt day of the paſſover on the 6th of March following. But this being before the equinox, another intercalation of the month Veadar muſt have been made. And ſo after the ſame manner it went through all other years; whereby it came to paſs, that the firſt of Niſan, which was the

---

[a] Talmud in Roſh Haſhanah. Maimonides in Kidduſh Ha.Hod.ſh. Selden de Anno Civili veterum Judæorum.

the beginning of their year, always was within 15 days before, or 15 days after the vernal equinox, that is, within the compass of 30 days in the whole, sooner or later; and according as that was fixed, so were fixed also the beginnings of all their other months, and all the fasts and feasts observed in them. But this inartificial way of forming their months and years, was in use among them only while they lived in their own land, and there might easily receive notice of what was ordained in this matter by those who had the care and ordering of it: for when they became dispersed through all nations, they were forced to make use of cycles and astronomical calculations for the fixing of their new moons and intercalations, and the times of their feasts, fasts, and other observances, that so they might be every where uniform herein. The first cycle they made use of for this purpose [a] was that of 84 years: by this they fixed their Paschal feast, and by that their whole year besides; and the use hereof the primitive Christians borrowed from them, and, for some of the first centuries, fixed their Easter in every year according to it: but this, after some time, being found to be faulty, Meto's cycle of 19 years [b] was, after the council of Nice, brought into use by them for this purpose instead of the other; and the Jews, following their example herein, almost about the same time, came into the same usage also; and upon this cycle is founded the present form of their year. The first who began to work it into this shape, [c] was Rabbi Samuel, rector of the Jewish school at Sora in Mesopotamia: Rabbi Adda, who was a great astronomer, pursued his scheme; and after him Rabbi Hillel, about the year of our Lord 360, brought it to that perfection in which now it is; and being Nasi, or prince of their sanhedrim, he gave it the authority of his sanction, and by virtue thereof it hath ever since been observed by them, and they say always is to be observed to the coming of the Messiah. According to this form [d] there are, within the compass of the said 19 years cycle, seven intercalated years, consisting of 13 months, and 12 common years, consisting of 12 months. Their intercalated years are the 3d, the 6th, the 8th, the 11th, the 14th, the 17th, and the 19th of that cycle; and when one round of this cycle is over, they begin another; and so constantly, according to it, fix their new moons (at which all their months begin) and all their fasts and feasts in every year. And this form of their year, it must be acknowledged, is very exactly and astronomically contrived, and may truly be reckoned the greatest piece of art and ingenuity that is to be found among that people. They who would throughly understand it, may read Maimonides's tract Kiddush

---

[a] Vide Bucherium de antiquo Paschali Judæorum Cyclo.

[b] *Epistola Ambrosii* 83. *ad episcopos per Æmiliam constitutos.* It was by the council of Nice referred to the church of Alexandria every year to fix the time of Easter, and they did it by Meto's cycle of 19 years.

[c] Juchasin; Shalsheleth Haccabala; & Zemach David, & ex iisdem Morinus in exercitat. Prima in Pentateuchum Samaritanum, cap. 3.

[d] Talmud in Rosh Hashanah. Maimonides in Kiddush Hachodesh, & Seldenus de Anno Civili veterum Judæorum.

dush Hachodesh, which hath been published in a very good Latin translation by Lewis de Veil, under the title, De Consecratione Calendarum, where he will find it very exactly and perspicuously described.

These having been the forms of the Jewish year, that is, the inartificial form used by the ancients in the land of Canaan, and the artificial and astronomical form now in use among the moderns throughout all their dispersions; according to neither of them can the days of the Jewish months be fixed to any certain days of the months in the Julian year: for, in both of them, the months being lunar, and the intercalations made of one whole lunar month at once, the days of those months, to the full extent of one full lunar month, fell sometimes sooner, and sometimes later in the solar form. Since the Jewish kalendar hath been fixed by Rabbi Hillel, upon the certain foundations of astronomy, tables may indeed be made, which may point out to what day in that kalendar every day in the Julian year shall answer: but this cannot be done for the time before; because, while they went inartificially to work in this matter by the phasis and appearance of the moon, both for the beginning of their months and years, and the making of their intercalations, they did not always do it exactly; but often varied from the astronomical truth herein. And this latter having been their way through all the times of which this History treats, we cannot, when we find the day of any Jewish month mentioned either in the scriptures, or in Josephus, reduce it exactly to its time in the Julian year, or there fix it any nearer, than within the compass of a month sooner or later. Kepler indeed holds, that the Jewish year was a solar year, consisting of 12 months of 30 days each, and an addition of five days after the last of them; and our countrymen Archbishop Usher, and Mr Lydiat, two of the most eminent chronologers that any age hath produced, go into the same opinion. Such a year, I acknowledge, was in use among the Chaldeans, from whom Abraham was descended; and also among the Egyptians, with whom the Israelites long lived: and I doubt not, but that, before their coming out of the land of Egypt, they also reckoned their time by the same form. For the time of the flood is manifestly computed by it [a] in the book of Genesis, an hundred and fifty days being there made equal to five months, which proves those months to have been thirty-day months. But that the Israelites made use of this sort of year, after their coming out of Egypt, can never be made consisting with the Mosaical law. According to that, their year must be made up of months purely lunar, and could no otherwise, than by an intercalary month, be reduced to the solar form: and there being a necessity of making this intercalation for the keeping of their festivals to their proper seasons, by this means it comes to pass, that the beginnings of their months cannot be fixed to any certain day in the Julian kalendar, but they fell always within the compass of 30 days sooner or later therein. That the thing may appear

[a] Chap. vii. 11. compared with chap. viii. 3. 4.

appear the clearer to the reader, I shall express it in this following scheme, wherein the first column gives the names of the Jewish months, and the second of the Julian months, within the compass of which the said Jewish months set over against them have always sooner or later their beginning and ending; and this is the nearest view that can be given of the correspondency of the one with the other.

1 Nisan	{ March / April.	5 Ab	{ July / August.	9 Cisleu	{ November. / December.
2 Jair	{ April / May.	6 Elul	{ August / September.	10 Tebeth	{ December. / January.
3 Sivan	{ May / June.	7 Tizri	{ September / October.	11 Shebat	{ January / February.
4 Tamuz	{ June / July.	8 Merchesvan	{ October / November.	12 Adar	{ February / March.

The 13th month called Veadar, or the second Adar, answered most the end of our March, it being then only intercalated, or cast in, when the beginning of Nisan would otherwise be carried back into the end of February.

I have, in the series of this History, taken no notice either of the jubilees, or the sabbatical years of the Jews, both because of the uselessness, and also of the uncertainty of them. They are useless, because they help not to the explaining of any thing, either in the holy scriptures, or the histories of the times which I treat of; and they are uncertain, because it doth not appear when or how they were observed. It is acknowledged by most learned men, that the jubilees were no more regarded after the Babylonish captivity: and it is manifest from scripture, that the sabbatical years were wholly neglected for many ages before it. For the desolation, which happened to the country of Judea, under that captivity, is said, in the second book of Chronicles (chap. xxxvi. 21.), to have been brought upon it for this very reason, that the land might enjoy its sabbaths, that is, those sabbatical years of rest, which the Jews, in neglecting the law of God concerning this matter, had deprived it of: and therefore, if we reckon to this desolation only the 52 years, that were from the destruction of the city and temple of Jerusalem, to the end of the Babylonish captivity (in which the land was wholly desolated), this will prove the observing of those sabbatical years to have been neglected for 364 years before that captivity. But, if we add hereto the other 18 years of that captivity, in which it was only in part desolated, and take in the whole 70 years of it into this reckoning, it will then carry up the time of this neglect much higher, even to 490 years before that captivity: and, as to the jubilees, there is no mention made of them any where through the whole scriptures, saving only in that law where they are enjoined; neither is there of their sabbatical years, saving only in the same law, and the place in Chronicles above mentioned. There are indeed two other places of scripture which some understand concerning them (that is, 2 Kings xix. 29. and Jeremiah xxxiv.

xxxiv. 8—10.) But both thefe paffages do better admit of other interpretations: for what is faid in the former of thefe, feems rather to refer to the defolations of the war, and the interruption of agriculture through the violences and calamity of it, than to a fabbatical year; and fo Grotius and other learned men underftand it. And what is faid in the other by Jeremiah, about the releafe of fervants, doth not infer a fabbatical year, nor a jubilee neither: for every Hebrew fervant [a] was to be releafed in the 7th year of his fervitude, though it were neither a jubilee, nor a fabbatical year; and therefore this inftance infers neither of them: and thofe who undertake to interpret the law which enjoins thefe jubilees and fabbatical years, very much differ concerning them, both as to the time and manner of their obfervance. Some will have the reckoning, both of the fabbatical years and the jubilees, to commence from the firft entering of the Ifraelites into the land of Canaan; and therefore place the firft fabbatical year in the 7th year after that entrance, and the firft jubilee alfo according hereto: but others fay, that the land was feven years in conquering and dividing, and that the 8th year was the firft in which the Ifraelites began to fow and reap in it; and that therefore the 14th year was the firft fabbatical year: and according to this reckoning they put the firft fabbatical year, and the firft jubilee, feven years later than the former, and fo the numbers of all the reft that follow. And then, as to the time of the jubilee, there is this difpute, whether it be the fame with the feventh fabbatical year, or the next year after. The reafon of this difpute is, becaufe if it be on the year after the 7th fabbatical year, then there will be two fabbatical years together, (for the year of jubilee was alfo [b] a fabbatical year); and in this cafe there would be the lofs of two crops together; and then it will be afked, how could the people be fupported? And they who, notwithftanding this objection, determine for the year next after the 7th fabbatical year to have been the year of jubilee, though [c] they have the fcripture on their fide in this particular, yet are not agreed where to begin the next week of years (or Shemittah, as the Jews call it) after that 7th fabbatical year; that is, whether the year of jubilee, or the next year after it, was to be the firft year of that week or Shemittah. If the jubilee year were the firft year of that week, then there would have been but five years for them to fow and reap in between the jubilee (which was alfo a fabbatical year) and the next fabbatical year after; whereas [d] the fcripture faith they were to have fix. And if the firft year of the next Shemittah were the next year after the jubilee, then the Shemittahs would not always fucceed in an exact feries immediately one after the other; but after the 7th Shemittah, the year of jubilee would intervene between that and the next; which difagreeth with the opinion of many. However, it is indeed the truth of the matter, and I know no objection

[a] Exodus xxi. 2.
[b] Levit. xxv. 11.
[c] Levit. xxv. 10.
[d] Levit. xxv. 3.

jection against it, but that it exposeth the error of those, who, thinking that the sabbatical years did always happen each exactly on the 7th year after the former, have in that order and series placed them in their chronological computations, without considering, that after every 49th year a jubilee year did intervene between the Shemittah that then ended, and the beginning of the next that followed. But they act most out of way in this matter, who would confine Daniel's prophecy of the 70 weeks to so many Shemittahs, as if these 70 weeks fell in exactly with 70 Shemittahs, that is, that the first week began with the first year of a Shemittah or sabbatical week, and ended with a sabbatical year, which was the last of a Shemittah; and so all the rest down to the last of the whole number: and to this end some have perplexed themselves in vain to find out sabbatical years to suit their hypotheses, and fix them to times to which they did never belong; whereas the prophecy means no more, than by the 70 weeks to express 70 times 7 years, that is, 490 in the whole, without any relation had either to Shemittahs or sabbatical years. And were it otherwise, the 70 weeks of Daniel, besides the 70 Shemittahs, must have contained 9 years more for the 9 jubilees, which must have happened within the compass of the said 70 Shemittahs, and thereby make the whole number of those weeks to be 499 years; which no one that I know of hath ever yet said. And therefore, since there is nothing certain to be known concerning these sabbatical years and jubilees of the Jews, as to their ancient observance of them, and consequently there can be no use made of them, for the explication either of scripture or history, I have not troubled the reader with them in the body of this History; and I wish I have not troubled him too far in saying so much of them here in the Preface.

In the series of this History, having often endeavoured to reduce the sums of money mentioned therein to the value they would bear with us in this present age, whether gold or silver, I think it requisite to lay down the rules whereby I make this reduction. It is to be observed, therefore, in order hereto, that, among the ancients, the way of reckoning their money was by talents. So the Hebrews, so the Babylonians, so the Greeks, and so the Romans, did reckon; and of these talents they had subdivisions, which were usually into minas and drachms, *i. e.* of their talents into minas, and of their minas into drachms. The Hebrews had, besides these, their shekels and half shekels, or bekas, and the Romans their denarii; which last were very near of the same value with the drachms of the Greeks. What was the value of an Hebrew talent appears from Exodus xxxviii. 25, 26.; for there 603,550 persons being taxed at an half shekel an head, they must have paid in the whole 301,775 shekels; and that sum is there said to amount to 100 talents, and 1775 shekels over: if, therefore, you deduct the 1775 shekels from the number 301,775, and divide the remaining sum, *i. e.* 300,000, by 100, this will prove each of those talents to contain 3000 shekels. Each of these shekels
weighed

weighed about three shillings of our money, and 60 of them, [a] Ezekiel tells us, made a mina, and therefore 50 of those minas made a talent. And as to their drachms, it appears, by the gospel of St Matthew, that it was the fourth part of a shekel, that is, nine pence of our money: for there (chap. xvii. 24.) the tribute money annually paid to the temple by every Jew (which was [b] half a shekel) is called Διδραχμον, (i. e. the two drachm piece); and therefore, if an half shekel contained two drachms, a drachm must have been the quarter part of a shekel, and every shekel must have contained four of them: and so Josephus tells us it did; for he [c] saith, that a shekel contained four Attic drachms; which is not exactly to be understood according to the weight, but according to the valuation in the currency of common payments: for, according to the weight, the heaviest Attic drachms did not exceed eight pence farthing half farthing of our money, and an Hebrew drachm, as I have said, was nine pence; but what the Attic drachm fell short of the Hebrew in weight might be made up in the fineness, and its ready currency in all countries (which last the Hebrew drachm could not have), and so might be made equivalent in common estimation among the Jews. Allowing, therefore, a drachm, as well Attic as Jewish, as valued in Judea, to be equivalent to nine pence of our money, a beka, or half shekel, will be equal to one shilling and six pence, a shekel three shillings, a mina nine pounds, and a talent 450 pounds. So was it in the time of Moses and Ezekiel, and so was it the same, in the time of Josephus, among that people; for [d] he tells us, that an Hebrew mina contained two litras and an half, which comes exactly to nine pounds of our money; for a litra, being the same with a Roman libra, contained 12 ounces Troy weight, that is, 96 drachms, and therefore two litras and an half must contain 240 drachms, which being estimated at nine pence a drachm, according to the Jewish valuation, comes exactly to 60 shekels, or nine pounds of our money. And this account exactly agrees with that of Alexandria; for [e] the Alexandrian talent contained 12,000 Attic drachms, and 12,000 Attic drachms, according to the Jewish valuation, being 12,000 of our nine pences, they amount to 450 pounds of Sterling money, which is the same value with the Mosaic talent. But here it is to be observed, that, though the Alexandrian talent amounted to 12,000 Attic drachms, yet they themselves reckoned it but at 6000 drachms, because every Alexandrian drachm contained [f] two Attic drachms; and therefore, the Septuagint version being made by the Alexandrian Jews, they there render the Hebrew word shekel by the Greek Διδραχμον, which signifieth two drachms; because two Alexandrian drachms make a shekel, two of them amounting to as much as four

Attic

---

[a] Chap. xlv. 12. [b] Talmud in Shekalim. [c] Antiq. lib. 3 c. 9.
[d] Joseph. Antiq. lib 14. cap. 12.
[e] Festus Pompeius, Dionysius Halicarnasseus etiam dicit, talentum Alexandrinum continere 125 libras Romanas; libræ autem Romanæ 125 continent drachmas Atticas 12,000.
[f] Varro æstimat drachmas Alexandrinas duplo superasse Atticasve Tyriasve.

Attic drachms; and therefore, computing the Alexandrian money according to the same method in which we have computed the Jewish, it will be as followeth: one drachm of Alexandria will be of our money eighteen pence; one didrachm, or shekel, consisting of two drachms of Alexandria, or four of Attica, will be three shillings; one mina, consisting of 60 didrachms, or shekels, will be nine pounds; and one talent, consisting of 50 minas, will be 450 pounds, which is the talent of [a] Moses, and so also it is the talent of [b] Josephus; for he tells us, that an Hebrew talent contained an hundred Greek (i. e. Attic) minas; for those 50 minas, which here make an Alexandrian talent, would be 100 Attic minas in the like method of valuation, the Alexandrian talent containing double as much as the Attic talent, both in the whole, and also in all its parts, in whatsoever method both shall be equally distributed. Among the Greeks, the established rule was, [c] that 100 drachms made a mina, and 60 minas a talent; but, in some different states, their drachms being different, accordingly their minas and talents were within the same proportion different also. But the money of Attica was the standard by which all the rest were valued, according as they more or less differed from it; and therefore, it being of most note, wherever any Greek historian speaks of talents, minas, or drachms, if they be simply mentioned, it is always to be understood of talents, minas, or drachms, of Attica, and never of the talents, minas, or drachms, of any other place, unless it be expressed. Mr Brerewood, going by the goldsmiths weights, [d] reckons an Attic drachm to be the same with a dram now in use in their shops, that is, the eighth part of an ounce; and therefore lays it at the value of seven pence halfpenny of our money, or the eighth part of a crown, which is, or ought to be, an ounce weight. But Dr Bernard, going more accurately to work, [e] lays the middle sort of Attic drachms at eight pence farthing of our money, and the minas or talents accordingly in the proportions above mentioned. The Babylonian talent, according to [f] Pollux, contained 7000 of those drachms. The Roman talent [g] contained 72 Italic minas, which were the same with the Roman libras; and 96 Roman denariuses, each being of the value of seven pence halfpenny of our money, made a Roman libra. But all the valuations I have hitherto mentioned must be understood only of silver money, and not of gold; for that was much higher. The proportion of gold to silver was among the ancients most commonly as ten to one; sometimes it was raised to be as eleven to one, and sometimes as twelve, and sometimes as thirteen to one. In the time of King Edward I. it was here in England at the value of

ten

---

[a] Exod. xxxviii. 25. 26.
[b] Antiq. lib. 3. c. 7.
[c] Julii Pollucis Onomasticon, lib. 10. c. 6.
[d] In libro de Ponderibus et Pretiis Veterum Nummorum.
[e] In libro de Mensuris et Ponderibus Antiquis.
[f] Lib. 10. c 6. p. 437.
[g] Festus Pompeius.

ten to one; but it is now gotten at sixteen to one, and so I value it in all the reductions which I make in this History of ancient sums to the present value. But, to make the whole of this matter the easier to the reader, I will lay all of it before him, for his clear view, in this following table of valuations.

Hebrew Money.

	£.	s.	d.
An Hebrew drachm	0	0	9
Two drachms made a beka, or half shekel, which was the tribute money paid by every Jew to the temple	0	1	6
Two bekas made a shekel	0	3	0
Sixty shekels made a mina	9	0	0
Fifty minas made a talent	450	0	0
A talent of gold, sixteen to one	7200	0	0

Attic Money, according to Mr Brerewood.

	£.	s.	d.
An Attic drachm	0	0	7½
An hundred drachms made a mina	3	2	6
Sixty minas made a talent	187	10	0
A talent of gold, sixteen to one	3000	0	0

Attic Money, according to Dr Bernard.

	£.	s.	d.
An Attic drachm	0	0	8¼
An hundred drachms made a mina	3	8	9
Sixty minas made a talent	276	5	0
A talent of gold, sixteen to one	3300	0	0

Babylonish Money, according to Mr Brerewood.

	£.	s.	d.
A Babylonish talent of silver, containing 7000 Attic drachms	218	15	0
A Babylonish talent in gold, sixteen to one	3500	0	0

Babylonish Money, according to Dr Bernard.

	£.	s.	d.
A Babylonish talent in silver	240	12	6
A Babylonish talent in gold, sixteen to one	3850	0	0

Alexandrian Money.

	£.	s.	d.
A drachm of Alexandria, containing two Attic drachms, as valued by the Jews	0	1	6
A didrachm of Alexandria, containing two Alexandrian drachms, which was an Hebrew shekel	0	3	0
Sixty didrachms, or Hebrew shekels, made a mina	9	0	0
Fifty minas made a talent	450	0	0
A talent of gold, sixteen to one	7200	0	0

Roman Money.

	£.	s.	d.
Four sestertiuses made a Roman denarius	0	0	7½
Ninety-six Roman denariuses made an Italic mina, which was the same with a Roman libra	3	0	0
Seventy-two Roman libras made a talent	216	0	0

If any desire a fuller account of the money of the ancients, he may read Mr Brerewood *De Ponderibus et Pretiis veterum Nummorum*, Bishop Cumberland of the Jewish Measures, Weights, and Monies, Dr Bernard *De Mensuris et Ponderibus Antiquis*, and others that have written of this argument. It sufficeth for my present purpose, that I here insert so much as may serve for a key to those passages in the ensuing History, where any sum of money, or any quantity of gold or silver, is mentioned.

So little mention having been made of Zoroastres by the western
writers,

writers, whether Greek or Latin, the reader may perchance be surprised to find so much said of him in this History, and his time placed so much later than is vulgarly reckoned. But, how sparingly soever the Greeks or Latins may have been in speaking of him, what hath been wanting in them hath been sufficiently supplied by the Persians and Arabs, who have given us large accounts of him, and have placed his time where truly it was, that is, in the time of Darius Hystaspes, king of Persia. Whatsoever we find written of him by the Arabs is taken from the Persians: for it was not till after the time of Mahomet that the Arabs had any literature among them; but the Persians had it long before: for we find in scripture [a], that the Persians had books and registers, in which all the actions of their kings, and the histories of their reigns, were carefully recorded; and Ctesias [b] tells us the same, and that it was out of those books and registers that he extracted his history, which he wrote of the Assyrian and Persian affairs [c], in 23 books; and Persia being the country which was the scene of all Zoroastres's doings, there it is that we may most likely expect the best account of him. And since he was there the founder and great patriarch of the religion which was received and reigned in that country, from the time of Darius Hystaspes to the death of Yazdejerd, for near 1150 years, and consequently was among them (as he still is among the remainder of that sect) in the same esteem and veneration that Mahomet is among the Mahometans, no wonder that much hath been said of him by their writers; and, if those writers have been as ancient as those of the Greeks and other nations, I know not why they should not have the same authority. I acknowledge many fabulous things have crept into their writings concerning him, as there have into the Roman legends of their saints, and for the same reason, that is, to create in vulgar minds the greater veneration for him. What I have out of the latter, I am beholden for to Dr Hyde's book, *De Religione veterum Persarum*, for I understand not the Persian language. All that could be gotten out of both these sorts of writers, concerning him or his religion, that carry with it any air of truth, is here carefully laid together; as also every thing else that is said of either of them, by the Greeks, or any other authentic writers: and, out of all this put together is made up that account which I have given of this famous impostor. And if the life of Mahomet, which I have formerly published, be compared herewith, it will appear hereby, how much of the way, which this latter impostor took for the propagating of his fraud, had been chalked out to him by the other. Both of them were very crafty knaves: but Zoroastres being a person of the greatest learning of his time, and the other so wholly ignorant of it, that he could neither write nor read, he was by much the more eminent of the two, though the other hath had the greater success in the propagation of his sect: the Magians scarce having

ever

[a] Ezra iv. 15. 19. v. 17. vi. 1. 2. Esther vi. 1.
[b] Apud Diodorum Siculum, lib. 2.
[c] Photius in Excerptis.

ever enlarged themselves beyond the present bounds of the kingdom of Persia, and some parts of Mesopotamia, Arabia, and India; whereas the Mahometans have overspread a great part of the world: for which they have been beholden to the prevailing power of two mighty empires erected by them, that is, that of the Saracens first, and next that of the Turks, who, having extended their conquests over many countries and kingdoms, have, by the power of the sword, subjugated the inhabitants to their religion, as well as to their empire.

To make this History the more clear, I have found it necessary to take in within its compass the affairs of all the other eastern nations, as well as those of the Jews, the latter not being throughly to be understood without the other: and, as far as the Grecian affairs have been complicated with those of Persia, Syria, or Egypt, I have been obliged to take notice of them also; and, without doing this, I could not lead the reader to so clear a view of the completion of those prophecies of the Old Testament which I have in the ensuing History explained: for how could the completion of the prophecy which we have of Xerxes, and his stirring up of all against the realm of Grecia (Daniel xi. 2.), be understood, without having an account of the war which he made against Grecia? Or how could the fulfilling of the prophecies which were delivered of Alexander, his swift victories, and his breaking by them the power of Persia (Dan. vii. 6. viii. 5. 6. 21. x. 20. and xi. 3. 4.) be brought into a clear light, without laying before the reader the whole series of those wars whereby it was effected! Or how could the verification of the prophecies concerning the four successors of Alexander, written by the same prophet (Dan. viii. 8. and xi. 4.) be fully evidenced, without giving a thorough narrative of all those transactions and wars, whereby it was brought to pass, that the empire of that great conqueror was at length divided among four of his chief commanders? The instance given in these particulars may serve to satisfy the reader as to all the rest.

To make all things the easier to the English reader, for whom I chiefly design this work, I have carefully avoided troubling him with any exotic words in the text; and, where I have been forced, in some places, to insert Hebrew words, I have chosen, for his sake, to do it in English letters. All things else, that may be above a mere English reader, I have referred to the notes and quotations at the bottom of the page; and in them I quote every thing in English, where the English reader can examine what I quote, and there only where he cannot are the references and quotations in any other language.

Several have in Latin written, by way of annals, of the times of which I treat, as Torniellus, Salianus, Capellus, and others. But, above all of this kind, are Archbishop Usher's Annals of the Old and New Testament, which is the exactest and most perfect work of chronology that hath been published; to which, I acknowledge, I have been much beholden; and, although I have not always concurred with him, yet I have, for the most part, especially in the or-

dering

dering and settling the years to which I refer the actions that are related: for I look on what he hath done before me herein to be the surest and safest clue I could conduct myself by, through all the intricate labyrinths of ancient times; and therefore I have generally followed him in the fixing of the years, excepting only where I saw very good reason to do otherwise. But, as to the other annalists I have mentioned, I have found it for the most part loss of time to consult them.

If I have been too large in my explication of the prophecy of Daniel's seventy weeks, or in the account which I have given of the Hebrew scriptures, or in any other discourse of like nature, occasionally intermixed in this work, the importance of the subject must be my excuse. For the chief design of this History, and my main end in writing it, being to clear the way to the better understanding of the holy scriptures, both of the Old and the New Testament, I have thought myself obliged, in the pursuit hereof, to handle every thing to the full, as it came in my way, that might any ways tend hereto. And if the reader receiveth any benefit from it, let him give God the praise, who hath enabled me, under a very calamitous and broken state of health, to finish this first part of my design, and still to go on with my studies, for the completing of the other.

NORWICH,
Aug. 1. 1715.

HUMPHREY PRIDEAUX.

[a] Diodorus Siculus, lib. 2. Athenæus, lib. 12. Herodotus, lib. 1. Justin. lib. 1. c. 3.

IN

THE HISTORY

OF

THE JEWS AND NEIGHBOURING NATIONS,

FROM

The Declenfion of the Kingdoms of ISRAEL *and* JUDAH,
to the Time of CHRIST.

BOOK I.

THE ancient empire of the Affyrians, which had governed Afia for above thirteen hundred years, being diffolved on the death of Sardanapalus, there Anno 747. arofe up [a] two empires in its ftead; the one founded by Arbaces, governor of Media, and the other by Belefis, governor of Babylon, who were the two principal commanders that headed the confpiracy, whereby the former empire was brought to an end; which they having, on their fuccefs, parted among themfelves, Belefis had Babylon, Chaldea, and Arabia, and Arbaces all the reft. This happened in the feventh year after the building of Rome, and in the fecond year of the eighth Olympiad, which was the feven hundred and forty-feventh year before Chrift, *i. e.* before the beginning of the vulgar æra, by which we now compute the years from his incarnation.

VOL. I.   A   Arbaces

[a] Diodorus Siculus, lib. 2. Athenæus, lib. 12. Herodotus, lib. 1. Juftin. lib. 1. c. 3.

Arbaces is in scripture called [a] Tiglath-Pilefer and [b] Thilgath-Pilnefer; in [c] Elian, Thilgamus; and by [d] Caftor, Ninus junior. He fixed his royal feat at Nineveh, the same place where the former Assyrian kings had their residence, and there he governed his new erected empire nineteen years.

Belefis is the same with Nabonassar, from the beginning of whose reign at Babylon commenceth the famous astronomical æra, from him called the æra of Nabonaffer. He is by [e] Nicolas Damascenus called Nanibrus, and in the [f] holy scripture Baladan, being the father of Merodac or Mordac-Empadus, who sent an embassy to King Hezekiah, to congratulate him on his recovery from his sickness; which will be hereafter spoken of.

And these two empires God was pleased to raise up to be his instruments in their turns to punish the iniquities of his own people; the first for the overthrowing of the kingdom of Israel, and the other for the overthrowing of the kingdom of Judah; as shall be shewn in the sequel of this history.

An. 742.
Ahaz 1.

In the sixth year of Tiglath-Pilefer [g], Ahaz began to reign over Judah; who being a very wicked and impious prince, God stirred up against him Rezin, king of Syria, and Pekah, king of Israel, who, confederating together, invaded his land with a great army, and, having harassed it all over, pent him up in Jerusalem, and there besieged him.

Their design was [h], on the taking of that city, to have wholly extirpated the house of David, and to have set up a new king over Judah, the son of Tabeal. Who this person was, is no where said in scripture; but he seemeth to have been some potent and factious Jew, who, having revolted from his master, the king of Judah, excited and stirred up this war against him, out of an ambitious aim of plucking him down from his throne, and reigning in his stead.

But it being the will of God only to punish Ahaz for his wickedness, and not the whole family of David, for which he had always, for the sake of David, expressed mercy and favour, he was pleased to prevent the mischief, by blasting the whole design; and therefore he sent the prophet Isaiah unto Ahaz, to encourage him valiantly to withstand the enemy in the defence of the city, and to assure him that they should not prevail against him; and for this he gave him two signs, the one to be accomplished speedily, and the other some ages after.

The

---

[a] 2 Kings xv. 29. & xxvi. 7. 16.
[b] 1 Chron. v. 6. 2 Chr. xxviii. 20.
[c] Hist. Animal. lib. 12. c. 21.
[d] Euseb. Chron. p. 46.
[e] In Eclogis Valesii, p. 426, &c.
[f] Isaiah xxxx. 1.
[g] 2 Kings xvi. 2 Chron. xxviii.
[h] Isaiah vii.

The firſt was, that the prophet ſhould take him a wife, who ſhould immediately on that marriage conceive a ſon, and that, before that ſon ſhould be of age to diſcern between good and evil, both theſe kings ſhould be cut off from the land; which accordingly came to paſs: For the prophet [a] immediately after taking a wife, before Maher-ſhalal-haſh-baz, the ſon born to him of that marriage, arrived at the age of diſcerning between good and evil, both theſe kings were ſlain; Rezin in the third year of Ahaz, and Pekah the next year after.

The other ſign was, that [b] a virgin ſhould conceive, and bear a ſon, who ſhould be called Emmanuel, that is, God with us, the Meſſias that was promiſed, God manifeſted in our nature, and for a while here dwelling with us to accompliſh the great work of our ſalvation. Which prophecy was then delivered to comfort and ſupport the drooping and deſponding ſpirits of the houſe of David; who ſeeing ſo great a force armed againſt them, and intending their deſtruction, were under terrible apprehenſions, as if their utter extirpation were then at hand. From which deſpair this prophecy fully relieved them, in aſſuring them, that their houſe ſhould ſtand, and continue, till this prediction ſhould be accompliſhed, and the Meſſias born of their race, in ſuch manner as was hereby foretold.

After this, the two kings, according to the words of the prophet, failing of their deſign, were forced to raiſe the ſiege, and return home, without prevailing in the enterpriſe which they had undertaken.

But [c] Ahaz, after this, inſtead of being reformed by the mercy, growing more wicked and perverſe than before, in abſolutely rejecting the God of Iſrael, and cleaving to the worſt abominations of the heathen nations round him, even to the making of his ſons paſs through the fire to Molech; the next year after; [d] God brought again upon him the ſame two confederated kings, from whom he had delivered him the former year, who, coming with forces better appointed, and councils better concerted than before, divided themſelves into three armies; the firſt under Rezin, king of Syria, the ſecond under Pekah, king of Iſrael, and the third under Zichri, a mighty man of Ephraim; and with theſe three armies, the more to diſtract him, they invaded him in three different parts of his kingdom at the ſame time. Rezin, in his ravage, having loaded his army with ſpoils, and taken a vaſt number of captives, returned with them to Damaſcus, thinking it his beſt

An. 741.
Ahaz 1.

---

[a] Iſaiah viii.
[b] Iſaiah vii. 14. Matth. i. 23.
[c] 2 Chron. xxviii. 2—5.
[d] 2 Kings xvi. 2 Chron. xxviii.

best interest there to secure what he had gotten. Pekah with his army marched directly against Ahaz, who had got together the main strength of his kingdom to oppose this invasion, and thereby for some time did put a stop to the progress of this part of the enemies forces; but at length, being encouraged by the departure of Rezin to give them battle, he was overthrown with a most terrible destruction, an hundred and twenty thousand of his men being slain in that day. Of which blow Zichri taking the advantage, led his forces to Jerusalem, and took the royal city, where he slew Maaseiah the king's son, and most of the chief governors and great men of the kingdom, whom he found there. And both these armies of Israel, on their return, carried with them vast spoils, and above two hundred thousand persons, whom they had taken captive, with intention to have sold them for bondmen and bondwomen. But a prophet from God having severely rebuked them for this their excessive cruelty against their brethren, whom God had delivered into their hands, the elders of the land, fearing the like wrath upon themselves for the punishment hereof, would not permit them to bring the captives to Samaria; whereon they were clothed, and relieved out of the spoils, and again sent back unto their own homes.

And the land was no sooner delivered from these enemies, but it was again invaded by others, who treated it with the same cruelty: For the Edomites and the Philistines, who next bordered on it, the former on the south, and the other on the west, seeing Judah brought thus low, took the advantage to seize on those parts which lay next unto them, and, by ravages and inroads, did all the mischief to the rest that lay in their power.

An. 740.
Ahaz 5.

But Ahaz, continuing still hardened in his iniquity, notwithstanding all this which he had suffered for the punishment of it, would not seek the Lord his God, or return unto him from his evil ways, but putting his confidence rather in man, pillaged the temple of all the gold and silver that was found therein, and sent it to Tiglath-Pileser, king of Assyria, to engage him to come to his assistance against his enemies, promising thereon to become his servant, and pay tribute unto him.

The king of Assyria, having an opportunity hereby offered unto him of adding Syria and Palestine to his empire, readily laid hold of the invitation, and marched with a great army into those parts; where, having slain Rezin in battle, he took Damascus, and reduced all that country under his dominion; and hereby he put an end to the kingdom of the Syrians in Damascus, after it had lasted there for ten generations, that is,

from

from the time of Rezon, the son of Eliadah, who first founded it, while Solomon was king over Israel.

After this, Tiglath-Pilefer [b] marched against Pekah, and seized all that belonged to Israel beyond Jordan, and also all the land of Galilee, and then went forward towards Jerusalem, but rather to get more money of Ahaz, than to afford him any real help; for he assisted him not for the recovery of any of those places which had been taken from him during the war, either by the Philistines, Edomites, or other enemies, but when he had got from him all that he could (for the raising of which Ahaz cut the vessels of the temple into pieces, and melted them down), he marched back to Damascus, and there wintered, without doing any thing more for him; so that, in reality, he was rather distressed, than any way helped by this alliance, the land being almost as much exhausted by the presents and subsidies, which were extorted from him by this his pretended friend and ally, as it was by the ravages and pillages of his open enemies. And, moreover, two lasting mischiefs followed hereon: For, 1*st*, Instead of two petty princes, whom he had afore for his neighbours, and with either of which he was well able to cope, he had now this mighty king for his borderer, against whom no power of the land was sufficient to make any resistance; and the ill effect hereof both Israel and Judah did afterwards sufficiently feel; for it became at length to both of them the cause of their destruction. 2*dly*, From this time the Jews were excluded all their traffic into the Southern sea, which had hitherto been one of the chiefest foundations of their riches.

This they had long carried on through the Red sea, and the straits of Babelmandel, not only to the coasts of Africa on the west, but also to those of Arabia, Persia, and India, on the east, and reaped a prodigious profit from it. King David was the first [c] who began it; for having [d] conquered the kingdom of Edom, and reduced it to be a province of his empire, he thereby became master of two sea-port towns on the Red sea, Elath and Esion-geber [e], which then belonged to that kingdom; and, seeing the advantage which might be made of the situation of these two places, he wisely took the benefit of it, and there begun this traffic. There are two places mentioned in scripture, to which it was from thence carried on, that is, Ophir and Tarshish. From the former of these David in his time drew great profit; for the three thousand talents of gold of Ophir, which he is said

(1 Chron.

[a] 1 Kings xi. 23—25.
[b] 2 Kings xvi. 2 Chron. xxviii.
[c] Eupolemus apud Euseb. Præp. Evang. lib. 9.
[d] 2 Sam. viii. 14. 1 Kings xi. 15. 16. 1 Chron. xviii. 13.
[e] 1 Kings ix. 26. 2 Chron. viii. 17.

(1 Chron. xxix. 4.) to have given to the houfe of God, feem to be of that gold of Ophir, which he himfelf had by his fleets in feveral voyages brought to him from thence: for what he had referved for this work out of the fpoils of war, the tributes of the conquered nations, and the public revenues of his kingdom, is before mentioned (c. xxiv. 14.) and amounted to [a] a prodigious fum. The three thoufand talents of the gold of Ophir, which he added, was over and above this, and *out of his own proper goods*, or private eftate, which he had befides what belonged to him as a king. And how he could increafe that fo far, as out of that only to be able to give fo great a fum, can fcarce any other way be accounted for, than by the great returns, which were made him from this traffic: for the gold alone amounted to [b] above one and twenty millions of our money, befides the feven thoufand talents of refined [c] filver, which were included in the fame gift. After David [d] Solomon carried on the fame traffic to Ophir, and had from thence in one voyage [e] four hundred and fifty talents of gold. And if Solomon got fo much in one voyage, well might David have gained the fum above mentioned, in the feveral voyages which were made thither for him, from the time that he had fubdued the land of Edom, to the time of his death, which was at leaft twenty-five years. But it muft be acknowledged, that Solomon much improved this trade, not only by his greater wifdom, but alfo by his great application to all the bufinefs of it. For, not being perplexed and incumbered with fuch wars, as his father David was, he had more leifure to attend thereto. And therefore, for the better fettling of it, he went [f] in perfon to Elath and Efiongeber, and there took care by his own infpection for the building of his fhips, the fortifying

---

[a] This fum is fo prodigious, as gives reafon to think that the talents, whereby that fum is reckoned were another fort of talents of a far lefs value than the Mofaic talents, of which an account is given in the Preface For what is faid to be given by David (1 Chron. xxii. 14—16. & xxix. 3—5.) and contributed by his princes (xxix. 6—8.) toward the building of the temple at Jerufalem, if valued by thefe talents, exceeded the value of eight hundred millions of our money, which was enough wherewith to have built all that temple of folid filver.

[b] For three thoufand Hebrew talents of gold, reduced to our money, amount to twenty-one millions and fix hundred thoufand pounds Sterling.

[c] 1 Chron. xxix. 4.

[d] 1 Kings ix. 26—28. & x. 11. 22. 2 Chron. viii. 17. 18. & x. 10—21.

[e] 2 Chron. viii. 18. The 450 talents here mentioned amount to three millions two hundred and forty thoufand pounds of our prefent Sterling money.

[f] 2 Chron. viii. 17.

tifying of both those ports, and the settling of every thing else, which might tend to the successful carrying on of this traffic, not only to Ophir, but to all other parts, where the sea, on which these ports lay, opened a passage. But his chiefest care was to plant those two towns with such inhabitants, as might be best able to serve him in this design. For which purpose he brought thither from the sea-coasts of Palestine as many as he could get of those who had been there used to the sea, especially of the Tyrians[a], whom his friend and ally Hiram, king of Tyre, from thence furnished him with in great numbers: and these were the most useful to him in this affair; for they being in those days, and for many ages after, the most skilful of all others in sea affairs, they were the best able to navigate his ships, and conduct his fleets, through long voyages. But the use of the compass not being then known, the way of navigation was in those times only by coasting, which often made a voyage to be of three years, which now may be finished almost in three months. However this trade succeeded so far, and grew to so high a pitch, under the wise management of Solomon, that thereby he drew to these two ports, and from thence to Jerusalem, all the trade of Africa, Arabia, Persia, and India, which was the chief fountain of those immense riches, which he acquired, and [b] whereby he exceeded all the kings of the earth in his time, as much as he did by his wisdom; so that [c] he made silver to be at Jerusalem, as the stones of the street, by reason of the great plenty with which it there abounded during his reign. After the division of the kingdom, Edom being of that part which remained to the house of David, they still continued to carry on this trade from [d] those two ports, especially from Esiongeber, which they chiefly made use of till the time of Jehosaphat. But he having there lost his fleet, which he had prepared to sail from thence to Ophir in partnership with Ahaziah, king of Israel, this spoiled the credit of that harbour. For there being nigh the mouth of it [e] a ridge of rocks, as this fleet was passing out of the port, they were by a sudden gust of wind, which God sent on purpose for the punishment of this confederacy, driven upon those rocks where [f] they were all broken to pieces and lost. And therefore, for the avoiding of the like mischief for the future, the

---

[a] 1 Kings ix. 27. 2 Chron. viii. 18. & ix. 10. 21.
[b] 1 Kings x. 23. 2 Chron. ix. 22.
[c] 1 Kings x. 27. 2 Chron. ix. 27.
[d] 1 Kings xxii. 48. 2 Chron. xx. 36.
[e] Because of these rocks it had the name of Esiongeber, which signified the back-bone of a man, for these rocks resembled it.
[f] 1 Kings xxii. 48. 2 Chron. xx. 36. 37.

the station of the king's ships was thenceforth removed to Elath, from whence Jehosaphat, the next year after, sent out another fleet for the same place. For whereas it is said, that he lost the first fleet for confederating with the idolatrous king of Israel, and we are told [a] in another place of his sending forth a fleet for Ophir, in which he would not permit Ahaziah to have any partnership with him. This plainly proves the sending out of two fleets by Jehosaphat, the first in partnership with Ahaziah, and the other without it. And thus this affair was carried on from the time of David till the death of Jehosaphat. For till then the land of Edom [b] was all in the hands of the kings of Judah, and was wholly governed by a deputy or viceroy there placed by them. But when Jehoram succeeded Jehosaphat, and God, for the punishment of the exceeding great wickedness of that prince had withdrawn his protection from him, Esau, according to the prophecy of Isaac [c] did break the yoke of Jacob from off his neck, after having served him (as foretold by that prophecy) for several generations, that is, from the time of David till then. For, on Jehoram's having revolted from God [d], the Edomites revolted from him, and having expelled his viceroy, chose them a king of their own, and under his conduct recovered their ancient liberty, and were not after that any more subject to the kings of Judah. And from this time the Jewish traffic through the Red sea had an interruption, till the reign of Uzziah. But he, in the very beginning of his reign, having [e] recovered Elath again to Judah, fortified it anew, and, having driven out the Edomites, planted it again with his own people, and there renewed their old traffic; which was from thence carried on and continued till the reign of Ahaz. But then Rezin, king of Damascus, having, in conjuction with Pekah, king of Israel, oppressed and weakened Judah to that degree which I have mentioned, he took the advantage of it to seize Elath, and, driving [f] out the Jews from thence, planted it with Syrians, purposing thereby to draw to himself the whole profit of that traffic of the Southern seas, which the kings of Judah had hitherto reaped, by having that port. But the next year after Tiglath-Pileser having conquered Rezin, and subdued the kingdom of Damascus, he seized with it Elath, as then belonging to his new conquest, and without having any regard to his friend and ally king Ahaz, or the just claim which he had thereto, kept it ever after, and thereby put an end to all that great profit, which the Jews till then had

reaped

---

[a] 1 Kings xxii. 49.
[b] 1 Kings xxii. 47.
[c] Gen. xxvii. 40.
[d] 2 Kings viii. 20, 22.
[e] 2 Kings xiv. 22. 2 Chron. xxvi. 2.
[f] 2 Kings xvi. 6.

reaped from this traffic, and transferred it to the Syrians, which became a great diminution of their wealth: for although they did not always carry it on with the same full gales of prosperity, as in the time of King Solomon, yet it was constantly, as long as they had it, of very great advantage to them; for it included all the trade of India, Persia, Africa, and Arabia, which was carried on through the Red sea. But, after Rezin had thus dispossessed them of it, they never had it any more restored to them, but were ever after wholly excluded from it. From thenceforth all the merchandise that came that way, instead of being brought to Jerusalem, was carried elsewhere; but at what place the Syrians fixed their principal mart for it, while it was in their hands, is no where said. But at length we find the whole of this trade ingrossed by the Tyrians, who, managing it from the same port, made it, by the way [a] of Rhinocorura (a sea-port town lying between the confines of Egypt and Palestine), center all at Tyre, and from thence they furnished all the western parts of the world with the wares of Persia, India, Africa, and Arabia, which thus by the way of the Red sea they traded to; and hereby they exceedingly enriched themselves during the Persian empire, under the favour and protection of whose kings they had they full possession of this trade. But when the Ptolemies prevailed in Egypt, they did, by building [b] Berenice, Myos-Hormos, and other ports on the Egyptian or western side of the Red sea (for Elath and Esiongeber lay on the eastern), and by sending forth fleets from thence to all those countries, to which the Tyrians traded from Elath, soon drew all this trade into that kingdom, and there fixed the chief mart of it at Alexandria [c], which was thereby made the greatest mart in the world, and there it continued for a great many ages after, and all the traffic, which the western parts of the world from that time had with Persia, India, Arabia, and the eastern coasts of Africa, was wholly carried on through the Red sea, and the mouth of the Nile, till a way was found [d], a little above two hundred years since, of sailing to those parts by the way of the Cape of Good Hope. After this, the Portuguese for some time managed this trade; but now it is in a manner wholly got into the hands of the English and Dutch. And this is a full account of the East India trade, from the time it was first begun by David and Solomon, to our present age.

But though it be by all agreed, that the trade to Ophir and Tarshish was the same that is now in the hands of our East India merchants, yet there are great disputes among learned men

in

[a] Strabo, lib. 16.
[b] Strabo, lib. 17.
[c] Strabo, lib. 17. p. 798.
[d] A. D. 1497.

in what parts of the eastern world these two places lay. Some will have Ophir to have been the island of Zocatora, which lies on the eastern coasts of Africa, a little without the straits of Babelmandel. Others will have it to be the island anciently called Taprobana, now Ceylon; and, for its being an island, they have the authority of Eupolemus (an ancient author quoted by Eusebius) on their side: for speaking of David, he saith of him [a], 'That he built ships at Elath, a city of Arabia, and from thence sent metal-men to the island of Urphe, or Ophir, situated in the Red sea, which was fruitful in yielding abundance of gold, and the metal-men brought it from thence to Judea.' But this being a question no way to be decided but from the scriptures, all that is to be observed from thence is, *1st*, That from Elath to Tarshish was a voyage [b] of three years, going and coming: but in what compass of time the voyage to Ophir was completed is not said; and that therefore Tarshish might be somewhere in the East Indies, but Ophir might be anywhere nearer home within the reach of those seas. *2dly*, That the commodities brought from Tarshish were [c] "gold, and silver, and ivory, and apes, and peacocks;" and those of Ophir [d] "were gold, and almug trees, and precious stones." And therefore any place in the Southern or great Indian sea, at the distance of a then three years voyage from Elath, which can best furnish the merchants with gold, silver, ivory, apes, and peacocks, may be guessed to be the Tarshish of the holy scriptures; and any place within the compass of the same Southern sea, that can best furnish them with gold, almug trees, and precious stones, and in that quantity of gold as Solomon brought home in one voyage, may be guessed to be the Ophir in the said holy scriptures mentioned. Only thus much I cannot forbear to say, that if the southern part of Arabia did furnish the world in those times [e] with the best gold, and in the greatest quantity, as good authors say, they that would have the Ophir of the holy scriptures to be there situated, seem, of all others, to have the best foundation for their conjecture. But more than conjecture no one can have in this matter.

But,

---

[a] Apud Euseb. Præp. Evang. lib. 9.
[b] 1 Kings x. 22. 2 Chron. ix. 21.
[c] 1 Kings x. 22.
[d] 1 Kings x. 11.
[e] Agatharcides, (p. 60. edit. Oxon.), tells us, that the Alileans and Cassandrins, in the southern parts of Arabia, had gold in that plenty among them, that they would give double the weight of gold for iron, triple its weight for brass, and ten times its weight for silver, and that, in digging the earth, they found it in gobbets of pure gold, which needed no refining, and that the least of them were as big as olive stones, but others much larger. No other author speaks of any other place in th world where it was ever found in the like plenty.

But, for the better underſtanding of what Eupolemus above
ſaith of Ophir, 'that it was an iſland in the Red ſea,' it is proper
here to take notice, that he doth not there mean the Arabian
gulf, which lieth between Arabia and Egypt, and is now commonly called the Red ſea; but [a] the great Southern ocean, which,
extending itſelf between India and Africa, waſheth up to the
coaſt of Arabia and Perſia, where it appearing of a reddiſh colour, by reaſon of the fierceneſs of the ſun-beams conſtantly
beating upon it in that hot climate, it was therefore called the
Red ſea; and this alone was that which was truly and properly
called ſo by the ancients: for the Arabian gulf, which hath now
obtained that name, was never for any ſuch redneſs of it ſo called; for neither the water (as ſome will have it) nor the ſand
(as others ſay) hath there any appearance of that colour, nor
was it ever by any of the eaſterns formerly ſo called. Throughout the whole ſcripture of the Old Teſtament [b] it is called Yam
Suph, that is, the Weedy Sea, by reaſon of the great quantity
of ſea-weed which is therein; and the ſame name it alſo hath
in the ancient Syriac verſion, as well as in the Targum or Chaldee paraphraſes. But, among the ancient inhabitants of the
countries adjoining, it was called Yam Edom, *i. e.* the Sea of
Edom: for the ſons of Edom having poſſeſſed all that country,
which, lying between the Red ſea and the lake of Sodom, was
by the Greeks called Arabia Petrea, they then named it, from
their father Edom, the land of Edom; and becauſe that which
we now call the Red ſea waſhed upon it, thence it was called
the ſea of Edom, or, in the dialect of the Greeks, the Edomean
or Idumean ſea, in the ſame manner as that which waſheth upon
Pamphylia was called the Pamphylian ſea, and that which waſheth upon Tyrrhenia the Tyrrhenian ſea, and ſo in abundance
of other inſtances. But the Greeks, who took this name from
the Phœnicians, finding it by them to be called Yam Edom,
inſtead of rendering it the ſea of Edom, or the Idumean ſea, as
they ought, miſtook the word Edom to be an appellative inſtead of a proper name; and therefore rendered it ἐρυθρὰ θάλασσα,
that is, the Red ſea; for Edom, in the language of that country ſignified red; and it is ſaid in ſcripture, that Eſau [c] having ſold his birth-right to his brother Jacob for a meſs of red
pottage, he was for that reaſon called Edom, that is, the Red.
And Strabo [d], Pliny [e], Mela [f], and others [g], ſay, that this ſea

was

---

[a] Dionyſii Periegeſis, v. 38. &
Comment. Euſtathii in eundem.
Strabo, lib. 16. p. 765. Agathemeri
Geographia, lib. 2. c. 11.
[b] See Exod. x. 19. xiii 18. &c.
[c] Gen. xxv. 30.

[d] Lib. 16. p. 766.
[e] Lib. 6. c. 23.
[f] Lib. 3. c. 8.
[g] Agatharcides, edit. Ox. p. 2.
Q. Curtius, lib. 8. c. 9. & lib. 10.
c. 1. Philoſtratus, lib. 3. c. 15. Ar-

was called so, not from any redness that was in it, but from a great king, called Erythrus, who reigned in the country adjoining upon it; which name Erythrus, signifying the same in Greek that Edom did in the Phœnician and Hebrew languages, that is, the red, this plainly proves, that the great king Erythrus could be none other than Edom, who having planted his posterity in the country, as I have said [a], from him it was called the land of Edom, or, with a Greek termination, Edomea, or Idumea, and from that land the sea which washed upon it was called the sea of Edom; but the Greeks translating Edom as an appellative into the word red, which it signified, instead of rendering it in the same sound, as a proper name; from this mistake it was by them called the Red sea, and that name it hath retained ever since.

But fully to clear what hath been above said, it is necessary farther to observe, that the Idumea mentioned by Strabo, Josephus, Pliny, Ptolemy, and other ancient writers, was not that land of Edom, or Idumea, which gave name to the Red sea, but another ancient Idumea, which was vastly larger than that Idumea which those authors describe; for [b] it included all that land, which was afterwards, from Petra, the metropolis of it, called Arabia Petrea: for all this was inhabited by the sons of Edom, and from thence it was anciently called the land of Edom. But, [c] on a sedition which arose among them, a party going off from the rest, while the land of Judea lay desolate during the Babylonish captivity, they planted themselves on the south-western part of that country, where they were called Idumeans; and that land alone which they there possessed was the Idumea which those authors mention. Those who remained behind, joining themselves to the Ishmaelites, were, from Nebaioth, or Nabath, the [d] son of Ishmael, called Nabathæans, and the country which they possessed Nabathea; and by that name we often hear of them in the ancient Greek and Latin writers.

An. 739.
Ahaz 4.

But to return from whence I have digressed, Ahaz, having gone so far with Tiglath-Pileser, as hath been said, found it necessary for him to overlook all injuries to avoid provoking greater; and therefore, carrying on the compliment towards him as if he had really been that friend

and

rianus in Rerum Indicarum libro, p. 579, edit. Blanc.
[a] See Fuller's Miscellanies, lib. 4. c. 20.
[b] That it reached to the Red sea appears from 2 Chron. viii. 17. for Elath and Eziongeber, cities of Edom, were ports on the Red sea.
[c] Strabo, lib. 16. p. 760.
[d] Gen. xxv. 13.

and protector, which he pretended to be as foon as he heard that he was returned to Damafcus, [a] he went thither to him, to pay him that refpect and obeifance, which, after having owned him as his protector and fovereign, he did now, as his client and tributary, owe unto him.

While he was at Damafcus on this occafion, [b] he faw there an idolatrous altar, of a form which he was much pleafed with; whereupon, caufing a pattern of it to be taken, he fent it to Urijah, the high prieft, at Jerufalem, to have another there made like unto it; and, on his return, having removed the altar of the Lord out of its place in the temple, ordered this new altar to be fet up in its ftead; and thenceforth giving himfelf wholly up to idolatry [c], inftead of the God of Ifrael, he worfhipped the gods of the Syrians, and the gods of the other nations round him, faying, that they helped their people, and that therefore he would worfhip them, that they might help him alfo. And accordingly, having filled Jerufalem and all Judea with their idols and their altars, he would fuffer no other god, but them only, to be worfhipped in the land; whereby, having excluded the only true God, the Lord his Creator, whom alone he ought to have adored, he caufed his temple to be fhut up, and utterly fuppreffed his worfhip throughout all his kingdom. And this he did with an air and profeffion of anger and defiance, for that he had not delivered him in his diftrefs, when the Syrians and Ifraelites came againft him, as if it were in his power to revenge himfelf upon the Almighty, and execute his wrath upon him that made him; to fuch an extravagant height of folly and madnefs had his impiety carried him beyond all that had reigned before him in Jerufalem; and in this he continued, till at length he perifhed in it, being cut off in the flower of his age, before he had outlived half his days.

Tiglath-Pilefer, on his return into Affyria, carried with him great numbers of the people, whom he had taken captive in the kingdom of Damafcus, and in the land of Ifrael. Thofe of Damafcus he planted [d] in Kir, and thofe of Ifrael [e] in Halah, and Habor, and Hara, and on the river Gozan in the land of the Medes. Kir was a city in the hither part of Media; but Halah, Habor, Hara, and the river Gozan, were farther remote. And herein was accomplifhed the prophecy of the prophet Amos [f] againft Ifrael, wherein he foretold, in the days of Uzziah, the grandfather of Ahaz, that God would caufe them to go into captivity beyond Damafcus, that is, unto places

beyond

---

[a] 2 Kings xvi. 10.
[b] 2 Kings xvi. 10—16.
[c] 2 Kings xvi. 2 Chron. xxviii. 22—25.
[d] 2 Kings xvi. 9.
[e] 1 Chron. v. 26.
[f] Amos v. 26, 27.

beyond where those of Damascus should be carried. St Stephen [a], quoting this prophecy, renders it beyond Babylon. So the common editions of the Greek Testament have it, and it is certainly true; for what was beyond Kir was also beyond Babylon, for Kir was beyond Babylon: But Wicelius's [b] edition hath Damascus in St Stephen's speech also, and, no doubt, he had ancient copies which he followed herein.

The planting of the colonies by Tiglath-Pileser in those cities of the Medes plainly proves Media to have been then under the king of Assyria: For, otherwise, what had he to do to plant colonies in that country: And therefore Tiglath-Pileser and Arbaces were not two distinct kings, whereof one had Media, and the other Assyria, as [c] Archbishop Usher supposeth, but must both be the same person expressed under these two distinct names. And [d] Diodorus Siculus positively tells us, that Arbaces had Assyria, as well as Media, for his share in the partition of the former empire; and therefore there is no room for a Tiglath-Pileser, or a Ninus junior, distinct from him, to reign in Assyria during his time, but it must necessarily be one and the same person, that was signified by all these different names.

Pekah, by this conquest which the Assyrians made upon him, being stript of so large a part of his kingdom, was hereby brought lower than he had afore brought King Ahaz. For he had now scarce any thing left, but the city of Samaria, and the territories of the tribe of Ephraim, and the half tribe of Manasseh only; which bringing him into contempt with his people, as well as raising their indignation against him (as is commonly the case of unfortunate princes) Hoshea, the son of Elah [e], rose up against him, and slew him, after he had reigned in Samaria twenty years; and hereby was fully accomplished that prophecy of Isaiah [f] concerning him, which is above related. After this the elders of the land seem to have taken the government into their hands; for Hoshea had not the kingdom till nine years after, that is, towards the end of the twelfth year of Ahaz.

An. 629.
Ahaz 14.

In the fourteenth year of Ahaz died Tiglath-Pileser, king of Assyria, after he had reigned [g] nineteen years; and Salmaneser, his son, (who in [h] Tobit is called Enemesser, and in [i] Hosea, Shalmon), reigned in his stead. And, as soon as he was settled in the throne, he came into Syria

[a] Acts vii. 43.
[b] See Dr Mill's Greek Testament, Acts vii. 43.
[c] Annales Veteris Testamenti sub anno Mundi 3257.
[d] Lib. 2.
[e] 2 Kings xv. 30.
[f] Ca. vii. 16.
[g] Castor apud Euseb. Chron. p. 46.
[h] Chap. i. 2.
[i] Chap. x. 14.

ria and Palestine, and there subjected Samaria to his dominion, making Hoshea, the king thereof, to become his vassal, and pay tribute unto him. In this expedition, among other prey which he took and carried away with him [a], was the golden calf, which Jeroboam had set up in Bethel, and had been there, ever since his time, worshipped by the ten tribes of Israel, that had revolted with him from the house of David. The other golden calf, which was at the same time set up by him in Dan, had been taken thence [b], about ten years before, by Tiglath-Pileser, in the invasion which he then made upon Galilee, in which province that city stood. And therefore the apostate Israelites, being now deprived of the idols which they had so long worshipped, began again to return to the Lord their God, and to go up to Jerusalem there to worship before him; and Hosheah encouraged them herein. For whereas [c] "the kings of Israel had hitherto maintained guards upon the frontiers to hinder all under their subjection from going up to Jerusalem to worship there," Hoshea took away those guards, and gave free liberty to all to worship the Lord their God according to his laws, in that place, which he had chosen; and therefore when Hezekiah invited all Israel, that is, all those of the ten revolted tribes, as well as the other two, to come up to his passover, Hoshea hindered them not [d], but permitted all that would to go up thereto. And when those of his subjects, who were at that festival, did, on their return, out of their zeal for the true worship of their God [e], break in pieces the images, cut down the groves, demolish the high places, and absolutely destroyed all other monuments of idolatry throughout the whole kingdom of Samaria, as will be hereafter related, Hoshea forbade them not, but in all likelihood gave his consent to it, and concurred with them herein. For he being king, without his encouraging it, and giving his authority for it, it could not have been done. And therefore he hath, as to religion, the best character given him in scripture of all that reigned before him over Israel from the division of the kingdom. For although he were not perfect in the true worship of God, and therefore it is said of him [f], That "he did evil in the sight of the Lord," yet it is subjoined, in the next words, "but not so as the kings of Israel which were before him." By which it appears, that his ways were less offensive to God, than were the ways of any of those that had reigned before him in that kingdom. However, still he was far from being perfectly righteous, which this alone sufficiently

[a] Seder Olam Rabba, c. xxii.
[b] 2 Kings xvii.
[c] Seder Olam Rabba, c. xxii.
[d] 2 Chron. xxx. 10. 18.
[e] 2 Chron. xxxi. 1.
[f] 2 Chron. xxvii. 2.

sufficiently proves, that he treacherously slew his master to reign in his stead.

Ahaz, in the 16th year of his reign, being smitten of God for his iniquities, [a] died in the thirty-sixth year of his age, and was buried in the city of David, but not with a royal burial; in the sepulchres of the kings. For, from this honour he was excluded, because of his wicked reign, as were Jehoram and Joash before him, and Manasseh and Ammon after him, for the same reason; it being the usage of the Jews to lay this mark of infamy upon those that reigned wickedly over them.

An. 727. Ahaz 16. Hezek. 1.

After Ahaz, reigned [b] Hezekiah his son, a very worthy and religious prince. He had, in the last year of his father's reign, been admitted a partner with him in the kingdom, while he was languishing (as it may be supposed) under the sickness of which he died. However, as long as his father lived he could make no alteration in that evil course of affairs, which he had put both church and state into. But, as soon as he was dead, and Hezekiah had the whole power in his hands, he immediately set himself with all his might to work a thorough reformation on both.

The first thing which he did, was, to open the house of God, which his father had impiously shut up, and restore the true worship therein; in order whereto he called the priests and Levites together, out of all parts of the land, to attend their duty in the temple, ordering them to remove his father's new altar, and to restore the altar of the Lord to its place again, and purge the temple of all other pollutions, with which it had been profaned, during the reign of his father. But it not being, till the end of the former year, that Ahaz died, the beginning of the first month of the ensuing year, (which is called Nisan, and corresponds partly with March, and partly with April, in our kalendar), was the soonest that they could be employed in this work; so that it not being completed till the 16th day of that month, the passover could not be kept that year in its regular time, which ought to have been begun on the 14th day of the said month of Nisan.

An. 726. Hezek. 2.

However, the house of the Lord being now sanctified, and made fit for the service of God, Hezekiah went up thither on the 17th day of that month, with the rulers and great men of his kingdom, where, the people being gathered together, he offered sin-offerings for the kingdom, and the sanctuary, and for Judah, to make atonement to God for them, and for all Israel; and after that he offered peace-offerings, and in all other particulars restored

---

[a] 2 Kings xvi. 20. 2 Chron. xxviii. 27. [b] 2 Kings xviii. 2 Chron. xxix.

restored the service of God in the same manner as it had been performed in the purest times, that had been before him; and there was great joy among all the good people of the land thereon.

And seeing the passover could not be kept on the regular time this year, because neither the temple, nor the priests, nor the people, were sanctified in order hereto, and in this case ᵃ the law of Moses allowed a second passover to be kept from the 14th day of the second month; King Hezekiah, having taken counsel hereon with the chief priests, and his princes, and all the congregation in Jerusalem, ᵇ decreed, that this second passover should be kept by all the congregation of Israel, instead of the first; and accordingly he sent messengers to carry notice hereof, not only through all Judah, but also through all the other tribes of Israel, and to invite all that were of Israel, to come to it. And accordingly, on the day appointed, there was at Jerusalem a very great concourse of people from all parts met together to solemnise the holy festival, and that as well from those tribes that had separated from the house of David, as from those who had stuck to it; for although many of Ephraim and Manasseh, and the rest of those tribes, laughed at Hezekiah's messengers, when they invited them to this solemnity, because of the impious contempt which through long disusage they had contracted of it; yet a great multitude, even from those parts, came to it, and very religiously joined in the observance of it, whereby it became the greatest passover that had been solemnised at Jerusalem since the days of King Solomon. And, because they had long neglected the observance of this solemn festival, to make some amends for it, they now doubled the time of its continuance; for, whereas the law directs it to be observed only seven days, they kept it fourteen, with much joy and gladness of heart; and, resolving from thenceforth to serve the God of Israel only, as soon as the solemnity was ended, they went out into all the coasts of Judah and Benjamin, and brake the images in pieces, and cut down the groves, and threw down the high places and the altars, and absolutely destroyed all the monuments of idolatry which were any where to be found, either in Jerusalem, Judea, or any of the coasts belonging thereto. And those of the other tribes, on their return home, did the same in all the rest of Israel; so that the true worship of God was again universally restored throughout all the land, and they might have received a blessing proportionable hereto, had they with the same zeal persisted in it.

And the brazen serpent, which Moses had set up in the wilderness, having been by many, in the preceding times of iniquity,

Vol. I.   B   quity;

ᵃ Numb. ix. 10, 11.   ᵇ 2 Chron. xxx.

quity, made the object of idolatrous worſhip [a], Hezekiah caufed this alſo to be deſtroyed; whereas, otherwiſe, it might have ſerved, as well as the pot of manna, and Aaron's rod, to have been a monument of the miraculous mercy of God ſhewn to his people on their coming out of Egypt, and for this reaſon it ſeems to have been ſo long preſerved.

But, notwithſtanding it is thus poſitively ſaid in the holy ſcripture, that the brazen ſerpent was deſtroyed by Hezekiah in the manner as I have related; yet the impudence of the Romaniſts is ſuch [b], that in the church of St Ambroſe at Milan, they now keep and ſhew to their Devoto's a brazen ſerpent, which they pretend to be the very ſame that Moſes did ſet up in the wilderneſs; and, upon this belief, an idolatrous devotion is there paid to it, as groſs as was that of the Jews, for which Hezekiah caufed it to be deſtroyed. But it muſt not be denied, that, among their learned men, there are thoſe who acknowledge the cheat, and diſclaim it.

About the beginning of the reign of Hezekiah [c], Sabacon, the Ethiopian, having invaded Egypt, and taken Boccharis, the king of that country, priſoner, caufed him with great cruelty to be burnt alive, and then, ſeizing his kingdom, reigned there in his ſtead. This is the ſame, who in ſcripture is called [d] So. And he having thus ſettled himſelf in Egypt, and after ſome time grown very potent there, Hoſhea, king of Samaria, entered into confederacy with him, hoping by his aſſiſtance to ſhake off the yoke of Aſſyria; and, in confidence hereof, he withdrew his ſubjection from Salmaneſer, and would pay him no more tribute, nor bring any more preſents unto him, as he had formerly uſed every year to do. Whereon [e] Salmaneſer, in the beginning of the fourth year of Hezekiah, marched with an army againſt him, and having ſubdued all the country round, pent him up in Samaria, and there beſieged him three years; at the end of which he took the city, and thereon putting Hoſhea in chains, he ſhut him up in priſon all his days, and carried the people into captivity, placing them in Halah, and in Habor, and in the other cities of the Medes, where Tiglath-Pileſer had before placed thoſe whom he had carried into captivity out of the ſame land.

An. 724.
Hezek. 4.

An. 721.
Hezek. 7.

In

---

[a] 2 Kings xviii. 4.
[b] Vid. Sigoni hiſtoriam de regno Italiæ, lib. 7. Torniellum in Annalibus ſub A. M. 3315. tom. 2. p. 105. Buxtorfii hiſtoriam ſerpentis aenei. cap. 6. &c.
[c] Herodot. lib. 2. African. apud Cyncellum, p. 74. Euſeb. in Chronic.
[d] 2 Kings xvii. 4.
[e] 2 Kings xviii.

In this captivity [a], Tobit, being taken out of his city of Thisbe, in the tribe of Naphtali, was, with Anna his wife, and Tobias his son, carried into Assyria, where he became purveyor to King Salmaneser. But the rest of his brethren were carried into Media, as is above said, and planted there, as particularly were Gabael in Rages, and Raguel in Ecbatana, which proves Media to have been still under the king of Assyria, and that there was no king in Media in those days distinct from the king of Assyria.

There is, in the 15th and 16th chapters of Isaiah, a very terrible prophecy against Moab, bearing date in the first year of Hezekiah ; wherein it was foretold, that within three years Arne and Kir-Harasheth, the two principal cities of that country, should be destroyed, and all the rest of it brought to contempt, ruin, and desolation ; which must have been executed the same year that Samaria was first besieged. It seemeth most likely, that Salmaneser, to secure himself from any disturbance on that side, first invaded Moab ; and, having destroyed these two cities, brought all the rest of that country under his subjection, and placed garrisons therein, sufficient to put a stop to all incursions of the Arabs, which might that way be made upon him, before he would begin that siege ; for, otherwise, he could not have been able to carry it on with success.

In the same year that Samaria was taken, [b] Mardoc-Empadus began his reign at Babylon. He was the son of Belesis, or Baladin, or Nabonassar (for by all these names was he called), and was the same [c], who in scripture is called Merodach-Baladan, the son of Baladan. But, after the death of his father, several other princes had succeeded in Babylon before the crown came to him. For [d] Nabonassar dying when he had sat in the throne fourteen years, after him reigned Nadeus two years ; and after him Chinzerus and Porus jointly five years ; and then after them Jugæus five years. But of these, there being nothing on record besides their names in the canon of Ptolemy, we have not hitherto taken any notice of them. After Jugæus succeeded Mardoc-Empadus, in the 27th year after the beginning of his father's kingdom in Babylon, and reigned twelve years.

While Salmaneser was engaged in the siege of Samaria, Hezekiah took the opportunity of recovering what had been lost from his kingdom in the reign of his father. And therefore [e], making war upon the Philistines, he not only regained all the cities of Judah, which they had seized during the time that Pekah and
Rezin

---

[a] Tobit chap. i.
[b] Canon Ptolemæi.
[c] Is. xxxix. 1.
[d] Canon Ptolemæi.
[e] 2 Kings xviii. 8. Josephus Antiq. lib. 9. c. 13.

Rezin diſtreſſed the land, but alſo diſpoſſeſſed them of almoſt all their own country, excepting Gaza and Gath.

As ſoon as the ſiege of Samaria was over, Salmaneſer ſent to Hezekiah to demand the tribute, which Ahaz had agreed to pay for the kingdom of Judea, in the time of Tiglath-Pileſer, his father; but [a] Hezekiah, truſting in the Lord his God; would not hearken unto him ; neither did he pay him any tribute, or ſend any preſents unto him ; which would immediately have brought Salmaneſer upon him with all his power, but that he was diverted by another war.

An. 720.
Hezek. 8.

For [b] Elulæus, king of Tyre, ſeeing the Philiſtines brought low by the war which Hezekiah had lately made upon them, laid hold of the opportunity of reducing Gath again under his obedience, which had ſome time before revolted from him: Whereupon the Gittites, applying themſelves to Salmaneſer, engaged him in their cauſe : ſo that he marched with his whole army againſt the Tyrians. Whereon Sidon, Ace, (afterwards called Ptolemais, and now Acon), and the other maritime towns of Phœnicia, which till then had been ſubject to the Tyrians, revolted from them, and ſubmitted to Salmaneſer. But the Tyrians having, in a ſea fight, with twelve ſhips only, beaten the Aſſyrian and Phœnician fleets both joined together, which conſiſted of ſixty ſhips, this gave them ſuch a reputation in naval affairs, and made their name ſo terrible in this ſort of war, that Salmaneſer would not venture to cope with them any more at ſea ; but turning the war into a ſiege, left an army to block up the city, and returned into Aſſyria. The forces which he left there much diſtreſſed the place, by ſtopping their aqueducts, and cutting off all the conveyances of water to them. To relieve themſelves in this exigency, they digged wells, from whence they drew up the water, and by the help of them held out five years ; at the end of which Salmaneſer dying, this delivered them for that time. But they being over puffed up with this ſucceſs, and growing very inſolent hereon, this provoked that prophecy againſt them in the 23d chapter of Iſaiah, which foretold the miſerable overthrow, that ſhould afterwards happen unto them ; and was accordingly effected by Nebuchadnezzar, king of Babylon, as will be hereafter ſhewn.

An. 715.
Hezek. 13.

In the ninth year of Hezekiah, died Sabacon, or So, king of Egypt, after he had reigned in that country, [c] eight years ; and

Seve-

---

[a] 2 Kings xviii. 7.
[b] Annales Menandri apud Joſephum Antiq. lib. 9. c. 14. et contra Appionem, lib. 1.
[c] Africanus apud Syncellum, p. 74.

Sevechus [a], his son, whom Herodotus [b] calleth Sethon, reigned in his stead.

Salmanefer, king of Assyria, being dead, after he had reigned fourteen years, Sennacherib, [c] his son, succeeded him in the kingdom, and reigned about eight years. He is the same whom the prophet Isaiah (c. xx. 1.) called Sargon. As soon as he was settled in the throne, he renewed the demand, which his father had made upon Hezekiah for the tribute, which Ahaz had agreed to pay in the reign of Tiglath-Pilefer, his grandfather; and, [d] on his refusal to comply with him herein, denounced war against him, and marched with a great army into Judea to fall upon him. This was in the fourteenth year of the reign of King Hezekiah.

An. 714.
Hezek. 14.

In this same year, [e] Hezekiah, falling sick of the pestilence, had a message from God, by the prophet Isaiah, to set his house in order, and prepare for death; but, on his hearty prayer to God, he obtained another message from him, by the same prophet, which promised him life for fifteen years longer, and also deliverance from the Assyrians, who were then coming against him; and, to give him thorough assurance hereof, by a miraculous sign, God did, at his request, make the sun go backward ten degrees upon the sun dial of Ahaz. And, accordingly, a lump of figs having been, by the prophet's direction, made into a plaster, and laid to the pestilential boil, he recovered within three days, and went up to the house of God, to return thanks unto him for so wonderful a deliverance.

Merodach-Baladan, king of Babylon (the same who in Ptolemy's canon is called Mardoc-Empadus) hearing of this miraculous recovery, [f] sent ambassadors unto him, to congratulate him hereon; which Hezekiah was much pleased with. Their coming on this occasion, seemeth principally to have been for two reasons. The first, to inquire about the miracle of the sun's retrogradation, (for the Chaldeans, being above all other nations then given to the study of astronomy, were very curious in their inquiries after such matters); and the other, to enter into an alliance with him against Sennacherib, whose growing power the Babylonians had reason to fear, as well as the Jews. And to make the Babylonians put the greater value upon his alliance on this account, seems to be the reason, that Hezekiah shewed those ambassadors from them all the riches of his house, his treasures, his armoury, and all his stores,

An. 713.
Hezek. 15.

---

[a] Africanus, p. 74.   [b] Africanus, lib. 2.   [c] Tobit. i. 15.
[d] 2 Kings xviii. 2 Chron. xxxii. If. xxxvi.
[e] 2 Kings xx. 2 Chron. xxxii. 24. If. xxxviii.
[f] 2 Kings xx. If. xxxix.

stores and strength for war. But by this he having expressed the vanity and pride of his mind, God sent him, by the prophet Isaiah, a rebuking message for it, and also a prophecy of what the Babylonians should afterwards do unto his family, in order to the humbling of that pride, with which his heart was then elated.

Towards the end of the 14th year of Hezekiah's reign, [a] Sennacherib came up with a great army against the fenced cities of Judah, and took several of them, and laid siege to Lachish, threatening Jerusalem itself next. Whereon Hezekiah, taking advice of his princes and chief counsellors, made all manner of preparations for its defence; repairing the walls, and making new ones, where they were wanting, and fortifying them with towers, and all other works and buildings, necessary for their defence. And he provided also darts and shields in great abundance, and all other arms and artillery, which might be any way useful for the defending of the place, and the annoying of the enemy on their coming against it. And he caused all the people to be inrolled and marshalled for the war, that were fit and able for it; placing over them captains of experience, to instruct them in all military exercises, and to conduct and lead them forth against the enemy, whenever there should be an occasion for it. And he took care also to stop up all the wells, that were without the walls of Jerusalem, for a great compass round the city, and diverted all brooks and water-courses from coming that way; thereby to distress the enemy for want of water, should they come and set down before that place. And farther, to strengthen himself the more, against so potent and formidable an enemy, he entered into alliance with the king of Egypt for their mutual defence. But [b] the prophet Isaiah condemned this alliance, as carrying with it a distrust in God, telling the Jews, that they should confide in him alone for their deliverance, who would himself come down to fight for Mount Zion, and deliver and preserve Jerusalem from the power of the enemy, that was then risen up against it: and that whatsoever trust they should place in Egypt, should all come to nothing, and be of no benefit to them, but rather turn to their shame, their reproach, and their confusion; and so in the event it accordingly happened.

However, Sennacherib being informed of all these preparations, which Hezekiah had made for his defence, and perceiving thereby how difficult a work it would be to take so strong a city, when so well appointed, and provided for its defence, he became inclined to hearken to terms of accommodation; and therefore, on Hezekiah's sending to treat with him, it was agreed, that
Hezekiah

[a] 2 Kings xx. 2 Chron. xxxii. Is. xxxvi. [b] Is. xxx. xxxi.

Hezekiah paying unto him [a] three hundred talents of silver, and thirty talents of gold for the present, and duly rendering his tribute for the future, there should be peace. But when Sennacherib had received the money, he had little regard to this agreement, but soon after broke it, and again renewed the war as will be hereafter shown. However, for the present, he gave him some respite, and marched against Egypt; and, the better to open his way into that country, [b] he sent Tartan, one of his generals, before him to take Ashdod, or Azotus: from the taking of which place, the prophet Isaiah dates the beginning of the war which Sennacherib had with the Egyptians; wherein, according as that prophet [c] had foretold, he much afflicted that people three years together, destroying their cities, and carrying multitudes of them into captivity. At that time Sevechus, the son of Sabacon, or So, the Ethiopian, was king of Egypt, whom Herodotus [d] calls Sethon, and represents him as a prince of so foolish a conduct, as was most likely to bring such a calamity upon his kingdom, whensoever it should be assaulted by an enemy. For, affecting the office of a priest, he neglected that of a king, and causing himself to be consecrated chief pontif of Vulcan, gave himself wholly up to superstition; and, having no regard to the warlike defence of his kingdom, he so far neglected and discouraged the military order which was there maintained for it, that he took from them their tenures, which, in the time of the former kings, his predecessors, had been allowed them for their support; which gave them such a just cause of offence and indignation against him, that, when he had need for their valour on this occasion, they would not fight for him; whereon he was forced to raise an army of such raw and unexperienced men as he could get out of the shopkeepers, tradesmen, labourers, and such like people; which being wholly unable to cope with such an army of veterans as Sennacherib brought against them, he did with great ease over-run the country, and work what devastation in it he pleased. And at this time seems to have been brought upon No-Amon, a famous city in Egypt, that destruction which the prophet Nahum speaks of (ch. iii. 10.),

B 4 where

[a] An Hebrew talent, according to the scripture, Exod. xxxviii. 25—27. containing 3000 shekels, and every shekel being 3 shillings of our money, these 300 talents of silver must contain of our money one hundred thirty-five thousand pound, and the 30 talents of gold, two hundred and sixteen thousand pound. So the whole sum here paid by Hezekiah amounted to three hundred fifty one thousand pound of our money.
[b] Is. xx. 1.
[c] Is. xx. 3. 4. Josephus Antiq. lib. 10. c. 1. 2.
[d] Herod. lib. 2.

where he tells us that her inhabitants were carried into captivity, her young children dashed in pieces in the top of her streets, and her great men divided by lot among the conquerors, and put into chains, to be led away as slaves and captives. All which, he tells us, happened, while Egypt and Ethiopia were her strength, which plainly points out unto us this time, when an Ethiopian prince reigned over Egypt. Sabacon, or So, the father of Sevechus, was an Ethiopian, who made himself king of Egypt by conquest; and therefore, during his and his son's reign, Egypt and Ethiopia were as one country, and they mutually helped each other, an instance whereof will not be wanting in this war.

No-Amon in Egypt was [a] the same with Thebes, famous for its hundred gates, and vast number of inhabitants. The Greeks called it Diospolis, or the city of Jupiter, because of a famous temple built there to Jupiter; and for the same reason was it called No-Amon by the Egyptians, for Amon was the name of Jupiter among that people.

It is to be observed, that the destruction of No-Amon, mentioned in Nahum, must have been some time before that of Nineveh; for the former is historically related by him as past, and the other only prophetically foretold as to come; and therefore Nineveh, having been destroyed in the 29th year of Josiah, as will hereafter be shewn, this destruction of No-Amon must have been long before, and in no time more likely than when Sennacherib made this war upon Egypt, and harassed it from one end to the other, for three years together. They who refer this destruction of No-Amon, spoken of by Nahum, to the invasion of Nebuchadnezzar, place it after the destruction of Nineveh, and thereby make one part of the text inconsistent with the other.

But Sennacherib did not end this war with the same success as he begun it; for, [b] having laid siege to Pelusium, and spent much time in it, he was at length forced to break up from thence, and retreat out of Egypt, because of Tirhakah, king of Ethiopia; for he being come into Egypt with a great army, to help Sevechus, his kinsman, was on a full march towards Pelusium, to relieve the place, which Sennacherib hearing of, durst not abide his coming, but raised the siege, and returning into Judea, encamped again at [c] Lachish, where he renewed the war with Hezekiah, notwithstanding the agreement of peace which he had afore made with him; and, to let him know as much, he sent Tartan, Rabsaris, and

An. 710.
Hezek. 18.

Rab-

---

[a] Vide Bochart. Phaleg. part 1. lib. 1. c. 1.
[b] Joseph. Antiq. lib. 10. c. 1.
[c] 2 Kings xviii. 17. 18. &c. 2 Chron. xxxii. 9. 10. &c. Isaiah xxxvi.

Rabshakeh, three of his principal captains, with that proud and blasphemous message, which we have at full recited [a] in two places of the holy scripture. It was delivered to the king's officers, from under the walls of Jerusalem, in the hearing of all the people, and in the Hebrew tongue: for they hoped thereby to draw the people to a revolt; but they, failing of success herein, returned to Sennacherib without their design. The person appointed to deliver this message was Rabshakeh, who, by his ready speaking of the Hebrew tongue, seems to have been an apostate Jew, or else one of the captivity of Israel. By office he was the king's chief cup-bearer, as his name imports. On their return, they found Sennacherib decamped from Lachish, and laying siege at Libnah; where, hearing that Tirhakah, on his finding him gone from Pelusium, was marching after him, as in pursuit of one flying from him, he led forth his army against him, and gave him a great overthrow; for it was [b] from God, by the prophet Isaiah before, laid as a burden upon Egypt, and as a burden upon Ethiopia, thus to be punished by him, and he was no more than as God's executioner herein. But, before [c] he went forth to this last war, he sent again to Hezekiah, adding a most blasphemous letter to his former message, defying therein, both him, and also the Lord his God, in a most impious manner; which justly provoked the wrath of God against him, to that degree, as brought a most dismal destruction upon him, to the cutting off of almost all his army: for when, swelling with his fresh victory over the Ethiopians, he was on his full march towards Jerusalem, with thorough purpose utterly to destroy that place, and all in it, an angel of the Lord went forth, and, in one night, smote in the camp of the Assyrians an hundred fourscore and five thousand men; so that, when he arose in the morning, he found almost all his army dead corpses; with which being terrified, he fled out of Judea in great confusion, and made all the haste he could back again to Nineveh, where he dwelt all the remainder of his life, in dishonour, shame, and regret. This happened in the 18th year of King Hezekiah, and four years after Sennacherib first came into those parts. After this, Hezekiah reigned the rest of his time in great peace and prosperity, being feared and honoured by all the nations round him, by reason of the favour which they saw he had with the Lord his God, in the great and wonderful deliverance which he had vouchsafed unto him; so that none of them, after this, would any more lift up their hand against him.

The

---

[a] 2 Kings xviii. 19, 20. &c. Is. xxxvi. 4. 5. &c.
[b] Is. xviii. and xx.
[c] Is. xxxvii. 2 Kings xix. 2 Chron. xxxii.

The Babylonish Talmud hath it, that this destruction upon the army of the Assyrians was executed by lightning; and some of the Targums are quoted for saying the same thing. But it seemeth most likely, that it was effected by bringing on them the hot wind which [a] is frequent in those parts, and often, when it lights among a multitude, destroys great numbers of them in a moment, as it frequently happens in those vast caravans of the Mahometans who go their annual pilgrimages to Mecca. And the words of [b] Isaiah, which threatened Sennacherib with a blast, that God would send upon him, seem to denote this thing.

Herodotus [c] gives us, from the relation of the Egyptian priests, some kind of a disguised account of this deliverance from the Assyrians in a fabulous application of it to the city of Pelusium, instead of Jerusalem, and to Sethon, the Egyptian king, instead of Hezekiah; by whose piety he saith it was obtained, that, while the king of Assyria laid siege to Pelusium, a great number of rats were miraculously sent into his army, which in one night did eat all their shield-straps, quivers, and bow-strings; so that, on their rising the next morning, finding themselves without arms for the carrying on of the war, they were forced to raise the siege and be gone. And it is particularly to be remarked, that Herodotus calls the king of Assyria, to whom he saith this happened, by the same name of Sennacherib, as the scriptures do, and the time in both doth also well agree; which plainly shews, that it is the same fact that is referred to by Herodotus, although much disguised in the relation; which may easily be accounted for, when we consider, that it comes to us through the hands of such as had the greatest aversion both to the nation and the religion of the Jews, and therefore would relate nothing in such manner as might give any reputation to either.

After this terrible blow, and the loss of so great an army, Sennacherib was so weakened, that he had no way of again recovering himself; which making him to fall into contempt among his subjects, several of his provinces revolted from him, and particularly Media, which was the largest and the most considerable of all his empire. For the Medes, when they heard in how low a condition he was returned to Nineveh, immediately shook off his yoke, and set [d] up for themselves,

An. 709.
Hezek. 12.

---

[a] Thevenot's Travels, part 2. book 1. c. 20. & p. 2. b. 2. c. 16. & p. 1. b. 2. c. 20. This wind is by the prophet Jeremiah, c. li. 1. called "A destroying wind," where the Arabick version renders it, "An hot pestilential wind."
[b] If. xxxvii. 7. 2 Kings xix 7.
[c] Lib. 2.
[d] Herodotus, lib. 1.

themselves, in a sort of democratical government; but soon growing sick of the confusions which this caused among them, they were forced to have recourse to monarchy for the remedy, and the next year after chose Deioces for their king, whom they had formerly made great use of as a common arbitrator of their differences, and, for the great proof which he had given of his justice and abilities on such occasions, they advanced him to this dignity. He began his reign in the 19th year of King Hezekiah; and having repaired, beautified, and enlarged, the city of Ecbatana, he made it the royal seat of his kingdom, and reigned there with great wisdom, honour, and prosperity, 53 years; during which time, it growing to be a great city, he is for this reason reckoned by the Greeks to have been the founder of it.

The same year [a] Arkianus began his reign at Babylon, after the decease of Mardoch-Empadus, or Merodach-Baladan, who ended his life with the former year, after having reigned over the Babylonians twelve years.

Sennacherib, after his return to Nineveh, being inflamed with rage for his great loss and disappointment, as if he would revenge himself upon his subjects for it, grew thenceforth [b] very cruel and tyrannical in the management of his government, especially towards the Jews and Israelites, abundance of whom he caused every day to be slain and cast into the streets: by which savage humour having made himself so intolerable, that he could be no longer borne by his own family, his two eldest sons [c], Adramelech and Sharezar, conspired against him, and, falling upon him while he was worshipping in the house of Nisroch, his god, they there slew him with the sword; and thereon having made their escape into the land of Armenia, Esarhaddon, his third son, reigned in his stead. Some commentators [d] will have it, that he had vowed to sacrifice these his two sons to appease his gods, and make them the more favourable to him for the restoration of his affairs, and that it was to prevent this that they thus sacrificed him. But for this there is no other foundation, but that scarce any thing else can be thought of which can afford any excuse for so wicked and barbarous a parricide.

Esarhaddon began his reign over Assyria about the 22d year of King Hezekiah, which was the last of the reign of Sevechus, or Sethon, in the kingdom of Egypt; who dying, after he had reigned fourteen years, An. 706. Hezek. 22.

[a] Can. Ptol.
[b] Tobit i. 18.
[c] 2 Kings xix. 37. 2 Chron. xxxii. 21. Is. xxxvii. 38.
[d] Bishop Patrick on 2 Kings xix. 37. Saliar us sub anno ante Christum 729.

years [a], was succeeded by Tirhakah, the same who came with the Ethiopian army to his help. He was the third and last of that race that reigned in Egypt.

In the 23d year of Hezekiah, Arkianus dying without is-
An. 705. Hezek 23. sue, there followed an [b] interregnum of two years, in the kingdom of Babylon, before they could agree upon a successor. At length [b] Belibus, being advanced to the throne, sat in it three years. After him succeeded [b] Apronadius, and reigned six years.

The same year that Apronadius began his reign at Babylon,
An. 699. Hezek. 29. Hezekiah ended his at Jerusalem: for [c] he died there, after he had reigned twenty and nine years; and all Judah and Jerusalem did him honour at his death; for they buried him, with great solemnity, in the chiefest and highest place of the sepulchres of the sons of David, expressing thereby, that they looked on him as the worthiest and best of all that had reigned over them of that family, since him that was the first founder of it.

The burial-place, called the sepulchres of the kings of the house of David (which hath been afore spoken of) was a very sumptuous and stately thing [d]. It lies now without the walls of Jerusalem, but, as is supposed, was formerly [e] within them, before that city was destroyed by the Romans. It consists of a large court of about 120 feet square, with a gallery, or cloyster, on the left hand, which court and gallery, with the pillars that supported it, were cut out of the solid marble rock. At the end of the gallery there is a narrow passage or hole, through which there is an entrance into a large room or hall, of about twenty-four feet square, within which there are several lesser rooms one within another, with stone doors opening into them; all which rooms, with the great room, were all likewise cut out of the solid marble rock. In the sides of those lesser rooms are several niches, in which the corpses of the deceased kings were deposited in stone coffins. In the innermost, or chiefest of these rooms, was the body of

Hezekiah

[a] Africanus apud Syncellum, p. 74.

[b] Ptol. Can.

[c] 2 Kings xx. 21. 2 Chron. xxxii. 33.

[d] Thevenot's Travels, part 1. book 2. c. 40. Maundrel's Journey from Aleppo to Jerusalem, p. 76.

[e] Maimonides in his tract, Beth Habbechirah, c. 7. saith, in Jerusalem, they do not allow a sepulchre, except the sepulchres of the house of David, and the sepulchre of Huldah the prophetess, which were there from the days of the former prophets. *This proves these sepulchres to have been within the walls of Jerusalem, and that the words of scripture which place them in the city of David are strictly to be understood.*

Hezekiah laid in a nich, perchance cut of purpofe at that time for it, in the upper end of that room, to do him the greater honour; and all this remains entire even to this day. It feems to have been the work of King Solomon, for it could not have been made without vaſt expence; and it is the only true remainder of old Jerufalem which is now to be feen in that place.

Hezekiah, during his reign, much improved the city of Jerufalem, not only [a] by new fortifying of it, erecting magazines therein, and filling them with all manner of armoury, which were of ufe in thofe days, but alfo by building [b] a new aqueduct, which was of great convenience to the inhabitants for the fupplying of them with water: and, for the [c] better promoting of religion, he maintained fkilful fcribes to collate together and write out copies of the holy fcripture; and it is particularly mentioned, that the Proverbs of Solomon were thus collected together and wrote out by thofe men.

And in his time the [d] Simeonites, being ſtraitened in their habitations, much enlarged their borders toward the fouth: for falling on the Amalekites, who dwelt in part of Mount Seir, and in the rich valley adjoining, they fmote them, and utterly deſtroyed them, and dwelt in their rooms.

But it was the misfortune of this good king Hezeziah to be fucceeded by a fon who was the wickedeſt and worſt of the whole race: for after him reigned [e] Manaffeh, who being a minor only 12 years old, at his coming to the crown, had the misfortune to fall into the hands of fuch of the nobility for his guardians and chief miniſters, who, being ill affected to his father's reformation, took care to breed him up in the greateſt averfion to it that they were able, corrupting his youth with the worſt of principles, both as to religion and government; fo that, when he grew up, he proved the moſt impious towards God, and moſt tyrannical and wicked towards his fubjects, of any that had ever reigned, either in Jerufalem or Samaria, over the tribes of Ifrael; for he not only reſtored all the idolatry of Ahaz, but went much beyond him in every abomination, whereby the true worſhip of God might be fuppreffed, and his moſt holy name difhonoured in the land; for whereas Ahaz did only fhut up the houfe of God, he converted it into a houfe of all manner of idolatrous profanation, fetting up an image in the fanctuary, and erecting altars for Baalim, and all

An. 698.
Manaf. 1.

[a] 2 Chron. xxxii. 5. Eccleſiaſticus xlviii. 17.
[b] 2 Kings xx. 20. 2 Chron. xxxii. 30. Eccleſiaſticus xlviii. 1.
[c] Prov. xxv. 1.
[d] 1 Chron. iv. 39.---43.
[e] 2 Kings xxi. 2 Chron. xxxiii.

all the hoft of heaven, in both its courts; and he alfo practifed witchcrafts, and inchantments, and dealt with familiar fpirits, and made his children pafs through the fire to Molech, and filled Judah and Jerufalem with his high places, idols, groves, and altars erected to falfe gods, and brought in all manner of other idolatrous profanations, whereby the true religion might be moft corrupted, and all manner of impiety be moft promoted, in the kingdom: and, to all thefe ways of abomination, he made Judah and Jerufalem to conform, raifing a terrible perfecution againft all that would not comply with him herein, whereby he filled the whole land with innocent blood, of which he did fhed very much in the carrying on of thefe and his other wicked purpofes. And when God fent his prophets to him, to tell him of thefe his iniquities, and to exhort him to depart from them, he treated them with contempt and outrage, and feveral [a] of them he put to death; and, particularly, it is faid, that Ifaiah the prophet, on this account, fuffered martyrdom under him, by being cruelly fawn afunder. This was [b] an old tradition among the Jews; and the holy apoftle, St Paul, in his epiftle to the Hebrews (c. xi. 37.) having among the torments undergone by the prophets and martyrs of foregoing times, reckoned that of being fawn afunder, he [c] is generally thought in that place to have had refpect hereto. By which horrid iniquities and abominations, God was fo juftly incenfed againft the land, that he declared hereon, [d] that he would ftretch out over Jerufalem the line of Samaria, and the plummet of the houfe of Ahab, and wipe Jerufalem clean of all its inhabitants, as a man wipeth a difh, and turneth it when empty upfide down. Which, accordingly, was executed upon it, in the deftruction of that city, and the defolation which was brought upon all Judah at the fame time. And among all the iniquities that drew down thefe heavy judgements upon that city and land, the fins of Manaffeh are always reckoned as [e] the moft provoking caufe; by which an eftimate may be beft made of the greatnefs of them.

In the fifth year of Manaffeh died Apronadius, king of Babylon, and was fucceeded by [f] Regibilus, who reigned only one year. After him, Mefeffimordacus had the kingdom, and held it four years.

An. 694.
Manaf. 5.

In

---

[a] Jofephus Antiq. lib. 10. c. 4.
[b] Talmud. Hierofol. in Sanhedrin, fol. 28. col. 3. Talm. Babylon. in Jevammoth, fol. 49. col. 2. et in Sanhedrin, fol. 103. col. 2. Shalfhelleth Hakkabbalah, fol. 19. col. 1. Yaikut Lib. Regum, fol. 38. col. 4.
[c] Vid. Juftin. Martyr. in Dialogo cum Tryphone. Hieronymum in Efaiam, c. 20. & 57. Epiphanium, et alios.
[d] 2 Kings xxi. 13.
[e] 2 Kings xxiii. 26. & xxiv. 3. Jer. xv. 4.
[f] Canon Ptolemæi.

In the 11th year of Manaſſeh [a] died Tirhakah, king of Egypt, after he had reigned there eighteen years, who was the laſt of the Ethiopian kings that reigned in that country. The Egyptians, after his death, not being able to agree about the ſucceſſion, continued for [b] two years together in a ſtate of anarchy and great confuſion till [c] at length, twelve of the principal nobility conſpiring together, ſeized the kingdom, and, dividing it among themſelves into twelve parts, governed it by joint confederacy fifteen years.

An. 688.
Manaſ. 11.

The ſame year that this happened in Egypt, by the death of Tirhakah, the like happened in Babylon, by the death of Meſeſſimordacus. For, he leaving no ſon behind him to inherit the kingdom, [d] an interregnum of anarchy and confuſion followed there, for eight years together; of which Eſarhaddon, king of Aſſyria, taking the advantage, ſeized Babylon; and adding it to his former empire, thenceforth reigned over [e] both for thirteen years. He is in the canon of Ptolemy, called Aſſar-Adinus. And in the ſcriptures he is ſpoken of as king of [f] Babylon and Aſſyria jointly together. In Ezra he is called [g] Aſnappar, and hath there the honourable epithets of the great and noble added to his name by the author of that book; which argues him to have been a prince of great excellency and worth in his time, and far exceeding all others, that had reigned before him in either of the kingdoms.

An. 680.
Manaſ. 19.

In the 22d year of Manaſſeh, Eſarhaddon, after he had now entered on the fourth year of his reign in Babylon, and fully ſettled his authority there, began to ſet his thoughts on the recovery of what had been loſt to the empire of the Aſſyrians, in Syria and Paleſtine, on the deſtruction of his father's army in Judea, and on that doleful retreat, which thereon he was forced to make from thence; and, being encouraged to this undertaking by the great augmentation of ſtrength which he had acquired, by adding Babylon and
Chaldea

An. 677.
Manaſ. 22.

[a] Africanus apud Syncellum, p. 74.
[b] Diodorus Siculus, lib. 1.
[c] Herodotus, lib. 2. Diodorus Siculus, lib. 1.
[d] Canon Ptolemæi.
[e] Canon Ptolemæi.
[f] He is ſaid, as king of Aſſyria, to have brought a colony out of Babylon into Samaria, 2 Kings xvii. 24. Ezra iv. 9. 10. which he could not have done, if he had not been king of Babylon, as well as of Aſſyria, at that time. And in 2 Chron. xxxiii. 11. he is ſaid, as king of Aſſyria, to have taken Manaſſeh priſoner, and to have carried him to Babylon, which argues him, at that time, to have been king of Babylon alſo.
[g] Ezra iv. 10.

Chaldea to his former kingdom of Affyria, he prepared a great army, and marched into thofe parts, and again added them to the Affyrian empire. And then was accomplifhed the prophecy which was fpoken by Ifaiah, in the firft year of Ahaz, againft Samaria, [a] that, within threefcore and five years, Ephraim fhould be abfolutely broken, fo as from thenceforth to be no more a people. For this year, being exactly fixty-five years from the firft of Ahaz, Efarhaddon, after he had fettled all affairs in Syria, marched into the land of Ifrael, and there taking captive all thofe who were the remains of the former captivity (excepting only fome few, who efcaped his hands, and continued ftill in the land), carried them away into Babylon and Affyria; and then, to prevent the land from becoming defolate, he brought others from [b] Babylon, and from Cutha, and from Avah, and Hamath, and Sephervaim, to dwell in the cities of Samaria in their ftead. And fo the ten tribes of Ifrael, which had feparated from the houfe of David, were brought to a full and utter deftruction, and never after recovered themfelves again. For thofe who were thus carried away, as well in this as in the former captivities (excepting only fome few, who, joining themfelves to the Jews in the land of their captivity, returned with them), foon going into the ufages and idolatry of the nations among whom they were planted, to which they were too much addicted while in their own land, after a while, became wholly abforbed and fwallowed up in them; and thenceforth, utterly lofing their name, their language, and their memorial, were never after any more fpoken of. And whereas there is a fect of Samaritans ftill remaining in Samaria, Sichem, and other towns thereabout, even to this day, who ftill have the law of Mofes in a character peculiar to themfelves, and in a dialect very little, if any thing at all, different from that of the Jews; yet thefe are not of the defcendants of the Ifraelites, but of thofe nations which Eferhaddon brought to dwell in that country in their ftead, after the others had been carried thence into captivity; and, for this reafon, the Jews call them by no other name than that of Cuthites (the name of one of thofe nations whom Efarhaddon had planted there), and have that utter hatred and averfion to them, that, reckoning them among the worft of heretics, they exprefs on all occafions a greater deteftation of them than they do even of the Chriftians themfelves.

Efarhaddon, after he had thus poffeffed himfelf of the land of Ifrael, fent fome of his princes, with part of his army, into Judea, to reduce that country alfo under his fubjection; who

having

[a] If. vii. 8.   [b] 2 Kings xvii. 24. Ezra iv. 2. 10.

having vanquished Manasseh in ª battle, and taken him, hid in a thicket of thorns, brought him prisoner to Esarhaddon, who bound him in fetters, and carried him to Babylon; where, his chains and his prison having brought him to himself, and a due sense of his great sin, wherewith he had sinned against the Lord his God, he returned unto him with repentance and prayer, and in his affliction, greatly humbled himself before him: whereon, God being intreated of by him, he mollified the heart of the king of Babylon towards him, so that, on a treaty, he was again restored to his liberty, and returned to Jerusalem; and then, knowing the Lord to be God, he abolished all those idolatrous profanations, both out of the temple, and out of all other parts of the land, which he had in his wickedness introduced into them, and again restored in all things the reformation of King Hezekiah, his father, and walked according thereto all the remainder of his life, worshipping the Lord his God only, and none other. And all Judah conformed to him herein; so that he continued in prosperity after this to the end of his reign, which was the longest of any of the kings that had sat on the throne of David, either before or after him: for he reigned full fifty-five years, and, these being all reckoned to his reign without any chasm, it is argued from hence, that his captivity at Babylon could not have been long; but that he was, within a very short time after, again released from it.

And to this time may be referred the completion of the prophecy of Isaiah concerning ᵇ the removal of Shebna, the chief minister of state, and the advancement of Eliakim, the son of Hilkiah, in his place. Both of them had been ministers of state under King Hezekiah, Shebna having been his scribe or secretary, and Eliakim the master of his household. And their history, as far as may be collected from the words of the prophet, appears to be thus. Shebna, being a very wicked man, was a fit person to serve the lusts and evil inclinations of Manasseh in the first part of his reign, and therefore was made his first minister of state; and Eliakim, who was of a quite contrary character, was quite laid aside. But on the revolution that happened on the coming of the army of the Assyrians, Shebna ᶜ was taken prisoner with his master, and carried to Babylon, and there detained in captivity ᵈ to his death. And therefore Manasseh, on his repentance, and return to Jerusalem, having resolved on other measures, called for Eliakim, and put the management of all his affairs into his hands; who, being a person of great wisdom, justice,

Vol. I.   C   and

ª 2 Chron. xxxiii. 11. Josephus Antiq. lib. 10. c. 4.
ᵇ Is. xxii. 15.—25.
ᶜ Is. xxii. 17.
ᵈ Is. xxii. 18.

and piety, soon re-established them upon the same foot as they had been in the days of Hezekiah, and so preserved them in peace and prosperity all his time, to the great honour of the king, and the good of all his people; and therefore he hath the character given him, of being [a] a father to the inhabitants of Jerusalem, and to all the house of Judah, and that, [b] having the key and government of the house of David upon his shoulders, he was the great support of it all his days. This Eliakim is supposed to have been of the pontifical family, and to have himself, in the time of Manasseh, borne the office of high priest, and to have been the same who is mentioned by the name of Joakim, or Eliakim, in the history of Judith, as high priest at that time; for Joakim and Eliakim are both the same name, being both of the same signification in the Hebrew tongue, and therefore the said high priest in Judith is, in the Syriac version, and also in Jerome's Latin version of that book, called promiscuously by both these names. But of this more will be said hereafter in its proper place.

The nations which Esarhaddon had brought to dwell in the cities of Samaria, instead of the Israelites, who had been carried thence, being, on their settling in that country [c], much infested with lions; and the king of Babylon being told, that it was because they worshipped not the God of the country, he ordered, that one of the priests, which had been carried thence, should be sent back to teach these new inhabitants how to worship the God of Israel. But they only took him hereon into the number of their former deities, and worshipped him jointly with the gods of the nations from whence they came; and in this corruption of joining the worship of their false gods with that of the true, they continued, till the building of the Samaritan temple on Mount Gerizzim by Sanballat; but, on that occasion, abundance of Jews falling off to them, they reduced them from this idolatry, to the worship of the true God only, as shall be hereafter related; and they have continued in the same worship ever since, even to this day.

An. 676.
Manas. 23.

In the eight and twentieth year of the reign of Manasseh, the twelve confederated sovereigns of Egypt, after they had jointly reigned there fifteen years, falling [d] out among themselves, expelled Psammitichus, one of their number, out of his share, which he had hitherto had with them in the government of the kingdom, and drove him into banishment; whereon, flying into the fens near the sea, he lay hid

An. 671.
Manas. 28.

---

[a] Isaiah xxii. 21.   [c] 2 Kings xvii.
[b] Isaiah xxii. 22.   [d] Herodot. lib. 2. Diodorus Siculus, lib. 1.

hid there, till, having gotten together out of the Arabian freebooters, and the pirates of Caria and Ionia, such a number of soldiers, as with the Egyptians of his party, made a considerable army, he marched with it against the other eleven, and, having overthrown them in battle, slew several of them, and drove the rest out of the land; and thereon, seizing the whole kingdom to himself, reigned over it in great prosperity fifty and four years.

As soon as he was well settled in the kingdom, he [a] entered into a war with the king of Assyria, about the boundaries of their two empires, which lasted many years: for, after the Assyrians had conquered Syria, Palestine only separating their respective territories, it became a constant bone of contention between them, as it was between the Ptolemys and the Seleucidæ afterwards, both parties striving which of the two should have the mastery of this province; and, according as they prevailed, sometimes the one, and sometimes the other possessed themselves of it. From the time of Hezekiah, it appears to have been in the hands of the Egyptians till the captivity of Manasseh. But, when Esarhaddon had conquered Judea, and carried the king prisoner to Babylon (as hath been above mentioned), it is plain, that, from thenceforth the king of Assyria became master of all, even to the very entry of Egypt; and the Egyptians, being at that time divided under several princes, and in civil wars among themselves, were in no capacity to put a stop to this progress. But when Psammitichus had gained the whole monarchy to himself, and again settled the affairs of that kingdom upon its former foundation (which happened about seven years after the captivity of Manasseh), he thought it time to look to the frontiers of his kingdom, and secure them as well as he could against the power of this growing neighbour, and therefore marched with an army into Palestine for this purpose; but, in the entry thereof, he found Ashdod, one of the first towns of that country, so strong a barrier against him, that it [b] cost him a blockade of nine and twenty years, before he could make himself master of it.

An. 670.
Manass. 29.

This place had formerly been [c] one of the five capital cities of the country of the Philistines. After this, the Egyptians got possession of it, and, by well fortifying of it, made it so strong a barrier of their empire on that side, that Sennacherib could not enter Egypt, till [d] he had, by Tartan, one of his generals, made himself master of it; and, when he had gotten it into his possession, finding the importance of the place, he added so much

to

---

[a] Herodotus, lib. 2.
[b] Herodotus, lib. 2.
[c] 1 Samuel vi. 17.
[d] Isaiah xx. 1.

to its strength, that, notwithstanding his unfortunate retreat out of Egypt, and the terrible loss of his army in Judea, immediately after, the Assyrians still kept it even to this time; and it was not without that long and tedious siege, which I have mentioned, that the Egyptians at last became again masters of it. And, when they had gotten it, they found it in such a manner wasted and reduced by so long a war, that it did them but little service afterwards; it being then no more than the carcase of that city, which it had formerly been. And therefore the prophet Jeremiah, speaking of it, calls it [a] "the remnant of Ashdod," intimating thereby, that it was then only the poor remains of what it had been in times foregoing.

But, notwithstanding this long siege, the whole war did not rest there. While part of the army lay at the blockade, the rest carried on the war against the other parts of Palestine; and so it continued many years, which obliged Manasseh [b] to fortify Jerusalem anew, and to put strong garrisons into all his frontier towns against them; for, since his release from the captivity of the Assyrians, and the restoration of his kingdom again to him, he was obliged to become their homager, and engage on their side in this war against the Egyptians, although they had been his former allies. And the better to enable him to support himself herein, and also the more firmly to fix him in his fidelity to them, they seem at this time to have put under his command all the other parts of the land of Canaan, that is, all that had been formerly possessed by the kings of Samaria, as well as what belonged to him as king of Judah; for it is certain, that Josiah, his grandson, had all this (as will be hereafter shewn), that is, not only the two tribes which made up the kingdom of Judah, but also all that had formerly been possessed by the other ten under the kings of Israel. And the most probable account that can be given of his coming by all this, is, that it was all given to Manasseh on this occasion, to hold in homage of the kings of Assyria, and that, after his death, it was continued to his son and grandson on the same conditions; in the performance of which that good and just prince, King Josiah, afterwards lost his life, as will be shewn in its proper place.

In the 31st year of Manasseh died Esarhaddon, after he had reigned, with great felicity, thirty-nine years over the Assyrians, and thirteen over the Babylonians; and [c] Saosduchinus, his son, reigned in his stead. He is the same who in the book of Judith is called [d] Nabuchodonosor. In the beginning of the 12th year of his reign, which was

An. 668.
Manas. 31.

---

[a] Jeremiah xxv. 20.
[b] 2 Chron. xxxiii. 14.
[c] Canon. Ptol.
[d] Judith i. 1.

was the 43d of Manasseh, [a] he fought a great battle in the plains of Ragau, with Deioces, king of Media (who in the book of Judith is called [b] Arphaxad), and, having overthrown him, and put him to flight, pursued after him to the adjacent mountains, where he made his retreat, and there, having overtaken him, he cut him off, and all his army; and thereon following his blow, and making the best of the advantage he had gotten, he made himself master of many of the cities of Media, and among them took [c] Ecbatana itself, the royal seat of the Median empire; and, after having miserably defaced it, returned in great triumph to Nineveh, and there took his pleasure in banquetting and feasting, both he and his army, for an hundred and twenty days.

An. 656.
Manaf. 43.

After this time of feasting was over, [d] he called his officers, nobles, and chief counsellors together, to take an account of what tributary countries and provinces had not gone with him to the war, for he had summoned them all to attend him herein; and, finding that none of the western countries had paid any regard to his commands in this matter, he made a decree, that Holofernes, the chief captain of his army, should go forth, to execute the wrath of his lord upon them for it. And, accordingly, the next year after, he marched westward with an army of an hundred and twenty thousand foot, and twelve thousand horse, and there wasted and destroyed a great many of those nations; till at length coming into Judea, and laying siege to Bethulia, he was there destroyed, and all his army cut in pieces, in the manner as is in the book of Judith at full related.

An. 655.
Manaf. 44.

That Arphaxad in the said book of Judith was Deioces, and Nabuchodonosor, Saosduchinus, appears from hence, that Arphaxad is said to be that king of Media, who was the [e] founder of Ecbatana, which all other writers agree to have been Deioces; and the beginning of the 12th year of Saosduchinus exactly agreeth with the last year of Deioces, when this battle of Ragau is said to have been fought. And there are several particulars in that history, which make it utterly inconsistent with any other times; for it was while [f] Nineveh was the metropolis of the Assyrian empire, it was while [g] the Persians, Syrians, Phœnicians, Cilicians, and Egyptians, were subject to them; it was while the [h] Median empire was in being, and not long after the building of Ecbatana; none of which could be

C 3

---

[a] Judith i. 5.
[b] Judith i. 1.
[c] Judith i. 14.
[d] Judith ii.
[e] Judith i. 1. 2.
[f] Judith i. 1.
[g] Judith i. 7—10.
[h] Judith i. 1. 2.

be after the captivity of Judah, where some would place this history. For, before that time, Nineveh had been long destroyed, and both the Assyrian and Median empires had been wholly extinguished, and the Persians, instead of being subject to the Assyrians, had made themselves lords over them, and over all the other nations of the East, from the Hellespont to the river Indus; for so far they had extended and established their empire, before the Jews were returned from the Babylonish captivity, and settled again in their own country. And therefore we must go much higher than the times after that captivity, to find a proper scene for the matters in that book related; and it can be no where laid more agreeably both with scripture and prophane history, than in the time where I have placed it.

This book of Judith was originally written [a] in the Chaldee language, by some Jew of Babylon (which is not now extant), and from thence, at the desire of Paula and Eustochium, was, by St Jerome, translated into the Latin tongue; which is the translation that is now extant in the vulgar Latin edition of the Bible, of which he himself saith, in the preface before it, that he did not translate it word for word, but only rendered it according to the sense of the author; and that, cutting off all the corruptions of various readings, which he found in different copies, he did put only that into the translation, which he judged to be the true and entire sense of the original. But, besides this translation of St Jerome, there are two others, one in Greek, and the other in Syriac. That which is in Greek is attributed to Theodotion, who flourished in the time of Commodus, who was made Roman emperor in the year of Christ 180. But it must be much ancienter; for Clemens Romanus, in his epistle to the Corinthians (which was wrote near 120 years before), brings a quotation out of it. The Syriac translation was made from the Greek, and so was also the English, which we at present have among the apocryphal writings in our Bible. And it is to be observed, that all these three versions last mentioned, have several particulars, which are not in Jerome's; and some of these seem to be those various readings, which he professeth to have cut off as corruptions of the text: and particularly that which is added in the 13th verse of the first chapter, appears to be of this sort; for there the battle of Ragau is placed in the 17th year of Nabuchodonosor, which is directly contradictory to what is in the former part of the same chapter, for there it is positively said, that it was in the 12th year of his reign And, agreeable hereto, Jerome's version placeth the expedition of Holofernes

---

[a] Hieronymi Præfatio in Librum Judith.

lofernes (that was the next year after) in the 13th year of Nabuchodonofer, which is the truth of the matter; whereas the other, following the blunder of the former contradiction, makes another, by placing it in the 18th year of his reign, and so renders that part of the history wholly inconsistent with itself. And therefore certainly, in this particular, Jerome's version is to be preferred, which gives good reason to think, that it ought to be so in all the rest, wherever there is any difference between them.

But still, whether the book be a true or a feigned history, is what learned men are not agreed in. The Romanists will have it all to be true; for they have received it into the canon of divine writ. But, on the other hand, it is the opinion of [a] Grotius, that it is wholly a parabolical fiction, written in the time of Antiochus Epiphanes, when he came into Judea to raise a persecution against the Jewish church; and that the design of it was, to confirm the Jews under that persecution in their hopes that God would send them a deliverance: 'That therein, by
' Judith is meant Judea; by Bethulia, the temple or house
' of God; and by the sword, which went out from thence,
' the prayers of the saints; that Nabuchodonofor doth there
' denote the devil; and the kingdom of Affyria, the devil's
' kingdom, pride: that by Holofernes is there meant the in-
' strument or agent of the devil in that persecution; Antio-
' chus Epiphanes, who made himself master of Judea, that
' fair widow, so called, because destitute of relief: that Elia-
' kim signifies God, who would arise in her defence, and at
' length cut off that instrument of the devil who would have
' corrupted her.' This particular explication of the parable (as he will have it to be) is, I confess, the peculiar fancy of this great man: But otherwise there are abundance of other learned writers among the Protestants, who agree with him in the general, that this book is rather a parabolical than a real history, made for the instructing and comforting of the people of the Jews under that figure, and not to give them a narrative of any thing really done; and their reason for it is, that they think it utterly inconsistent with all times, where it hath been endeavoured to be placed, either before or after the captivity of the Jews. My putting it in the time of Manasseh takes off all the objections which are brought to prove its inconsistency with the times after the captivity, which, I confess, are unanswerable.

But where it here stands, the objections from the other part still remain; and they are these following: 1st, That Joakim or Eliakim

[a] In Præfatione ad Annotationes in Librum Judith.

Eliakiam (for they are acknowledged to be both [a] the same name) is said in the history of Judith to have been then high priest; but there is none of that name to be found, either in the scriptures or in Josephus, that was high priest before the captivity. 2*dly*, Achior the Amonite, in his speech to Holofernes (ch. v. ver. 18), there speaks of the temple as having been lately cast to the ground, which was not done till the last year of the reign of Zedekiah; and therefore this cannot be consistent with any time before it; and the 3d verse of chapter iv. plainly puts it after the captivity; for there the text is, that the people of the Jews were newly returned from their captivity, when Holofernes invaded Judea. 3*dly*, The chief management of the public affairs of the state are in that book placed wholly in the high priest, without any mention made of the king throughout the whole of it, or implying in the least, that there was then any such government in the land; which renders it wholly inconsistent with any other times than those in which there was no king in Judah. 4*thly*, That, in the conclusion of the book, Judith is said to have lived an hundred and five years; and that none made the children of Israel any more afraid in all her days, nor a long time after her death. But supposing her to have been 45 years old when she went out to Holofernes (and in an older age she cannot well be supposed to have beauty enough to charm such a man), to make her an hundred and five years old, there must be 60 years more added to her life, which will carry down her death to the 4th year of Zedekiah, when the state of the Jews had for several years been exceedingly disturbed by the Babylonians, and was, within a little while after, totally subverted by them; which makes both her life and her death absolutely inconsistent with the times in which they are above placed.

To the first of these objections it may be answered, 1*st*, That though there be no such person as Joakim, or Eliakim, named in scripture to have been high priest before the captivity, yet this is no argument but that there might have been such an one; for the scripture no where professeth to give us an exact catalogue of all such as had been high priests till the captivity. That which looks most like it is what we have in the 6th chapter of the first book of Chronicles. But that is only a direct lineal descent of the pontifical family from Aaron to Jozadack, the son of Seraiah, who was high priest at the captivity, and not a

catalogue

---

[a] For they are both of the same signification, El being the name of God in one, as Jehovah is the other, and the latter part of the name is the same in both; and therefore, as Jehoiakim, or Joakim, king of Judah, is called also Eliakim, so this high priest is, in the version of Jerome, called promiscuously by both names.

catalogue of such as had borne the pontifical office; for several are in that pedigree who never were high priests, and several are left out that were. The high priests of the family of Eli are instances of the latter; for they are left out of that pedigree, though they were high priests: and those of the true race, who were excluded by them, are instances of the former; for they are in it, though they never were high priests. And it is very likely, that, from the time of Solomon to the captivity, many more such instances might have happened to hinder that pedigree from being an exact catalogue of the high priests: for, on the minority, or some other unqualifying defect of the right heir, the next collateral must have been admitted to the office, whose name could not come into the pedigree; and, on the failing of an elder branch (as might have happened), the heir of the next collateral branch must have come into the office; and then the ancestors of the collateral successor must be in the pedigree, though they never had been in the office, and those of the elder branch, though they had been in the office, could not be in the pedigree, because it had failed. For it is only the pedigree of Jozadack, the son of Seraiah, who was high priest at the captivity, which is in a direct line from Aaron, that is given us in the 6th chapter of the first book of Chronicles: and it being the usage of the Jews, in their pedigrees, to pass from a remote ancestor to a remote descendant, by leaving out those who are between, of which abundance of instances might be given in scripture, it is possible this also might have happened in this case. And thus much is certain, that four high priests named in scripture are not in that pedigree, *i. e.* Jehoidah, and Zechariah his son, who were high priests in the reign of Joash; Azariah, who was high priest in the reign of Uzziah; and Urijah, who was high priest in the reign of Ahaz, kings of Judah. There are indeed two Azariahs named in that pedigree, besides the Azariah who was the father of Seraiah; but neither of these two could be the Azariah that was high priest in the time of Uzziah: for ^a Amariah, the son of the last of the said two Azariahs in that pedigree, was high priest in the time of Jehosaphat, five generations before. As to the pedigrees of the high priests in Ezra and Nehemiah, they are but imperfect parts of that which we have in the 6th chapter of the 1st book of Chronicles. As for the catalogue of Josephus, it is so corrupted, that scarce five of the names in it agree with any thing that we have in scripture. And therefore, putting all this together, Joakim or Eliakim might have been high priest in the time of Manasseh, though there be no mention of him as such, by either of his names, either in the holy scriptures or

---

^a 2 Chron. xix. 11.

in the history of Josephus. But, 2*dly*, That this Joakim or Eliakim (for both, as hath been afore observed, is the same name) is not named in scripture, is not certainly true: for there are some who will have Eliakim, the son of Hilkiah, that is afore spoken of, to have been the person, and understand what is said in If. xxii. 21. of the robe and the girdle, which he was to put on, as meant of the pontifical robe and girdle; and therefore infer from hence, that he was high priest: and [a] St Jerome and St Cyril, among the ancients, both were of this opinion. And it must be said, that what is there prophesied of him by Isaiah, that God would commit the government of the state to his hands, in the room of Shebnah, who was chief minister before him; and that he should be a father to the inhabitants of Jerusalem, and to the house of Judah; and that the key of the house of David should be laid upon his shoulder, to open and to shut without controul, as he should think fit, doth very well agree with that part which Joakim is said to have acted in the book of Judith. But that he was the same person is what I durst not from that, which is brought to prove it, lay much stress upon; neither is there any need of it for the satisfying of this objection, what I have else said being sufficient for it.

2*dly*, As to the objection from ch. iv. ver. 3. of Judith, and from the speech of Achior (ch. v. ver. 18.), the words on which they are founded are not in Jerome's version; and therefore it is most likely they were put into the Greek version (from whence the English is taken) from some of those corrupted copies of the original which Jerome complains of: for in his version) which he made from the best corrected copies of the original Chaldee), ver. 3. of chapter iv. is wholly left out, as are also those words of ch. v. ver. 18. which speak of *the temple's having been cast to the ground*. And although there be words still remaining in Jerome's version, as well as in our English, which speak of the captivity and dispersion of the Jews, and their late restoration again to their own land; yet they are none other than what may be better understood of the Assyrian captivity, in the time of Manasseh, than of the Babylonish, which happened afterwards. As to the third objection, it is possible Manasseh might be then engaged in the defence of some other part of his kingdom, and therefore had intrusted Joakim with the management of all affairs at Jerusalem during his absence. And if he were the Eliakim mentioned in the 22d chapter of Isaiah, and, as chief minister of state, was then invested with all that amplitude of trust and power as is there described, that might be reason enough for him only to be made

mention

---

[a] In Isaiam xxii.

mention of in this tranfaction, without naming of his mafter at all therein.

But, *laftly*, To give a fatisfactory anfwer to the fourth objection, I muft confefs is not in my power. Could we put this hiftory fo far back, as the minority of Manaffeh, this would not only afford us an anfwer to this objection, but would alfo give us a much clearer one to the laft preceding. For, then there would be reafon enough, not to mention the minor king, but only the chief minifter and guardian of the kingdom, in the tranfacting of the whole affair: and the death of Judith would, on this fuppofition, be at fuch a diftance from the deftruction of the Jewifh ftate, as not to make this objection unanfwerable. But the wickednefs of the pupil will not allow him to have been bred under fo good a man for his governor, as Eliakim is defcribed to be. And what is faid in the 18th and 19th verfes of the fifth chapter of Judith, concerning the captivity and reftoration of the Jews, and is retained alfo in Jerome's verfion, muft neceffarily refer the matters therein related, to thofe times which followed the captivity of Manaffeh, and the reftoration of him and his people again to their own land. And the chronology of this hiftory will not permit the beginning of it to fall any where elfe, but in the 12th year of Saofduchinus, and the laft of Deioces; and thefe two characters of the time exactly concurring, according to Herodotus and Ptolemy, do unavoidably determine us to fix it here. However, our not being able to clear this difficulty, is not a fufficient reafon for us to reject the whole hiftory. There is fcarce any hiftory written, but what, to the next age after, may appear, as to time, place, and other circumftances, with thofe feeming inconfiftencies, as cannot then be eafily reconciled, when the memory of men begin to fail concerning them. And how much more then, may we be apt to blunder, when we take our view at the diftance of above two thoufand years, and have no other light to difcern the fo far diftant object by, than fuch glimmerings from broken fcraps of hiftory, as leave us next door to groping in the dark for whatfoever knowledge we get by them? That which feemeth moft probable in this cafe is, that the writer of this book, the more to magnify his heroine, attributed too long a continuance to that peace, which was by her obtained for the land: [a] for, according to this account,

[a] For, allowing her to have been 45 years old at the time of her killing Holofernes, there muft be 60 years after to the time of her death, and " a long time after" in the text (Judith xvj. 25.) cannot imply lefs than 20 years more. But if we fuppofe her to be but 25 at the killing of Holofernes (which is more likely) it will carry down the computation even beyond the deftruction of Jerufalem, which makes the objection much ftronger.

account, it must have lasted at least eighty years: which being what they never had enjoyed from the time they were a nation, or what scarce any other nation ever had, I would rather choose to allow a fiction in this particular, than for the sake of it condemn the whole book as such, which seemeth to carry with it the air of a true history in all other particulars.

However, I must acknowledge, that what is above said in the defence of this book, for its being a true history, doth not so far clear the matter, especially in respect of the fourth objection, but that if any one will still contend, that it is only a religious romance, and not a true history; that, according to the intention of the author, the scene of it was put under the reign of Xerxes, when [a] Joakim, the son of Joshua, was high priest, and the civil government of Judea, as well as the ecclesiastical, was in the hands of that officer; and that the inconsistency of so many particulars in that book, with the state and transactions of those times, was only from the ignorance of the author in the history of the said times, and his unskilfulness in placing the scene of his story in them; I say, if any one will insist on all this, notwithstanding what is above said, I shall not enter into any controversy with him about it; only thus much I must insist on, that if it be a true history (which I am inclined most to think, though I will not be positive in it), it can fall no where else, but in the time where I have laid it.

After the death of Deioces, [b] Phraortes his son succeeded in the kingdom of Media, and reigned over it twenty-two years.

An. 648.
Manas.51.
In the fifty-first year of Manasseh, died [c] Saosduchinus, king of Babylon and Assyria, and Chyniladanus reigned in his stead.

An. 644.
Manas.55.
Manasseh, king of Judah, after he had reigned fifty-five years, and lived sixty-seven, [d] died at Jerusalem; and notwithstanding his signal repentance, since his former wickedness had been so great, they would not allow him the honour of being buried in the sepulchres of the sons of David, but laid him in a grave made for him in his own garden.

An. 643.
Ammon 1.
After Manasseh reigned Ammon his son; who, imitating the first part of his father's reign, rather than the latter, gave himself up to all manner of wickedness and impiety; whereon the servants of his house conspired against him, and slew him after he had reigned two years.

But

---

[a] Nehemiah xii. 10. 26.
[b] Herodotus lib. 1.
[c] Canon Ptolemæi.
[d] 2 Kings xxi. 18. 2 Chron. xxxiii. 20.

But the people of the land severely revenged the murder; putting them all to death, that had any hand in it. However, they would not give him in his burial the honour of a place among the sepulchres of the sons of David, but buried him in the garden by his father; which shews, that though they condemned the wickedness of his reign, they would not allow of the violence that was offered to his person; though it may well be supposed, that nothing less than the highest tyranny and oppression could have provoked his own domestics to it.

After the death of Ammon, [a] Josiah his son succeeded him in the kingdom, being then but eight years old. But having the happiness to fall under the conduct of better guardians in his minority, than did Manasseh his grandfather, he proved, when grown up, a prince of very extraordinary worth; equalling in piety, virtue, and goodness, if not exceeding herein, the best of his predecessors. An. 640. Josiah 1.

Although Ammon reigned but two years, yet the beginning of the reign of Josiah, is here put at the distance of three years from the beginning of the first year of Ammon, because the odd months of the reign of Hezekiah, Manasseh, and Ammon, over and above the round number of years, which they are said to have reigned, do by this time amount to a whole year more, which the chronology of the ensuing history makes necessary to be here supposed.

In the 6th year of Josiah, [b] Phraortes, king of Media, having brought under him all the upper Asia (which is all that lay north of Mount Taurus, from Media to the river Halys), and made the Persians also to become subject unto him, elated his thoughts on these successes, to the revenging of himself upon the Assyrians for his father's death, and accordingly marched with a great army against them, and, having made himself master of the country, laid siege to Nineveh itself, the capital of the empire. But he had there the misfortune to meet with the same ill fate that his father had in the former war; for, being overthrown in the attempt, he and all his army perished in it. An. 635. Josiah 6.

Josiah, in the [c] 8th year of his reign, being now sixteen years old, took on him the administration of the kingdom, and, beginning with the reformation of religion, endeavoured to purge it of all those corruptions, which had been introduced in the time of Ammon and Manasseh, his father, and grandfather; and did set his heart to seek the Lord his God with all his might, as did David his father. An. 663. Josiah 8.

Cyaxares

---
[a] 2 Kings xxii. 2 Chron. xxxiv.   [c] 2 Chron. xxxiv. 3.
[b] Herodotus, lib. 1.

Cyaxares, the son of Phraortes [a], having succeeded his father in the kingdom of Media, as soon as he had well settled himself in the government, drew together a great army to be revenged on the Assyrians for the late loss, and, having overthrown them in a great battle, led the Medes the second time to the siege of Nineveh; but, before he could make any progress therein, he was called off to defend his own territories against a new enemy. For the Scythians, from the parts about the Palus Meotis, passing round the Caucasus, had made a great inroad upon them; whereby he was forced to leave Nineveh to march against them. But he had not the same success in this war, which he had against the Assyrians; for the Scythians, having vanquished him in battle, dispossessed him of all the upper Asia, and reigned there twenty-eight years; during which time, they enlarged their conquests into Syria, and as far as the borders of Egypt. But there Psammitichus, king of Egypt, having met them, prevailed with intreaties and large gifts, that they proceeded no farther; and thereby saved his country from this dangerous invasion. In this expedition, they seized [b] on Bethshean, a city in the territories of the tribe of Manasseh on this side Jordan, and kept it as long as they continued in Asia; and therefore, from them it was afterwards called Cythopolis, or the city of the Scythians But how far the ravages of those barbarians might affect Judea is no where said, although there can be no doubt, but that those parts, as well as the rest of Palestine, both in their march to the borders of Egypt, and also in their return from thence, must have suffered much by them. It is related of them, that in their passage through the land of the Philistines, on their return from Egypt, some of the stragglers robbed [c] the temple of Venus at Askelon, and that for the punishment hereof they and their posterity were afflicted with emerods for a long while after; which lets us know, that the Philistines had till then still preserved the memory of what they had formerly suffered on the account of the [d] ark of God. For, from that time, it seems, they looked on this disease, as the proper punishment from the hand of God, for all such like sacrilegious impieties: and for this reason assigned it to the Scythians in their histories, on their charging of them there with this crime.

Josiah, in the [e] 12th year of his reign, being now twenty years old, and having farther improved himself in the knowledge of God and his laws, proceeded according hereto farther to perfect that reformation,

An. 629.
Josiah 12.

which

---

[a] Herodotus, lib. 1.
[b] Syncellus, p. 214.
[c] Herodotus, lib. 1.
[d] 1 Sam. v.
[e] 2 Chron. xxxiv. 3. 4. 5. &c.

which he had begun. And therefore, making a strict inquiry, by a general progress through the land, after all the relics of idolatry which might be any where remaining therein, he broke down all the altars of Baalim with the idols erected on high before them, and all the high-places, and cut down the groves and broke in pieces all the carved images, and the molten images, and digged up the graves of the idolatrous priests, and burnt their bones upon all places of idolatrous worship, thereby to pollute and defile them for ever; and when he had thus cleansed all Judah and Jerusalem, he went into the cities of Ephraim and Manasseh, and all the rest of the land, that had formerly been possessed by the ten tribes of Israel (for all this was then subject to him), and there did the same thing.

In the 13th year of Josiah, [a] Jeremiah was called to the prophetic office, which he afterwards executed for above 40 years, in warning Judah and Jerusalem of the wrath of God impending on them for their iniquities, and in calling them to repentance for the averting of it; till at length, on their continuing wholly obdurate in their evil ways, it was poured out in full measure upon both in a most calamitous destruction.

An. 628.
Josiah 13.

In the 15th year of Josiah, Chyniladanus, king of Babylon and Assyria, having, by his effeminacy and unprofitableness in the state, made himself contemptible to his people, [b] Nabopollassar, who was general of his army, took this advantage to set up for himself, and, being a Babylonian by birth, made use of his interest there to seize that part of the Assyrian empire, and reigned king of Babylon twenty-one years.

An. 626.
Josiah 15.

Josiah, [c] in the 18th year of his reign, took especial care for the repairing of the house of God, and therefore sent several of the chief officers of his court to take an account of the money collected for it, and to lay his command upon Hilkiah the high priest, that he should see it be forthwith laid out in the doing of the work; so that all might be put in thorough repair. The high priest, in pursuance of this order, took a general view of the house, to see what was necessary to be done; and, while he was thus examining every place, he found the authentic copy of the law of Moses. This ought to have been laid up [d] on the side of the ark of the covenant in the most holy place; but it was taken out thence and hid

An. 623.
Josiah 18.

[a] Jer. i. 2. and xxv. 3.
[b] Alexander Polyhistor apud Eusebium in Chronico, p. 46. et apud Syncellum, p. 210.
[c] 2 Kings xxii. 2 Chron. xxxiv.
[d] Deut. xxxi. 26.

hid elfewhere in the time of Manaſſeh, as it is conjectured, that it might not be deſtroyed by him in the time of his iniquity. This book Hilkiah ſent to the king by Shaphan the ſcribe, who, on his delivering of it to the king, did, by his command, read ſome part of it to him. The place, which on the opening of the book he happened on, was (ſay the Jewiſh doctors) that part of the 28th chapter of Deuteronomy, wherein are denounced the curſes of God againſt the people of Iſrael, and againſt the king in particular (ver. 26.), in caſe they ſhould not keep the law which he had commanded them. On the hearing of this, Joſiah rent his clothes through grief, and was ſeized with great fear and conſternation, on the account both of himſelf and his people, as knowing how much they and their fathers had tranſgreſſed this law, and dreading the curſes denounced againſt them for it. To eaſe his mind under this trouble and anxiety of his thoughts, he ſent Hilkiah the high prieſt with ſeveral of his officers to Huldah the propheteſs, to inquire of the Lord. The anſwer, which they brought back, was a ſentence of deſtruction upon Judah and Jeruſalem; but that as to Joſiah, becauſe of his repentance, the execution of it ſhould be delayed till after his days. However, the good king, to appeaſe the wrath of God, as much as lay in his power, called together a ſolemn aſſembly of all the elders and people of Judah and Jeruſalem; and, going up with them to the temple, cauſed the law of God to be there read to them, and after that both king and people publicly entered into a ſolemn covenant to walk after the Lord, and to keep his commandments, and his teſtimonies, and his ſtatutes, with all their heart and all their ſoul; and to perform all the words of the covenant that were written in that book. And after this he made another progreſs through the land to purge it of all other abominations of idolatry or other wickedneſs, which might be ſtill remaining in it, which he throughly rooted out in all parts of his kingdom in ſuch manner, as is in the 23d chapter of the 2d book of Kings at large related. And particularly he deſtroyed the altar and high-place, which Jeroboam had built at Bethel, firſt polluting them by burning on them the bones of men, taken out of their ſepulchres near adjoining, and then breaking down the altar, and burning the high-place, and the grove, and ſtamping them all to powder; whereby he fulfilled what had been [a] prophefied of him by name many ages before in the time of Jeroboam. And he did the ſame in all the reſt of the cities of Samaria, deſtroying every remainder of idolatry, which he could any where find in any of them. And, when the next paſſover approached, he cauſed that feaſt to be kept with ſo great a ſolemnity and concourſe

[a] 2 Kings xiii. 2.

courſe of people from all parts of the land, that it not only exceeded the paſſover of Hezekiah, which is afore mentioned, but all other paſſovers from the days of Samuel the prophet to that time.

By the behaviour both of the high prieſt, as well as of the king, at the finding of the book of the law, it plainly appears, that neither of them had ſeen any copy of it before; which ſhews into how corrupt a ſtate the church of the Jews was then ſunk, till this good king reformed it: for although Hezekiah [a] kept ſcribes on purpoſe to collect together and write out copies of the holy ſcriptures, yet, through the iniquity of the times that after followed in the reigns of Manaſſeh and Ammon, they had either been ſo deſtroyed, or elſe ſo neglected and loſt, that there were then none of them left in the land, unleſs in ſome few private hands, where they were kept up and concealed till this copy was found in the temple: and therefore, after this time (by the care, we may be aſſured, of this religious prince), were written out thoſe copies of the law, and other holy ſcriptures then in being, which were preſerved after the captivity, and out of which Ezra made his edition of them, in ſuch a manner as will be hereafter related.

In the 24th year of Joſiah, [b] died Pſammitichus, king of Egypt, after he had reigned fifty-four years, and was ſucceeded by Necus, his ſon, the ſame who in ſcripture is called Pharaoh Necho, and often mentioned there under that name. He made an attempt to join the Nile and the Red ſea, by drawing a canal from the one to the other; but, after he had conſumed an hundred and twenty thouſand men in the work, he was forced to deſiſt from it. But he had better ſucceſs in another undertaking; for, having gotten ſome of the experteſt of the Phœnician ſailors into his ſervice, he [c] ſent them out by the Red ſea through the ſtraits of Babelmandel, to diſcover the coaſts of Africa; who, having ſailed round it, came home the third year through the ſtraits of Gibraltar, and the Mediterranean ſea, which was a very extraordinary voyage to be made in thoſe days, when the uſe of the loadſtone was not known. This voyage was performed about two thouſand one hundred years before Vaſquez de Gama, a Portugueſe, by diſcovering the Cape of Good Hope, A.D. 1497, found out the ſame way from hence to the Indies, by which theſe Phœnicians came from thence. Since that, it hath been made the common paſſage thither from all theſe weſtern parts of the world.

An. 617.
Joſiah 24.

In the 29th year of the reign of Joſiah, which was the 23d
of

---

[a] Prov. xxv. 1. [b] Herodot. lib. 1. [c] Herodot. lib. 4.

of Cyaxares in the kingdom of Media, [a] Nabopollafar, king of Babylon, having made an affinity with
Aſtyages, the eldeſt ſon of Cyaxares, by the marriage
of Nebuchadnezzar, his ſon, with Amyitis, the daughter of Aſtyages, entered into a confederacy with him againſt the Aſſyrians; and thereon, joining their forces together, they beſieged
Nineveh; and, after having taken the place, and ſlain Saracus
the king (who was either the ſucceſſor of Chyniladanus, or he
himſelf under another name), to gratify the Medes, they utterly deſtroyed that great and ancient city; and from that time
Babylon became the ſole metropolis of the Aſſyrian empire.
From the time that Eſarhaddon obtained the kingdom of Babylon [b], both cities equally had this honour, the kings ſometimes reſiding at Nineveh, and ſometimes at Babylon; but after this Nineveh loſt it for ever: for, although there was another city afterwards erected out of the ruins of old Nineveh,
which for a long time bore the ſame name, yet it never attained
to the grandeur and glory of the former. It is at this day called
[c] Moſul, and is only famous for being the ſeat of the patriarch
of the Neſtorians, of which ſect are moſt of the Chriſtians
in thoſe parts. It is ſituated on the weſt ſide of the river Tigris, where was anciently only a ſuburb of the old Nineveh;
for the city itſelf ſtood on the eaſt ſide of the river, where are
to be ſeen ſome of its ruins of great extent even unto this day.
According to [d] Diodorus Siculus, the circuit of Nineveh was
480 furlongs, which make 60 of our miles. And hence it is,
that it is ſaid in Jonah to be a city [e] of three days journey,
that is in compaſs, for 20 miles is as much as a man can well
go in a day. Strabo [f] ſaith of it, that it was much bigger
than Babylon; and in the ſame place he tells us, that the circuit of Babylon was 385 furlongs, that is, 48 of our miles.
The phraſe *much bigger* may well extend to the other twelve
miles to make it up ſixty.

In this deſtruction of Nineveh was fulfilled the prophecies
of [g] Jonah, [h] Nahum, and [i] Zephaniah, againſt it. And we
are told in the book of [k] Tobit, that Tobias his ſon lived to
hear of it, and that it was accompliſhed by Nabuchodonoſor
and Aſſuerus, which exactly agrees with the account which,
out of Alexander Polyhiſtor, I have juſt above given of it. For
that

An. 612.
Joſiah 29.

---

[a] Euſebii Chronicon, p. 124. A-
lexander Polyhiſtor apud Syncellum, p. 210. et apud Euſebium in
Chronico, p. 46. Herodot. lib. 1.

[b] Strabo, lib. 16. p. 734.

[c] Thevenot's Travels, part 2.
book 2. c. 11. p. 50.

[d] Lib. 2.

[e] Jonah iii. 3.

[f] Lib. 16. p. 737.

[g] Chap. iii.

[h] Chap. ii. and iii.

[i] Chap. ii. 13.

[k] Chap. xiv. 15.

that the Affuerus here mentioned was Aftyages, appears from Daniel; for Darius the Mede, who was Cyaxares, the fon of Aftyages, is there called the fon [a] of Ahafuerus: and Nabuchodonofor was a name among the Babylonians commonly given to their kings, as that of Pharaoh was among the Egyptians. And that Nabopollafar in particular was fo called, not only appears from [b] the rabbinical writings of the Jews, but alfo from Jofephus himfelf, a writer, by reafon of his antiquity, of much better authority in this matter. For, in his Antiquities, where he is fpeaking of this fame king, he [c] calls him in a quotation, which is there brought out of Berofus, by the name of Nabuchodonofor; and afterwards, [d] in his book againft Apion, repeating the fame quotation, he there calls him Nabullafar, the fame by contraction with Nabopollafar; which plainly proves him to have been called by both thefe names. I know there are thofe who take upon them, from this paffage in the book againft Apion, to mend that in the Antiquities, and put Nabopollafar in both places; but I fee no reafon for it but their own fancy. Others may, with as good authority, from the paffage in the Antiquities, mend that in the book againft Apion, and put Nabuchodonofor in both places. It is certain the books of Tobit and Judith can never be reconciled with any other ancient writings, either facred or profane, which relate to thofe times, unlefs we allow Nabuchodonofor to have been a name common to the kings of Babylon.

The [e] archbifhop of Armagh hath put this deftruction of Nineveh 14 years earlier, that is, in the laft year of Chyniladanus in the canon of Ptolemy, for no other reafon, I fuppofe, but that he reckoned that the end of his life and the end of his reign in that canon happened both at the fame time, and both together in the deftruction of that city: whereas, the computation of that canon being by the years of the kings that reigned at Babylon, Chyniladanus's reign there muft end where Nabopollafar's begun, whether he then died or no, as it is moft probable he did not, but that he continued to hold the kingdom of Affyria after he had loft that of Babylon, and that it was not till fome time after that lofs that Nineveh was deftroyed: for Eufebius placeth the deftruction of Nineveh in the 23d year of the reign of Cyaxares; and to put it back 14 years, to the laft of Chyniladanus

[a] Daniel ix. 1.
[b] In Juchafin, Nebuchadnezar is called Nebuchadnezzar, the fon of Nebuchadnezzar, fol. 136.; and David Gaoz, under the year of the world 3285, calls the father Nebuchadnezzar the firft, and the fon Nebuchadnezzar the fecond.
[c] Jofephus Antiq. lib. 10. c. 11.
[d] Lib. 1.
[e] In Annalibus Veteris Teftamenti fub anno mundi.

danus in the canon, will make it fall in the 9th year of Cyaxares, which is too early either for his son Astyages to have a daughter marriageable, or for Nebuchadnezzar to be of age sufficient to take her to wife: for, after this rate, Nebuchadnezzar must be allowed to have been [a] at the least 85 years old at the time of his death, and Astyages much older, which is an age very unlikely for such to live, who usually waste their lives, both by luxury and fatigue, much faster than other men.

At the destruction of this city of Nineveh ended the book of Tobit. It was first written [b] in Chaldee by some Babylonian Jew, and seems, in its original draught, to have been the memoirs of the family to which it relates; first begun by Tobit, then continued by Tobias, and lastly finished by some other of the family, and afterwards digested by the Chaldee author into that form in which we now have it. Jerome [b] translated it out of the Chaldee into Latin, and his translation is that which we have in the vulgar Latin edition of the Bible. But there is a Greek version much ancienter than this; for we find it made use of by Polycarp, Clemens Alexandrinus, and other fathers, who were before Jerome; and from this hath been made the Syriac version, and also that which we have in English among the apocryphal writers in our Bible. But the Chaldee original is not now extant. The Hebrew copies which go about of this book, as well as that of Judith, seem both to be of [c] a modern composure. It being easier to settle the chronology of this book than that of the book of Judith, it hath met with much less opposition from learned men, and is generally looked on, both by Jews and Christians, as a genuine and true history; though, as to some matters in it (as particularly that of the angel's accompanying of Tobias in a long journey under the shape of Azarias, the story of Raguel's daughter, the frighting away of the devil by the smoke of the heart and liver of a fish, and the curing of Tobit's blindness by the gall of the same fish), it is much less reconcileable to a rational credibility; for these things look more like the fictions of Homer than the writings of a sacred historian, and give an objection against this book which doth not lie against the other. However, it may excellently well serve to represent unto us the duties of charity and patience, in the example of Tobit's ready helping his brethren in distress to the utmost of his power,

[a] For, according to this account, this marriage must have been 21 years before Nebuchadnezzar began to reign, and he reigned 43 years; and it must also have been 31 years before Astyages began to reign, and he reigned 30 years.
[b] Præfatio Hieronymi in Tobiam.
[c] They are generally thought to have been made by Munster.

power, and his bearing with a pious submission the calamities of his captivity, poverty, and blindness, as long as inflicted upon him. The Latin and Greek versions of this book, which I have mentioned, do much differ, each having some particulars in it which are wanting in the other. But here the Latin version must give place to the Greek. For [a] Jerome made it, before he himself understood Chaldee, by the help of a learned Jew, from whose mouth, he tells us, he wrote down in Latin what the other rendered into Hebrew from the original, and in this manner finished the whole work in one day's time; and a work so done must undoubtedly have abundance of mistakes as well as inaccuracies in it. But his translation [b] of Judith was made afterwards, when, by his further studies in the oriental languages, he had rendered himself as much master of the Chaldee as he was before of the Hebrew; and he did it with great care, comparing diligently many various copies, and making use only of such as he found to be the best; and therefore his version of that book may well deserve an authority beyond the Greek, which cannot be claimed for the other. If the copy which Jerome translated his Tobit from were a true copy, and he were not mistaken in the version, there is one passage in it which absolutely overthrows the whole authority of the book: for (ch. xiv. 7.) there is mention made of the temple of Jerusalem as then burnt and destroyed, which makes the whole of it utterly inconsistent with the times in which it is placed. The Greek version, as also the English, which is taken from it, I acknowledge, speak only prophetically of it, as of that which was to be done, and not historically, as of that which was already done, as Jerome's doth. However, this Latin edition is that which the church of Rome hath canonized. If the historical ground-plot of the book be true, which is the most that can be said of it, yet certainly it is interlarded with many fictions of the invention of him that wrote it.

The Babylonians and the Medes having thus destroyed Nineveh, as is above related, they became so formidable hereon, as raised the jealousy of all their neighbours; and therefore, to put a stop to their growing greatness, [c] Necho, king of Egypt, in the 31st year of King Josiah, marched with a great army towards the Euphrates to make war upon them. The words of Josephus are, [d] 'That it was to make war upon the Medes and 'Babylonians, who had dissolved the Assyrian empire;' which plainly shews, that this war was commenced immediately upon

that

[a] Hieronymi Præfatio in Tobiam.
[b] Hieronymi Præfatio in Librum Judith.
[c] Herodotus, lib. 2. Josephus Antiq. lib. 10. c. 6.
[d] Josephus Antiq. lib. 10. c. 6.

that diffolution, and confequently, that the deftruction of Nineveh, whereby this diffolution was brought to pafs, was juft before this war, in the year where, according to Eufebius, I have placed it.

On Necho's taking his way through Judea, [a] Jofiah refolved to impede his march; and therefore, getting together his forces, he pofted himfelf in the valley of Megiddo, there to ftop his paffage: whereon Necho fent ambaffadors unto him, to let him know, that he had no defign upon him, that the war he was engaged in was againft others; and therefore advifed him not to meddle with him, left it fhould turn to his hurt. But Jofiah not hearkening thereto, on Necho's marching up to the place where he was pofted to ftop his paffage, it there came to a battle between them; wherein Jofiah was not only overthrown, but alfo unfortunately received a wound, of which, on his return to Jerufalem, he there died, after he had reigned thirty-one years.

An. 610.
Jofiah 31.

It is the notion of many, that Jofiah engaged rafhly and unadvifedly in this war, upon an over confidence in the merit of his own righteoufnefs; as if God, for this reafon, muft neceffarily have given him fuccefs in every war which he fhould engage himfelf in. But this would be a prefumption very unworthy of fo religious a perfon. There was another reafon that engaged him in this undertaking, which hath been above hinted at. From the time of Manaffeh's reftoration, the kings of Judah were homagers to the kings of Babylon, and bound by oath to adhere to them againft all their enemies, efpecially againft the Egyptians, and to defend that border of their empire againft them; and, for this purpofe, they feem to have had conferred on them, the reft of the land of Canaan, that which had formerly been poffeffed by the other ten tribes, till conquered from them by the Affyrians. It is certain Jofiah had the whole land of Ifrael in the fame extent in which it had been held by David and Solomon, before it was divided into two kingdoms. For his reformation went through all of it; and it was executed by him, not only in Bethel (where one of Jeroboam's calves ftood), but alfo in every other part thereof, and with the fame fovereign authority as in Judea itfelf; and therefore he muft have been king of the whole. And it is to be remarked, that the battle was fought, not within the territories of Judea, but at Megiddo, a town of the tribe of Manaffeh, lying in the middle of the kingdom of Ifrael, where Jofiah would have had nothing to do, had he not been king of that kingdom alfo, as well as of the other of Judah: and he could have had it no otherwife, but by grant from the king of Babylon,

[a] 2 Kings xxxiii. 29. 30. 2 Chron. xxxv. 20.---25.

Babylon, a province of whose empire it was made by the conquest of it, first begun by Tiglath-Pileser, and afterwards finished by Salmaneser and Esarhaddon. And if this grant was not upon the express conditions which I have mentioned, yet whatsoever other terms there were of this concession, most certainly fidelity to the sovereign paramount, and a steady adherence to his interest, against all his enemies, was always required in such cases, and an oath of God exacted for the performance hereof. And it is not to be doubted, but that Josiah had taken such an oath to Nabopollasar, the then reigning king of Babylon, as Jehoiakim and Zedekiah afterwards did to Nebuchadnezzar, his son and successor in that empire; and therefore, should Josiah, when under such an obligation, have permitted an enemy of the king of Babylon to pass through his country to make war upon him, without any opposition, it would plainly have amounted to a breach of his oath, and a violation of that fidelity which he had in the name of his God sworn unto him, which so good and just a man as Josiah was could not but absolutely detest. For, although the Romanists make nothing of breaking faith with heretics, yet the breaking of faith with an heathen was condemned [a] by God himself in Jehoiakim and Zedekiah; and most certainly it would have been condemned in Josiah also, had he become guilty of it; which being what a person so well instructed in religion as Josiah was could not but be thoroughly convinced of, the sense which he had of his duty, in this particular, seems solely to have been that which engaged him in this war, in which he perished: and with him perished all the glory, honour, and prosperity of the Jewish nation; for, after that, nothing else ensued but a dismal scene of God's judgements upon the land, till, at length, all Judah and Jerusalem were swallowed up by them in a woful destruction.

The death of so excellent a prince was deservedly lamented by all his people, and by none more than by Jeremiah, the prophet, who had a thorough sense of the greatness of the loss, and also a full foresight of the great calamities that were afterwards to follow upon the whole people of the Jews; and therefore, while his heart was full with the view of both, he wrote [b] a song of lamentation upon this doleful occasion, as he afterwards did another upon the destruction of Jerusalem. This [c] last is that which we still have; the other is not now extant.

Megiddo, where the battle was fought, was a city [d] in the tribe

---

[a] Ezek. xvi. 13—19.   [b] 2 Chron. xxxv. 25.
[c] This last, referring throughout to the destruction of Jerusalem, could not be that which was wrote upon the death of Josiah.
[d] Joshua xvii. 11. Judges i. 27.

tribe of Manaffeh, on this fide Jordan, which is by Herodotus called Magdolum, nigh it was the town of Hadad-Rimmon, afterwards called ᵃ Maximianopolis; and therefore the lamentation for the death of Jofiah is in fcripture called the " Lamentation of Hadad-Rimmon in the valley of Megiddo;" which was fo great for this excellent prince, and fo long continued, ᵇ that the lamentation of Hadad-Rimmon afterwards became a proverbial phrafe for the expreffing of any extraordinary forrow.

This great and general mourning of all the people of Ifrael for the death of this prince, and the prophet Jeremiah's joining fo pathetically with them herein, fheweth in how great a reputation he was with them, which he would not have deferved, had he engaged in this war contrary to the words of that prophet, fpoken to him from the mouth of the Lord, as the apocryphal writer of the firft book of ᶜ Efdras, and others from him, fay; for then he would have died in rebellion againft God, and difobedience to his command; and then neither God's prophet, nor God's people, could, in this cafe, without finning againft God, have expreffed fo great an efteem for him as this mourning implied; and therefore this mourning alone is a fufficient proof of the contrary. Befides, it is to be obferved, that no part of canonical fcripture gives us the leaft intimation of it; nor can we from thence have any reafon or ground to believe, that there was any fuch word from the Lord by the prophet Jeremiah, or any other prophet, to recal Jofiah from this war. All that is faid of it is from the apocryphal book I have mentioned; of which it may be truly faid, that where it is not a tranfcript from Ezra, or fome other canonical fcripture, it is no more than a bundle of fables, too abfurd for the belief of the Romanifts themfelves (for they have not taken this book into their canonical fcripture, though they have thofe of Tobit and of Bel and the Dragon); and therefore it is deferving of no man's regard in this particular.

It is faid indeed (2 Chr. xxxv. 21.) that Necho fent meffengers to Jofiah, to tell him, that he was fent of God on this expedition; that God was with him in it; and that to meddle with him would be to meddle with God; and that therefore he ought to forbear, that God deftroy him not; and (ver. 22.) that Jofiah hearkened not to the word of Necho from the mouth of God. And, from all this put together, fome would infer, that Jofiah was difobedient to the word of God, in going to that war. But this is utterly inconfiftent with the character which is given us in fcripture of that religious and excellent prince; and therefore what is here faid muft not be underftood of the true God,

the

ᵃ Hieronymus.   ᵇ Zechariah xii. 11.   ᶜ Chap. i. 28.

the Lord Jehovah, who was the God of Ifrael, but of the Egyptian gods, whofe oracles Jofiah had no reafon to have any regard to. For Necho, being an heathen prince, knew not the Lord Jehovah, nor ever confulted his prophets or his oracles: the Egyptian gods were thofe only whom he worfhipped, and whofe oracles he confulted; and therefore when he faith he was fent of God on this expedition, and that God was with him, he meant none other than his falfe Egyptian gods, whom he ferved: for, wherever the word God occurs in this text, it is not expreffed in the Hebrew original by the word Jehovah, which is the proper name of the true God, but by the word Elohim, which, being in the plural number, is equally applicable to the falfe gods of the heathens, as well as to the true God, who was the God of Ifrael; and, in the fcriptures of the Old Teftament, it is equally ufed for the expreffing of the one as well as the other. For, wherever there is occafion therein to fpeak of thofe falfe gods, it is by the word Elohim that they are there mentioned. And, whereas it is faid (ver. 22.), that "Jofiah hearkened not to the words of Necho from the mouth of God," (and from hence it is chiefly inferred, that the meffage which Necho fent to Jofiah was truly from God), it is to be obferved, that the phrafe, which we render *from the mouth of God*, is, in the Hebrew original Mippi Elohim, *i. e.* from the mouth of Elohim, which may be interpreted of the falfe gods, as well as of the true God (as hath been already faid), and much rather, in this place, of the former, than of the latter. For, wherever elfe, [a] through the whole Hebrew text of the holy fcriptures, there is mention made of any word coming from the mouth of God, he is there mentioned by the name Jehovah, which determines it to be the true God; and this is the only place, in the whole Hebrew Bible, where, in the ufe of this phrafe, it is expreffed otherwife, that is, by the name Elohim, and not by the name Jehovah; which change in the phrafe, in this place, is a fufficient proof to me, that there muft be here a change in the fignification alfo, and that the word, which is here faid to come from the mouth of Elohim, is not the fame with the word which is, every where elfe, in the ufe of this phrafe in fcripture, faid to come from the mouth of Jehovah, but that Elohim muft, in this place, fignify the falfe gods of the Egyptians; and that from their falfe oracles only Necho had this word which he fent to Jofiah. For what had he to do with any word from the true God, who knew him not, nor ever worfhipped him? Or how could any fuch revelation come to him,

---

[a] See Deut. viii. 3. Jofh. ix. 14. 1 Kings xiii. 21. 2 Chr. xxxvi. 12. If. i. 20. xl. 5. lviii. 14. lxii. 2. Jer. ix. 12. & xxiii. 16. Micah iv. 4.

him, who knew not any of his prophets, or ever confulted them? And therefore, moft certainly, the word which is here faid to come Mippi Elohim, *i. e.* from the mouth of Elohim, muft be underftood only of Necho's Elohim, that is, of thofe falfe Egyptian gods, whofe oracles he confulted, before he undertook this expedition, as it was than ufual with heathen princes, on fuch occafions, to confult the falfe deluding oracles of the gods they worfhipped. And had it been here Mippi Jehovah, *i. e.* from the mouth of Jehovah, inftead of Mippi Elohim, confidering who fent the meffage, it would not have much mended the matter; for Jofiah would have had no reafon to believe it from fuch a meffenger. When Sennacherib came up againft Judah, he fent Hezekiah word, [a] that the Lord (Jehovah in the Hebrew) faid unto him, Go up againft this land, and deftroy it. But it was not reckoned a fault in Hezekiah, that he believed him not, neither could it be reckoned a fault in Jofiah in doing the fame. For it is certain, that Sennacherib, in fo pretending, lied to King Hezekiah; and, why might not Jofiah then have as good reafon to conclude that Necho, in the like pretence, might have lied alfo unto him? for God ufed not to fend his word to his fervants by fuch meffengers. But Necho's pretence was not fo large as Sennacherib's; for Sennacherib pretended to be fent by Jehovah, the certain name of the true God, but Necho pretended to be fent only by Elohim, which may be interpreted of his falfe Egyptian gods, as well as of the true God. And it feems clear he could mean none other than the former by that word in this text; and therefore Jofiah could not be liable to any blame, in not hearkening to any words which came from them.

After the death of Jofiah, [b] the people of the land took Jehoahaz, his fon, who was alfo called Shallum, and made him king in his ftead. He was much unlike his father, for he did that which was evil in the fight of the Lord, and therefore he was foon tumbled down from his throne into a prifon, where he ended his days with mifery and difgrace in a ftrange land.

For Pharaoh-Necho, [c] having had the good fuccefs, in his expedition, to beat the Babylonians at the Euphrates; and having thereon taken Carchemifh, a great city in thofe parts, and fecured it to himfelf with a good garrifon, after three months returned again towards Egypt, and hearing, in his way, that Jehoahaz had taken upon him to be king of Judah, without his confent, [d] he fent for him to Riblah in Syria, and, on his arrival,

---

[a] 2 Kings xviii. 25. If. xxxvi. 10.
[b] 2 Kings xxiii. 31. 2 Chron. xxxvi. 1.
[c] Jofephus Antiq. lib. 10. c. 6.
[d] 2 Kings xxiii. 33. 2 Chron. xxxvi. 3. 4.

val, caused him to be put in chains, and sent him prisoner into Egypt, where he died; and then, proceeding on in his way, came to Jerusalem, where he made [a] Jehoiakim, another of the sons of Josiah, king, instead of his brother, and put the land to an annual tribute of an [b] hundred talents of silver, and a talent of gold; and after that returned with great triumph into his own kingdom.

Herodotus, making mention of this expedition of Necho's, and also of the battle which he fought at Megiddo (or Magdolum, as he calleth it), [c] saith, that, after the victory there obtained by him, he took the great city Cadytis, which city he afterwards describes to be a mountainous city in Palestine, of the bigness of Sardis in Lydia, the chief city of all Lesser Asia in those times; by which description, this city, Cadytis, could be none other than Jerusalem; for that is situated in the mountains of Palestine, and there was then no other city in those parts which could be equalled to Sardis but that only: and it is certain, from scripture, that, after this battle, Necho did take Jerusalem, for he [d] was there when he made Jehoiakim king. There is, I confess, no mention of this name, either in the scriptures, or in Josephus; but that it was however called so, in the time of Herodotus, by the Syrians and Arabians, doth appear from this, that it is called by them, and all the eastern nations, by no other name but one of the same original, and the same signification, even to this day; for Jerusalem is a name now altogether as strange among them, as Cadytis is to us. They [e] all call it by the name of Al-kuds, which signifies the same that Cadytis doth, that is, The Holy: For, from the time that Solomon built the temple at Jerusalem, and it was thereby made to all Israel the common place of their religious worship, this epithet of The Holy was commonly given unto it; and therefore we find it thenceforth called, in the sacred writings of the Old Testament, [f] Air Hakkodesh, *i. e.* the City of Holiness, or the Holy City, and so also in [g] several places in the New Testament. And this same title

they

---

[a] This Jehoiakim was elder brother to Jehoahaz; for the latter was but 23 years old when the other was 25. 2 Kings xxiii. 31. 36. and yet the people, on the death of Josiah, chose Jehoahaz to succeed him.

[b] The whole annual tribute, as here taxed, came to 52,200 l. of our money.

[c] Herodotus, lib. 22.

[d] 2 Chron. xxxvi. 3.

[e] Golii Notæ ad Alfraganum, p. 137. Sandy's Travels, b. 3. p. 155. Baudrandi Geographia, sub voce Hierosolyma.

[f] Neh. xi. 1. & 18. Is. xlviii. 2. and c. lii. 1. Dan. ix. 24.

[g] Matth. iv. 5. & xxvii. 53. Rev. xxi. 2.

they gave it in their coins, for the inscription of their shekels (many of which are still extant) was [a] Jerusalem Kedushah, *i.e.* Jerusalem the Holy; and this coin going current among the neighbouring nations, especially after the Babylonish captivity had made a dispersion of that people over all the East, it carried this name with it among them; and they from hence called this city by both names, Jerusalem Kedushah, and at length, for shortness sake, Kedushah only, and the Syrians (who in their dialect usually turned the Hebrew *sh* into *th,* Kedutha. And the Syriac, in the time of Herodotus, being the only language that was then spoken in Palestine (the Hebrew having been no more used there, or any where else, as a vulgar language, after the Babylonish captivity), he found it, when he travelled through that country, to be called there in the Syriac dialect Kedutha, from whence, by giving it a Greek termination, he made it, in the Greek language, Καδυτις, or Cadytis, in his history, which he wrote about the time that Nehemiah ended his twelve years government at Jerusalem. And, for the same reason that it was called Kedushah, or Kedutha, in Syria and Palestine, the Arabs, in their language, called it [b] Bait Alackdes, *i. e.* the Holy Buildings, or the Holy City, and often, with another adjective of the same root, and the same signification, Bait Alkuds, and at length simply Alkuds, *i. e.* the Holy, by which name only [c] it is now called by the Turks, Arabs, and all other nations of the Mahometan religion in those parts. And that it may not look strange to prove an ancient name by the modern name which is now given that place, it is necessary I acquaint the reader, that the Arabs being the ancientest nation in the world (who have never been by any conquest dispossessed, or driven out of their country, but have there always remained in a continued descent from the first planters of it even to this day), and being also as little given to make changes in their manners and usages, as they are as to their country, they have still retained those names of places which were at first given them, and on their getting the empire of the East, restored them again to many of them, after they had been for several ages extinct, by the intermediate changes that had happened in them. And thus [d] the ancient metropolis of Egypt, which, from Mizraim, the son of Ham, the first planter of that country after the flood, was called Mesri,
and

[a] See Lightfoot's Works, vol. 1. p. 497. and vol. 2. p. 303. and Walton's Apparatus before the Polyglot Bible, p. 36. 37.

[b] Golii Notæ ad Alfraganum, p. 137.

[c] Sandy's Travels. b. 3. p. 155. Baudrandi Geog. sub voce Hierosolyma.

[d] Bocharti Phaleg. part 1. lib. 4. c. 24. Golii Notæ ad Alfraganum, p. 152, 153, &c.

and afterwards for many ages had the name of Memphis, was, on the Arabs making themselves masters of Egypt again, called Mesri, and hath retained that name ever since, though, by the building of Cairo on the other side of the Nile over against it (for Mesri stands on the west side of that river), that ancient and once noble city is now brought in a manner to desolation. And for the same reason the city of Tyrus, which was anciently called [a] Zor or Zur (from whence the whole country of Syria had its name), hath, since it fell into the hands of the Arabs, on the erecting of the empire in the east, been again called [b] Sor, and is at this day known by no other name in those parts. And by the same means the city of Palmyra hath again recovered the old name of Tadmor, by which it was called [c] in the time of Solomon, and is now known in the east by no other name: and abundance of other like instances might be given in the east to this purpose, and the like may be found nearer home. For it is well known that the Welsh, in their language, do still call all the cities in England by the old British names, by which they were called 1300 years ago, before the Saxons dispossessed them of this country; and should they recover it again, and here get the dominion over it as formerly, no doubt they would again restore to all places here the same British names, by which they still call them.

Jehoiakim, on his taking on him the kingdom, followed the example of his brother [d] in doing that which was evil; for he went on in his steps to relax all the good order and discipline of his father, as the other had done, and the people (who never went heartily into that good king's reformation), gladly laying hold hereof, did let themselves loose to the full bent of their own depraved inclinations; and run into all manner of iniquity; whereon the prophet Jeremiah, being sent of God, [e] first went into the king's house, and there proclaimed God's judgements against him and his family, if he went on in his iniquities, and did not amend and repent of them; and after that [f] he went up into the temple, and there spoke to all the people that came up thither to worship, after the same manner, declaring unto them, that if they would turn from their evil ways, God would turn from his wrath, and repent of

An. 609.
Jehoiak. 1.

the

---

[a] So it is called in the original Hebrew text of the Old Testament, wherever there is mention of this city therein.
[b] Golii notæ ad Alfraganum, p. 130. and 131. Baudrandi Geog. sub voce Tyrus. Thevenot's Travels, b. 2. c. 60. p. 220.
[c] 1 Kings ix. 18. 2 Chron. viii. 4.
[d] 2 Kings xxiii. 37. 2 Chron. xxxvi. 5.
[e] Jer. xxii.
[f] Jer. xxvi.

the evil which he purposed to bring upon them; but that, if they would not hearken unto him to walk in the law of God, and keep his commandments, then the wrath of God should be poured out upon them, and both that city and the temple should be brought to utter desolation: which angering the priests that then attended in the temple, they laid hold of him, and brought him before the king's council to have him put to death. But Ahikam, one of the chief lords of the council, so befriended Jeremiah, that he brought him off, and got him discharged by the general suffrage, not only of the princes, but also of all the elders of the people that were then present. This Ahikam was [a] the father of Gedaliah, that was afterwards made governor of the land under the Chaldeans, and the son of Shaphan the scribe (who was [b] chief minister of state under King Josiah) and brother [c] to Gemariah, [d] Elasah, and [e] Jazaniah, who were great men in those days, and members also of the council with him; and therefore, in conjunction with them, he had a great interest there, which he made use of on this occasion to deliver the prophet from that mischief which was intended against him.

But [f] Uriah, another prophet of the Lord, who had this same year prophesied after the same manner, could not so come off. For Jehoiakim was so incensed against him for it, that he sought to put him to death; whereon Uriah fled into Egypt. But this did not secure him from his revenge; for he sent into Egypt after him, and, having procured him to be there seized, brought him up from thence, and slew him at Jerusalem; which became a further enhancing of his iniquity, and also of God's wrath against him for it.

About the same time also prophesied the prophet Habakkuk, and Zephaniah, who, being called to the prophetic office in the reign of Josiah, continued (as seems most likely) to this time; for they prophesied the same things that Jeremiah did, and upon the same occasion, [g] that is, destruction and desolation upon Judah and Jerusalem, because of the many heinous sins they were then guilty of. Zephaniah doth not name the Chaldeans, who were to be the executioners of this wrath of God upon them, but [h] Habakkuk doth. As to Habakkuk, neither the time in which he lived, nor the parents from whom he was descended, are any where named in scripture; but he prophesying the coming

---

[a] 2 Kings xxv. 22.
[b] 2 Kings xxii.
[c] Jer. xxxvi. 10.
[d] Jer. xxix. 3.
[e] Ezek. viii. 11. From which place it is inferred, that Jazaniah was then president of the Sanhedrim.
[f] Jer. xxvi. 20—23.
[g] Hab. i. 1—11. Zeph. i. 1—18.
[h] Hab. i. 5.

ming of the Chaldeans in the same manner as Jeremiah did, this gives reason to conjecture that he lived in the same time. Of Zephaniah it is directly said, [a] that he prophesied in the time of Josiah, and in his pedigree (which is also given us) his father's grandfather is called [a] Hezekiah, which, some taking to be King Hezekiah, do therefore reckon this prophet to have been of royal descent.

In the third year of Jehoiakim, [b] Nabopollasar, king of Babylon, finding that, on Necho's taking of Carchemish, all Syria and Palestine had revolted to him, and that he being old and infirm, was unable to march thither himself to reduce them; he took Nebuchadnezzar his son into partnership with him in the empire, and [c] sent him with an army into those parts; and from hence the Jewish computation of the years of Nebuchadnezzar's reign begins, that is, from the end of the third year of Jehoiakim: for it was about the end of that year that this was done; and therefore, according to the Jews, [d] the fourth year of Jehoiakim was the first year of Nebuchadnezzar; but, according to the Babylonians, his reign is not reckoned to begin till after his father's death, which happened two years afterwards; and both computations being found in scripture, it is necessary to say so much here for the reconciling of them.

An. 607.
Jehoiak. 3.

In the 4th year of Jehoiakim, Nebuchadnezzar [e] having beaten the army of Necho, king of Egypt, at the Euphrates, and retaken Carchemish, marched towards Syria and Palestine, to recover those provinces again to the Babylonish empire; on whose approach [f] the Rechabites, who, according to the institution of Jonadab, the son of Rechab, their father, had always abstained from wine, and hitherto only lived in tents, finding no security from this invasion in the open country, retired for their safety to Jerusalem, where was transacted between them and Jeremiah what we find related in the 35th chapter of his prophecies.

An. 606.
Jehoiak. 4.

This very [g] same year Jeremiah prophesied of the coming of Nebuchadnezzar against Judah and Jerusalem, that the whole land should be delivered into his hands, and that a captivity of seventy years continuance should after that ensue upon the people of the Jews; and he also delivered several other prophecies
of

---

[a] Zephaniah i. 1.
[b] Berosus apud Joseph. Ant. lib. 10. c. 11. et contra Apion. lib. 1.
[c] Daniel i. 1.
[d] Jer. xxv. 1. Which same 4th year was the 23d from the 13th of Josiah, when Jeremiah first began to prophesy, ver. 3.
[e] Jer. xlvi. 1.   [f] Jer. xxxv. 6.—11.   [g] Jer. xxv.

of the many calamities and woful defolations, that were then ready to be brought upon them, intending thereby, if poffible, to bring them to repentance, that fo the wrath of God might be diverted from them.

But, all this working nothing upon their hardened and obdurate hearts, God commanded him [a] to collect together, and write in a roll, all the words of prophecy which had been fpoken by him againft Ifrael, Judah, and the nations, from the 13th year of Jofiah (when he was firft called to the prophetic office) to that time; whereon Jeremiah called to him Baruch, the fon of Neriah, a chief difciple of his, who, being a ready fcribe, wrote from his mouth all as God had commanded, and then went with the roll, which he had thus written, up into the temple, and there read it, in the hearing of all the people, on the great faft of the expiation, when all Judah and Jerufalem were affembled together at that folemnity; for Jeremiah, being then fhut up in prifon for his former prophefying, could not go up thither himfelf, and therefore, by God's command, Baruch was fent to do it in his ftead; and at his firft reading of the roll, whether it were that Jehoiakim and his princes were then abfent to take care of the borders of the kingdom, which Nebuchadnezzar was then juft ready to invade, or that, amidft the diftractions which ufually happen on fuch impending dangers, men's minds were otherwife engaged, no refentments were at that time expreffed either againft the prophet or his difciple on this occafion. But Baruch being very much affrighted and difmayed at the threats of the roll, which he had thus wrote and publicly read, the word of prophecy, which we have in the 45th chapter of Jeremiah, was fent from God on purpofe to comfort him, and a promife is therein given him, that amidft all the calamities, deftructions, and defolations, which, according to the words of the roll, fhould be certainly brought upon Judah and Jeruf.lem, he fhould be fure to find a deliverance; for that none of them fhould reach him, but God would give him his life for a prey, in all places wherefoever he fhould go.

The great faft of the expiation, wherein Baruch read the roll, as is above related, was annually kept by the Jews [b] on the tenth day of the month Tizri, which anfwers to our September. Immediately after that Nebuchadnezzar invaded Judea; and, having laid fiege to Jerufalem, [c] made himfelf mafter of it in the ninth month, called Cifleu, which anfwers to our November, on the 18th day of that month, (for on that day is ftill kept by the Jews an annual faft in commemoration of it even to this day), and,

---

[a] Jeremiah xxxvi. [b] Leviticus xvi. 29. and xxiii. 27.
[c] Dan. i. 2. 2 Chron. xxxvi. 6.

and, having then taken Jehoiakim prisoner, he put him in chains, to carry him to Babylon. But he having [a] humbled himself to Nebuchadnezzar, and submitted to become his tributary, and thereon sworn fealty to him, he was again restored to his kingdom; and Nebuchadnezzar marched from Jerusalem for the farther prosecuting of his victories against the Egyptians.

But, before he removed from Jerusalem, he had caused great numbers of the people to be sent captive to Babylon, and particularly [b] gave order to Ashpenaz, the master of his eunuchs, that he should make choice out of the children of the royal family, and of the nobility of the land, such as he found to be of the fairest countenance, and the quickest parts, to be carried to Babylon, and there made eunuchs in his palace; whereby was fulfilled the word of the Lord spoken by [c] Isaiah the prophet to Hezekiah, king of Judah, above an hundred years before. At the same time also, he [d] carried away a great part of the vessels of the house of the Lord to put them in the house of Bel, his god, at Babylon. And therefore, the people being thus carried into captivity, the sons of the royal family, and of the nobility of the land made eunuchs and slaves in the palace of the king of Babylon, the vessels of the temple carried thither, and the king made a tributary, and the whole land now brought into vassalage under the Babylonians, from hence must be reckoned the beginning of the seventy years of the Babylonish captivity, [e] foretold by the prophet Jeremiah; and the fourth year of Jehoiakim must be the first year in that computation.

Among the number of the children, that were carried away in this captivity by the master of the eunuchs, were [f] Daniel, Hananiah, Mishael, and Azariah. Daniel they called Belteshazzar, and the other three, Shadrach, Meshach, and Abednego. Some, indeed, do place their captivity some years latter, but that is absolutely inconsistent with what is elsewhere said in scripture. For these children, after their carrying away to Babylon, were to be [g] three years under the tuition of the master of the eunuchs, to be instructed by him in the language and the learning of the Chaldeans, before they were to be admitted to the presence of the king, to stand and serve before him. But in the second [h] year of Nebuchadnezzar's reign at Babylon, from his father's death (which was but the 4th year after his first taking of Jerusalem), Daniel had not only admission and freedom of access

[a] 2 Kings xxiv. 1.
[b] Daniel i. 3.
[c] Is. xxxix. 7. 2 Kings xx. 18.
[d] Daniel i. 2.
[e] Jer. xxv. 11. & xxix. 10.
[f] Daniel i. 6.
[g] Daniel i. 5.
[h] Daniel ii. 16.

cefs to the prefence of the king, but we find him [a] there interpreting of his dream, and immediately thereon advanced to be chief [b] of the governors of the wife men, and ruler over all the province of Babylon: for which truft lefs than four years inftruction in the language, laws, ufages, and learning of the country can fcarce be thought fufficient to qualify him, nor could he any fooner be old enough for it; for he was but a youth when he was firft carried away from Jerufalem. And therefore all this put together doth neceffarily determine the time of Daniel's and the other children's carrying away to Babylon to the year where I have placed it; and, if we will make fcripture confiftent with fcripture, it could not poffibly have been any later. Daniel, fpeaking of the captivity, [c] begins the hiftory of it from the 3d year of Jehoiakim, which placeth it back ftill a year farther than I have done: and this is an objection on the other hand; but the anfwer hereto is eafy. Daniel begins his computation from the time that Nebuchadnezzar was fent from Babylon by his father on this expedition, which was in the latter end of the 3d year of Jehoiakim: after that, two months at leaft muft have been fpent in his march to the borders of Syria. There, in the 4th year of Jehoiakim (we fuppofe in the beginning of that year) he fought the Egyptians; and, having overthrown them in battle, beficged Carchemifh, and took it: after this, he reduced all the provinces and cities of Syria and Phœnicia, in which having employed the greateft part of the year (and a great deal of work it was to do within that time), in the beginning of October, he came and laid fiege to Jerufalem, and, about a month after, took the city: and from hence we date the beginning of Daniel's fervitude, and alfo the beginning of the feventy years of the Babylonifh captivity; and therefore do reckon that year to have been the frft of both.

The Scythians, who had now for 28 years held all the Upper Afia (that is, the two Armenia's, Cappadocia, Pontus, Colchis, and Iberia), were this year again [d] driven out of it. The Medes, whom they had difpoffeffed of thefe provinces, had long endeavoured to recover them by open force; but finding themfelves unable to fucceed this way, they at length accomplifhed it by treachery: for, under the covert of a peace (which they had made on purpofe to carry on the fraud), they invited the greateft part of them to a feaft, where, having made them drunk, they flew them all; after which, having eafily fubdued the reft, they recovered from them all that they had loft, and again extended their empire to the river Halys, which had been the ancient borders of it towards the weft.

After

[a] Dan. ii. 31. [b] Dan. ii. 48. [c] Dan. i. 1. [d] Herodot. lib. 1.

After the Chaldeans were gone from Jerusalem, Jehoiakim, instead of being amended by those heavy chastisements which by their hand God had inflicted on him and his kingdom, rather grew worse under them in all those ways of wickedness and impiety which he had afore practised; and Judah and Jerusalem kept pace with him herein, to the farther provoking of God's wrath, and the hastening of their own destruction. However, no means were omitted to reclaim them; and Jeremiah the prophet, who was particularly sent to them for this purpose, was constantly calling upon them, and exhorting them to turn unto the Lord their God, that so his wrath might be turned from them, and they saved from the destruction which was coming upon them, of which he ceased not continually to warn them. And they having, on the ninth month, called Cisleu, proclaimed a public fast to be held on the 18th day of the same, because of the calamity which they had suffered thereon, in the taking of Jerusalem by the Chaldeans the year foregoing (which hath ever since been annually observed by them in commemoration hereof, as hath been afore said), the prophet, laying hold of this opportunity, when all Judah and Jerusalem were met together to keep this solemnity, [a] sent Baruch again up into the temple with the roll of his prophecies, there to read it a second time in the hearing of all of them, making thereby another trial, if, by the terrors of these prophecies, it were possible to fright them into their duty. And it being God's command, by the mouth of his prophet, Baruch accordingly went up into the temple on the said fast-day, and, entering into the chamber of Gemariah the scribe (which was the room where the king's council used to sit in the temple, near the east gate of the same), did there, from a window aloft, read, in the hearing of all the people, then gathered together in the court below, all the words of the said roll: which Micaiah, the son of Gemariah, who was then present, hearing, went immediately to the king's house, and there informed the lords of the council of it; whereon they sent for Baruch, and caused him to sit down, and read the roll over to them; at the hearing whereof, and the threats therein contained, they, being much affrighted, inquired of Baruch the manner of his writing of it; and being informed that it was all dictated to him from the mouth of the prophet, they ordered him to leave the roll and depart, advising, that he and Jeremiah should immediately go and hide themselves, where no one might find them; and then went in to the king, and informed

An. 605.
Jehoiak. 5.

---

[a] Jeremiah xxxvi. 9, 10, &c.

formed him of all that had paſſed; whereon he ſent for the roll, and cauſed it to be read to him; but after he had heard three or four leaves of it, as he was ſitting by the fire in the winter parlour, he took it and cut it with a pen-knife, and caſt it into the fire that was there before him, till it was all conſumed, notwithſtanding ſome of the lords of the council intreated him to the contrary; and immediately thereon, iſſued out an order to have Baruch and Jeremiah ſeized; but having hid themſelves, as adviſed by the council, they could not be found.

The Jews keep an annual faſt even to this day for the burning of this roll: the day marked for it in their kalendar is the 29th day of [a] Ciſleu, eleven days after that, which they keep for that faſt, on which it was read in the temple. But, the reading of the roll on the faſt of the 18th of Ciſleu, and the burning of it according to the account given hereof by Jeremiah, ſeem immediately to have followed each other.

After the burning of this roll, another by God's eſpecial command was forthwith written in the ſame manner, from the mouth of the prophet, by the hand of Baruch, wherein was contained all that was in the former roll; and there were added many other like words, and particularly that prophecy in reſpect of Jehoiakim and his houſe, which is, for this impious fact, in the 30th and 31ſt verſes of the 36th chapter of Jeremiah, denounced againſt them.

In making the roll to be read twice in the temple by Baruch, I confeſs, I differ from moſt that have commented upon this place of ſcripture. But as the reading of the roll by Baruch is, in the 36th chapter of Jeremiah, twice related, ſo it is plain to me, that it was twice done: for in the firſt relation, [b] it is ſaid to be done in the 4th year of Jehoiakim, and, in the ſecond, it is [c] ſaid to be done in the 5th; which plainly denotes two different times. And, in the firſt relation, Jeremiah [d] is ſaid to be ſhut up in priſon, when the roll was read; but, in the ſecond relation, it plainly appears, he was out of priſon, for [e] he was then at full liberty to go out of the way and hide himſelf. For theſe reaſons I take it for certain, that the roll was twice read: and I have Archbiſhop Uſher with me in the ſame opinion, whoſe judgement muſt always be of the greateſt weight in ſuch matters.

Nebuchadnezzar, after his departure from Jeruſalem, employed all this year in carrying on his war againſt the Egyptians, in which he had that ſucceſs, that before the enſuing winter, he had driven

---

[a] Ciſleu is the 9th month in the Jewiſh year, and anſwers to our November.
[b] Jer. xxxvi. 1. [c] Jer xxxvi. 9. [d] Jer. xxxvi. 5. [e] Jer. xxxvi. 26.

driven them out of all Syria and Paleſtine, and brought in ſubjection to him, ᵃ from the river Euphrates to the river of Egypt, all that formerly belonged to the king of Egypt, *i. e.* all Syria and Paleſtine. For, as the river Euphrates was the boundary of Syria towards the north-eaſt; ſo the river of Egypt was the boundary of Paleſtine towards the ſouth-weſt. This river of Egypt, which is ſo often mentioned in ſcripture as the boundary of the land of Canaan, or Paleſtine, towards Egypt, was not the Nile, as many ſuppoſe, but a ſmall river, which, running through the deſart that lies between theſe two countries, was anciently reckoned the common boundary of both. And thus far the land reached, which was promiſed to the ſeed of Abraham (Gen. xv. 18.), and was afterwards by lot divided among them, Joſhua xv. 4.

Towards the end of the 5th year of Jehoiakim, died Nabopollaſar, king of Babylon, and father of Nebuchadnezzar, after he had reigned ᵇ one and twenty years, which Nebuchadnezzar being informed of, ᶜ he immediately, with a few only of his followers, haſtened through the deſart the neareſt way to Babylon, leaving the groſs of his army, with the priſoners and prey, to be brought after him by his generals. On his arrival at the palace, he received the government from the hands of thoſe who had carefully reſerved it for him, and thereon ſucceeded his father in the whole empire, which contained Chaldea, Aſſyria, Arabia, Syria, and Paleſtine, and reigned over it, according to Ptolemy, forty-three years; the firſt of which begins from the January following, which is the Babyloniſh account, from which the Jewiſh account differs two years, as reckoning his reign from the time he was admitted to be partner with his father. From hence we have a double computation of the years of his reign, the Jewiſh and the Babyloniſh; Daniel follows the latter, but all other parts of ſcripture that make mention of him, the other.

An. 604.
Jehoiak. 6.

In the ſeventh year of Jehoiakim, which was the ſecond year of Nebuchadnezzar, according to the Babyloniſh account, and the fourth according to the Jewiſh, Daniel ᵈ revealed unto Nebuchadnezzar his dream, and alſo unfolded to him the interpretation of it, in the manner as we have it at large related in the 2d chapter of Daniel; whereon he was advanced to great honour, being made chief of the governors over all the wiſe men of Babylon, and alſo chief ruler over

An. 603.
Jehoiak. 7.

ᵃ 2 Kings xxiv. 7.
ᵇ Canon Ptolemæi.
ᶜ Beroſus apud Joſeph. Antiq. lib. 10. c. 11. et contra Apionem, lib. 1.
ᵈ Daniel ii.

over the whole province of Babylon, and one of the chief lords of the council, who always continued in the king's court, he being then about the age of twenty-two. And, in his prosperity, he was not forgetful of his three companions, who had been brought to Babylon with him, Shadrach, Meshach, and Abednego; but, having spoken to the king in their behalf, procured, that they were preferred to places of great honour under him in the province of Babylon. These afterwards made themselves very signally known to the king, and also to the whole empire of Babylon, by their constancy to their religion, in refusing to worship the golden image which Nebuchadnezzar had set up, and by the wonderful deliverance which God wrought for them thereon; which deservedly recommending them to the king's highest regard, they were thereon much higher advanced: the whole history hereof is at full related in the 3d chapter of Daniel.

The same year, Jehoiakim, after he had served the king of Babylon three years, [a] rebelled against him, and, refusing to pay him any more tribute, renewed his confederacy with Pharaoh Necho, king of Egypt, in opposition to him. Whereon Nebuchadezzar, not being then at leisure, by reason of other engagements, to come himself and chastise him, sent orders to all his lieutenants and governors of provinces in those parts to make war upon him; which brought upon Jehoiakim inroads and invasions from every quarter, [b] the Ammonites, the Moabites, the Syrians, the Arabians, and all the other nations round him, who had subjected themselves to the Babylonish yoke, infesting him with incursions, and harassing him with depredations on every side: and thus they continued to do for three years together, till at length, in the 11th year of his reign, all parties joined together against him; [c] they shut him up in Jerusalem, where, in the prosecution of the siege, having taken him prisoner in some sally (it may be supposed) which he made upon them, they slew him with the sword, and then cast out his dead body into the high-way, without one of the gates of Jerusalem, allowing it no other burial, [d] as the prophet Jeremiah had foretold, than that of an ass, that is, to be cast forth into a place of the greatest contempt, there to rot and be consumed to dust in the open air.

An. 599.
Jehoiak. 11.

The year before, [e] died his confederate, on whom he chiefly depended, Pharaoh Necho, king of Egypt, after he had reigned 16 years, and Psammis his son succeeded him in the kingdom.

Jehoiakim

[a] 2 Kings xxiv. 1.
[b] 2 Kings xxiv. 2.
[c] 2 Kings xxiv. 10.
[d] Jeremiah xxii. 18. 19. & xxxvi. 30.
[e] Herodot. lib. 2.

Jehoiakim being dead, [a] Jehoiachin his fon (who is alfo called Jeconiah, and Coniah) reigned in his ftead, who doing evil in the fight of the Lord, in the fame manner as his Father had done; this provoked [b] a very bitter declaration of God's wrath againft him, by the mouth of the prophet Jeremiah, and it was as bitterly executed upon him. For after Jehoiakim's death, the fervants of Nebuchadnezzar (that is, his lieutenants and governors of the provinces, that were under his fubjection in thofe parts) ftill [c] continued to block up Jerufalem; and, after three months, Nebuchadnezzar himfelf came thither in perfon with his royal army, and caufed the place to be begirt with a clofe fiege on every fide; whereon Jehoiachin, finding himfelf unable to defend it, went out to Nebuchadnezzar with his mother, and his princes and fervants, and delivered himfelf into his hands. But hereby, he obtained no other favour than to fave his life, for, being immediately put in chains, he was carried to Babylon, and there continued fhut up in prifon till the death of Nebuchadnezzar, which was full feven and thirty years.

An. 98.
Jehoiachin.
Zedekiah.

Nebuchadnezzar, having hereon made himfelf mafter of Jerufalem, [d] took thence all the treafures of the houfe of the Lord, and the treafures of the king's houfe, and cut in pieces the veffels of gold, which Solomon, king of Ifrael, had made in the temple of the Lord, and carried them to Babylon; and he alfo carried thither with him a vaft number of captives, Jehoiachin the king, his mother, and his wives, and his officers, and princes, and all the mighty men of valour, even to the number of ten thoufand men, out of Jerufalem only, befides the fmiths, and the carpenters, and other artificers; and, out of the reft of the land, of the mighty men feven thoufand, and of the crafts-men and fmiths one thoufand, befides three thoufand twenty and three, [e] which had been carried away the year before out of the open country, before the fiege of Jerufalem was begun. With the mighty men of valour he recruited his army, and the artificers he employed in the carrying on of his building at Babylon; of which we fhall fpeak hereafter.

In this captivity [f] was carried away to Babylon Ezekiel the prophet, the fon of Buzi, of the houfe of Aaron, and therefore the æra whereby he reckons throughout all his prophecies is from this captivity.

[a] 2 Kings xxiv. 6. 2 Chron. xxxvi. 9.
[b] Jer. xxii. 24.— 30.
[c] 2 Kings xxiv. 10. 11.
[d] 2 Kings xxiv. 13.—16.
[e] Jer. lii. 28.
[f] Ezek. xl. 1.

After this great carrying away of the Jews into [a] captivity, the poorer sort of the people being still left in the land, Nebuchadnezzar made Mattaniah, the son of Josiah, and uncle of Jehoiachin, king over them, taking of him a solemn oath to be true and faithful unto him; and, to engage him the more to be so, he changed his name from Mattaniah to Zedekiah, which signifieth *the justice of the Lord*, intending by this name to put him continually in mind of the vengeance which he was to expect from the justice of the Lord his God, if he violated that fidelity, which he had in his name sworn unto him.

Zedekiah, being thus made king, reigned eleven years in Jerusalem; but his ways being evil in the sight of the Lord, as were those of his nephew and brothers that reigned before him, he did thereby so far fill up the measure of the iniquities of his forefathers, that they at length drew down upon Judah and Jerusalem that terrible destruction in which his reign ended.

And thus was concluded the second war which Nebuchadnezzar had with the Jews. Three years he managed it by his lieutenants and governors of the neighbouring provinces of his empire. In the fourth year he came himself in person, and put an end to it in the captivity of Jehoiachin, and the taking of Jerusalem. What hindered him from coming sooner is not said; only it appears, that, in the tenth year of Jehoiakim, he was engaged in an arbitration between the Medes and Lydians. The occasion was this. After [b] the Medes had recovered all the upper Asia out of the hand of the Scythians, and again extended their borders to the river Halys, which was the common boundary between them and the Lydians, it was not long before there happened a war between these two nations, which was managed for five years together with various success. In the sixth year they engaged each other with the utmost of their strength, intending to make that battle decisive of the quarrel, that was between them. But, in the midst of it, while the fortune of the day seemed to hang in an equal balance between them, there happened an eclipse, which overspread both armies with darkness; whereon, being frightened with what had happened, they both desisted from fighting any longer, and agreed to refer the controversy to the arbitration of two neighbouring princes. The Lydians chose Siennesis, king of Cilicia, and the Medes, [c] Nebuchadnezzar, king of Babylon, who agreed a peace between them on the terms, that Astyages, son to Cyaxares, king of Media, should take to wife Arienna, the daughter of Halyattis, king of

the

---

[a] 2 Kings xxiv. 17. 2 Chron. xxxvi. 10.
[b] Herodotus, lib. 1.
[c] He is, by Herodotus, lib. 1. called Labynetus.

the Lydians; of which marriage, within a year after, was born Cyaxares, who is called Darius the Median in the book of Daniel. This eclipse was foretold by Thales the Milesian; and it happened on the 20th of September, according to the Julian account, in the 147th year of Nabonassar, and in the ninth of the reign of Jehoiakim, king of Judah, which was the year before Christ 601.

The same year that Cyaxares was born to Astyages, he gave his daughter Mandana, whom he had by a former wife, in marriage to Cymbyses, king of Persia; of whom the next year after (which was the last year of Jehoiakim) was born Cyrus, the famous founder of the Persian monarchy, and the restorer of the Jews to their country, their temple, and their former state.

Jehoiachin being thus carried into captivity, and Zedekiah settled in the throne, Jeremiah had, in [a] a vision, under the type of two baskets of figs, foreshewn unto him the restoration which God would again give to them who were carried into captivity, and the misery and desolation which should befal them, with their king, that were still in the land; that the captivity of the former should become a means of preservation unto them, while the liberty which the others were left in should serve only to lead them to their utter ruin; as accordingly it befel them in the destruction of Jerusalem, and the utter devastation of the land, which happened a few years afterwards.

The same year God also foreshewed to Jeremiah the confusion which he would bring upon [b] Elam (a kingdom lying upon the river Ulai, eastward beyond the Tigris), and the restoration which he would afterwards give thereto; which accordingly came to pass: for it was [c] conquered by Nebuchadnezzar, and subjected to him, in the same manner as Judah was. But afterwards, joining with Cyrus, it helped to conquer and subdue the Babylonians, who had before conquered them; and [d] Shushan, which was the chief city of that province, was thenceforth made the metropolis of the Persian empire, and had the throne of the kingdom placed in it.

After the departure of Nebuchadnezzar out of Judea and Syria, Zedekiah having settled himself in the kingdom, [e] the kings of the Ammonites, and of the Moabites, and of the Edomites, and of the Zidonians, and the Tyrians, and of the other neighbouring nations, sent their ambassadors to Jerusalem, to congratulate Zedekiah on his accession to the throne, and then proposed to him a league against the king of Babylon, for the

shaking

---

[a] Jeremiah xxiv.
[b] Jeremiah xlix. 34.—39.
[c] Xen. Cyropæd. lib. 6.
[d] Strabo, lib. 15. p. 727.
[e] Jeremiah xxvii.

shaking off his yoke, and the hindering of him from any more returning into those parts. Whereon Jeremiah, by the command of God, made him yokes and bonds, and sent them by the said ambassadors to their respective masters, with this message from God, That God had given all their countries unto the king of Babylon, and that they should serve him, and his son, and his son's son, and that, if they would submit to his yoke, and become obedient to him, it should be well with them, and their land, but, if otherwise, they should be consumed and destroyed before him. And he spake also to King Zedekiah according to the same words; which had that influence on him, that he did not then enter into the league that was proposed to him by the ambassadors of those princes. But afterwards, when it was farther strengthened, by the joining of the Egyptians and other nations in it, and he and his people began to be tired with the heavy burden and oppression of the Babylonish domination over them, he also was drawn into this confederacy; which ended in the absolute ruin both of him and his kingdom, as will be hereafter related.

Zedekiah, about the second year of his reign, [a] sent Elasah the son of Shaphan, and Gemariah the son of Hilkiah, to Babylon, on an embassy to King Nebuchadnezzar. By them Jeremiah wrote a letter to the Jews of the captivity in Babylon. The occasion of which was, Ahab the son of Kilaiah, and Zedekiah the son of Maaseiah, two of the captivity among the Jews at Babylon, taking upon them to be prophets sent to them from God, fed them with lying prophecies, and false promises of a speedy restoration, whereon they neglected to make any settlements in the places assigned them for their habitation, either by building of houses, cultivating their land, marrying of wives, or doing any thing else for their own interest and welfare in the country where they were carried, out of a vain expectation of a speedy return. To remedy this evil, Jeremiah wrote to them to let them know, that they were deceived by those who made them entertain such false hopes: that, by the appointment of God, their captivity at Babylon was to last seventy years; and those who remained in Judah and Jerusalem should be so far from being able to affect any restoration for them, that God would speedily send against them the sword, the famine, and the pestilence, for the consuming of the greatest part of them, and scatter the rest over the face of the earth, to be a curse, and an astonishment, and an hissing, and a reproach, among the nations, whither he would drive them. And therefore he exhorts them to provide for themselves in the country

An. 597.
Zedek. 2.

[a] Jeremiah xxix.

country whether they are carried, as settled inhabitants of the same, and comport themselves there, according to all the duties which belong to them as such, without expecting any return till the time that God had appointed. And as to their false prophets, who had prophesied a lie unto them, he denounced God's curse against them in a speedy and fearful destruction; which accordingly was soon after executed upon them: for Nebuchadnezzar finding that they disturbed the people by their vain prophecies, and hindered them from making settlements for themselves in the places where he had planted them, caused them to be seized, and roasted to death in the fire. The [a] latter Jews say, that these two men were the two elders who would have corrupted Susannah, and that Nebuchadnezzar commanded them to be burnt for this reason. The whole foundation of this conceit is, that Jeremiah, in the 23d verse of the chapter where he writes hereof, accuseth them for committing adultery with their neighbours wives; from whence they conjecture all the rest.

These letters being read to the people of the captivity at Babylon, such as were loath to be dispossessed of their vain hopes, were much offended at them; and therefore Semaiah, the Nehelemite, another false pretender to prophecy among them, writing their as well as his own sentiments hereof, sent back letters by the same ambassadors, directing them to Zephaniah, the son of Maaseiah, the second priest, and to all the priests, and people at Jerusalem, wherein he complained of Jeremiah for writing the said letters, and required them to rebuke him for the same; which letters being read to Jeremiah, the word of God came unto him, which denounced a very severe punishment upon Semaiah for the same.

In the fourth year of Zedekiah, and the fifth month of that year, Hananiah, the son of Azur of Gibeon, [b] took upon him to prophesy falsely in the name of the Lord, that within two full years God would bring back all the vessels of the house of the Lord, and King Jeconiah, and all the captives again to Jerusalem; whereon, the word of the Lord came to Jeremiah concerning Hananiah, that seeing he had spoken to the people of Judah in the name of the Lord, who sent him not, and had made them thereby to trust in a lie, he should be smitten of God, and die before the year should expire; and accordingly, he died the same year, in the seventh month, which was within two months after.

An. 595.
Zedek. 4.

The same year, Jeremiah had revealed unto him the prophecies, which we have in the 50th and 51st chapters of Jeremiah, concerning God's judgements that were to be executed upon
Chaldea

[a] Vide Gemaram in Sanhedrin. [b] Jer. xxviii.

Chaldea and Babylon, by the Medes and Persians. All which Jeremiah wrote in a book, and [a] delivered it to Seraiah, the son of Neriah, and brother of Baruch, who was then sent to Babylon by Zedekiah, commanding him, that, when he should come to Babylon, he should there read the same upon the banks of Euphrates; and that, when he should have there made an end of reading it, he should bind a stone to it, and cast it into the midst of the river, to denote thereby, that, as that should sink, so should Babylon also sink, and never rise any more; which hath since been fully verified, about two thousand years having now passed since Babylon hath been wholly desolated, and without an inhabitant.

Baruch seemeth to have gone with his brother in this journey to Babylon; for he is [b] said, in the apocryphal book that bears his name, to have read that book at Babylon, in the hearing of King Jeconiah, or Jehoiachin, and of the elders and people of the Jews then at Babylon, on the fifth year after the taking of Jerusalem by the Chaldeans; which can be understood of no other taking of it, than that wherein Jehoiachin was made a captive: for, after the last taking of it, in the eleventh of Zedekiah, Baruch could not be in Babylon; for, after that, he went into Egypt with Jeremiah, from whence it is not likely that he did ever return. And farther, it is said, in this very book of Baruch, that, after the reading of his book, as aforesaid, a collection was made at Babylon of money, which was sent to Jerusalem, to Joakim, the high priest, the son of Hilkiah, the son of Shallum, and to the priests, and to all the people that were found with him at Jerusalem, to buy burnt-offerings, and sin-offerings, and incense, and to prepare the mincha, and to offer upon the altar of the Lord their God; nothing of which could be true after the last taking of Jerusalem by the Chaldeans: for then the city and temple were burnt and utterly destroyed; and after that there was no high priest, altar, altar-service, or people, to be found at Jerusalem, till the return of the Jews again thither, after the end of their 70 years captivity. And, if there were any such person as Joakim (for he is no where else named), since he is here said to be the son of Hilkiah, the son of Shallum, he must have been the uncle of Seraiah, who was high priest at the burning of the temple, and grandson to the same Hilkiah; and therefore he must have been high priest before Seraiah, if there were any such person in that office at all: for it is certain, there were none such in it after him, during the life of Jeconiah. But of what authority this book is, or by whom it was written, whether any thing related therein be historically true, or the whole

[a] Jer. li. 59...64.   [b] Baruch i. 1...4.

whole of it a fiction, is altogether uncertain. Grotius [a] thinks it wholly feigned, by some hellenistical Jew, under Baruch's name, and so do many others; and it cannot be denied, but that they have strong reasons on their side. The subject of the book is an epistle sent, or feigned to be sent, by King Jehoiachin, and the Jews in captivity with him at Babylon, to their brethren, the Jews that were still left in Judah and Jerusalem: with an historical preface premised; in which it is related, how Baruch, being then at Babylon, did, in the name of the said king, and the people by their appointment, draw up the said epistle, and afterwards read it to them for their approbation; and how that, the collection being then made, which is above mentioned, the epistle, with the money, was sent to Jerusalem. There are three copies of it, one in Greek, and the other two in Syriac; whereof one agreeth with the Greek, but the other very much differs from it. But in what language it was originally written, or whether one of these be not the original, or which of them may be so, is what no one can say. Jerome [b] rejected it wholly, because it is not to be found among the Jews, and calls the epistle annexed to it ψευδόγραφον, *i.e.* a false or feigned writing. The most that can be said for it is, that Cyril of Jerusalem, and the Laodicean council, held A.D. 364, both name Baruch among the canonical books of holy scripture; for, in both the catalogues which are given us by them of these canonical books, are these words, *Jeremias, cum Baruch, Lamentationibus, et Epistola*, i.e. " Jeremiah, with Baruch, the Lamentations, and the Epistle;" whereby may seem to be meant the prophecies of Jeremiah, the lamentations of Jeremiah, the book of Baruch, with the epistle of Jeremiah at the end of it, as they are all laid together in the vulgar Latin edition of the Bible. The answer given hereto is, that these words were intended by them to express no more than Jeremiah's prophecies and lamentations only; that by the epistle is meant none other than the epistle in the 29th chapter of Jeremiah; and that Baruch's name is added, only because of the part which he bore in collecting all these together, and adding the last chapter to the book of his prophecies; which is supposed to be Baruch's, because the prophecies of Jeremiah end with the chapter before, that is, the 51st, as it is positively said in the last words of it; and it must be said, that since neither in St Cyril, nor in the Laodicean council, any of the other apocryphal books are named, it is very unlikely, that, by the name of Baruch in either of them, should be meant the apocryphal book, so named; which hath the least pretence of any of them to be canonical,

---

[a] In Comment. ad Baruch.   [b] In Præfatione ad Jeremiam.

canonical, as it appeared by the difficulty which ᵃ the Trentine fathers found to make it so.

In the 5th year of Zedekiah, which was also the 5th year of Jehoiachin's captivity, and the 30th from the great reformation made in the 18th year of King Josiah, Ezekiel ᵇ was called of God to be a prophet among the Jews of the captivity. And this same year he saw the vision of the four cherubims, and the four wheels, which is related in the 1st chapter of his prophecies. The same year were also revealed unto him ᶜ the 390 years of God's utmost forbearance of the house of Israel, and the 40 years of God's utmost forbearance of the house of Judah, and the judgement which, after that, God would inflict upon both; as the whole is contained in the 4th, 5th, 6th, and 7th chapters of his prophecies.

An. 594. Zedek. 5.

In the same year ᵈ died Cyaxares, king of Media, after he had reigned 40 years; and Astyages his son, who in scripture is called Ahasuerus, reigned in his stead.

In the same year ᵉ died also Psammis, king of Egypt, in an expedition which he made against the Ethiopians; and Apries his son, the same who in scripture is called Pharaoh Hophra, succeeded him in that kingdom, and reigned 25 years.

In the same year Ezekiel, being in a vision, was carried to Jerusalem, and there shewn all the several sorts of idolatry which were practised by the Jews in that place, had revealed unto him the punishments which God would inflict upon them for those abominations; and this makes up the subject of the 8th, 9th, 10th, and 11th chapters of his prophecies. But, at the same time, God promised to those ᶠ of the captivity, who, avoiding these abominations, kept themselves steady and faithful to his service, that he would become a sanctuary unto them in the strange land where they were carried, and bring them back again unto the land of Israel, and there make them flourish in peace and righteousness, as in former times. All ᵍ which the prophet declared to the Jews at Babylon, among whom he dwelt.

In the 7th year of Zedekiah, God did, both by types and words of revelation, foreshew unto Ezekiel the taking of Jerusalem by the Chaldeans, Zedekiah's flight from thence by night, the putting out of his eyes, and his imprisonment and death at Babylon; and also the carrying away of the Jews at the same time into captivity,

An. 592. Zedek. 7.

the

ᵃ The history of Trent, book 2. p. 144.
ᵇ Ezek. i. 1. 2. 3. &c.
ᶜ Ezek. iv. 4. 5. 6. &c.
ᵈ Herodot. lib. 1.
ᵉ Herodot. lib. 26.
ᶠ Ezek. xi. 15—21.
ᵍ Ezek. xi. 25.

the desolation of their country, and the many and great calamities which should befal them for their iniquities: and this is the subject of the 12th chapter of his prophecies. And what is contained in the seven following chapters was also the same year revealed unto him, and relates mostly to the same subject.

At this time Daniel was grown to so great a perfection and eminency in all righteousness, holiness, and piety of life, in the sight both of God and man, that [a] he is by God himself equalled with Noah and Job, and reckoned with these two to make up the three, who, of all the saints that had till then lived upon the earth, had the greatest power to prevail with God in their prayers for others. And yet he was then but a young man; for, allowing him to be eighteen when he was carried away to Babylon, among other children, to be there educated, and brought up for the service of the king (and a greater will not agree with this character), thirty-two at this time must have been the utmost of his age. But he dedicated the prime and vigour of his life to the service of God; and that is the best time to make proficiency therein.

Zedekiah, having in the 7th year of his reign [b] sent ambassadors into Egypt, made a confederacy with Pharaoh Hophra, king of Egypt; and therefore, the next year, after breaking the oath of fidelity which he had sworn in the name of the Lord his God unto Nebuchadnezzar, king of Babylon, he rebelled against him; which drew on him that war which ended in his ruin, and in the ruin of all Judah and Jerusalem with him, in that calamitous destruction in which both were involved hereby. *An. 591. Zedek. 8.*

In the 9th year of Zedekiah, [c] Nebuchadnezzar, having drawn together a great army out of all the nations under his dominion, marched against him, to punish him for his perfidy and rebellion. But, on his coming into Syria, finding that the Ammonites had also entered into the same confederacy with Egypt against him, he was [d] in a doubt for some time which of these two people he should first fall upon, them, or the Jews; whereon he committed the decision of the matter to his diviners, who, consulting by the entrails of their sacrifices, their teraphim, and their arrows, determined for the carrying of the war against the Jews. This way of divining by arrows was usual among these idolaters. The manner of it, Jerome [e] tells us, was thus: They wrote on several *An. 590. Zedek. 9.*

---

[a] Ezek xiv. 14. 20.   [b] Ezek. xvii. 15.
[c] 2 Kings xxv. 1.   2 Chron. xxxvi. 17.   Jer. xxxix. 1. lii. 4.
[d] Ezek. xxi. 19---24.   [e] In Comment. in Ezek. xxi.

ral arrows the names of the cities they intended to make war against, and then, putting them promiscuously all together into a quiver, they caused them to be drawn out thence in the manner as they draw lots; and that city, whose name was on the arrow first drawn, was the first they assaulted. And by this way of divination, the war being determined against Judah, Nebuchadnezzar immediately marched his army into that country, and in a few days [a] took all the cities thereof, excepting only Lachish, Azekah, and Jerusalem: Whereon, the Jews at Jerusalem, being terrified with these losses, and the apprehensions of a siege, then ready to be laid to that place, made a shew of returning unto the Lord their God, and entered into a solemn covenant, thenceforth to serve him only, and faithfully observe all his laws. And, in pursuance hereof, [b] proclamation was made, that every man should let his man-servant, and every man his maid-servant, being an Hebrew or an Hebrewess, go free [c], according to the law of God; and every man did according hereto.

On the [d] tenth month of the same year, and the tenth day of the month (which was about the end of our December, Nebuchadnezzar, with all his numerous army, laid siege to Jerusalem, and blocked it close up on every side; in memory whereof, the tenth day of Tebeth, which is their tenth month, hath ever since been observed [e] by the Jews, as a day of solemn fast even to this time.

On the same [f] tenth day of the tenth month, in which this siege began at Jerusalem, was the same revealed to Ezekiel in Chaldea; where, by the type of a boiling pot, was foreshewn unto him the dismal destruction which should thereby be brought upon that city. And the [g] same night, the wife of the prophet, who was the desire of his eyes, was, by a sudden stroke of death, taken from him; and he was forbid by God to make any manner of mourning for her, or appear with any of the usual signs of it upon him, thereby to foreshew, that the holy city, the temple, and the sanctuary, which were dearer to them than any wife can be in the eyes of her husband, should not only, by a speedy and sudden stroke of destruction, be taken from them, but that the calamity ensuing thereon should be such, and so great, as should not allow them as much as to mourn for the loss of them.

In the beginning of the tenth year of Zedekiah, [h] the prophet

[a] Jer. xxxiv. 7.
[b] Jer. xxxiv. 8—10.
[c] Deut. xv. 12.
[d] 2 Kings xxv. 1. Jer. xxxix. 1. lii. 4.
[e] Zech. viii. 19.
[f] Ezek. xxiv. 1, 2.
[g] Ezek. xxiv. 16—18.
[h] Jer. xxxiv.

phet Jeremiah, being sent of God, declared unto him, that the Babylonians, who were now besieging of the city, should certainly take it, and burn it with fire, and take him prisoner, and carry him to Babylon; and that he should die there. Whereon [a] Zedekiah, being much displeased, put him in prison, and, while he was shut up there, even in this very year, [b] he purchased of Hanameel, his uncle's son, a field in Anathoth; thereby to foreshew, that although Judah and Jerusalem should be laid desolate, and the inhabitants led into captivity, yet there should be a restoration, when lands and possessions should be again enjoyed by the legal owners of them, in the same manner as in former times.

An. 589.
Zedekiah 10.

Pharaoh Hophra [c] coming out of Egypt with a great army to the relief of Zedekiah, Nebuchadnezzar raised the siege of Jerusalem to march against him. But, before he went on this expedition, [d] he sent all the captive Jews which he then had in his camp to Babylon, the number of which were 832 persons.

On the departure of the Chaldeans from Jerusalem, Jeremiah being again set at liberty, [e] Zedekiah sent unto him Jehucal, the son of Shelemiah, and Zephaniah, the son of Maaseiah, the priest, to inquire of the Lord by him, and to desire him to pray for him and his people. To whom the prophet returned an answer from God, that the Egyptians, whom they did depend upon, would certainly deceive them; that their army would again return into Egypt, without giving them any help at all; and that thereon the Chaldeans would again renew the siege, take the city, and burn it with fire.

But the general opinion of the people being, that the Chaldeans were gone for good and all, and would return no more to renew the war against them, they [f] repented of the covenant of reformation, which they had entered into before God, when they were in fear of them; and caused every man's servant, and every man's handmaid, whom they had set at liberty, again to return into servitude, to be unto them again for servants and for handmaids, contrary to the law of the Lord, and the covenant, which they had lately entered into with him, to walk according to it. For [g] which inhuman and unjust act, and their impious breach of the covenant lately made with God, Jeremiah proclaimed liberty to the sword, the famine, and the pestilence, to execute the wrath of God upon them, and their king, and their princes, and all Judah and Jerusalem, to their utter destruction.

VOL. I.   F   While

[a] Jer xxxii. 1.—5.
[b] Jer. xxxii. 7.—17.
[c] Jer. xxxvii. 5.
[d] Jer. lii. 29.
[e] Jer. xxxvii. 3.—10.
[f] Jer. xxxv. 11.
[g] Jer. xxxiv. 17.—22

While the Chaldeans were yet abſent from Jeruſalem, [a] Jeremiah intending to retire to Anathoth, his native place, that thereby he might avoid the ſiege, which he knew would be again renewed on the return of the Chaldeans from their expedition againſt the Egyptians, put himſelf on his journey thither ; but, as he was paſſing the gate of the city that led that way, the captain, that kept guard there, ſeized him for a deſerter, as if his intentions were to fall away to the Chaldeans; whereon he was again put in priſon, in the houſe of Jonathan the ſcribe, which they had made the common jail of the city, where he remained many days

The Egyptians, on the coming of the Chaldeans againſt them, durſt not ſtay to engage in battle with ſo numerous and well appointed an army; but, [b] withdrawing on their approach, retired again into their own country, treacherouſly leaving Zedekiah and his people to periſh in that war which they had drawn them into. Whereon [c] the prophet Ezekiel, reproaching them for their perfidy, in thus becoming a ſtaff of reed to thoſe, whom by oaths and covenants of alliance they had made to lean and confide on them, denounced God's judgements againſt them, to be executed both upon king and people, in war, confuſion, and deſolation, for forty years enſuing, for the puniſhment hereof: and [d] alſo foretold, how, after that, they ſhould ſink low, and become a mean and baſe people, and ſhould no more have a prince of their own to reign over them. Which hath accordingly come to paſs: for, not long after the expiration of the ſaid forty years, they were made a province of the Perſian empire, and have been governed by ſtrangers ever ſince ; for, on the failure of the Perſian empire, they became ſubject to the Macedonians, and after them to the Romans, and after the Romans to the Saracens, and then to the Mamalukes, and are now a province of the Turkiſh empire.

On the retreat of the Egyptians, Nebuchadnezzar [e] returned to Jeruſalem, and again renewed the ſiege of that place; which laſted about a year, from the ſecond inveſting of it, to the time when it was taken.

The ſiege being thus renewed, Zedekiah [f] ſent for Jeremiah out of priſon, to conſult with him, and inquire of him, what word there was from God concerning the preſent ſtate of his affairs? to which he found there was no other anſwer, but that he was to be delivered into the hands of the king of Babylon. However, at the intreaty of the prophet, he was prevailed with

not

[a] Jer. xxxvii. 11.—15.
[b] Jer. xxxvii. 7.
[c] Ezek. xxix.
[d] Ezek. xxx. 13.
[e] Jer. xxxvii. 8.
[f] Jer. xxxvii. 17.—21.

not to send him back again to the common jail of the city, lest he should die there by reason of the noisomness of the place; and therefore, instead thereof, he was ordered to the prison of the king's court, where he continued, with the allowance of a certain portion of bread out of the common store, till the city was taken.

Zedekiah, finding himself in the siege much pressed by the Chaldeans, [a] sent messengers to Jeremiah, farther to inquire of the Lord by him concerning the present war. To which he answered, that the word of the Lord concerning him was, that God, being very much provoked against him, and his people, for their iniquities, would fight against the city, and smite it; that both king and people should be delivered into the hands of the king of Babylon; that those who continued in the city, during the siege, should perish by the pestilence, the famine, and the sword; but that those who should go out, and fall to the Chaldeans, should have their lives given them for a prey. At which answer [b], several of the princes and chief commanders about the king, being very much offended, pressed the king against him, as one that weakened the hands of the men of war, and of all the people, and sought their hurt more than their good: whereon he being delivered into their hands, they cast him into a dungeon, where he must have perished, but that [c] Ebedmelech, an eunuch of the court, having intreated the king in his behalf, delivered him thence; for which charitable act he had a message sent him from God of mercy and deliverance unto him. After this, [d] Zedekiah, sending for Jeremiah into the temple, there secretly inquired of him; but had no other answer, than what had been afore given him, saving only, that the prophet told him, that, if he would go forthwith and deliver himself into the hands of the king of Babylon's princes, who commanded at the carrying on of the siege, this was the only way whereby he might save both himself and the city; and he earnestly pressed him hereto. But Zedekiah would not hearken unto him herein; but sent him back again to prison, and after that no more consulted with him.

In the 11th year of Zedekiah, in the beginning of the year, God declared, by the prophet Ezekiel, his judgements against Tyre, for their insulting on the calamitous state of Judah and Jerusalem; foreshewing, that the same calamities should be also brought upon them by the same Nebuchadnezzar, into whose hands God would deliver them; and this is the subject of the 26th, 27th, and 28th chapters of his prophecies; in the last of which God particularly upbraideth

An. 588.
Zedek. 11.

---

[a] Jer. xxi. 1.—14.
[b] Jer. xxxviii. 1.—6.
[c] Jer. xxxviii. 7.—13.
[d] Jer. xxxviii. 14.—23.

upbraideth Ithobal, then king of Tyre, with the insolent and proud conceit he had of his own knowledge and understanding, having puffed up himself herewith, as [a] " if he were wiser than Daniel; and that there was no secret that could be hid from him:" which sheweth to how great an height the fame of Daniel's wisdom was at that time grown, since it now became spoken of, by way of proverb, through all the east; and yet, according to the account above given of his age, he could not at this time exceed 36 years. And, in the conclusion of the 28th chapter, the like judgements are denounced also against Sidon, and for the same reason.

The same year God declared, by the same prophet, his judgements against Pharaoh and the Egyptians: that he would bring the king of Babylon against them, and deliver them into his hands; and that, notwithstanding their greatness and pride, they should no more escape his revenging hand than the Assyrians had done before them, who were higher and greater than they. And this is the subject of the 30th and 31st chapters of his prophecies.

In the 4th month, on the 9th day of the month, of the same 11th year of Zedekiah, [b] Jerusalem was taken by the Chaldeans, after the siege had lasted, from their last setting down before it, about a year. Hereon Zedekiah, with his men of war, fled away; and, having broken through the camp of the enemy, endeavoured to make his escape over Jordan: but, being pursued after, he was overtaken in the plains of Jericho: whereon, all his army being scattered from him, he was taken prisoner, and carried to the king of Babylon at Riblah in Syria, where he then resided; who, having caused his sons, and all his princes that were taken with him, to be slain before his face, commanded his eyes to be put out, and then bound him in fetters of brass, and sent him to Babylon, where he died in prison: and hereby was fulfilled the [c] prophecy of the prophet Ezekiel concerning him, That he should be brought to Babylon in the land of the Chaldeans, yet should not see the place, though he should die there.

In the 5th month, on the 7th day of the month (i.e. towards the end of our July), came [d] Nebuzaradan, captain of the guards, to the king of Babylon, to Jerusalem; and, after having taken out all the vessels of the house of the Lord, and gathered together all the riches that could be found, either in the king's house, or in any of the other houses of the city, he did, on the 10th

---

[a] Ezekiel xxviii. 3.
[b] 2 Kings xxv. 4. 2 Chr. xxxvi. 17. Jer. xxxix. :—10. lii. 6 —11.
[c] Ezek. xii. 13.
[d] 2 Kings xxv. 8...17. Jer. lii. 12...23.

10th day of the fame month, purfuant to the command of his mafter, fet both the temple and city on fire, and abfolutely confumed and deftroyed them both, overthrowing all the walls, fortreffes, and towers, belonging thereto, and wholly razing and levelling to the ground every building therein, till he had brought all to a thorough and perfect defolation; and fo it continued for 52 years after, till, by the favour of Cyrus, the Jews being releafed from their captivity, and reftored again to their own land, repaired thefe ruins, and built again their holy city. In memory of this calamity, they keep two fafts, even to this day, the 17th of the 4th month (which falls in our June) for the deftruction of Jerufalem, and the 9th of the 5th month (which falls in our July) for the deftruction of the temple; both which are made mention of [a] in the prophecies of the prophet Zechariah, under the names of the faft of the 4th month, and the faft of the 5th month, and are there fpoken of as annually obferved from the deftruction of Jerufalem to his time, which was 70 years after. Jofephus [b] remarks, that the burning of the temple by Nebuchadnezzar happened on the very fame day of the year on which it was afterwards again burned by Titus.

Nebuzaradan, having thus deftroyed the city and the temple of Jerufalem, made all the people he found there captives. Of thefe [c], he took Seraiah the high prieft, and Zephaniah the fecond prieft, and about 70 others of the principal perfons he found in the place, and carried them to Riblah to Nebuchadnezzar, who caufed them all there to be put to death. Of [d] the reft of the people, he left the poorer fort to till the ground, and drefs their vineyards, and made Gedaliah, the fon of Ahikam, governor over them, and all the other he carried away to Babylon.

But concerning Jeremiah, [e] Nebuchadnezzar gave particular charge to Nebuzaradan, that he fhould offer him no hurt, but look well to him, and do for him in all things according as he fhould defire. And therefore, as foon as he came to Jerufalem, with commiffion to deftroy the place, he and the princes that were with him fent and took him out of prifon, where he had lain bound from the time that Zedekiah had put him there, and reftored him to his liberty; and, having carried him with him as far as Ramah, on his return to Nebuchadnezzar, he then gave him his option, whether he would go with him to Babylon, where

[a] Zechariah viii. 19.
[b] De Bello Judaico, lib. vii. c. 10.
[c] 2 Kings xxv. 18.---21. Jer. lii. 24.---27.
[d] 2 Kings xxv. 22—25. Jer. xxxix. 9, 10, & lii. 15. 16.
[e] Jer. xxxix. 11.—14. & xl. 1.—6.

where he should be well looked after, and maintained at the king's charge, or else remain in the land; and he having chosen the latter, Nebuzaradan gave him victuals and a reward, and sent him back to Gedaliah the son of Ahikam, with an especial charge to take care of him.

After Nebuchadnezzar was returned to Babylon, [a] all those who before, for fear of the Chaldeans, had taken refuge among the neighbouring nations, or had hid themselves in the fields and the deserts, after their escape, on the dispersion of Zedekiah's army in the plains of Jericho, hearing that Gedaliah was made governor of the land, resorted to him; and, he having promised them protection, and sworn unto them, that they should be safe under his government, they settled themselves again in the land, and gathered in the fruits of it. The chief among these were Johanan and Jonathan the sons of Kereah, Seraiah the son of Tanhumeth, Azariah the son of Hoshaiah, Ishmael the son of Nethaniah, and others.

But [b] Ishmael came to him only out of a treacherous design; for, being of the seed-royal, he reckoned to make himself king of the land, now the Chaldeans were gone; and, for the accomplishing of it, had formed a conspiracy to kill Gedaliah, and seize the government; and Baalis, the king of the Ammonites, was confederated with him herein. But Johanan, the son of Kereah, having got notice of it, he, and all the chief men of the rest of the people, went to Gedaliah, and informed him of it, proposing to kill Ishmael, and thereby deliver him from the mischief that was intended against him. But Gedaliah being of a very benign disposition, and not easy to entertain jealousies of any one, would not believe this of Ishmael, but still carried on a friendly correspondence with him; [c] of which Ishmael, taking the advantage, came to him in the seventh month, which answers to our September, when the people were most of them scattered abroad from him to gather in the fruits of the land, and while they were eating and drinking together at an entertainment, which Gedaliah had in a very friendly manner made for him and his men, they rose upon him, and slew him, and, at the same time, slew also a great number of the Jews and Chaldeans, whom they found with him in Mizpah, and took the rest captive. And the next day, hearing of eighty men, who were going on a religious account, with offerings and incense [d] to the house of God, they craftily drew them

---

[a] Jer. xl. 7.—12.   [b] Jer. xl. 13.—16.   [c] Jer. xli.

[d] *i.e.* At Jerusalem; for though the temple were destroyed, yet the people that were left, continued to offer sacrifices and worship there on the place where it stood, as long as they remained in the land.

them into Mizpah, and there flew them all, excepting ten of them, who offered their stores for the redemption of their lives. And then taking with them all the captives, among whom were the daughters of King Zedekiah, they departed thence to go over to the Ammonites. But Johanan the son of Kereah, and the rest of the captains, hearing of this wicked fact, immediately armed as many of the people as they could get together, and pursued after Ishmael; and, having overtaken him at Gibeon, retook all the captives; but he and eight of his men escaped to the Ammonites. This murder of Gedaliah happened two months after the destruction of the city and temple of Jerusalem, in the said seventh month, and on the 30th day of the month. For that day the Jews have kept as a fast in commemoration of this calamity ever since; and [a] Zechariah also makes mention of it as observed in his time, calling it by the name of the *fast of the seventh month*; and they had reason to keep a fast for it, for it was the completion of their ruin.

After this great misfortune, [b] Johanan the son of Kereah, and the people that were left, fearing the king of Babylon, because of the murder of Gedaliah whom he had made governor of the land, departed from Mizpah, to flee into the land of Egypt, and came to Bethlehem in their way thither: where they stopping a while consulted the prophet Jeremiah (whom they had carried with them) about their intended journey, and desired him to inquire of God in their behalf; who, after ten days, having received an answer from God, called them together, and told them, that if they would tarry in the land, all should go well with them, and God would shew mercy unto them, and incline the heart of the king of Babylon to be favourable unto them; but if they would not hearken unto the word of the Lord, but would, notwithstanding his word now delivered to the contrary, set their faces to go into the land of Egypt, that then the sword and famine should follow close after them thither, and they should be all there destroyed. But all this was of no effect with them: for, their hearts being violently bent to go into Egypt, they would not hearken to the word of the Lord spoken to them by the mouth of his prophet, but told Jeremiah, that the answer which he gave them, was not from God, but was suggested to him by Baruch the son of Neriah for their hurt. And therefore Johanan the son of Kereah, and the rest of the captains of the forces, took all the remnant of Judah, that were returned, from all nations whither they had been driven, again to dwell in the land, and all the persons whom Nebuzaradan had

left

---

[a] Zechariah viii. 19.   [b] Jeremiah lii.

left with Gedaliah, even men, women, and children, and the king's daughters, and alſo Jeremiah the prophet, and Baruch the ſon of Neriah, and went into Egypt, and ſettled in that country, till the plagues and judgements which God had threatened them with, for their diſobedience to his word, there overtook them, to their utter deſtruction. And thus ended this unfortunate year, in which the temple and city of Jeruſalem were deſtroyed, and the whole land of Judah brought in a manner to utter deſolation for the ſins thereof.

THE

OLD AND NEW TESTAMENT

CONNECTED,

IN

THE HISTORY

OF

THE JEWS AND NEIGHBOURING NATIONS,

FROM

The Declenſion of the Kingdoms of ISRAEL *and* JUDAH,
to the Time of CHRIST.

BOOK II.

IN the 12th year of the captivity of Jehoiachin, one eſcaping from Jeruſalem [a] came to Ezekiel in the land of the Chaldeans, and told him of the deſtruction of the city; whereon he propheſied deſolation to the reſt of the land of Judah, and utter deſtruction to the remainder of the Jews who were left therein.   An. 587. Nebuchadnezzar 18.

The ſame year Ezekiel propheſied againſt Egypt, and Pharaoh Hophra, the king thereof, that God would bring againſt him Nebuchadnezzar, king of Babylon, who ſhould lay the land deſolate; and that he and all his armies ſhould be brought to deſtruction, and periſh, like as other nations whom God had cut off for their iniquities: which is the ſubject of the 32d chapter of his prophecies.

The Jews which went into Egypt, [b] having ſettled at Migdol, and Tahpanhes, and Noph, and in the country of Pathros,
(*i. e.*

[a] Ezek. xxxiii. 21—29.   [b] Jer. xliv. 1.

(*i. e.* at [a] Magdalum by the Red sea, at Daphne near Pelusium, at Memphis, and in the country of Thebais), gave themselves there wholly up to idolatry, [b] worshipping the queen of heaven, and other false deities of the land, and burning incense unto them, without having any more regard to the Lord their God. Whereon the [c] prophet Jeremiah cried aloud against this impiety, unto those among whom he lived, that is, those who had settled [d] in the land of Pathros or Thebais. (For this being the farthest from Judea of all the places where they had obtained settlements in that country, they had carried him thither, the better to take from him all opportunity of again returning from them). But all his exhortations were of no other effect, than to draw from them a declaration, that [e] they would worship the Lord no more, but would go on in their idolatry: for they told him, that it had been best with them, when they practised it in Judah and Jerusalem; that it was since their leaving of it off, that all their calamities had happened unto them; and that therefore, they would no more hearken unto any thing, that he should deliver unto them in the name of the Lord. Whereon [f] the word of the Lord came unto the prophet, denouncing utter destruction unto them by the sword, and by the famine, that thereby all of them, that is, all the men of Judah then dwelling in Egypt, should be consumed, excepting only some few, who should make their escape into the land of Judah. And, for a sign hereof, it was foretold unto them by the same prophet, that Pharaoh Hophra, king of Egypt, in whom they trusted, should be given into the hands of his enemies, who sought his life, in the same manner as Zedekiah was given into the hands of Nebuchadnezzar, that sought his life; that so, when this should be brought to pass in their eyes, they might be assured thereby, that all these words, which the Lord hath spoken against them, should certainly be fulfilled upon them; as accordingly they were, about 18 years afterwards.

After this there is no more mention of Jeremiah. It is most likely that he died in Egypt soon after, he being then much advanced in years: (For he had now prophesied 41 years from the 13th of Josiah), and also much broken (as we may well suppose) by the calamities which happened to himself and his country. Tertullian, Epiphanius, Dorotheus, Jerome, and Zonaras, tell us, that he was stoned to death by the Jews, for preaching

against

---

[a] Vide Boch. Phal. p. 1. lib. 4. c. 27.
[b] Jer. xliv. 8. 15.---19.
[c] Jer xliv. 1—15.
[d] Jer. xliv. 15.
[e] Jer. xliv. 16---19.
[f] Jer. xliv. 26---30.

against their idolatry. And of this some interpret St Paul's ἐλιθάσθησαν (*i. e.* they were stoned), Heb. xi. 37.: but others say, that he was put to death by Pharaoh Hophra, because of his prophecy against him. But these seem to be traditions, founded rather on conjecture, than on any certain account of the matter.

Nebuchadnezzar, being returned to Babylon after the end of the Jewish war, and the full settling of his affairs in Syria and Palestine, did, out of the spoils which he had taken in that expedition, [a] make that golden image to the honour of Bel his god, which he did set up, and dedicate to him in the plain of Dura: the history of which is at large related in the 3d chapter of Daniel: but how Daniel escaped the fiery furnace, which his three friends on that occasion were condemned unto, is made a matter of inquiry by some. That he did not fall down and worship the idol, is most certain; it absolutely disagreeing with the character of that holy religious man, to make himself guilty of so high an offence against God, as such a compliance would have amounted unto; either, therefore, he was absent, or else, if present, was not accused. The latter seems most probable; for Nebuchadnezzar, having summoned all his princes, counsellors, governors, captains, and all other his officers and ministers, to be present, and assisting at the solemnity of this dedication, it is not likely, that Daniel, who was one of the chiefest of them, should be allowed to be absent. That he was present, therefore, seems most probable: but his enemies thought it fittest not to begin with him, because of the great authority he had with the king; but rather to fall first on his three friends, and thereby pave the way for their more successful reaching of him after it But what was in the interim miraculously done in their case, quashed all further accusation about this matter; and for that reason it was, that Daniel is not at all spoken of in it.

Nebuchadnezzar, in the 21st year of his reign, according to the Jewish account, which was the 19th according to the Babylonish account, and the second from the destruction of Jerusalem, came again into Syria, and laid [b] siege to Tyre, Ithobal being then king of

An. 586.
Nebuchad-
nezzar. 19.

that

---

[a] In the Greek version of Daniel, chap. iii. 1. this is said to have been done in the 18th year of Nebuchadnezzar. But this is not in the original text; for in that no year at all is mentioned: and therefore it is most probable it crept into it from some marginal comment, for which, I doubt not, there was some very good authority For, it could in no year of that king's reign fall more likely; and therefore according hereto I have here placed it

[b] Josephus Antiquities book 10. chap. 11. et contra Apionem lib. 1.

that city; which found him hard work for thirteen years together, it being so long before he could make himself master of the place: for it was a strong and wealthy city, which had never as yet submitted to any foreign empire, and was [a] of great fame in those days for its traffic and merchandise, whereby several of its inhabitants had made themselves as great [b] as princes in riches and splendour. It [c] was built by the Zidonians, 240 years before the building of the temple of Solomon at Jerusalem: For Zidon [d] being then conquered and taken by the Philistines of Askelon, many of the inhabitants escaping thence in their ships, built Tyre; and therefore it was called by the prophet Isaiah [e] the daughter of Zidon: but it soon out-grew its mother in largeness, riches, and power, and was thereby enabled to withstand for so many years the power of this mighty king, to whom all the east had then submitted.

While Nebuchadnezzar lay at this siege, Nebuzaradan, the captain of his guards, being sent out by him with part of his army, invaded the land of Israel, to take revenge, as it may be supposed, for the death of Gedaliah, there being no other reason why he should fall on the poor remains of those miserable people, whom he himself had left and settled there. In which expedition [f] Nebuzaradan, seizing upon all of the race of Israel that he could meet with in the land, made them all captives, and sent them to Babylon. But they all amounted to no more than 745 persons, the rest having been all fled into Egypt, as hath been before related.

An. 584.
Nebuchadnezzar 21.

By this last captivity was fully completed the desolation of the land, no more of its former inhabitants being now left therein. And hereby were also completed the prophecies of Isaiah, Jeremiah, Ezekiel, and other prophets relating hereto; and particularly [g] that of Ezekiel, wherein God's forbearance of the house of Israel is limited to 390 days, and his forbearance of the house of Judah to 40 days. For, taking the days for years, according to the prophetic stile of scripture, from the apostasy of Jeroboam to the time of this last captivity, there will be just 390 years; and so long God bore the idolatry of the house of Israel: and from the 18th year of Josiah, [h] when the house of Judah entered into covenant with God to walk wholly in his ways, to the same time will be just 40 years; and so long God bore their walking contrary to that covenant. But now the stated time of his forbearance, in respect of both being fully completed,

[a] Ezek. xxvi. &. xxvii.
[b] Is. xxiii. 8.
[c] Joseph. Antiq. b. 8. c. 2.
[d] Justin lib. 18. c. 3.
[e] Is. xxiii. 12.
[f] Jer. lii. 30.
[g] Ezek. iv. 1---8.
[h] 2 Chron. xxxiv. 29---31.

pleted, he completed alſo the deſolation of both in this laſt captivity, in which both had an equal ſhare, part of them, who were now carried away, being of the houſe of Judah, and part of the houſe of Iſrael. There are others who end both the computations at the deſtruction of Jeruſalem; and, to make their hypotheſis good, they begin the 40 years of God's forbearance of the houſe of Judah from the miſſion of the prophet Jeremiah to preach repentance unto them, that is, from the 13th of Joſiah, [a] when he was firſt called to this office; from which time, to the laſt year of Zedekiah, when Jeruſalem was deſtroyed, were exactly 40 years. And as to the 390 years forbearance of the houſe of Iſrael, according as they compute the time from Jeroboam's apoſtaſy, they make this period to fall exactly right alſo, that is, to contain juſt 390 years from that time to the deſtruction of Jeruſalem. But this period relating purely to the houſe of Iſrael, as contradiſtinct from the houſe of Judah, in this prophecy, it cannot be well interpreted to end in the deſtruction of Jeruſalem, in which the houſe of Iſrael had no concern: for Jeruſalem was not within the kingdom of Iſrael, but within the kingdom of Judah, of which it was the metropolis; and therefore the latter only, and not the former, had their puniſhment in it. But this laſt equally affected both; and therefore here may well be ended the reckoning which belonged to both. As to the computing of the 40 years of God's forbearance of the houſe of Judah from the miſſion of Jeremiah to preach repentance unto them, it muſt be acknowledged, that from thence to the deſtruction of Jeruſalem, the number of years falls exactly right; and therefore, ſince [b] the 120 years of God's forbearance of the old world is reckoned from the like miſſion of Noah to preach repentance unto them, I ſhould be inclined to come into this opinion, and reckon the 40 years of this forbearance of Judah by the 40 years of Jeremiah's like preaching of repentance unto them; but it cannot be conceived, why Ezekiel ſhould reckon the time of his miſſion by an æra from the 18th year of Joſiah (for the 30th year on which he ſaith he was called to the prophetic office is certainly to be reckoned from thence), unleſs it be with reſpect to the 40 years of God's forbearance of the houſe of Judah in his own prophecies.

After this, Nebuzaradan [c] marched againſt the Ammonites; and, having deſtroyed Rabbah, their royal city, and by fire and ſword made great deſolation in that country, he carried their king, and their princes, and moſt of the chief of the land, into captivity: and this was done by way of juſt revenge for the

part

[a] Jer. i. 2.　　　　　[b] Gen. vi. 3.
[c] Jer. xlix. 1.—6. Ezek. xxv. 1.—7. Amos i. 14. 15.

part which they had in the murder of Gedaliah, the king of Babylon's governor in the land of Ifrael.

And, during this fiege of Tyre, the other neighbouring nations, that is, the Philiftines, the Moabites, the Edomites, and the Zidonians, feem alfo to have been haraffed and broken by the excurfions of the Babylonians, and to have had all thofe judgements executed upon them which we find, in the prophecies of [a] Jeremiah and [b] Ezekiel, to have been denounced againft them.

In the 14th year after the deftruction of Jerufalem, which was the 25th year of the captivity of Jehoiachin, were revealed unto the prophet Ezekiel all thofe vifions and prophecies concerning the future ftate of the church of God, which we have from the 40th chapter of his prophecies to the end of that book.

An. 574.
Nebuchad-
nezzar 31.

This fame year, the judgements which God had denounced, by the mouth of his prophets, againft Pharaoh Hophra, or Apries, king of Egypt, began to operate againft him. For [c] the Cyrenians, a colony of the Greeks, that had fettled in Africa, having taken from the Lybians (a neighbouring nation, lying between them and the Egyptians, and bordering upon both, a great part of their land), and divided it among themfelves, the Lybians made a furrender both of themfelves and their country into the hands of Apries, to obtain his protection. Hereon Apries fent a great army into Lybia, to wage war againft the Cyrenians; which, having the misfortune to be beaten and overthrown in battle, were almoft all cut off and deftroyed, fo that very few of them efcaped the carnage, and returned again into Egypt: whereon the Egyptians, entertaining an opinion, that this army was fent by Apries into Lybia of purpofe to be deftroyed, that he might, when rid of them, with the more eafe and fecurity govern the reft, became fo incenfed againft him, that a great many of them, embodying together, revolted from him. Apries, hearing of this, fent Amafis, an officer of his court, to appeafe them, and reduce them again to their duty. But, while he was fpeaking to them, they put on his head the enfigns of royalty, and declared him their king; which he accepting of ftaid among them, and increafed the revolt. At which Apries, being much incenfed, fent Paterbemis, another officer of his court, and one of the firft rank among his followers, to arreft Amafis, and bring him unto him; which he not being able to effect, in the midft of fo great an army of confpirators as he found about him, was, on his return, very cruelly and unworthily treated by Apries; for,

out

---

[a] Jer. xxvii. xxviii. xxix. [b] Ezek. xxv.
[c] Herodot. lib. 2. & 4. Diodorus Siculus, lib. 1. part 2.

out of anger for his not effecting that for which he sent him, though he had no power to accomplish it, he outrageously commanded his ears and his nose to be immediaately cut off. Which wrong and indignity offered to a person of his character and worth, so incensed the rest of the Egyptians, that they almost all joined with the conspirators in a general revolt from him. Whereon Apries, being forced to fly, made his escape into the Upper Egypt, towards the borders of Ethiopia; where he maintained himself for some years, while Amasis held all the rest.

But while this was a-doing in Egypt, at length, [a] in the 26th year of the captivity of Jehoiachin, which was the 15th after the destruction of Jerusalem, Nebuchadnezzar made himself master of Tyre, after a siege [b] of thirteen years continuance, and utterly destroyed the place, that is, the city, which was on the continent; the ruins of which were afterwards called Palæ-Tyrus, or Old Tyre. But, before it came to this extremity, the inhabitants had removed most of their effects into an island about half a mile distant from the shore, and there built them a new city. And therefore, when Nebuchadnezzar entered that, which he had so long besieged, he found little there wherewith to reward his soldiers in the spoil of the place, which they had so long laboured to take; and therefore, wrecking his anger upon the buildings, and the few inhabitants who were left in them, he razed the whole town to the ground, and slew all he found therein. After this it never more recovered its former glory; but the city on the island became the Tyre that was afterwards so famous by that name; the other on the continent never rising any higher, than to become a village by the name of Old Tyre, as was before said: That it was this Tyre only that Nebuchadnezzar besieged, and not the other on the island, appears from the description of the siege, which we have in Ezekiel. For thereby we find, that Nebuchadnezzar made [c] a fort against the place, and cast up a mount against it, and erected [d] engines of battery to break down its walls, which could not be said of the Tyre on the island; for that was all surrounded by the sea. And that he also took, and utterly destroyed that city, appears likewise from the writings [e] of the same prophet. But that the city on the island then escaped this fate, is manifest from the Phœnician histories; for in them, after the death of Ithobal (who was [f] slain in the

An. 573. Nebuchadnezzar 32.

conclusion

---

[a] Ezek. xxix. 17.
[b] Josephus Antiq. lib. 10. c. 11. et contra Apionem lib. 1.
[c] Ezek. xxvi. 8.
[d] Ezek. xxvi. 9.
[e] Ezek. xxvi. 4. and 9.—12.
[f] Ezek. xxviii. 8.---10

conclufion of this war), we are told [a] that Baal fucceeded in the kingdom, and reigned ten years, and that after him fucceeded feveral temporary magiftrates, one after another, who, by the name of judges, had the government of the place. It is moft probable, that, after Nebuchadnezzar had taken and deftroyed the old town, thofe who had retired into the ifland came to terms, and fubmitted to him; and that thereon Baal was deputed to be their king under him, and reigned ten years: that, at the end of the faid ten years (which happened in the very year that Nebuchadnezzar was again reftored after his diftraction), Baal being then dead or depofed, the government, to make it the more dependent on the Babylonians, was changed into that of temporary magiftrates; who, inftead of the name of kings, had only that of fuffetes, or judges, given unto them; which was a name well known among the Carthaginians, who were defcended of the Tyrians; for fo [b] their chief magiftrates were called. It had its derivation from the Hebrew word Shophetim, *i. e.* judges, which was the very name whereby the chief governors of Ifrael were called for feveral generations, before they had kings. And under this fort of government the Tyrians feem to have continued for feveral years after, till they were reftored to their former ftate by Darius Hyftafpis feventy years after; as will, in its proper place, be hereafter related.

And here I cannot but obferve, how exactly the chronology of the Phœnician annals agreeth with that of the holy fcriptures. Ezekiel placeth the taking of Tyre by Nebuchadnezzar in the 26th year of the captivity of Jehoiachin. For, in the firft month, and in the firft day of the month, of the 27th year, he fpeaketh (ch. xxix. 17. 18. &c.) of that city as newly taken by Nebuchadnezzar; and therefore the taking of it muft have been in the year before, that is, in the 26th of the faid captivity. This fell in the [c] 32d year of the reign of Nebuchadnezzar, according to the Babylonifh account; from which year, according to Ptolemy's canon, the firft year of Cyrus at Babylon will be the 36th, and fo, according to the Phœnician annals, will it be exactly the fame. For, [d] according to them, after the taking of Tyre by Nebuchadnezzar,

---

[a] Jofephus contra Apionem, lib. 1.

[b] Livius lib. 28. *Suffetes eorum qui fummus eft pœnis magiftratus.* Vide etiam ejufdem lib. 30. et lib. 34. ubi de fuffetibus ut de fummo apud Carthaginienfes magiftratu mentio fit.

[c] For the 37th year of the captivity of Jehoiachin being the laft (which was the 43d) year of the reign of Nebuchadnezzar (2 Kings xxv. 27. and Jer. lii. 31.) the 26th year of the faid captivity muft be in the 32d of Nebuchadnezzar.

[d] Jofephus contra Apionem, lib. 1.

Nebuchadnezzar, Baal had the government of it ten years, and Ecnibal two months, Coelbes ten months, Abbar three months, Mitgonus and Jeraſtratus ſix years, Balator one year, Merball four years, and Hirom twenty years, in whoſe 14th year, ſay the ſame annals, Cyrus began his empire. And, putting all theſe together, the 14th of Hirom will be exactly the 36th year from the 32d of Nebuchadnezzar, which was the 26th of the captivity of Jehoiachin, the year, according to Ezekiel, in which Tyre was taken. And therefore, it doth hereby appear, that the ſaid Phœnician annals place the taking of Tyre in the very ſame year that Ezekiel doth: for the 26th year from the captivity of Jehoiachin computed downward, in which Ezekiel placeth it, and the 36th year from the 14th of Hirom computed upward, in which the Phœnician annals place it, will be exactly the ſame year.

Nebuchadnezzar and his army having ſerved ſo long before Tyre, [a] " till every head was bald, and every ſhoulder peeled;" through the length and hardſhips of the war, and gotten little on the taking of the place to reward him and his army for their ſervice in executing the wrath of God upon the place, by reaſon that the Tyrians had ſaved the beſt of their effects in the iſland; God did, by the prophet Ezekiel, promiſe them the ſpoils of Egypt. And accordingly, this very ſame year, immediately after this ſiege was over, Nebuchadnezzar, taking the advantage of the inteſtine diviſions which were then in that country, by reaſon of the revolt of Amaſis, marched with his army thither, and over-running the whole land, from [b] Migdol, or Magdolum (which is at the firſt entering into Egypt), even to Syene (which is at the fartheſt end of it towards the borders of Ethiopia), he made [c] a miſerable ravage and devaſtation therein, ſlaying multitudes of the inhabitants, and reducing a great part of the country to ſuch a deſolation, as it did not recover from in [d] forty years after. After this Nebuchadnezzar having loaded himſelf and his army with the rich ſpoils of this country, and brought it all in ſubjection to him, he came to terms with Amaſis; and having confirmed him in the kingdom, as his deputy, returned to Babylon.

Vol. I. G During

[a] Ezek. xxix. 18—20. & xxx. 1—19.
[b] Ezek. xxx. 6. Where obſerve this paſſage (from the tower of Syene) in the Engliſh tranſlation of the Bible is wrong tranſlated. For the Hebrew word Migdol, which is there tranſlated tower, is the name of the city Magdolum, which was at the entrance of Egypt from Paleſtine, *i. e.* at the hither end of Egypt; whereas Syene was at the other end, upon the borders of Ethiopia: the tranſlation ought to be thus (from Migdol to Syene), that is, from one end of Egypt to the other.
[c] Ezek. xxix. 30—32.
[d] Ezek. xxix. 13.

During this ravage of the land of Egypt by the Babylonians, moſt of the Jews, who had fled thither after the murder of Gedaliah, fell into their hands. [a] Many of them they ſlew; others they carried captive with them to Babylon. The few that eſcaped ſaved themſelves by flying out of Egypt, and afterwards ſettled again in their own land at the end of the captivity.

After Nebuchadnezzar was gone out of Egypt, Apries, creeping out of his hiding places, got towards the ſeacoaſts, moſt likely into the parts of Lybia; and there [b] hiring an army of Carians, Ionians, and other foreigners, marched againſt Amaſis, and gave him battle near the city of Memphis; in which being vanquiſhed and taken priſoner, he was carried to the city of Sais, and there ſtrangled in his own palace. And hereby were completed all the prophecies of the prophets [c] Jeremiah, and [d] Ezekiel, which they had foretold both concerning him and his people; eſpecially that of Jeremiah, relating to his death, whereby it was foreſhewn, [e] "That God would give Pharaoh Hophra, king of Egypt, into the hands of his enemies, and into the hand of them that ſought his life, as he gave Zedekiah, king of Judah, into the hand of Nebuchadnezzar, his enemy, that ſought his life:" Which was exactly fulfilled, on his being taken priſoner, and executed by Amaſis in the manner as I have ſaid. It is remarked of him [f] by Herodotus, that he was of that pride and high conceit of himſelf, as to vaunt, that it was not in the power of God himſelf to diſpoſſeſs him of his kingdom, ſo ſurely he thought himſelf eſtabliſhed in it; and agreeably hereto is it, that the prophet Ezekiel chargeth him with ſaying, [g] "The river is mine, and I have made it." For the firſt 20 years of his reign, he had enjoyed as proſperous a fortune as moſt of his predeceſſors, having [h] had many ſucceſſes againſt the Cypriots, the Zidonians, the Philiſtines, and other nations; but after he took on himſelf, Caligula like, to be thought as a god, he fell from his former ſtate, and made that miſerable exit which I have related. After his death, [i] Amaſis, without any farther oppoſition, became poſſeſſed of the whole kingdom

An. 570. Nebuchadnezzar. 35.

---

[a] Jer. xliv. 27. 28.
[b] Herodotus, lib. 2. Diodorus Siculus, lib. 1. part 2.
[c] Chap. xliii. xliv. xlv.
[d] Chap. xxix. xxx. xxxi. xxxii.
[e] Jer. xliv. 30.
[f] Herodotus, lib. 2.
[g] Ezek. xxix. 9.
[h] Herodotus, lib. 2. Diodorus Siculus, lib. 1. part 2. Jer. xlvii. 1.
[i] Herodotus, ibid. Diodorus, ibid.

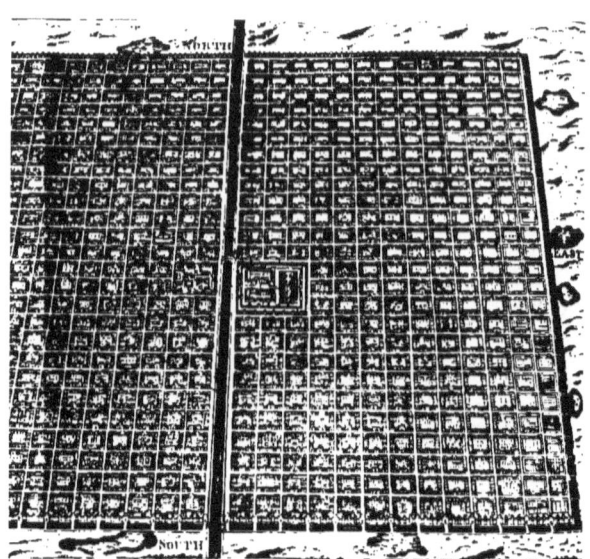

The PLAN of BABYLON.

kingdom of Egypt, and held it from the death of Apries, 44 years. This happened in the 19th year after the destruction of Jerusalem.

In the same 19th year, Nebuchadnezzar being returned from this Egyptian expedition to Babylon, had there the dream of the wonderful great tree, and the cutting down thereof; of which, and the interpretation of it, there is a full account in the 4th chapter of Daniel.

Nebuchadnezzar being now at rest from all his wars, and in full peace at home, applied himself to the finishing of his buildings at Babylon. [a] Semiramis is said by some, and [b] Belus by others, to have first founded this city. But by whomsoever it was first founded, it was Nebuchadnezzar that made it one of the wonders of the world. The [c] most famous works therein, were, 1*st*, the walls of the city; 2*dly*, the temple of Belus; 3*dly*, his palace, and the hanging gardens in it; 4*thly*, the banks of the river; and, 5*thly*, the artificial lake, and artificial canals made for the draining of that river. In the magnificence and expence of which works he much exceeded whatsoever had been done by any king before him. And, excepting the walls of China, nothing like it hath been since attempted, whereby any one else can be equalled to him herein.

1*st*, The walls were every way prodigious: for they [d] were in thickness 87 feet, in height 350 feet, and in compass 480 furlongs, which make sixty of our miles. This is Herodotus's account of them, who was himself at Babylon, and is the most ancient author that hath wrote of this matter. And although there are others that differ from him herein, yet the most that agree in any measures of those walls, give us [e] the same, or very near the same, he doth. Those who lay the height of them at 50 cubits, speak of them only as they were, after the time of Darius Hystaspis: for the Babylonians having revolted from him and, in confidence of their strong walls, stood out against him in a long siege, after he had taken the place; to [f] prevent their rebellion for the future, he took away their gates, and beat down their walls to the height last mentioned; and beyond this they were never after raised. These walls were drawn round the city in the form of [f] an exact square, each side of which was

---

[a] Herodot. lib. 1. Ctesias, Justin, lib. 1. c. 2.
[b] Q. Curtius, lib. 5. c. 1. Abydenus ex Megasthene apud Euseb. Præp. Evang. lib.
[c] Berosus apud Joseph. Antiq. lib. 10. c. 11. Abydenus apud Euseb. Præp. Evang. lib. 9.
[d] Herodotus, lib. 1.
[e] Plinius, lib. 6. c. 26. Philostratus, lib. i. c. 18.
[f] Herodotus, lib. 3.

was 120 furlongs, or 15 miles in length, and [a] all built of large bricks, cemented together with bitumen, a glutinous flime arifing out of the earth in that country, which binds in building much ftronger and firmer than lime, and foon grows much harder than the brick or ftones themfelves which it cements together. Thefe walls were furrounded on the outfide with a vaft ditch filled with water, and lined with bricks on both fides, after the manner of a fcarp or counterfcarp, and the earth which was dug out of it, made the bricks, wherewith the walls were built; and therefore, from the vaft height and breadth of the walls may be inferred the greatnefs of the ditch. In every fide of this great fquare were 25 gates, that is, an 100 in all, which were all made of folid brafs; and hence it is, that, when God promifed to Cyrus the conqueft of Babylon, he tells him, "that he would break in pieces before him the gates of brafs," (If. xlv. 2.). Between every two of thefe gates, were three towers, and four more at the four corners of this great fquare, and three between each of thefe corners and the next gate on either fide; and every one of thefe towers was ten feet higher than the walls. But this is to be underftood only [b] of thofe parts of the wall where there was need of towers: for fome parts of them lying againft moraffes always full of water, where they could not be approached by an enemy, they had there no need of any towers at all for their defence; and therefore in them there were none built; for the whole number of them amounted to no more than 250; whereas, had the fame uniform order been obferved in their difpofition all round, there muft have been many more. From the 25 gates on each fide of this great fquare, went 25 ftreets in ftraight lines to the gates, which were directly over againft them in the other fide oppofite to it. So that the whole number of the ftreets were 50, each fifteen miles long, whereof 25 went one way, and 25 the other, [c] directly croffing each other at right angles. And befides thefe, there were alfo four half ftreets, which were built but of one fide, as having the wall on the other. Thefe went round the four fides of the city next the walls, and [d] were each of them 200 feet broad, and the reft were about 150. By thefe ftreets thus croffing each other, the whole city was cut out into 676 fquares, each of which was four furlongs and an half on every fide, that is, two miles and a quarter in compafs. Round thefe fquares, on every fide, towards the

ftreets,

[a] Herodot. lib. 1. Q. Curtius, lib. 5. c. 1. Strabo, lib. 16. Diod. Sic. lib. 3. Arianus de Expeditione Alexandri, lib. 7.
[b] Diodorus Siculus, lib. 2.
[c] Herodotus, lib. 1.
[d] *Two Plethra*, faith Diodorus, that is 200 feet, for a plethrum contained 100 feet.

streets, stood the houses, all built 3 or 4 stories high, and beautified [a] with all manner of adornments towards the streets. The space within, in the middle of each square, was all void ground, employed for yards, gardens, and other such uses. A branch of the river Euphrates did run quite cross the city, entering in on the north side, and going out on the south; over which, in the middle of the city, was a bridge of [b] a furlong in length, and thirty feet in breadth, built with [c] wonderful art, to supply the defect of a foundation in the bottom of the river, which was all sandy. At the two ends of the bridge were [d] two palaces, the old palace on the east side, and the new palace on the west side of the river; the former of these took up [e] four of the squares above mentioned, and the other [f] nine of them; and the temple of Belus, which stood next the old palace, took up another of these squares. The whole city stood on a [g] large flat or plain, in a very fat and deep soil. That part of it [h] which was on the east side of the river, was the old city; the other on the west side was added by Nebuchadnezzar. Both together were included within that vast square I have mentioned. The pattern hereof seemeth to have been taken from Nineveh, that having been exactly [i] 480 furlongs round, as this was. For Nebuchadnezzar having, in conjunction with his father, destroyed that old royal seat of the Assyrian empire, resolved to make this which he intended should succeed it in that dignity altogether as large; only, whereas Nineveh was [k] in the form of parallelogram, he made Babylon in that of an exact square; which figure rendered it somewhat the larger of the two. To fill this great and large city with inhabitants, was the reason that Nebuchadnezzar, out of Judea and other conquered countries, carried so great a number of captives thither. And could he have made it as populous as it was great, there was no country in all the east could better, than that in which it stood, have maintained

[a] Herodotus, lib. 1. Philostratus, lib. 1.
[b] Strabo saith, that the river which passed through Babylon, was a furlong broad (lib. 16.): but Diodorus saith (lib. 2.) that the bridge was five furlongs long; if so, it must be much longer than the river was broad.
[c] Diodorus Siculus, lib. 2. Q. Curtius, lib. 5. c. 1. Philostratus, lib. 1. c. 18. Herodotus, lib. 1.
[d] Berosus apud Joseph. Antiq. lib. 10. c. 11. Herodotus, lib. 1. Diodor. Sic. lib. 2. Q. Curtius, lib. 5. c. 1. Philostratus, lib. 1. c. 18.
[e] It was 30 furlongs in compass, Diodorus Sicul. lib. 2.
[f] It was 60 furlongs in compass, Diodor. ibid.
[g] Herodotus, lib. 1.
[h] Diodorus Siculus, lib. 2.
[i] Diodorus, ibid.
[k] Two of its sides were each 150 furlongs long, and the other but 80 each, Diodor. ibid.

ed so great a number of people, as must then have been in it: for the fertility of this province was so great, [a] that it yielded to the Persian kings, during their reign over Asia, half as much as did all that large empire besides; the common return of their tillage being between two and three hundred fold every crop. But it never happened to have been [b] fully inhabited; it not having had time enough to grow up thereto; for, within 25 years after the death of Nebuchadnezzar, the royal seat of the empire was removed from thence to Shushan by Cyrus; which did put an end to the growing glory of Babylon; for after that it never more flourished. When Alexander came to Babylon, Curtius tells us, [b] no more than 90 furlongs of it was then built; which can no otherwise be understood, than of so much in length; and if we allow the breadth to be as much as the length (which is the utmost that can be allowed), it will follow, that no more than 8100 square furlongs were then built upon; but the whole space within the walls contained 14400 square furlongs; and therefore there must have been 6300 square furlongs that were unbuilt, which Curtius [b] tells us were plowed and sown. And, besides this, the houses were not contiguous, but all built with a void space on each side between house and house. And the same historian tells us, this was done because this way of building seemed to them the safest. His words are, *Ac ne totam quidem urbem tectis occupaverunt, per 90 stadia, habitatur; nec omnia continua sunt, credo quia tutius visum est pluribus locis spargi;* i. e. 'Neither was the whole city built upon, for the space of 90 furlongs it was inhabited; but the houses were not contiguous, because they thought it safest to be dispersed in many places distant from each other.' Which words (they thought it safest) are to be understood, not as if they did this for the better securing of their houses from fire, as some interpret them, but chiefly for the better preserving of health. For hereby, in cities situated in such hot countries, those suffocations and other inconveniences are avoided, which must necessarily attend such as there dwell in houses closely built together. For which reason Delhi, the capital of India, and several other cities in those warmer parts of the world, are thus built; the usage of those places being, that such a stated space of ground be left void between every house and house, that is built in them. And old Rome was built after the same manner. So that, putting all this together, it will appear, that Babylon was so large a city, rather in scheme than in reality. For, according to this account, it must be by much the larger part that was never built; and therefore, in this respect, it must give place to Nineveh, which was as many furlongs

[a] Herodotus, lib. 1.   [b] Q. Curtius, lib. 5. c. 1.

longs in circuit, as the other and without any void ground in it that we are told of. And the number of its infants at the same time, which could not difcern between their right hand and their left, which the fcriptures tell us were 120,000 in the time of Jonah, doth fufficiently prove it was fully inhabited. It was intended indeed, that Babylon fhould have exceeded it in every thing. But Nebuchadnezzar did not live long enough, nor the Babylonifh empire laft long enough, to finifh the fcheme that was firft drawn of it.

The next great work of Nebuchadnezzar at Babylon was the temple [a] of Belus. But that which was moft remarkable in it, was none of his work, but was built many ages before. It was a wonderful tower that ftood in the middle of it. At the foundation, [b] it was a fquare of a furlong on each fide, that is, half a mile in the whole compafs, and confifted of eight towers, one built above over the other. Some following a miftake of the Latin verfion of Herodotus, wherein the loweft of thefe towers is faid to be a furlong thick and a furlong high, will have each of thefe towers to have been a furlong high, which amounts to a mile in the whole. But the Greek of Herodotus, which is the authentic text of that author, faith no fuch thing, but only, that it was a furlong long and a furlong broad, without mentioning any thing of its height at all. And Strabo, in his defcription of it, calling it a pyramid, becaufe of its decreafing or benching-in at every tower, [c] faith of the whole, that it was a furlong high, and a furlong on every fide. To reckon every tower a furlong, and the whole a mile high, would fhock any man's belief, were the authority of both thefe authors for it, much more, when there is none at all. Taking it only as it is defcribed by Strabo, it was prodigous enough: for, according to his demenfions only, without adding any thing further, it was one of the moft wonderful works in the world, and much exceeding the greateft of the pyramids of Egypt, which hath been thought to excel all other works in the world befides. For [d] although it fell fhort of that pyramid at the bafis, (where that was a fquare of 700 feet on every fide, and this but of 600), yet it far exceeded it in the height; the perpendicular meafure of the faid pyramid being no more than 481 feet, whereas that of the other, was full 600; and therefore it was higher than that pyramid by 119 feet, which is one quarter of the whole. And therefore it was not without reafon, that [e] Bochartus afferts it to have been the very same

[a] Berofus apud Jofephum Antiq. lib. 10. c. 11.
[b] Herodotus, lib. 1.
[c] Strabo, lib. 16.
[d] See Mr Greave's defcription of the pyramids, p. 68. 69.
[e] Phaleg. part 1. lib. 1. c. 9.

same tower which was there built at the confusion of tongues. For it was prodigious enough to answer the scriptures description of it; and it is particularly attested by several authors to have been all built [a] of bricks and bitumen, as the scriptures tell us the tower of Babel was. Herodotus saith, that the going up to it was by stairs on the outside round it; from whence it seems most likely, that the whole ascent to it was by the benching-in drawn in a flopping line from the bottom to the top eight times round it; that this made the appearance of eight towers one above another, in the same manner as we have the tower of Babel commonly described in pictures; saving only, that whereas that is usually pictured round, this was square For such a benching-in drawn in a slope eight times round in manner as aforesaid, would make the whole seem on every side as consisting of eight towers, and the upper tower to be so much less than that next below it, as the breadth of the benching-in amounted to. These eight towers being as so many stories one above another, were each of them 75 feet high, and in them were many great rooms with arched roofs supported by pillars. All which were made parts of the temple, after the tower became consecrated to that idolatrous use. The uppermost story of all was that which was most sacred, and where their chiefest devotions were performed. Over the whole, on the top of the tower, was an observatory, [c] by the benefit of which it was, that the Babylonians advanced their skill in astronomy beyond all other nations, and came to so early a perfection in it, as is related. For when Alexander took Babylon, Calisthenes the philosopher, who accompanied him thither, found they had astronomical observations for 1903 years backwards from that time: which carrieth up the account as high as the 115th year after the flood, which was within 15 years after the tower of Babel was built. For the confusion of tongues, which followed immediately after the building of that tower, happened in the year wherein Peleg was born, which was 101 years after the flood, and 14 years after that these observations began. This account Calisthenes sent from Babylon into Greece, to his master Aristotle; as Symplicius, from the authority of Porphyry, delivers it unto us in his second book De Cœlo. Till the time of Nebuchadnezzar, the temple of Belus contained no more than this tower only, and the rooms in it served all the occasions of that idolatrous worship. But [c] he enlarged it, by vast buildings erected round it, in [d] a square

---

[a] Strabo, lib. 16. Herodotus, lib. 1. Diodor. Sic. lib. 2. Arrian. de Expeditione Alexandri, lib. 7.
[b] Diodor. Sic. lib. 2. p. 98.
[c] Berosus apud Josephum Antiq. lib. 10. c. 11.
[d] Herodotus, lib. 1.

square of two furlongs on every side, and a mile in circumference, which was 1800 feet more than [a] the square at the temple of Jerusalem: for that was but 3000 feet round; whereas this was, according to this account, 4800. And, on the outside of all these buildings, there was a wall inclosing the whole, which may be supposed to have been of equal extent with the square in which it stood, that is, two miles and an half in compass; in which were several gates leading into the temple, all [b] of solid brass; and the brasen sea, the brasen pillars, and the other brasen vessels, which were carried to Babylon from the temple of Jerusalem, seem to have been employed to the making of them. For it is said, that Nebuchadnezzar did put all the sacred vessels, which he carried from Jerusalem, [c] into the house of his god at Babylon, that is, into this house or temple of Bel; for that was the name of the great god of the Babylonians. He is supposed to have been the same with Nimrod, and to have been called Bel from his dominion, and Nimrod from his rebellion: for Bel, or Baal, which is the same name, signifieth lord, and Nimrod, a rebel, in the Jewish and Chaldean languages: the former was his Babylonish name, by reason of his empire in that place, and the latter his scripture name, by reason of his rebellion, in revolting from God to follow his own wicked designs. This temple stood till the time of Xerxes: but he, on his return from his Grecian expedition, [d] demolished the whole of it, and laid it all in rubbish; having first plundered it of all its immense riches, among which were several images or statues of massy gold, and one of them is said, by [e] Diodorus Siculus, to have been 40 feet high, which might perchance have been that which Nebuchadnezzar consecrated in the plains of Dura. Nebuchadnezzar's golden image is said indeed in scripture to have been 60 cubits, *i. e.* 90 feet high: But that must be understood of the image and pedestal both together: for that image being said to have been but six cubits broad or thick, it is impossible that the image could have been 60 cubits high; for that makes its height to be ten times its breadth or thickness, which exceeds all the proportions of a man, no man's height being above six times his thickness, measuring the slenderest man living at his waist. But where the breadth of this image was measured is not said: perchance it was

---

[a] For it was a square of 500 cubits on every side, and 2000 in the whole, *i. e.* 3000 feet. See Lightfoot's description of the temple of Jerusalem.
[b] Herodot. lib. 1.
[c] Dan. i. 2. 2 Chron. xxxvi. 7.
[d] Strabo, lib. 16. p. 738. Herodot. lib. 1. Arrianus de Expeditione Alexandri, lib. 7.
[e] Lib. 2.

was from shoulder to shoulder; and then the proportion of six cubits breadth will bring down the height exactly to the measure which Diodorus hath mentioned: for the usual height of a man being four and a half of his breadth between the shoulders, if the image were six cubits broad between the shoulders, it must, according to this proportion, have been 27 cubits high, which is 40½ feet. Besides, Diodorus [a] tells us, that this image of 40 feet high, contained 1000 Babylonish talents of gold, which, according to Pollux (who, in his Onomasticon, reckons a Babylonish talent to contain 7000 Attic drachma's, *i. e.* 875 ounces) [b] amounts to three millions and an half of our money. But, if we advance the height of the statue to 90 feet without the pedestal, it will increase the value to a sum incredible; and therefore it is necessary to take the pedestal also into the height mentioned by Daniel. Other images and sacred utensils were also in that temple, all of solid gold. Those that are particularly mentioned by Diodorus contain 5030 talents, which, with the 1000 talents in the image above mentioned, amount to above 21 millions of our money. And, besides this, we may well suppose the value of as much more in treasure and utensils not mentioned, which was a vast sum. But it was the collection of near 2000 years; for so long that temple had stood. All this Xerxes took away, when he destroyed it. And perchance to recruit himself with the plunder, after the vast expence which he had been at in his Grecian expedition, was that which chiefly excited him to the destruction of it, what other reason soever might be pretended for it. Alexander, on his return to Babylon from his Indian expedition, [c] purposed again to have rebuilt it: and, in order hereto, he did set 10,000 men on work to rid the place of its rubbish: but, after they had laboured herein two months, Alexander died, before they had perfected much of the undertaking; and this did put an end to all farther proceedings in that design. Had he lived, and made that city the seat of his empire, as it was [d] supposed he would, the glory of Babylon would no doubt have been advanced by him to the utmost height that ever Nebuchadnezzar intended to have brought it to, and it would again have been the queen of the East.

Next this temple, [e] on the same east side of the river, stood the

[a] Lib. 2.

[b] This is according to the lowest computation, valuing an Attic drachm at no more than seven pence halfpenny, whereas Dr Bernard reckons it to be eight pence farthing, which would amount the sum much higher.

[c] Strabo, lib. 16. Josephus contra Apionem, lib. 1. Arrianus de Expeditione Alexandri, lib. 7.

[d] Strabo, lib. 15. p. 731.

[e] Diodor. Sic. lib. 2. Philostrat. lib. 1. c. 18.

the old palace of the kings of Babylon, being four miles in
compafs. Exactly over againft it, on the other fide of the
river, [a] ftood the new palace; and this was that [b] which Nebuchadnezzar built. It was four times as big as the former,
as being [c] eight miles in compafs. It was furrounded with
three walls, one within another, and ftrongly fortified, according to the way of thofe times. But what was moft wonderful in it were the hanging gardens, which were of fo celebrated a name among the Greeks. They [d] contained a fquare
of four plethra (that is, of 400 feet) on every fide, and were
carried up aloft into the air, in the manner of feveral large
terraces, one above another, till the higheft equalled the height
of the walls of the city. The afcent was from terrace to terrace, by ftairs ten feet wide. The whole pile was fuftained
by vaft arches built upon arches, one above another, and
ftrengthened by a wall, furrounding it on every fide, of 22
feet in thicknefs. The floors of every one of thefe terraces
were laid in the fame manner; which was thus: On the top
of the arches were firft laid large flat ftones, 16 feet long, and
four broad, and over them was a layer of reed, mixed with
a great quantity of bitumen, over which were two rows of
bricks, clofely cemented together by plafter, and then over all
were laid thick fheets of lead, and, laftly, upon the lead was
laid the mould of the garden: and all this floorage was contrived to keep the moifture of the mould from running away
down through the arches. The mould or earth laid hereon was
of that depth, as to have room enough for the greateft trees to
take rooting in it; and fuch were planted all over it in every
terrace, as were alfo all other trees, plants, and flowers, that
were proper for a garden of pleafure. In the upper terrace
there was an aqueduct or engine, whereby water was drawn
up out of the river, which from thence watered the whole
garden. Amyitis, the wife of Nebuchadnezzar, having been
bred in Media (for fhe was the daughter of Aftyages, the king
of that country, as hath been before related), had been much
taken with the mountainous and woody parts of that country,
and therefore defired to have fomething like it at Babylon: and
to gratify her herein was the reafon of erecting this monftrous
work of vanity.

The other works attributed to him, by [e] Berofus and [f] Abydenus, were the banks of the river, and the artificial canals,
and

[a] Diodor. Sic. lib. 2. Philoftratus, lib. 1. c. 18.
[b] Berofus apud Jofeph. lib. 10. c. 11.
[c] Diodor. lib. 2. Herodot. lib. 1.
[d] Diodor. Sic. lib. 2. Strabo, lib. 16. Q. Curtius, lib. 5. c. 1.
[e] Apud Jofeph. Antiq. lib. 10. c. 11. et contra Apionem, lib. 1.
[f] Apud Eufebium Præpar. Evang. lib. 9.

and artificial lake, which were made for draining of it in the times of overflows: for, [a] on the coming on of the summer, the sun melting the snow on the mountains of Armenia, from thence there is always a great overflow of water during the months of June, July, and August, which, running into the Euphrates, makes it overflow all its banks during that season, in the same manner as doth the river Nile in Egypt; whereby the city and country of Babylon suffering great damage, for [b] the preventing hereof, he did, a great way up the stream, cut out of it, on the east side, two artificial canals, thereby to drain off these overflowings into the Tigris, before they should reach Babylon. The [c] farthest of these was the current which did run into the Tigris near Seleucia, and the other that which, taking its course between the last mentioned and Babylon, discharged itself into the same river over against Apamia; which being very large, and navigable for great vessels, [d] was from thence called Naharmalcha, that is, in the Chaldean language, the royal river. This is said to have been made by [e] Gobaris, or Gobrias, who, being the governor of the province, had the overseeing of the work committed to his care, and seemeth to have been the same who afterwards, on a great wrong done him, revolted from the Babylonians to Cyrus, as will be hereafter related. And, for the farther securing of the country, Nebuchadnezzar built [f] also prodigious banks of brick and bitumen on each side of the river, to keep it within its channel, which [g] were carried along from the head of the said canals down to the city, and some way below it. But the most wonderful part of the work was within the city itself: for there, [h] on each side of the river, he built from the bottom of it a great wall, for its bank, of brick and bitumen, which was of the same thickness with the walls of the city; and, over against every street that crossed the said river, he made, on each side, a brasen gate in the said wall, and stairs leading down from it to the river, from whence the citizens used to pass by boat from one side to the other, which was the only passage they had over the river, till the bridge was built, which I have above mentioned. The gates were open by day, but always

[a] Strabo, lib. 16. Plin. lib. 5. c. 26. Arrianus de Expeditione Alexandri, lib. 7. Q. Curtius, lib. 5. c. 1.
[b] Abydenus apud Euseb. Præp. Evang. lib. 9.
[c] Ptol. lib. 5. c. 18. Plin. lib. 5. c. 26.
[d] Abydenus, ibid. Ptol. ibid. Plin. lib. 6. c. 26. Polybius, lib. 5. Ammianus Marcellinus, lib. 24. Strabo, lib. 16. p. 747. Isidorus Characenus de Stathmis Parthicis.
[e] Plin. lib. 6. c. 26.
[f] Abydenus, ibid.
[g] Herodotus, lib. 1.
[h] Berosus apud Joseph. Antiq. lib. 10. c. 11.

ways shut by night. And this prodigious work [a] was carried on, on both sides of the river, to the length of 160 furlongs, which is 20 miles of our measure; and therefore must have been begun two miles and an half above the city, and continued down two miles and an half below it; for through the city was no more than 15 miles. While these banks were a building, the river was turned another way: for which purpose, to the west of Babylon [b], was made a prodigious artificial lake, which was, [c] according to the lowest computation, 40 miles square, and 160 in compass; and in depth 35 feet, saith Herodotus; 75, saith Megasthenes. The former seems to measure from the surface of the sides, and the other from the top of the banks that were cast up upon them. And into this lake was the whole river turned by an artificial canal cut from the west side of it, till all the said work was finished, and then it was returned again into its own former channel. But that the said river, in the time of its increase, might not, through the gates above mentioned, overflow the city, this lake, with the canal leading thereto, was still preserved, and proved the best and the most effectual means to prevent it; for whenever the river rose to such an height, as to endanger this overflowing, it always discharged itself, by this canal, into the lake, through a passage in the bank of the river, at the head of the said canal, made there of a pitch fit for this purpose, whereby it was prevented from ever rising any higher below that place. And the water received into the lake, at the time of these overflowings, was there kept all the year, as in a common reservatory, for the benefit of the country, to be let out by sluices, at all convenient times, for the watering of the lands below it. So it equally served the convenience of Babylon, and also the convenience of that part of the province, in improving their lands, and making them the more fertile and beneficial to them; though at last it became the cause of great mischief to both: for it afforded to Cyrus the means of taking the city, and, in the effecting thereof, became the cause of drowning a great part of that country, which was never after again recovered; of both which an account will be hereafter given in its proper place. Berosus, Megasthenes, and Abydenus, attribute all these works to Nebuchadnezzar; but Herodotus tells us, that the bridge, the river banks, and the lake, were the work of Nitocris, his daughter-in-law.

[a] Diodorus, lib. 2. p. 96.
[b] Abydenus, ibid. Herodotus, lib. 1. Diodorus, ibid.
[c] According to Herodotus, this lake was 420 furlongs square, i.e. 52 miles and an half on every side, and then the whole compass must be 210 miles; but, according to Megasthenes, the whole compass was but 40 parasanga, i.e. 160 miles, for each parasanga contained 4 of our miles

in-law. Perhaps Nitocris finished what Nebuchadnezzar had left unperfected at his death, and this procured her, with that historian, the honour of the whole.

All the flat whereon Babylon stood being, by reason of so many rivers and canals running through it, made in many places marshy, especially near the said rivers and canals, this caused it to abound much in willows; and therefore it is called in scripture, *The valley of willows*, (for so the words, Is. xv. 7. which we translate, *the brook of the willows*, ought to be rendered): and, for the same reason, the Jews (Psal. cxxxvii. 1. 2.) are said, when they were by the rivers of Babylon, in the land of their captivity, to have hung their harps upon the willows, that is, because of the abundance of them which grew by those rivers.

At the end [a] of twelve months after Nebuchadnezzar's last dream, while he was walking in his palace at Babylon, most likely in his hanging gardens, and in the uppermost terrace of them, from whence he might have a full prospect of the whole city, he, proudly boasting of his great works done therein, said, [b] " Is not this great Babylon, which I have built for the house of the kingdom, by the might of my power, and for the honour of my majesty?" But, while the words were yet in his mouth, there came a voice to him from heaven to rebuke his pride, which told him, that his kingdom was departed from him, and that he should be driven from the society of men, and thenceforth, for seven years, have his dwelling with the wild beasts of the field, there to live like them in a brutal manner. And immediately hereon, his senses being taken from him, he fell into a distracted condition; and, continuing so for seven years, he lived abroad in the fields, eating grass like the oxen, and taking his lodgings on the ground, in the open air, as they did, till his hair was grown like eagles feathers, and his nails like birds claws. But, at the end of seven years, his understanding returning unto him, he was restored again to his kingdom, and his former majesty and honour re-established on him.

An. 569.
Nebuchad-
nezzar 36.

An. 563.
Nebuchad-
nezzar 42.

And hereon, being made fully sensible of the almighty power of the God of heaven and earth, and that it is he only that doth all things according to his will, both in the armies of heaven, and among the inhabitants of the earth, and by his everlasting dominion disposeth of all things at his good pleasure, he did, by a public decree, make acknowledgement hereof through all the Babylonish empire, praising his almighty power, and magnifying his mercy in his late restoration shewn upon him.

After this he lived only one year, and died, having reigned, according

[a] Daniel iv.   [b] Daniel iv. 30.

according to the Babylonish account, from the death of his father, 43 years, and according to the Jewish account, from his first coming with an army into Syria, 45 years. His death happened about the end of the year, a little before the conclusion of the 37th year of the captivity of Jehoiachin. He was one of the greatest princes that had reigned in the east for many ages before him. Megasthenes [a] prefers him for his valour to Hercules. But his greatness, riches, and power, did in nothing more appear, than in his prodigious works at Babylon above described, which, for many ages after, were spoken of as the wonders of the world. He is [b] said at his death to have prophesied of the coming of the Persians, and their bringing of the Babylonians in subjection to them. But in this he spake no more, than what he had been informed of by Daniel the prophet, and, in the interpretation of his dreams, been assured by him should speedily come to pass, as accordingly it did within 23 years after.

An. 561. Nebuchadnezzar 43.

On the death of this great prince, [c] Evilmerodach his son succeeded him in the Babylonish empire; and, as soon as he was settled in the throne, he released Jehoiachin, king of Judah, out of prison, after he had lain there near 37 years, and promoted him to great honour in his palace, admitting him to eat bread continually at table, and placing him there before all the other kings and great men of his empire, that came to him to Babylon, and also made him a daily allowance to support him, with an equipage in all things else suitable hereto. Jerome [d] tells us, from an ancient tradition of the Jews, that Evilmerodach, having had the government of the Babylonish empire during his father's distraction, administered it so ill, that, as soon as the old king came again to himself, he put him in prison for it; and that the place of his imprisonment happening to be the same where Jehoiachin had long lain, he there entered into a particular acquaintance and friendship with him; and that this was the cause of the great kindness which he afterwards shewed him. And since the old historical traditions of the Jews [e] are often quoted in the New Testament, if this were such, it is not wholly to be disregarded, and that especially since the mal-administrations, which Evilmerodach

An. 561. Evilmerodach 1.

---

[a] Abydenus ib. Joseph. Antiq. lib. 10. c. 11. Strabo, lib. 15. p. 687.
[b] Abydenus ibid.
[c] 2 Kings xxv. 27. Jeremiah lii. 31. Berosus apud Josephum contra Apionem, lib. 1. et Euseb. Præp. Evang. lib. 9.
[d] Comment. in Esaiam xiv. 19.
[e] By St Stephen, Acts vii. By St Paul, Hebrews xi. 35.—37. and to Timothy, Eph. iii. 8. and by St Jude 9. 14. 15.

merodach was guilty of after his father's death, give reason e-
nough to believe, that he could not govern without them before.
For he [a] proved a very profligate and vicious prince, and for
that reason was called Evilmerodach, that is, foolish Merodach;
for his proper name was only Merodach. But, whatsoever was
the inducing reason, this favour he shewed to the captive prince,
as soon as his father was dead. So that the last year of Nebuchadnezzar's reign was the last of the 37 years of Jehoiachin's
captivity; and this shews us when it begun, and serves to the
connecting of the chronology of the Babylonish and Jewish history
in all other particulars. For which reason it may be useful to
have a particular state of this matter, which I take to have been
as followeth. In the 7th year of the reign of Nebuchadnezzar,
according to the Babylonish account, [b] in the beginning of the
Jewish year, that is, in the month of April according to our year,
Jehoiachin was carried captive to Babylon. And therefore the
first year of his captivity, beginning in the month of April, in
the 7th year of Nebuchadnezzar, the 37th year of it must begin
in the same month of April, in the 43d year of Nebuchadnezzar; towards the end whereof that great king dying, with the
beginning of the next year began the first year of the reign of
Evilmerodach; and the March following, [c] that is, on the 27th
day of the 12th or last month of the Jewish year, Jehoiachin was,
by the great favour of the new king released from his captivity,
in the manner as is above expressed, about a month before he
had fully completed 37 years in it.

An. 561.
Evilmero-
dach 1.
    In the same year, which was the first of Evilme-
rodach at Babylon, [d] Croesus succeeded Alyattes his
father in the kingdom of Lydia, and reigned there
14 years. This was the 28th year after the destruction of Jerusalem, and the 46th of the 70 years captivity of
Judah.

When Evilmerodach had reigned two years at Babylon, his
lusts, and his other wickedness, made him so intolerable, [e] that
at length even his own relations conspired against him, and put

An. 559.
Nerigliſſar 1.
    him to death, and [f] Nerigliſſar his sister's husband,
who was the head of the conspiracy against him,
reigned in his stead. And since it is said, that Jehoiachin was fed [g] by him until the day of his death, it is inferred

---

[a] Berosus ibid.
[b] 2 Chron. xxxvi. 10. For there it is said, that it was at the return of the year.
[c] 2 Kings xxxv. 27. Jer. lii. 31.
[d] Herodotus. lib. 1.

[e] Berosus ibid. Megasthenes apud Eusebium Præp. Evang. lib. 9.
[f] Berosus ibid. Ptol. in Canone. Josephus Antiq. lib. 10. c. 12. Megasthenes, ibid.
[g] Jer. lii. 33.

BOOK II.   THE OLD AND NEW TESTAMENT.   113

ferred from hence, that he did not outlive him, but that he either died a little before him, or elſe, as a favourite, was ſlain with him. The laſt ſeemeth moſt propable, as beſt agreeing with the prophecy of Jeremiah concerning him; for it is therein denounced againſt him, [a] that he ſhould not proſper in his days; which could not be ſo well verified of him, if he died in full poſſeſſion of all that proſperity which Evilmerodach advanced him unto.

On the death of Jehoiachin, Salathiel, his ſon, [b] became the nominal prince of the Jews after him. For, after the loſs of the authority, they ſtill kept up the title; and for a great many ages after, in the parts about Babylon, there was always one of the houſe of David, which, by the name of [c] *The Head of the captivity*, was acknowledged and honoured as a prince among that people, and had ſome ſort of juriſdiction, as far as it was conſiſtent with the government they were under, always inveſted in him, and ſometimes a ratification was obtained of it from the princes that reigned in that country. And it is ſaid, this [d] pageantry is ſtill kept up among them; and chiefly, it ſeems, that they may be furniſhed from hence with an anſwer to give the Chriſtians, when they urge the prophecy of Jacob againſt them: for, whenſoever, from that prophecy, it is preſſed upon them, that the Meſſiah muſt be come, becauſe the ſceptre is now departed from Judah, and there is no more a lawgiver among them from between his feet, we are commonly told of *This Head of the captivity*; their uſual anſwer being, that the ſceptre is ſtill preſerved among them in *The Head of the captivity*; and that they have alſo in their [e] Naſi, or prince of the Sanhedrim (another peageantry officer of theirs), a lawgiver from between the feet of Judah (that is of his ſeed) ſtill remaining in Iſrael. But if theſe officers are now ceaſed from among them, as ſome of them will acknowledge, then this anſwer muſt ceaſe alſo; and the prophecy returns in its full force upon them; and why do they then any longer reſiſt the power of it?

The ſame year that Evilmerodach was ſlain, died [f] Aſtyages, king of Media, and after him ſucceeded Cyaxares the ſecond, his ſon, in the civil government of the kingdom, and Cyrus, his grandſon, by his daughter Mandana in the military. Cyrus at

VOL. I.   H   this

---

[a] Jer. xxii. 30.   [b] 2 Eſdras v. 16.
[c] Vide Notas Conſtantini L'empereur ad Benj. Itinerarium, p. 192, &c.
[d] Vide Jacobi Altingi librum Shilo, lib. 1. c. 3. 13. 14. &c.   Et Seldenum de Synedriis, lib. 2. c. 7. §. 5.
[e] Vide Buxtorfii Lexicon Rabbinicum, p. 1399. & Seldenum de Synedriis, lib. 2. c. 6.
[f] Cyropedia, lib. 1.

this time was [a] 40 years old, and Cyaxares [b] 41. And from this year, thofe who reckon to Cyrus a reign of 30 years, begin that computation. For Nerigliffar, on his coming to the crown, [c] making great preparations for a war againft the Medes, Cyaxares called Cyrus out of Perfia to his affiftance, and on his arrival with an army of 30,000 Perfians, Cyaxares made him general of the Medes alfo, and fent him with the joint forces of both nations to make war againft the Babylonians. And from this time he was reckoned by all foreigners as king over both thefe nations; although, in reality the regal power was folly in Cyaxares, and Cyrus was no more than general of the confederate army under him. But, after his death, he fucceeded him in the kingdom of the Medes, as he did his father a little before in that of Perfia; which, with the countries he had conquered, made up the Perfian empire, of which he was the founder and firft monarch.

He was a very extraordinary perfon in the age in which he lived, for wifdom, valour, and virtue, and of a name famous in holy writ, not only for being [d] the reftorer of the ftate of Ifrael, but efpecially in being there appointed for it [e] by name many years before he was born; which is an honour therein given to none, fave only to him, and [f] Jofiah, king of Judah. He was born (as hath been already taken notice of) on the fame year in which Jehoiachin died. It is on all hands agreed, that his mother was Mandana, the daughter of Aftyages, king of the Medes, and his father Cambyfes a Perfian.

But whether this Cambyfes was king of that country, or only a private perfon, is not agreed. Herodotus, and thofe who follow him, allow him to have been no more than a private nobleman, of the family of Achæmenes, one of the moft antient in that country. But Xenophon's account makes him king of the Perfians, but fubjeét to the Medes. And not only in this particular, but alfo in moft things elfe concerning this great prince, the relations of thefe two hiftorians are very much different. But Herodotus's account of him containing narratives which are much more ftrange and furprifing, and confequently more diverting and acceptable to the reader, moft have chofen rather to follow him, than Xenophon, that have written after their times of this matter. Which humour was

much

[a] Cicero, lib. 1. De Divinatione dicit de Cyro—Ad Septuagefimum pervenit cum quadraginta annos natus regnare cœpiffet.
[b] For he was 62 when he began to reign in Babylon, after the death of Belfhazzar, Dan. v. 31. which being nine years before Cyrus's death (who lived 70 years), it muft follow that Cyrus was then 61, and therefore when he was 40, Cyaxares muft have been 41.
[c] Cyropedia, lib. 1. [d] Ezra i. [e] If. xliv. 28. & xlv. 1. [f] 1 Kings xlii. 2.

much forwarded by Plato, in his ª giving a character of Xenophon's history of Cyrus (in which he was also followed by Tully), ᵇ as if therein, under the name of Cyrus, he rather drew a description of what a worthy and just prince ought to be, than gave us a true history of what that prince really was. It must be acknowledged, that Xenophon being a great commander, as well as a great philosopher, did graft many of his maxims of war and policy into that history, and to make it a vehicle for this, perchance was his whole design in writing that book. But it doth not follow from hence, but that still the whole foundation and ground-plot of the work may be all true history. That he intended it for such, is plain; and that it was so, its agreeableness with the holy writ doth abundantly verify. And the true reason why he chose the life of Cyrus, before all others, for the purpose above mentioned, seemeth to be no other, but that he found the true history of that excellent and gallant prince to be above all others the fittest for those maxims of right policy and true princely virtue to correspond with, which he grafted upon it. And therefore, bating the military and political reflections, the descants, discourses, and speeches interspersed in that work, which must be acknowledged to have been all of Xenophon's addition, the remaining bare matters of fact I take to have been related by that author as the true history of Cyrus. And thus far I think him to have been an historian of much better credit in this matter than Herodotus. For Herodotus having travelled through Egypt, Syria, and several other countries, in order to the writing of his history, did as travellers use to do, that is, put down all relations upon trust, as he met with them, and no doubt he was imposed on in many of them. But Xenophon was a man of another character, ᶜ who wrote all things with great judgement, and due consideration; and having lived in the court of Cyrus the younger, a descendant of the Cyrus whom we now speak of, had opportunities of being better informed of what he wrote of this great prince, than Herodotus was; and confining himself to this argument only, no doubt, he examined all matters relating to it more thoroughly, and gave a more accurate and exact account of them, than could be expected from the other, who wrote of all things at large, as they came in his way. And for these reasons, in all things relating to this prince, I have chosen to follow Xenophon, rather than any of those who differ from him.

For the first ᵈ 12 years of his life, Cyrus lived in Persia

with

ᵃ De Legibus, lib. 3.   ᶜ Diog. Laertius in vita Xenophontis
ᵇ Ep. 1. ad Quintum fratrem.   ᵈ Cyropedia, lib. 1.

with his father, and was there educated, after the Perfian manner, in hardfhip and toil, and all fuch exercifes as would beſt tend to fit him for the fatigues of war, in which he exceeded all his contemporaries. But here it muſt be taken notice of, that the name of Perfia did then extend only to one province of that large country, which hath been fince fo called : for then the whole nation of the Perfians could number no more than [a] 120,000 men. But afterwards, when, by the wifdom and valour of Cyrus, they had obtained the empire of the Eaſt, the name of Perfia became enlarged with their fortunes; and it thenceforth took in all that vaſt tract, which is extended eaſt and weſt from the river Indus to the Tygris, and north and fouth from the Cafpian fea to the ocean; and fo much that name comprehends even to this day. After Cyrus was twelve years old, he was fent for into Media by Aſtyages, his grandfather, with whom he continued five years: and there, by the fweetnefs of his temper, his generous behaviour, and his conſtant endeavour to do good offices with his grandfather for all he could, he did fo win the hearts of the Medes to him, and gained fuch an intereſt among them, as did afterwards turn very much to his advantage, for the winning of that empire which he erected. In the 16th year of his age, Evilmerodach, the fon of Nebuchadnezzar, king of Babylon and Aſſyria, being abroad on an hunting expedition, a little before his marriage, for a fhew of his bravery, made an inroad into the territories of the Medes, which drew out [b] Aſtyages with his forces to oppofe him. On which occafion, Cyrus, accompanying his grandfather, then firſt entered the fchool of war ; in which he behaved himfelf fo well, that the victory which was at that time gained over the Aſſyrians was chiefly owing to his valour. The next year after, he went home to his father into Perfia, and there continued till the 40th year of his life ; at which time he was called forth to the aſſiſtance of his uncle Cyaxares, on the occafion which I have mentioned. Hereon he marched out of Perfia with his army, and behaved himſelf fo wifely, that, from this fmall beginning, in 20 years time, he made himfelf maſter of the greateſt empire that had ever been erected in the Eaſt to that time, and eſtabliſhed it with fuch wifdom, that, upon the ſtrength of this foundation only, it ſtood above 200 years, notwithſtanding what was done by his fucceffors

[a] Cyropedia, lib. 1.
[b] From hence it may be inferred, that Evilmerodach was not the fon of Nebuchadnezzar by Amytis, the daughter of Aſtyages, but by fome other wife, it not being likely that the grandfather and grandfon would thus engage in war againſt each other.

fors (the worst race of men that ever governed an empire) through all that time to overthrow it.

Nerigliffar, upon intelligence that Cyrus was come with so great an army to the assistance of the Medes, farther to strengthen himself against them, [a] sent ambassadors to the Lydians, Phrygians, Carians, Cappadocians, Cilicians, Paphlagonians, and other neighbouring nations, to call them to his aid; and, by representing to them the strength of the enemy, and the necessity of maintaining the balance of power against them, for the common good of Asia, drew them all into confederacy with him for the ensuing war. Whereon the king of Armenia, who had hitherto lived in subjection to the Medes, looking on them as ready to be swallowed up by so formidable a confederacy against them, thought this a fit time for the recovering of his liberty, and therefore [b] refused any longer to pay his tribute, or send his quota of auxiliaries for the war, on their being required of him; which being a matter that might be of dangerous consequence to the Medes, in the example it might give to other dependent states to do the same, Cyrus thought it necessary to crush this revolt with the utmost expedition; and therefore, marching immediately with the best of his horse, and covering his design under the pretence of an hunting match, [c] entered Armenia, before there was any intelligence of his coming, and, having surprised the revolted king, took him and all his family prisoners; and, after this, having seized the hills towards Chaldea, and planted good forts and garrisons on them, for the securing of the country against the enemy on that side, he came to new terms with the captive king; and, having received from him the tribute and auxiliaries which he demanded, he restored him again to his kingdom, and returned to the rest of his army in Media. This happened about the 3d year of the reign of Nerigliffar, and the 32d after the destruction of Jerusalem.

An. 588.
Nerigliffar 2.

An. 557.
Nerigliffar 3.

After both parties had now been for three years together forming their alliances, and making their preparations for the war, in the 4th year of Nerigliffar, the confederates on both sides being all drawn together, both armies took the field, [d] and it came to a fierce battle between them; in which Nerigliffar being slain, the rest of the Assyrian army was put to the rout, and Cyrus had the victory. Crœsus, king of Lydia, after the death of Nerigliffar, as being in dignity next to him, took upon him the command of

An. 556.
Nerigliffar 4.

---

[a] Cyropedia, lib. 1.
[b] Cyropedia, lib. 2.
[c] Cyropedia, lib. 3.
[d] Cyropedia, lib. 3. & 4.

of the vanquished army, and made as good a retreat with it as he could. But the next day following, Cyrus, pursuing after them, overtook them at a disadvantage, and put them to an absolute rout, taking their camp, and dispossessing them of all their baggage; which he effected chiefly by the assistance of the Hyrcanians, who had the night before revolted to him. Hereon Crœsus, taking his flight out of Assyria, made the best of his way into his own country. He, being aware of what might happen, had, the night before, sent away his women, and the best of his baggage; and therefore, in this respect, escaped much better than the rest of the confederates.

The death of Neriglissar was a great loss to the Babylonians; for he was [a] a very brave and excellent prince. The preparations which he made for the war shewed his wisdom, and his dying in it his valour. And there was nothing else wanting in him for his obtaining of better success in it; and, therefore, that he had it not, was owing to nothing else, but that he had to deal with the predominant fortune of Cyrus, whom God had designed for the empire of the East, and therefore nothing was to withstand him. But nothing made the loss of Neriglissar more appear, than the succeeding of Laborosoarchod his son in the kingdom after him: for he was [b] in every thing the reverse of his father, being given to all manner of wickedness, cruelty, and injustice, to which, on his advancement, to the throne he did let himself loose in the utmost excess, without any manner of restraint whatsoever, as if the regal office, which he was now advanced to, were for nothing else but to give him a privilege of doing, without controul, all the vile and flagitious things that he pleased. Two acts of his tyrannical violence towards two of his principal nobility, Gobrias and Gadates, are particularly mentioned. The only son of the former he slew at an hunting, to which he had invited him, for no other reason, but that he had thrown his dart with success at a wild beast, when he himself had missed it. And the other he caused to be castrated, only because one of his concubines had commended him for an handsome man. These wrongs done those two noblemen drove them, with the provinces which they governed, into a revolt to Cyrus; and the whole state of the Babylonish empire suffered by it: for Cyrus, encouraged hereby, [c] penetrated into the very heart of the enemy's country, first taking possession of the province, and garrisoning the castles of Gobrias, and afterward doing the same in the province and castles of Gadates. The Assyrian king was before him in the latter, to be revenged on Gadates

---

[a] Cyropedia, lib. 4. [b] Cyropedia, lib. 4. & 5. [c] Cyropedia, lib. 5.

dates for his revolt. But Cyrus, on his coming, having put him to the rout, and flain a great number of his men, forced him again to retreat to Babylon. After Cyrus had thus fpent the fummer in ravaging the whole country, and twice fhewn himfelf before the walls of Babylon, to provoke the enemy to battle, at the end of the year, he led back his army again towards Media; and, ending the campaign with the taking of three fortreffes on the frontiers, there entered into winter-quarters, and fent for Cyaxares, to come thither to him, that they might confult together about the future operations of the war.

As foon as Cyrus was retreated, Laborofoarchod, being now freed from the fear of the enemy, gave himfelf a thorough loofe to all the flagitious inclinations that were predominant in him; which carried him into fo many wicked and unjuft actions, like thofe, which Gobrias and Gadates had fuffered from him, that, being no longer tolerable, his [a] own people confpired againft him, and flew him, after he had reigned only nine months. He is not named in the canon of Ptolemy; for it is the method of that canon, to afcribe all the year to him that was king in the beginning of it, how foon foever he died after, and not to reckon the reign of the fucceffor, but from the firft day of the year enfuing; and therefore, if any king reigned in the interim, and did not live to the beginning of the next year, his name was not put into the canon at all. And this was the cafe of Laborofoarchod: for Nerigliffar his father being flain in battle, in the beginning of the fpring, the nine months of his fon's reign ended before the next year began: and therefore the whole of that year is reckoned to the laft of Nerigliffar, and the beginning of the next belonged to his fucceffor: and this was the reafon that he is not at all mentioned in that canon.

After him fucceeded [b] Nabonadius, and reigned feventeen years. [c] Berofus calls him Nabonnedus, Megafthenes [d] Nabonnidochus, Herodotus [e] Labynetus, and Jofephus [f] Naboandelus, who, he faith, is the fame with Belfhazzar. And there is as great a difference among writers, what he was, as well as what he was called. Some [g] will have him to be of the royal blood of Nebuchadnezzar, and [h] others no way at all related to him. And

An. 555.
Belfhaz. 1.

fome

[a] Berofus apud Jofephum contra Apionem, lib. 1. Megafthenes apud Eufeb. Præp. Evang. lib. 9. Jofephus Antiq. lib. 10. c. 11.
[b] Canon Ptolemæi.
[c] Apud Jofephum contra Apiorem, lib. 1.
[d] Apud Eufeb. Præp. Evang. lib. 9.
[e] Herodotus, lib. 1.
[f] Antiq. lib. 10. c. 11.
[g] Jofephus, ibid.
[h] Megafthenes, ibid.

some say [a] he was a Babylonian, and others [b] that he was of the seed of the Medes. And of those who allow him to have been of the royal family of Nebuchadnezzar, some will have it that he was his son, and others, that he was his grandson. For the clearing of this matter, these following particulars are to be taken notice of: 1*st*, That he is on all hands agreed to have been the last of the Babylonish kings. 2*dly*, That therefore he must have been the same who in scripture is called Belshazzar: for, immediately after the death of Belshazzar, the kingdom was given to the Medes and Persians (D..n. v. 28. 30. 31.). 3*dly*, That he was of the seed of Nebuchadnezzar; for he is called his son, and Nebuchadnezzar is said to be his father, in several places of the same 5th chapter of Daniel; and in the 2d book of Chronicles (chap. xxxvi. 20.), it is said that Nebuchadnezzar and his children, or offspring, reigned at Babylon till the kingdom of Persia. 4*thly*, That the nations of the East were to serve Nebuchadnezzar, and his son, and his son's son, according to the prophecy of Jeremiah (chap. xxvii. 7.); and therefore he must have had a son, and a son's son, successors to him in the throne of Babylon. 5*thly*, That as Evilmerodach was his son, so none but Belshazzar, of all the kings that reigned after him at Babylon, could be his son's son; for Neriglissar was only his daughter's husband, and Laborosoarchod was the son of Neriglissar; and therefore neither of them was either son, or son's son, to Nebuchadnezzar. 6*thly*, That this last king of Babylon is said, by [c] Herodotus, to be son to the great queen Nitocris; and therefore she must have been the wife of a king of Babylon to make her so: and he could have been none other than Evilmerodach; for by that king of Babylon only could she have a son, that was son's son to Nebuchadnezzar. And therefore, putting all this together, it appears, that this Nabonadius, the last king of Babylon, was the same with him that in scripture is called Belshazzar; and that he was the son of Evilmerodach, by Nitocris his queen, and so son's son to Nebuchadnezzar. And that whereas he is called the son of Nebuchadnezzar in the 5th chapter of Daniel, and Nebuchadnezzar is there called his father, this is to be understood in the large sense, wherein any ancestor upward is often called father, and any descendant downward son, according to the usual stile of scripture.

This new king came young to the crown; and, had he been wholly left to himself, the Babylonians would have gotten but

---

[a] Berosus, ibid.
[b] Scaliger in notis ad Fragmenta veterum Græcorum selecta, et de emendatione temporum, lib. 6. cap. De Regibus Babyloniis.
[c] Herodotus, lib. 1.

but little by the change: for he hath, in Zenophon, the character [a] of an impious prince; and it sufficiently appears, by what is said of him in Daniel, that he was so. But his mother, who was a woman [b] of great understanding and a masculine spirit, came in to their relief: for, while her son followed his pleasures, she took the main burden of the government upon her, and did all that could be done by human wisdom to preserve it. But God's appointed time for its fall approaching, it was beyond the power of any wisdom to prevent it.

On the coming of Cyaxares to Cyrus's camp, and [c] consultation thereon had between them concerning the future carrying on of the war, it was found, that, by ravaging and plundering the countries of the Babylonish empire, they did not at all enlarge their own; and therefore it was resolved to alter the method of the war for the future, and to apply themselves to the besieging of the fortresses, and the taking of their towns, that so they might make themselves masters of the country, and in this sort of war they employed themselves for the next seven years.

In the mean time [d] Nitocris did all that she could to fortify the country against them, and especially the city of Babylon; and therefore did set herself diligently to perfect all the works that Nebuchadnezzar had left unfinished there, especially the walls of the city, and the banks of the river within it. By this last she fortified the city as much against the river by walls and gates, as it was against the land; and, had it been in both places equally guarded, it could never have been taken. And, moreover, while the river was turned for the finishing of these banks and walls, she [e] caused a wonderful vault or gallery to be made under the river, leading cross it from the old palace to the new, 12 feet high, and 15 feet wide, and having covered it over with a strong arch, and over that with a layer of bitumen six feet thick, she turned the river again over it; for it is the nature of that bitumen, to petrify when water comes over it, and grow as hard as stone; and thereby the vault or gallery under was preserved from having any of the water of the river to pierce through into it. The use this was intended for, was to preserve a communication between the two palaces, whereof one stood on the one side of the river, and the other on the other side, that in case one of them were distressed (for they were both fortresses strongly fortified), it might be relieved from the other; or, in case either were taken, there might be a way to retreat from it to the other. But all these cautions and provisions served in no stead

---

[a] Cyropedia, lib. 7.
[b] Herodotus, lib. 1.
[f] Cyropedia, lib. 6.
[d] Herodotus, lib. 1.
[e] Herodotus, lib. 1. Diod. Sic. lib. 2. Philostratus, lib. 1. c. 18.

stead when the city was taken by furprife, becaufe, in that hurry and confufion which men were then in, none of them were made ufe of.

In the firſt year of this king's reign, which was the 34th after the deſtruction of Jeruſalem, Daniel had revealed unto him the viſion of the four monarchies, and of the kingdom of the Meſſiah that was to ſucceed after them; which is at full related in the 7th chapter of Daniel.

An. 555.
Belſhaz. 1.

In the 3d year of King Belſhazzar, Daniel ſaw the viſion of the ram and the he-goat, whereby were ſignified the overthrow of the Perſian empire by Alexander the Great, and the perſecution that was to be raiſed againſt the Jews by Antiochus Epiphanes, king of Syria. This viſion is at full related in the 8th chapter of Daniel; and it is there ſaid, that it was revealed unto him at Shuſhan, in the palace of the king of Babylon, while he attended there as a counſellor and miniſter of ſtate about the king's buſineſs; which ſhows, that Shuſhan, with the province of Elam, of which it was the metropolis, was then in the hands of the Babylonians. But, about three years after, Abradates, viceroy or prince of Shuſhan, revolting to Cyrus, it was thenceforth joined to the empire of the Medes and Perſians; and the Elamites came up with the Medes to beſiege Babylon, according to the prophecy of Iſaiah (ch. xxi. 2.); and Elam was again reſtored according to the prophecy of Jeremiah (ch. xlix. 39.); for it recovered its liberty again under the Perſians, which it had been deprived of under the Babylonians.

An. 553.
Belſhaz. 3.

The Medes and Perſians growing ſtill upon the Babylonians, and Cyrus making great progreſs in his conqueſts, by taking fortreſſes, towns, and provinces, from them, to put a ſtop to this prevailing ᵃ power, the king of Babylon, about the 5th year of his reign, taking a great part of his treaſure with him, goes into Lydia, to King Crœſus, his confederate, and, there by his aſſiſtance, framed a very formidable confederacy againſt the Medes and Perſians; and, with his money, hiring a very numerous army of Egyptians, Greeks, Thracians, and all the nations of Leſſer Aſia, he appointed Crœſus to be their general, and ſent him with them to invade Media, and then returned again to Babylon.

An. 551.
Belſhaz. 5.

Cyrus, having full intelligence of all theſe proceedings from one of his confidents, who, by his order, under the pretence of a deſerter, had gone over to the enemy, made ſuitable preparations to withſtand the ſtorm, and, when all was ready, marched

againſt

ᵃ Cyropedia, lib. 6.

against the enemy. By this time Crœsus [a] had passed over the river Halys, taken the city of Pteria, and in a manner destroyed all the country thereabout. But, before he could pass any farther, Cyrus came up with him, and, having engaged him in battle, put all his numerous army to flight; whereon Crœsus returning to Sardis, the chief city of his kingdom, dismissed all his auxiliaries to their respective homes, ordering them to be again with him by the beginning of the ensuing spring, and sent to all his allies for the raising of more forces to be ready against the same time, for the carrying on of the next year's war; not thinking that, in the interim, now winter being approaching, he should have any need of them. But Cyrus, pursuing the advantage of his victory, followed close after him into Lydia, and there came upon him just as he had dismissed his auxiliaries. However, Crœsus, getting together all his own forces, stood battle against him. But the Lydians being mostly horse, Cyrus brought his camels against them, whose smell the horses not being able to bear, they were all put into disorder by it; whereon the Lydians dismounting, fought on foot; but being soon overpowered, were forced to make their retreat to Sardis, where Cyrus immediately shut them up in a close siege.

An. 548.
Belshaz. 8.

While he lay there, he [b] celebrated the funeral of Abradates and Panthea his wife. He was prince of Shushan under the Babylonians, and had revolted to Cyrus about two years before, as hath been already mentioned. His wife, a very beautiful woman, [c] had been taken prisoner by Cyrus in his first battle against the Babylonians. Cyrus having treated her kindly, and kept her chastely for her husband, the [d] sense of this generosity drew over this prince to him; and he happening to be slain in this war, as he was fighting valiantly in his service, his wife, out of grief for his death, slew herself upon his dead body, and Cyrus took care to have them both honourably buried together, and a stately monument was erected over them near the river Pactolus, where it remained many ages after.

Crœsus, being shut up in Sardis, [e] sent to all his allies for succours; but Cyrus pressed the siege so vigorously, that he took the city before any of them could arrive to its relief, and Crœsus in it, whom he condemned to be burnt to death; and accordingly a great pile of wood was laid together, and he was placed on the top of it for the execution; in which extremity, calling to mind the

[a] Herodotus, lib. 1. Cyropedia, lib. 6.
[b] Cyropedia, lib. 7.
[c] Cyropedia, lib. 5.
[d] Cyropedia, lib. 6.
[e] Herodotus, lib. 1. Cyropedia, lib. 7.

the conference he formerly had with Solon, cried out with a great sigh, three times, Solon, Solon, Solon. This Solon [a] was a wise Athenian, and the greatest philosopher of his time, who coming to Sardis on some occasion, Crœsus, out of the vanity and pride of his mind, caused all his riches, treasures, and stores, to be shewn unto him, expecting that, on his having seen them, he should have applauded his felicity, and pronounced him of all men the most happy herein; but, on his discourse with him, Solon plainly told him, that he could pronounce no man happy, as long as he lived, because no one could foresee what might happen unto him before his death. Of the truth of which Crœsus being now thoroughly convinced by his present calamity, this made him call upon the name of Solon; whereon Cyrus, sending to know what he meant by it, had the whole story related to him; which excited in him such a sense of the uncertainty of all human felicity, and such a compassion for Crœsus, that he caused him to be taken down from the pile, just as fire had been put to it, and not only spared his life, but allowed him a very honourable subsistence, and made use of him as one of his chief counsellors all his life after; and, at his death, recommended him to his son Cambyses, as the person whose advice he would have him chiefly to follow. The taking of this city happened [b] in the first year of the 58th Olympiad, which was the 8th year of Belshazzar, and the 41st after the destruction of Jerusalem.

Crœsus being a very religious prince, according to the idolatrous superstition of those times, [c] entered not on this war without having first consulted all his gods, and taken their advice about it; and he had two oracular answers given him from them which chiefly conduced to lead him into this unfortunate undertaking, that cost him the loss of his kingdom. The one of them was, that Crœsus should then only think himself in [d] danger, when a mule should reign over the Medes; and the other, that when he should pass over Halys, to make war upon the Medes, he should overthrow a great empire. The first, from the impossibility of the thing that ever a mule should be a king, made him argue that he was for ever safe. The second made him believe, that the empire that he should overthrow, on his passing over the river Halys, should be the empire of the Medes. And this

[a] Plutarchus in vita Solonis, Herodotus, lib. 1.
[b] Solinus, cap. 7. Eusebius in Chronico.
[c] Herodotus, lib. 1. Cyropedia, lib. 7.
[d] Nebuchadnezzar prophesied of the coming of Cyrus under the same appellation, telling the Babylonians, at the time of his death, that a Persian mule should come and reduce them into servitude. So saith Megasthenes in Eusebius de Præp. Evang. lib. 9.

this chiefly encouraged him in this expedition, contrary to the advice of one of the wifeſt of his friends, who earneſtly diſſuaded him from it. But now all things having happened otherwiſe than theſe oracles had made him expect, he obtained leave of Cyrus to ſend meſſengers to the temples of thoſe gods who had thus miſled him, to expoſtulate with them about it. The anſwers which he had hereto were, that Cyrus was the mule intended by the oracle; for that he was born of two different kinds of people, of the Perſians by his father, and of the Medes by his mother, and was of the more noble kind by his mother. And the empire which he was to overthrow, by his paſſing over Halys, was his own. By ſuch falſe and fallacious oracles did thoſe evil ſpirits, from whom they proceeded, delude mankind in thoſe days; rendering their anſwers, when conſulted, in ſuch dubious and ambiguous terms, that whatſoever the event were, they might admit of an interpretation to agree with it.

After this Cyrus [a] continued ſome time in Leſſer Aſia, till he had brought all the ſeveral nations which inhabited in it, from the Egean ſea to the Euphrates, into thorough ſubjection to him. From hence he went into Syria and Arabia, and there did the ſame thing; and then marched into the upper countries of Aſia, and, having there alſo ſettled all things in a thorough obedience under his dominion, he again entered Aſſyria, and marched on towards Babylon, that being the only place of all the Eaſt which now held out againſt him: and, having overthrown Belſhazzar in battle, he ſhut him up in Babylon and there beſieged him. This happened in the ninth year after the taking of Sardis, and in the beginning of the ſixteenth year of Belſhazzar. But this ſiege proved a very difficult work: for the walls were high and impregnable, the number of men within to defend them very great, and they were fully furniſhed with all ſorts of proviſions for twenty years, and [b] the void ground within the walls was able both by tillage and paſturage to furniſh them with much more. And therefore the inhabitants, thinking themſelves ſecure in their walls and their ſtores, looked on the taking of the city by a ſiege as an impracticable thing; and therefore, from the top of their walls, ſcoffed at Cyrus, and derided him for every thing he did towards it. However he went on with the attempt; and firſt he drew a line of circumvallation round the city, making the ditch broad and deep, and by the help of the palm-trees, [c] which uſually grow in that country to the height of 100 feet, he erected

An. 540.
Belſhaz. 16.

towers

---

[a] Herodotus lib. 1. Cyropedia, lib. 7. [b] Vide Q. Curtium, lib. 5. c. 1.
[c] Cyropedia, lib. 7.

towers higher than the walls, thinking at firſt to have been able to take the place by aſſault; but finding little ſucceſs this way, he applied himſelf wholly to the ſtarving of it into a ſurrender, reckoning that the more people there were within, the ſooner the work would be done. But, that he might not over-fatigue his army, by detaining them all at this work, he divided all the forces of the empire into twelve parts, and appointed each its month to guard the trenches. But, after near two years had been waſted this way, and nothing effected, he at length lighted on a ſtratagem, which, with little difficulty, made him maſter of the place: for [a] underſtanding, that a great annual feſtival was to be kept at Babylon on a day approaching, and that it was uſual for the Babylonians on that ſolemnity to ſpend the whole night in revelling, drunkenneſs, and all manner of diſorders, he thought this a proper time to ſurpriſe them; and, for the effecting of it, he had this device: He ſent up a party of his men to the head of the canal leading to the great lake above deſcribed, with orders, at a time ſet, to break down the great bank or dam, which was between the river and that canal, and to turn the whole current that way into the lake. In the interim, getting all his forces together, he poſted one part of them at the place where the river ran into the city, and the other where it came out, with orders to enter the city that night by the channel of the river, as ſoon as they ſhould find it fordable. And then, toward the evening, he opened the head of the trenches on both ſides the river above the city, to let the water of it run into them. And, by this means, and the opening of the great dam, the river was ſo drained, that, by the middle of the night, it being then in a manner empty, both parties, according to their orders, entered the channel, the one having Gobrias, and the other Gadates, for their guides; and finding the gates leading down to the river, which uſed on all other nights to be ſhut, then all left open, through the neglect and diſorder of that time of looſeneſs, they aſcended through them into the city; and both parties being met at the palace, as had been concerted between them, they there ſurpriſed the guards, and ſlew them all: and when, on the noiſe, ſome that were within opened the gates to know what it meant, they ruſhed in upon them and took the palace; where, finding the king with his ſword drawn at the head of thoſe who were at hand to aſſiſt him, they ſlew him valiantly fighting for his life, and all thoſe that were with him. After this, proclamation being made of life and ſafety to all ſuch as ſhould bring in their arms, and of death to all that ſhould refuſe ſo to do, all

An. 539.
Belſhaz. 17.

quietly

[a] Herodotus, lib. 1. Cyropedia, lib. 7.

quietly yielded to the conquerors, and Cyrus, without any farther refiftance, became mafter of the place: and this concluded all his conquefts, after a war of 21 years; for fo long was it from his coming out of Perfia with his army, for the affiftance of Cyaxares, to his taking of Babylon; during all which time he lay abroad in the field, carrying on his conquefts from place to place, till at length he had fubdued all the Eaft, from the Egean fea to the river Indus, and thereby erected the greateft empire that had ever been in Afia to that time; which work was owing as much to his wifdom as his valour, for he equally excelled in both. And he was alfo a perfon of that great candour and humanity to all men, that he made greater conquefts by his courtefy, and his kind treatment of all he had to do with, than by his fword, whereby he did knit the hearts of all men to him; and in this foundation lay the greateft ftrength of his empire, when he firft erected it.

This account Herodotus and Zenophon both give of the taking of Babylon by Cyrus; and herein they exactly agree with the fcripture. For Daniel [a] tells us, that Belfhazzar made a great feaft for a thoufand of his lords, and for his wives, and for his concubines, and that in that very night he was flain, and Darius the Mede, that is, Cyaxares the uncle of Cyrus, took the kingdom; for Cyrus allowed him the title of all his conquefts, as long as he lived. In this feaft Belfhazzar having impioufly profaned the gold and filver veffels that were taken out of the temple of Jerufalem, in caufing them to be brought into the banqueting-houfe, and there drinking out of them, he and his lords, and his wives, and his concubines, God did, in a very extraordinary and wonderful manner, exprefs his wrath againft him for the wickednefs hereof; for he caufed an hand to appear on the wall, and there write a fentence of immediate deftruction againft him for it. The king faw the appearance of the hand that wrote it; for it was exactly over againft the place where he fat. And therefore, being exceedingly affrighted and troubled at it, he commanded all his wife men, magicians, and aftrologers, to be immediately called for, that they might read the writing, and make known unto him the meaning of it. But [b] none of them being able to do it, the queen-mother, on her hearing of this wonderful thing, came into the banqueting-houfe, and acquainted the king of the great fkill and ability of Daniel in fuch matters; whereon he being fent for, did read to the king the writing, and, boldly telling

---

[a] Daniel v.

[b] The reafon why they could not read it was, becaufe it was written in the old Hebrew letters, now called the Samaritan character, which the Babylonians knew nothing of.

ling him of his many iniquities and tranfgreffions againft the great God of heaven and earth, and particularly in profaning, at that banquet, the holy veffels, which had been confecrated to his fervice in his temple at Jerufalem, made him underftand, that this hand-writing was a fentence from heaven againft him for it, the interpretation of it being, that his kingdom was taken from him, and given to the Medes and Perfians. And it feemeth to have been immediately upon it that the palace was taken, and Belfhazzar flain; for [a] candles were lighted before the hand-writing appeared, fome time after this muft be required for the calling of the wife-men, the magicians, and aftrologers, and fome time muft be wafted in their trying in vain to read the writing. After that the queen-mother came from her apartment into the banqueting-houfe to direct the king to fend for Daniel, and then he was called for, perchance from fome diftant place. And by this time many hours of the night muft have been fpent; and therefore we may well fuppofe, that, by the time Daniel had interpreted the writing, the Perfians were got within the palace, and immediately excuted the contents of it, by flaying Belfhazzar, and all his lords, that were with him. The queen, that entered the banqueting-houfe to direct the king to call for Daniel, could not be his wife; for all his wives, and concubines, the text tells us, fat with him at the feaft; and therefore it muft have been Nitocris the queen-mother. And fhe feemeth to have been there called the queen, by way of eminency, becaufe fhe had the regency of the kingdom under her fon, which her great wifdom eminently qualified her for. And Belfhazzar feemeth to have left this entirely to her management: for when Daniel was called in before him, he did [b] not know him, though he was one of the chief minifters of ftate that [c] did the king's bufinefs in his palace, but afked of him whether he were Daniel. But Nitocris, who conftantly employed him in the public affairs of the kingdom, knew him well, and therefore advifed that he fhould be fent for on this occafion. This fhews Belfhazzar to have been a prince that wholly minded his pleafures, leaving all things elfe to others to be managed for him; which is a conduct too often followed by fuch princes who think kingdoms made for nothing elfe, but to ferve their pleafures, and gratify their lufts. And therefore that he held the crown 17 years, and againft fo potent an enemy as Cyrus, was wholly owing to the conduct of his mother, into whofe hands the management of his affairs fell: for fhe was a lady of the greateft wifdom of her time, and did the utmoft that could be done to fave the ftate of Babylon from ruin. And therefore, her name was long after of that fame

[a] Daniel v. 5.   [b] Daniel v. 13.   [c] Daniel viii. 27.

fame in thofe parts, that Herodotus fpeaks of her, as if fhe had been fovereign of the kingdom, in the fame manner as Semiramis is faid to have been, and attributes to her all thofe works about Babylon which [a] other authors afcribe to her fon. For, although they were done in his reign, it was fhe that did them, and therefore fhe had the beft title to the honour that was due for them; though, as hath been above hinted, the great lake, and the canal leading to it (which, though reckoned among the works of Nebuchadnezzar, muft at leaft have been finifhed by her, according to Herodotus), how wifely foever they were contrived for the benefit both of the city and country, turned to the great damage of both; for Cyrus, draining the river by this lake and canal, by that means took the city. And when, by the breaking down of the banks at the head of the canal, the river was turned that way, no care being taken afterwards again to reduce it to its former channel, by repairing the breach, [b] all the country on that fide was overflown and drowned by it; and the current, by long running this way, at length making the breach fo wide, as to become irreparable, unlefs by an expence as great as that whereby the bank was firft built, a whole province was loft by it; and the current which went to Babylon afterwards grew fo fhallow, as to be fcarce fit for the fmalleft navigation, which was a further damage to that place. Alexander, who intended to have made Babylon the feat of his empire, endeavoured to remedy this mifchief, and did accordingly fet himfelf to build the bank anew, which was on the weft fide of it; but, when he had carried it on the length of four miles, he was ftopped by fome difficulties that he met with in the work from the nature of the foil, which poffibly would have been overcome, had he lived; but his death, which happened a little after, put an end to this, as well as to all his other defigns. And, a while after, Babylon falling into decay, on the building of Seleucia in the neighbourhood, this work was never more thought of; but that country hath remained all bog and marfh ever fince. And no doubt this was one main reafon which helped forward the defertion of that place, efpecially when they found a new city built in the neighbourhood, in a much better fituation.

In the taking of Babylon ended the Babylonifh empire, after it had continued from the beginning of the reign of Nabonaffar (who firft founded it) 209 years. And here ended the power and pride of this great city, juft 50 years after it had deftroyed the city and temple of Jerufalem; and hereby were in a great meafure accomplifhed the many prophecies which were by the prophets

VOL. I. I Ifaiah,

[a] Berofus apud Jofeph. contra Apionem, lib. 1.
[b] Arrianus de Expeditione Alexandri, lib 7.

Isaiah, Jeremiah, Habakkuk, and Daniel, delivered against it. And here it is to be observed, that, in reference to the present besieging, and taking of the place, it was particularly foretold by them, that it [a] should be shut up, and besieged by the Medes, Elamites, and Armenians; that the river [b] should be dried up; that the city should be taken in the time [c] of a feast, while her princes and her wife men, her captains, and her rulers, and her mighty men, were drunken; and that they should be thereon made to sleep a perpetual sleep, from which they should not awake. And so accordingly all this came to pass, Belshazzar, and all his thousand princes, who were drunk with him at the feast, having [d] been all slain by Cyrus's soldiers when they took the palace. And so also was it particularly foretold, by the prophet Isaiah (xiv.), that God would make the country of Babylon *a possession for the bittern and pools of water* (v. 23.); which was accordingly fulfilled by the overflowing and drowning of it, on the breaking down of the great dam, in order to take the city; which I have above given an account of; and so also that God would cut off from that city *the son and the grandson* (v. 22.), that is, the son and grandson of their great king Nebuchadnezzar; and they were accordingly both cut off by violent deaths in the flower of their age, Evilmerodach the son before this time in the manner as hath been above related, and Belshazzar the grandson in the present taking of Babylon; and hereby the sceptre of Babylon was broken, as was foretold by the same prophecy (v. 5.): for it did never after any more bear rule. Where I read *the son and the grandson* (ver. 22.), it is, I confess, in the English translation *the son and the nephew*. But, in the 21st chapter of Genesis, ver. 23. the same Hebrew word *Neked* is translated *son's son*, and so it ought to have been translated here; for this is the proper signification of the word; which appears from the use of the same word, Job xviii. 19.: for Bildad, there speaking of the wicked, and the curse of God which shall be upon him, in the want of a posterity, expresseth it thus: *Lo ninlo velo Neked*, i. e. *he shall have neither son nor grandson*; for nephew, in the English signification of the word, whether brother's son, or sister's son, cannot be within the meaning of the text, the context not admitting it.

An. 538.
Darius the
Mede 1.

After the death of Belshazzar, Darius the Mede is said [e] in scripture to have taken the kingdom: for Cyrus, as long as his uncle lived, allowed him a joint title with him in the empire, although it was

---

[a] Is. xiii. 17. and xxi. 2. Jer li. 11. 27.—30.
[b] Jer. l. 38. and li. 36.
[c] Jer. li. 39. 57.
[d] Cyropedia, lib. 7.
[e] Daniel v. 31.

was all gained by his own valour, and, out of deference to him, yielded him the firft place of honour in it. But the whole power of the army, and the chief conduct of all affairs being ftill in his hands, he only was looked on as the fupreme governor of the empire, which he had erected; and therefore, there is no notice at all taken of Darius in the canon of Ptolemy, but, immediately after the death of Belfhazzar (who is there called Nabonadius), Cyrus is placed as the next fucceffor, as in truth and reality he was; the other having no more than the name and the fhadow of the fovereignty, excepting only in Media, which was his own proper dominion.

There are [a] fome who will have Darius the Median to have been Nabonadius, the laft Babylonifh king in the canon of Ptolemy. And their fcheme is, that, after the death of Evilmerodach, Nerigliffar fucceeded only as guardian to Laborofoarchod his fon, who was next heir in right of his mother, fhe having been daughter to Nebuchadnezzar; and that Laborofoarchod was the Belfhazzar of the fcriptures, who was flain in the night of the impious feftival, not by Cyrus (fay they), but by a confpiracy of his own people: that the fcriptures attribute to him the whole four years of Belfhazzar, which the canon of Ptolemy doth to Nerigliffar, (or Nericaffolaffar, as he is there called), becaufe Nerigliffar reigned only as guardian for him; and that hence it is, that we hear of the firft and the third year of Belfhazzar, [b] in Daniel, though Laborofoarchod reigned alone, after his father's death, only nine months: that, after his death, the Babylonians made choice of Nabonadius, who was no way of kin to the family of Nebuchadnezzar, but a Median by defcent; and that for this reafon only is he called Darius the Median in fcripture. As to what they fay of Nabonadius's not being of kin to the family of Nebuchadnezzar, it muft be confeffed, that the fragments of Megafthenes [c] may give them fome authority for it: but as for all the reft, it hath no other foundation but the imagination of them that fay it. And the whole is contrary to fcripture: for, 1ft, The hand-writing on the wall told Belfhazzar, that his kingdom fhould be divided, or rent from him, and be given to the [d] Medes and Perfians; and immediately after [e] the facred text tells us, that Belfhazzar was flain that night, and Darius the Median took the kingdom, who could be none other than Cyaxares, king of Media, who, in conjunction with Cyrus, the Perfian, conquered Babylon. 2dly, Therefore el-

I 2   fhazzar

---

[a] Scaliger, Calvifius, and others.
[b] Daniel vii. 1. &. viii. 1.
[c] Apud Eufeb. Præp. Evang lib. 9.
[d] Dan. v. 28.
[e] Dan. v. 30. 31.

shazzar must have been the last Babylonish king, and consequently the Nabonadius of Ptolemy. 3*dly*, This last king was not a stranger to the family of Nebuchadnezzar; for the sacred text makes him [a] his descendant. 4*thly*, Darius is said to have governed the kingdom by the laws [b] of the Medes and Persians; which cannot be supposed, till after the Medes and Persians had conquered that kingdom. Had this Darius been Nabonadius the Babylonish king, he would certainly have governed by the Babylonish laws, and not by the laws of his enemies, the Medes and Persians, who were in hostility against him all his reign, and sought his ruin. 5*thly*, Darius is said to have divided his empire into [c] 120 provinces, which could not have been true of the Babylonish empire, that never having been large enough for it. But it must be understood of the Persian empire only, which was vastly larger. And afterwards, on the conquest of Egypt by Cambyses, and of Thrace and India by Darius Hystaspis, it had seven other provinces added to its former number; and therefore, in the time of Esther, it consisted of 127 provinces. And this having been the division of the Persian empire at that time, it sufficiently proves the former to have been of the same empire also: for if the Persian empire from India to Ethiopia contained but 127 provinces, the empire of Babylon alone, which was not the seventh part of the other, could not contain 120. The testimony which Scaliger brings to prove Nabonadius to have been a Mede by descent, and by election made king of Babylon, is very absurd. In the prophecy of Nebuchadnezzar, delivered to the Babylonians a little before his death, concerning their future subjection to the Persians, which is preserved in the fragments of Megasthenes, there are these words: [d] 'A Persian mule shall come, who, by the help of your own gods fighting for him, shall bring slavery upon you, whose assistant, or fellow-causer herein, shall be the Mede.' By which Mede is plainly meant Cyaxares, king of Media, who was confederate with Cyrus in the war, wherein Babylon was conquered. But Scaliger saith it was Nabonadius; and hence proves that he was a Mede, and quotes this place in Megasthenes for it. If you ask him, why he saith this, his answer is, that the person, who is in that prophecy said to be the assistant of Cyrus, and fellow-causer with him in bringing servitude upon Babylon, must be Nabonadius, because he was an assistant and fellow-causer with him herein in being beaten and conquered by him. This argument needs no answer, it is sufficiently refuted by being related. And therefore Isaac Vossius

well

---

[a] Daniel v. 11. 13. 18. 22.
[b] Daniel vi. 8. 15.
[c] Daniel vi. 1.
[d] Apud Euseb. Præp. Evan. lib. 9.

well observes, that the arguments which Scaliger brings for this are *indigna Scaligero*, i. e. *unworthy of Scaliger*. Chronologia Sacra, p. 144.

After Cyrus had settled his affairs at Babylon, [a] he went into Persia, to make a visit to his father and mother, they being both yet living; and, on his return through Media, he there married the daughter of Cyaxares, having with her for her dowry the kingdom of Media, in reversion after her father's death; for she was his only child: and then with his new wife he went back to Babylon. And Cyaxares, being earnestly invited by him thither, accompanied him in the journey. On their arrival at Babylon, they there took counsel, in concert together, for the settling of the whole empire; and, [b] having divided it into the 120 provinces which I have before spoken of, they [c] distributed the government of them among those that had born with Cyrus the chief burden of the war, and best merited from him in it. Over these were appointed [d] three presidents, who, constantly residing at court, were to receive from them, from time to time, an account of all particulars relating to their respective government, and again remit to them the king's orders concerning them. And therefore, in these three, as the chief ministers of the king, was intrusted the superintendency and main government of the whole empire. And of them Daniel was made the first. To which preference, not only his great wisdom (which was of eminent fame all over the East), but also his seniority, and long experience in affairs, gave him the justest title: for he had now, from the second year of Nebuchadnezzar, been employed full 65 years as a prime minister of state under the kings of Babylon. However, this station advancing him to be the next person to the king in the whole empire, it stirred up so great an envy against him among the other courtiers, that they laid that snare for him, which cast him into the lions den. But he being there delivered by a miracle from all harm, this malicious contrivance ended in the destruction of its authors: and Daniel being thenceforth immoveably settled in the favour of Darius and Cyrus, [e] he prospered greatly in their time, as long as he lived.

In the first year of Darius, Daniel computing, that the seventy years of Judah's captivity, which were prophesied of by the prophet Jeremiah, were now drawing to an end, [f] earnestly prayed unto God, that he would remember his people, and grant restoration to Jerusalem, and make his face again to shine upon the holy city, and his sanctuary, which he had placed there.

Whereon,

---

[a] Cyropedia, lib 8.
[b] Daniel vi. 1.
[c] Cyropedia, lib. 8.
[d] Daniel vi. 2.
[e] Daniel vi. 28.
[f] Daniel ix.

Whereon, in a vision, he had assurance given him by the angel Gabriel, not only of the deliverance of Judah from their temporal captivity, under the Babylonians, but also of a much greater redemption, which God would give his church in his deliverance of them from their spiritual captivity under sin and Satan, to be accomplished at the end of 70 weeks, after the going forth of the commandment to rebuild Jerusalem, that is, at the end of 490 years. For, taking each day for an year, according as is usual in the prophetic stile of scripture, so many years 70 weeks of years will amount to, which is the clearest prophecy of the coming of the Messiah that we have in the Old Testament: for it determines it to the very time, on which he accordingly came, and by his death and passion, and resurrection from the dead, completed for us the great work of our salvation.

Cyrus, immediately on his return to Babylon, had issued out his orders [a] for all his forces to come thither to him, which, at a general muster, he found to be 120,000 horse, 2000 sithed chariots, and 600,000 foot. Of these having distributed into garrisons as many as were necessary for the defence of the several parts of the empire, he marched with the rest in an expedition into Syria, where he settled all those parts of the empire; reducing all under him as far as the Red sea, and the confines of Ethiopia. In the interim [b] Cyaxares (whom the scriptures call Darius the Median) staid at Babylon, and there governed the affairs of the empire, and during that time happened what hath been above related concerning Daniel's being cast into the lion's den, and his miraculous deliverance from it.

And, about the same time, seem to have been coined those famous pieces of gold called Darics [c] which, by reason of their fineness, were for several ages preferred before all other coin throughout all the East: for we are told that the author of this coin was [d] not Darius Hystaspis, as some have imagined, but an ancienter Darius. But there is no ancienter Darius mentioned to have reigned in the East, excepting only this Darius, whom the scripture calls Darius the Median. And therefore it is most likely, that he was the author of this coin, and that, during the two years that he reigned at Babylon, while Cyrus was absent from thence on his Syrian, Egyptian, and other expeditions, he caused it to be made there, out of the vast quantity of gold, which had been brought thither into the treasury, as the spoils of the war which he and Cyrus had been so long engaged in;

from.

---

[a] Cyropedia, lib. 8.
[b] Daniel v. 31.
[c] Herodotus, lib. 4. Plutarchus in Artaxerxe.
[d] Harpocration. Scholiastes Aristophanis ad Eccles. p. 741. 742. Suidas sub voce Δαρεικος.

from whence it became difperfed all over the Eaft, and alfo into Greece, where it was of great reputation. According [a] to Dr Bernard, it weighed two grains more than one of our guineas; but the finenefs added much more to its value; for it was in a manner all of pure gold, having none or at leaft very little alloy in it; and therefore may be well reckoned, as the proportion of gold and filver now ftands with us in refpect to each other, to be worth 25 fhillings of our money. In thofe [b] parts of fcripture which were written after the Babylonifh captivity, thefe pieces are mentioned by the name of Adarkonim, and in the Talmudifts by the name of [c] Darkonoth, both from the Greek Δαρεικοί, *i. e.* Darics. And it is to be obferved, that all thofe pieces of gold, which were afterwards coined of the fame weight and value by the fucceeding kings, not only of the Perfian but alfo of the Macedonian race, were all called Darics, from the Darius that was the firft author of them. And thefe were either whole Darics or half Darics, as with us there are guineas and half guineas.

But, about two years after, Cyaxares dying, and Cambyfes being alfo dead in Perfia, [d] Cyrus returned, and took on him the whole government of the empire; over which he reigned feven years. His reign is reckoned, from his firft coming out of Perfia, with an army for the affiftance of Cyaxares, to his death, to have been 30 years; from the taking of Babylon nine years, and from his being fole monarch of the whole empire, after the death of Cyaxares and Cambyfes, feven years. Tully [e] reckons by the firft account, [f] Ptolemy by the fecond, and [g] Xenophon by the third. And the firft of thefe feven years, is that firft year of Cyrus mentioned in the firft verfe of the book of Ezra, wherein an end was put to the captivity of Judah, and a licence given them, by a public decree of the king's, again to return into their own country. The feventy years, which Jeremiah had prophefied fhould be the continuance of this captivity, were now juft expired: for it began a year and two months before the death of Nabopollaffar, after that Nebuchadnezzar reigned 43 years, Evilmerodach two years, Nerigliffar four years, Belfhazzar 17 years, and Darius the Median two years; which being all put together, make juft 69 years and two months; and,

[a] De Ponderibus et Menfuris Antiquis, p. 171.
[b] 1 Chron. xxix. 7. and Ezra viii. 27.
[c] Vide Buxtorfii Lexicon Rabinicum, p. 577.
[d] Cyropedia, lib 8.
[e] De Divinatione, lib. 1.
[f] In Canone.
[g] Cyrop. lib. 8. Where Xenophon faith, that Cyrus reigned after the death of Cyaxares feven years.

and, if you add hereto ten months more to complete the said 70 years, it will carry down the end of them exactly into the same month, in the first year of Cyrus, in which it began in the last save one of Nabopollassar, *i. e.* in the 9th month of the Jewish year, which is the November of ours. For in that month Nebuchadnezzar first took Jerusalem, and carried great numbers of the people into captivity, as hath been before related. And that their release from it happened also in the same month may be thus inferred from scripture. The first time the Jews are found at Jerusalem after their return, was in their Nisan, *i. e.* in our April, as will hereafter be shewn. If you allow them four months for their march thither from Babylon (which was the time [a] in which Ezra performed the like march), the beginning of that march will fall in the middle of the December preceding. And if you allow a month's time after the decree of release for their preparing for that journey, it will fix the end of the said captivity, which they were then released from, exactly in the middle of the month of November, in the first year of Cyrus; which was the very time on which it began, just 70 years before. And that this first of Cyrus is not to be reckoned, with Ptolemy, from the taking of Babylon, and the death of Belshazzar, but with Zenophon, from the death of Darius the Mede, and the succession of Cyrus into the government of the whole empire, appears from hence, that this last is plainly the scripture reckoning: for therein, after the taking of Babylon, and the death of Belshazzar, Darius the Mede [b] is named in the succession before Cyrus the Persian, and the years [c] of the reign of Cyrus are not there reckoned, till the years of the reign of Darius had ceased; and therefore, according to scripture, the first of Cyrus cannot be till after the death of Darius.

There can be no doubt, but that this decree in favour of the Jews was obtained by Daniel. When Cyrus first came into Babylon, on his taking the city, he found him there an old minister of state, famed for his great wisdom all over the East, and long experienced in the management of the public affairs of the government; and such counsellors wise kings always seek for: and, moreover, his late reading of the wonderful hand-writing on the wall, which had puzzled all the wise men of Babylon besides, and the event which happened immediately after, exactly agreeable to his interpretation, had made a very great and fresh addition to his reputation; and therefore, on Cyrus's having made himself master of the city, he was soon called for, as a person that was best able to advise and direct about the settling of the government

---

[a] Ezra vii. 9.
[b] Daniel vi. 28.
[c] Compare Daniel ix. 1. with the 10th chap. ver. 1.

vernment on this revolution, and was confulted with in all the
meafures taken herein. On which occafion, he fo well approved
himfelf, that afterwards, on the fettling of the government of
the whole empire, he was made firft fuperintendant, or prime
minifter of ftate, over all the provinces of it, as hath been already fhewn: and when Cyrus returned from his Syrian expedition again to Babylon, he found a new addition to his fame,
from his miraculous deliverance from the lions den. All which
put together gave fufficient reafon for that wife and excellent
prince to have him in the higheft efteem; and therefore it is faid,
that [a] he profpered under him, as he did under Darius the Median, with whom, it appears, he was in the higheft favour and
efteem. And fince he had been fo earneft with God in prayer
for the reftoration of his people, as we find in the 9th chapter of
Daniel, it is not to be thought, that he was backward in his in-
terceffions for it with the king, efpecially when he was in fo great
favour, and of fo great authority with him. And, to induce
him the reader to grant his requeft, he fhewed him the prophecies of the prophet Ifaiah, [b] which fpake of him by name
150 years before he was born, as one whom God had defigned
to be a great conqueror, and king over many nations, and the
reftorer of his people, in caufing the temple to be built, and
the land of Judah and the city of Jerufalem to be again dwelt
in by its former inhabitants. That Cyrus had feen and read
thefe prophecies, [c] Jofephus tell us; and it is plain from fcripture that he did fo; for they are recited [d] in his decree in Ezra for the rebuilding of the temple. And who was there that
fhould fhew them unto him, but Daniel, who, in the ftation
that he was in, had conftant accefs unto him, and of all men
living had it moft at heart to fee thefe prophecies fulfilled, in
the reftoration of Sion? Befides Cyrus, in his late expedition
into Syria and Paleftine, having feen fo large and good a country as that of Judea lie wholly defolate, might juftly be
moved with a defire of having it again inhabited; for the
ftrength and riches of every empire being chiefly in the number of its fubjects, no wife prince would ever defire that any
part of his dominions fhould lie unpeopled. And who could
be more proper again to plant the defolated country of Judea
than its former inhabitants? They were firft carried out of Judea by Nebuchadnezzar to people and ftrengthen Babylon;
and perchance under this government of the Perfians, to which
the Babylonians were never well affected, the weakening and
difpeopling of Babylon might be as ftrong a reafon for their
being

---

[a] Dan. i. 21. & vi. 28.
[b] If. xliv. 28. & xlv. 1.
[c] Lib. 11. c. 1.
[d] Ezra i. 2.

being sent back again into their own country. But whatsoever second causes worked to it, God's over-ruling power, which turneth the hearts of princes which way he pleaseth, brought it to pass, that, in the first year of Cyrus's monarchy over the East, he issued out his royal decree for the rebuilding of the temple at Jerusalem, and the return of the Jews again into their own country. And hereon the state of Judah and Jerusalem began to be restored; of which an account will be given in the next book.

THE

THE

OLD AND NEW TESTAMENT

CONNECTED,

IN

THE HISTORY

OF

THE JEWS AND NEIGHBOURING NATIONS,

FROM

The Declenſion of the Kingdoms of ISRAEL *and* JUDAH, *to the Time of* CHRIST.

BOOK III.

CYRUS [a] having iſſued out his decree for the reſtoring of the Jews unto their own land, and the rebuilding of the temple at Jeruſalem, they gathered together out of the ſeveral parts of the kingdom of Babylon, to the number of 42,360 perſons, with their ſervants, which amounted to 7337 more.   An. 536. Cyrus 1.

Their chief leaders were [b] Zerubbabel, the ſon of Salathiel, the ſon of Jehoiachin, or Jeconias, king of Judah, and Jeſhua, the ſon of Jozadak, the high prieſt. Zerubbabel (whoſe Babyloniſh name was [c] Sheſhbazzar) was made [d] governor of the land, under the title of Tirſhatha, by commiſſion from Cyrus. But Jeſhua was high prieſt by lineal deſcent from the pontifical family; for [e] he was the ſon of Jozadak, who was the ſon of Seraiah,

[a] Ezra i. & ii.
[b] Ezra ii. 2.
[c] Ezra i. 8, 11.
[d] Ezra v. 14.
[e] 1 Chron. vi. 14, 15.

raiah, that was high prieſt when Jeruſalem was deſtroyed, and the temple burnt by the Chaldeans. Seraiah, being then taken priſoner by Nebuzaradan, and carried to Nebuchadnezzar to Riblah in Syria, was [a] then put to death by him: but Jozadak, his ſon being ſpared as to his life, [b] was only with the reſt led captive to Babylon, where he died before the decree of reſtoration came forth; and therefore the office of high prieſt was then in Joſhua his ſon, and under [c] that title he is named, next Zerubbabel, among the firſt of thoſe that returned. The reſt were [d] Nehemiah, Seraiah, Reelaia, Mordecai, Bilſham, Miſpar, Bigvai, Rehum, and Baanah, who were the prime leaders of the people, and the chief aſſiſtants to Zerubbabel, in the reſettling of them again in their own land, and are by the Jewiſh writers reckoned the chief men of the great ſynagogue; ſo they call the convention of elders which, they ſay, ſat at Jeruſalem after the return of the Jews, and did there again re-eſtabliſh all their affairs both as to church and ſtate, of which they ſpeak great things, as ſhall hereafter be ſhewn. But it is to be obſerved, that the Nehemiah and Mordecai above mentioned, were not the Nehemiah and Mordecai of whom there is ſo much ſaid in the books of Nehemiah and Eſther, but quite different perſons who bore the ſame name.

At the ſame time that Cyrus iſſued out his decree for the rebuilding of the temple at Jeruſalem, he [e] ordered all the veſſels to be reſtored which had been taken from thence. Nebuchadnezzar, on the burning of the former temple, had brought them to Babylon, and placed them there in the temple of Bel his god. From thence they were, according to Cyrus's order, by Mithredath, the king's treaſurer, delivered to Zerubbabel, who carried them back again to Jeruſalem. All the veſſels of gold and ſilver that were at this time reſtored were 5400; the remainder was brought back by Ezra, in the reign of Artaxerxes Longimanus, many years after.

And not only thoſe of Judah and Benjamin, but ſeveral alſo of the other tribes, took the benefit of this decree to return again into their own land: for [f] ſome of them who were carried away by Tiglath-Pileſer, Salmanezer, and Eſarhaddon, ſtill retained the true worſhip of God in a ſtrange land, and did not go into the idolatrous uſages and impieties of the heathens, among whom they were diſperſed, but joined themſelves to the Jews, when, by a like captivity, they were brought into the ſame parts;

---

[a] 2 Kings xxv. 18.
[b] 1 Chron. vi. 15.
[c] Ezra ii. 2. iii. 2. Hag. i. 12. and ii. 2.
[d] Ezra ii. 2. Neh. vii. 7.
[e] Ezra i. 7.---11.
[f] Tobit i. 11. 12. & xiv. 9.

parts; and some, after all the Assyrian captivities, were still left in the land. For we find some of them still there in the time of [a] Josiah, and they suffered the Babylonish captivity, as well as the Jews, till at length they were wholly carried away in the last of them by Nebuzaradan, in the [b] 23d year of Nebuchadnezzar. And many of them had long before [c] left their tribes for their religion, and, incorporating themselves with their brethren of Judah and Benjamin, dwelt in their cities, and there fell into the same calamity with them in their captivity under the Babylonians. And of all these a great number took the advantage of this decree again to return and dwell in their own cities; for both Cyrus's decree, as well as that of Artaxerxes, extended to all the house of Israel. The decree of Artaxerxes [d] is, by the name, to all the people of Israel, and that of Cyrus [e] is to all the people of the God of Israel, that is, as appears by the text, to all those that worshipped God at Jerusalem, which must be understood of the people of Israel, as well as of Judah; for that temple was built for both, and both had an equal right to worship God there. And therefore Ezra, when he returned, in the reign of Artaxerxes Longimanus, [f] sent a copy of the king's decree, whereby that favour was granted him through all Media, where the ten tribes were in captivity, as well as through all Chaldea and Assyria, where the Jews were in captivity; which plainly implies, that both of them were included in that decree, and that being a renewal of the decree of Cyrus, both must be understood of the same extent. And we are told in scripture, that, after the captivity, [g] some of the children of Ephraim and Manasseh dwelt in Jerusalem, as well as those of Judah and Benjamin. And it appears from several places [h] in the New Testament, that some of all the tribes were still in being among the Jews, even to the time of their last dispersion on the destruction of Jerusalem by the Romans, though then all were comprehended under the name of Jews, which, after the Babylonish captivity, became the general name of the whole nation, as that of Israelites was before. And this being premised, it solves the difficulty which ariseth from the difference that is between the general number, and the particulars of those that returned upon Cyrus's decree. For the general number, both in Ezra and Nehemiah, is said to be 42,360; but the particulars, as

reckoned

---

[a] 2 Chron. xxxiv. 9. & xxxv. 18.
[b] Jer. lii. 30.
[c] 2 Chron. xi. 16. xv. 9. & xxxi. 6.
[d] Ezra vii. 13.
[e] Ezra i. 3.
[f] Joseph. Antiq. lib. 11. c. 5.
[g] 1 Chron. ix. 3.
[h] Luke ii. 36. James i. 1. Acts xxvi. 7.

reckoned up in their several families in Ezra, amount only to 29,818, and in Nehemiah to 31,031. The meaning of which is, they are only the tribes of Judah, Benjamin, and Levi, that are reckoned by their families in both these places, [a] the rest being of the other tribes of Israel, are numbered only in the gross sum, and this is that which makes the gross sum so much exceed the particulars in both the computations. But how it comes to pass, that the particulars in Ezra differ from the particulars in Nehemiah, since there are several ways how this may be accounted for, and, we can only conjecture which of them may be the right, I shall not take upon me to determine.

Of the 24 courses of the priests that were carried away to Babylon, only [b] four returned, and they were the courses of Jedaiah, Immer, Pashur, and Harim, which made up the number of 4289 persons. The rest either tarried behind, or were extinct. However, the old number of the courses, as established by King David, were still kept up. For, of the four courses that returned, [c] each subdivided themselves into six, and the new courses taking the names of those that were wanting, still kept up the old titles; and hence it is, that after this Mattathias is said to have been of the [d] course of Joarib, and Zacharias, of the course [e] of Abia, though neither of these courses were of the number of those that returned. For the new courses took the names of the old ones, though they were not descended from them, and so they were continued by the same names under the second temple, as they had been under the first, only the fifth course, though of the number of these that returned, changed its name, and for that of Malchijah, under which it was first established, took the name of Pashur, that is, the name of the son, instead of that of the father; for, [f] Pashur was the son of Malchijah. It is a common saying among the Jews, that they were [g] only the bran, that is, the dregs of the people, that returned to Jerusalem after the end of the captivity, and that all the fine flower staid behind at Babylon. It is most certain, that, notwithstanding the several decrees that had been granted by the kings of Persia for the return of the Jews into their own land, there were a great many that waved taking the advantage of them, and continued still in Chaldea, Assyria, and other Eastern provinces, where they had been carried; and it is most likely, that they were of the best and richest of the nation that did so:

---

[a] Seder Olam Rabba, c. 29.
[b] Ezra ii. 36—39.
[c] Talmud. Hierosol. in Taanith.
[d] 2 Mac. ii. 1.
[e] Luke i. 5.
[f] 1 Chron. ix. 12. Nehem. xi. 12.
[g] Talmud Bab. in Kiddushim.

so: for, when they had gotten houses and lands in those parts, it cannot be supposed, that such would be very forward to leave good settlements to new-plant a country that had lain many years desolate. But of what sort soever they were, it is certain a great many staid behind, and never again returned into their own country. And if we may guess at their number, by the family of Aaron, they must have been many more than those who settled again in Judea; for of the 24 courses of the sons of Aaron, which were carried away, we find only four among those that returned, as hath been already taken notice of; and hereby it came to pass, that, during all the time of the second temple, and for a great many ages after, the number of the Jews in Chaldea, Assyria, and Persia, grew to be so very great, that they were all along thought to exceed the number of the Jews of Palestine, even in those times when that country was best inhabited by them.

Those who made this first return into Judea, arrived there in Nisan, the first month of the Jewish year (which answers to part of March and part of April in our kalendar); for the [a] second month of the next year is said to be in the second year after their return; and therefore, they must then have been a whole year in the land. As soon as they came thither, [b] they dispersed themselves according to their tribes, and the families of their fathers, into their several cities, and there betook themselves to rebuild their houses and again manure their lands, after they had now, from the destruction of Jerusalem, and the flight of the remainder of the people into Egypt, on the death of Gedaliah, lain desolate and uncultivated 52 years, according to the number of the sabbatical years, which they had neglected to observe; for, according to the Mosaical law, they ought to have left [c] their lands fallow every seventh year. But, among other commandments of God, this also they had neglected: and therefore, [d] God made the land lie desolate without inhabitants or cultivation, till it had enjoyed the full number of its sabbaths that it had been deprived of. And this tells us how long the Jews had neglected this law of the sabbatical year: for it is certain, the land was desolated only 52 years, that is, from the death of Gedaliah till the end of the 70 years captivity, in the first year of the empire of Cyrus. And 52 sabbatical years make 52 weeks of years, which amount to 364 years; which carries up the computation to the beginning of the reign of Asa; and therefore, from that time the Jews having

An. 535. Cyrus 2.

---

[a] Ezra iii. 8.
[b] Ezra ii. 1. iii. 70. & iii. 1. Neh. vii. 6.
[c] Lev. xxv. 2—4.
[d] Lev. xxvi. 34. 35. 43. 2 Chron. xxxvi. 21.

ving neglected to observe the sabbatical years, till they had deprived the land of 52 of them, God made that land lie desolate, without cultivation or inhabitants, just so many years, till he had restored to it that full rest, which the wickedness of its inhabitants had, contrary to the law of their God, denied unto it. If we reckon the whole seventy years of the captivity into those years of desolation, which were to make amends for the sabbatical years that the land had been deprived of, then we must reckon the observation of them to have been laid aside for 70 weeks of years, that is, 490 years. But this will carry back the omission higher up than the days of David and Samuel, in whose time it is not likely that such a breach of the law of God would have been permitted in the land.

On the seventh month, which is called the month Tisri, all the people which had returned to their several cities gathered together at [a] Jerusalem, and there, on the first [b] day of that month, celebrated the feast of trumpets. This month began about the time of the autumnal equinox, and was [c] formerly the first month of the year, till it was [d] changed at the time of the coming up of the children of Israel out of Egypt; for that happening in the month of Abib, afterwards called Nisan, that month, for this reason, had the honour given it, as thenceforth, to be reckoned among the Israelites for the first month of the year, that is, in all ecclesiastical matters. Before this time Tisri [e] was reckoned every where to begin the year, because from thence did commence (it was thought) [f] the beginning of all things; it being the general opinion among the ancients, that the world was created, and first began, at the time of the autumnal equinox. And for this reason the Jews do still, in their æra of the creation of the world, as well as in their æra of contracts, compute the beginning of the year from the first of Tisri, and all their bills, and bonds, and all other civil acts and contracts, are still dated among them according to the same computation. And from this month also they [g] began all their jubilees and sabbatical years. And therefore, although their ecclesiastical year began from Nisan, and all their festivals were reckoned according to it, yet their civil year was still reckoned from Tisri, and the first day of that month was their new-year's-day,

[a] Ezra iii. 1.
[b] Ezra iii. 6. Levit. xxiii. 24. Numb. xxix. 1.
[c] Exod. xxiii. 16. and xxxiv. 22.
[d] Exod. xii. 2.
[e] Chaldee Paraphrast on Exodus xii. 2.
[f] Vide Scaligerum de Emendatione Temporum, lib. 5. c De Conditu Mundi, p. 366, &c.
[g] Levit. xxv. 9.

day, and for the more solemn celebration of it, this feast of trumpets seems to have been appointed.

On the [a] 10th day of the same month was the great day of expiation, when the high priest made atonement for all the people of Israel; and on the [b] 15th day began the feast of tabernacles, and lasted till the 22d inclusively. During all which solemnities, the people staid at Jerusalem, and employed all that time to the best of their power to set forward the restoration of God's worship again in that place; toward which all that had riches contributed according to their abilities. And the [c] free-will offerings which were made on this occasion, besides 100 vestments for the priests, amounted to 61,000 drams of gold, and 5000 minas of silver, which in all comes to about 75,500 pounds of our money; for every dram of gold is worth 10 shillings of our money, and every mina of silver 9 pounds; for [d] it contained 60 shekels, and every [e] shekel of silver is worth of our money three shillings. And upon this fund they began the work. And a great sum it was to be raised by so small a number of people, and on their first return from their captivity, especially if they were only of the poorer sort, as the Rabbins say. It must be supposed, that these offerings were made by the whole nation of the Jews, that is, by those who staid behind, as well as by those who returned; otherwise it is scarce possible to solve the matter; for all having an equal interest in that temple, and the daily sacrifices there offered up having been in the behalf of all, it is very reasonable to suppose, that all did contribute to the building of it; and that especially seeing that, as long as that temple stood, [f] every Jew annually paid an half shekel, *i. e.* about 18 pence of our money, towards its repair, and the support of the daily service in it, into what parts soever they were dispersed through the whole world.

The first thing they did, was [g] to restore the altar of the Lord for burnt-offerings. This stood [h] in the middle of the inner court of the temple, exactly before the porch leading into the holy place; and hereon were made the daily offerings of the morning and evening service, and all other offerings, ordinary and extraordinary, which were offered up to God by fire. It had been beaten down and destroyed by the Babylonians at the burn-

Vol. I   K   ing

---

[a] Levit. xvi. 29. 30. and xxiii. 27. Numb. xxix. 7.
[b] Levit. xxiii. 34. Numb. xxix. 12. &c.
[c] Ezra ii. 69.
[d] Ezekiel xlv. 12.
[e] Vide Bernardum de Mensuris & Ponderibus antiquis, p. 129.
[f] Exod. xxx. 13—15. Maimonides in Shekalim, cap. 1. 2.
[g] Ezra iii. 3.
[h] See Lightfoot of the Temple, chap. 34.

ing of the temple, and in the same place was it now again restored. That it [a] was built, and stood in another place, with a tabernacle round it, till the rebuilding of the temple was fully finished and completed, is a fancy without a foundation. It was certainly built in its proper place, [b] that is, in the same place where it before stood, and there they daily offered sacrifices upon it, even before any thing else of the temple was built about it. It was [c] a large pile built all of unhewn stones, 32 cubits (*i. e.* 48 feet) square at the bottom; from thence it rising one cubit benched-in one cubit; and from thence, being 30 cubits square, it did rise five cubits, and benched-in one cubit; and from thence being 28 cubits square, it did rise three cubits, and benched-in two cubits; from whence it did rise one cubit, which was the hearth, upon which the offerings were burned, and the benching-in of two cubits breadth was the passage round it, on which the priests stood, when they tended the fire, and placed the sacrifices on it. So this hearth was a square of 24 cubits, or 36 feet, on every side, and one cubit high, which was all made of solid brass, and from hence it was called the [d] brazen altar. For it is not to be imagined, that it was all made of solid brass; for to make up so big a pile all of that metal would cost a vast sum of money. And besides, if it were so made, it would not only be against the law, but also impracticable, for the use intended. It would be against the law, because thereby they are commanded, that wheresoever they should make an altar, other than the portable altar of the tabernacle, they should make it [e] of earth or else of unhewn stone. And it would be impracticable for the use intended, because, if it were all of brass, the fire continually burning upon the top of it would so heat the whole, and especially that part of it next the hearth, that it would be impossible for the priests to stand on it, when they were come thither to officiate in tending the altar, and offering the sacrifices thereon; and that especially since they were always to officiate barefooted, without any thing at all upon their feet to fence them from the heat of it. It is not indeed any where commanded, that the priests should officiate barefooted; but among the garments assigned for the priests (Exod. xxviii.) shoes not being named, they were supposed therefore to be forbid, and the text saying,

---

[a] Bishop Patrick in his comment on first Chronicles, chap. 9.
[b] Ezra iii. 2. For there it is said, that they did set the altar upon its bases or foundations, *i. e.* upon the same bases or foundations, on which it before had stood.
[c] Middoth in Middoth. Maimonides in Beth Habbechira, c. 1. 2.
[d] 1 Kings viii. 64.
[e] Exod. xx. 24. 25.

DIFFERENT ALTARS OF BURNT OFFERINGS.

faying, (ver. 4.) *Thefe are the garments which they shall make;* this (they fay) excludes all that are not there named. And Mofes being commanded, at the burning bufh, [a] to put off his fhoes, for that the ground on which he ftood was holy, becaufe of the extraordinary prefence of God then in that place; this they make a further argument for it: for, fay they, the temple was all holy for the fame reafon, that is, becaufe of the extraordinary prefence of God there refiding in Shechinah over the mercy-feat. And for thefe reafons it was moft ftrictly exacted, that the priefts fhould be always barefooted in the temple, although their going there with their bare feet upon the marble pavement was very pernicious to the health of many of them. On the four corners of the altar, on the laft benching-in, where the priefts ftood, when they offered the facrifices, there were fixed four fmall pillars of a cubit height, and a cubit on every fide, in the form of an exact cube. And thefe were the horns of the altar fo often mentioned in fcripture. The middle of each of them was hollow, becaufe therein was to be put fome of the blood of the facrifices. The afcent up to the altar was by a gentle rifing on the fouth fide, called the Kibbefh, which was 32 cubits in length, and 16 in breadth, and landed upon the upper benching-in next the hearth, or the top of the altar; for [b] to go up to the altar by fteps was forbid by the law. The form of the whole will be beft underftood by the annexed draught.

But their zeal for the temple being that which had brought moft of them back again into Judea, the rebuilding of this was what they had their hearts moft intent upon. And therefore having employed the firft year [c] in preparing materials, and contracting with carpenters and mafons for the work, [d] in the fecond month of the fecond year they laid the foundation of the houfe; which was done with great folemnity: for Zerubbabel the governor, and Jefhua the high prieft, being prefent, with all the congregation, the trumpeters blew their trumpets, and muficians founded their inftruments, and fingers fung, all in praife to the Lord their God, and all the reft of the people fhouted for joy, while the firft ftones were laid; only the old men, who had feen the glory of the firft temple, and had no expectation that this, which was now a-building by a few poor exiles lately returned into their country, could ever equal that, which had all the riches of David and Solomon, two of the wealthieft princes of the eaft, expended in the erecting of it, wept at the remembrance of the old temple, while others rejoiced at the laying the foundations of the new. And indeed

An. 534.
Cyrus 3.

---

[a] Exod. iii. 5. Acts vii. 33.
[b] Exod. xx. 26.
[c] Ezra iii. 7.
[d] Ezra iii. 8—10, &c.

indeed the difference between the former temple and this, which was now a building, was so great, that God himself tells the prophet [a] Haggai, that the latter, in comparison with the former, was as nothing; so much did it come short of it. But this is not to be understood of its bigness: for the second temple was of the same dimensions with the first; it being built upon the very same foundations, and therefore it was exactly of the same length and breadth. Cyrus's commission may seem to make it broader; for that allows [b] 60 cubits to its breadth; whereas Solomon's temple is said to have been but [c] 20 cubits in breadth. But these different measures are to be understood in respect of the different distances between which the said measures were taken. The 20 cubits breadth, said of Solomon's temple, was only the breadth of the temple itself, measuring from the inside of the wall on the one side, to the inside of the wall on the other side. But the 60 cubits breadth in Cyrus's commission was the breadth of the whole building, measuring from the inside of the outer wall of it on the one side, to the inside of the outer wall on the other side. For [d] besides the temple itself, which contained the holy place, and the holy of holies, each 20 cubits broad, there were thick walls inclosing it on each side, and without them chambers on each side; then another wall, then a gallery, and then the outer walls of all inclosing the whole building, being 5 cubits thick; which altogether made up the whole breadth to be 70 cubits from out to out; from which deducting the 5 cubits breadth of the outer wall on each side, you have remaining the breadth of Cyrus's commission, that is, 60 cubits; which was the breadth of the whole building from the inside of one outer wall to the inside of the other. So that the difference of the said 20 cubits breadth, and of the said 60 cubits breadth, is no more than this, that one of them was measured from the inside to the inside of the inner walls, and the other from the inside to the inside of the outer walls of the said temple.

But the glory of Solomon's temple was not in the temple itself, much less in the bigness of it; for that alone, was but a small pile of building, [e] as containing no more than 150 feet in length, and 105 in breadth, taking the whole of it together from out to out; which is exceeded by many of our parish churches. The main grandeur and excellency of it consisted, 1*st*, In its ornaments, its workmanship being every where exceeding curious, and its overlayings vast and prodigious: for the overlaying of the holy of holies only, which was a room but 30 feet square,

---

[a] Haggai ii. 3.
[b] Ezra vi. 3.
[c] 1 Kings vi. 2. 2 Chron. iii. 3.
[d] See Lightfoot of the temple.
[e] See the representation of the temple, preceding page.

square, and 30 feet high, amounted ª to 600 talents of gold, which comes to 4,320,000 l. of our sterling money. 2*dly*, In its materials; for Solomon's temple was all built of new large stones, hewn out in the most curious and artful manner; whereas the second temple was mostly built of such stones only as they dug up out of the ruins of the former. 3*dly*, In its out-buildings; for the court, in which the temple stood, and that without it called the *court of the women*, were built round with stately buildings and cloysters; and the gates entering thereinto were very beautiful, and sumptuous; and the outer court, which was a large square encompassing all the rest, of 750 feet on every side, was surrounded with a most stately and magnificent cloyster, sustained by three rows of pillars on three sides of it, and by four on the fourth: and all the outbuildings then lay in their rubbish, without any prospect of a speedy reparation; and there could then be no such ornaments or materials in this new temple, as there were in the former. In process of time, indeed, all the out-buildings were restored, and such ornaments and materials were added, on Herod's repairing of it, that the second temple, after that, came little short herein of the former; and there ᵇ are some who will say, that it exceeded it. But still what was the main glory of the first temple, those extraordinary marks of the divine favour, with which it was honoured, were wholly wanting in the second. The Jews reckon them up in these ᶜ five particulars; 1. The ark of the covenant and the mercy-seat which was upon it; 2. The *Shechinah*, or divine presence; 3. The *Urim and Thummim*; 4. The holy fire upon the altar; and, 5. The spirit of prophecy.

I. The ark of the covenant was ᵈ a small chest, or coffer, three feet nine inches in length, and two feet three inches in breadth, and two feet three inches in height; in which were put the two tables of the law, as well as the broken ones (say the Rabbins) ᵉ as the whole; and that there was nothing else in it,

---

ª 2 Chron. iii. 8.
ᵇ R. Azarias in Meor Enaiim, part 3. c. 51.
ᶜ Talmud Bab. in Yoma, c. 1. f. 21. and Talmud Hierosol. in Taanith, c. 2. f. 65.
ᵈ Exod. xxv. 10—22.
ᵉ For the proof of this, they bring the 2d verse of the 10th chapter of Deuteronomy, which they read thus: *And I will write on the tables the words that were on the first table, which thou breakest, and hast put in the ark.* And it is true, the word is VESHAMATA, *i. e. and thou hast put*, in the preter tense; but it being with a *vau* before it, that turns the preter tense into the future, and therefore it must be read, *and thou shalt put them*, as in our translation, and not *and thou hast put them*, as the fautors of this opinion would have it.

it, when it was brought into Solomon's temple, is said in two places [a] of scripture. But the Rabbins raise a controversy concerning Aaron's rod and the pot of manna, and the original volume of the law written by Moses's own hand, whether they were not also in the ark. It is said of [b] Aaron's rod, and the pot [c] of manna, that they were laid up before the testimony; and it being agreed on all hands, that by the testimony are meant the two tables, those who interpret these words [*before the testimony*] in the strictest sense, will have the said rod and pot of manna to have been laid up immediately before the tables within the ark; for otherwise (say they) they would not have been laid up before the testimony, but before the ark. But others, who do not understand the word in so strict a sense, say, they were laid up in the holy of holies without the ark, in a place just before it; thinking that in this position, without the ark, they may be as well said to be laid up before the testimony or tables of the law, as if they had been placed immediately before them within the ark. But the holy apostle St Paul decides this controversy; for he positively tells us, *That* [d] *within the ark were the golden pot, that had manna, and Aaron's rod, and the tables of the covenant*. As to the book, or volume of the law, it being commanded to be put [e] *mitzzad*, i. e. *on the side* of the ark, those who interpret that word of the inside, place it within the ark, and those who interpret it of the outside, place it on the outside of it, in a case or coffer made of purpose for it, and laid on the right side, meaning, by the right side, that end of it which was on the right hand. And the last seem to be in the right as to this matter; for, 1*st*, The same word, [f] *mitzzad*, is made use of, where it is said, that the Philistines sent back the ark with an offering of jewels of gold put in a coffer *by the side of it*. And there it is certain that word must be understood of the outside, and not of the inside. 2*dly*, The ark was not of capacity enough to hold the volume of the whole law of Moses with the other things placed therein. 3*dly*, The end of laying up the original volume of the law in the temple was, that it might be reserved there, as the authentic copy, by which all others were to be corrected, and set right; and therefore, to answer this end, it must have been placed so, as that access might be

---

[a] 1 Kings viii. 9. 2 Chron. v. 10.

[b] Numb. xvii. 10.

[c] Exod. xvi. 33. where to lay up before the Lord, is, by the Jewish commentators, interpreted as the same with before the testimony of the Lord.

[d] Hebrews ix. 4. and hereto agree Abarbanel on 1 Kings viii. 9. & R. Levi Ben Gerfom.

[e] Deut. xxxi. 26.

[f] 1 Sam. vi. 8.

be had thereto on all occasions requiring it; which could not have been done, if it had been put within the ark, and shut up there by the cover of the mercy-seat over it, which was not to be removed. And, 4*thly*, When [a] Hilkiah the high priest, in the time of Josiah, found the copy of the law in the temple, there is nothing said of the ark; neither is it there spoken of, as taken from thence, but as found elsewhere in the temple. And therefore, putting all this together, it seems plain, that the volume of the law was not laid within the ark, but had a particular coffer, or repository of its own, in which it was placed on the side of it. And the word *mitzzad*, which answers to the Latin, *a latere*, cannot truly bear any other meaning in the Hebrew language. And therefore the Chaldee paraphrase, which goes under the name of Jonathan, Ben Uzziel, in paraphrasing on these words of Deuteronomy, [b] *Take this book of the law, and put it in the side of the ark of the covenant,* renders it thus, *Take the book of the law, and place it in a case, or coffer, on the right side of the ark of the covenant of the Lord your God.* Over [c] the ark was the mercy-seat, and it was the covering of it. It was all made of solid gold, and of the thickness (say the Rabbins) of an hand's breadth. At the two ends of it were two cherubims, looking inward towards each other, with wings expanded, which embracing the whole circumference of the mercy seat, did meet on each side in the middle; all which (say the [d] Rabbins) was made out of the same mass, without joining any of the parts by solder. [e] Here it was where the *Shechinah*, or divine presence, rested both in the tabernacle and temple, and was visibly seen in the appearance of a cloud over it: and from hence [f] the divine oracles were given out by an audible voice, as often as God was consulted in the behalf of his people. And hence it is, that God is so often said in scripture [g] to dwell between the cherubims, that is between the cherubims on the mercy-seat, because there was the seat or throne of the visible appearance of his glory among them. And [h] for this reason the high priest appeared before this mercy-seat once every year, on the great day of expiation, when he was to make his nearest approach to the divine presence, to mediate, and make atonement for the whole people of Israel. And all else of that nation, who served God according

[a] 2 Kings xxii. 8.
[b] Deut. xxxi. 26.
[c] Exod. xxv. 17.---22.
[d] R. Levi Ben Gersom, R. Solomon, Abarbanel, and others.
[e] Levit. xvi. 2.
[f] Exod. xxv. 22. Numb. vii. 89.
[g] 1 Sam. iv. 4. 2 Sam. vi. 2. 2 Kings xix. 15. 1 Chron. xiii. 6. Psal. lxxx. 1. & xc. 1.
[h] Levit. xvi. 29.---34. Numb. xxix. 7. Heb. ix. 7. Talmud in Yoma.

to the Levitical law, made it the centre of their worship, not only in the temple, when they came up thither to worship, but every where else in their difperfion through the whole world; whenever they prayed, [a] they turned their faces towards the place where the ark ftood, and directed all their devotions that way. And therefore the author of the book [b] Cozri juftly faith, that the ark, with the mercy-feat, and cherubim, were the foundation, root, heart, and marrow, of the whole temple, and all the Levitical worship therein performed. And therefore, had there nothing elfe of the firft temple been wanting in the fecond but the ark only, this alone would have been reafon enough for the old men to have wept, when they remembered the firft temple in which it was, and alfo for the faying of Haggai, That the [c] fecond temple was as nothing in comparifon of the firft; fo great a part had it in the glory of this temple, as long as it remained in it. However, the defect was fupplied as to the outward form: for in [d] the fecond temple, there was alfo an ark made of the fame fhape and dimenfions with the firft, and put in the fame place. But though it was there fubftituted in its ftead (as there was need that fuch an one fhould for the fervice that was annually performed before it on the great day of expiation), yet it had none of its prerogatives or honours conferred upon it; for there were no tables of the law, no Aaron's rod, no pot of manna in it, no appearance of the divine glory over it, no oracles given from it. The firft ark was made and confecrated by God's appointment, and had all thefe prerogatives and honours given unto it by him. But the fecond, being appointed and fubftituted by man only, to be in the ftead and place of the other, could have none of them. And the only ufe that was made of it, was to be a reprefentative of the former on the great day of expiation; and to be a repofitory of the holy fcriptures, that is, of the original copy of that collection which was made of them after the captivity, by Ezra and the men of the great fynagogue; as will be hereafter related: for when this copy was perfected, it was there laid up in it. And, in imitation hereof, the Jews, in all their fynagogues, have a like [e] ark or coffer, of the fame fize or form, in which they keep the fcriptures belonging to the fynagogue; and from whence they take it out with great folemnity, whenever they ufe it, and return it with the like, when they have done with it. That there was any ark at all in the fecond temple, many of the Jewifh writers do deny; and fay, that the whole

[a] 1 Kings viii. 48. Daniel v. 10.
[b] Part II. § 28.
[c] Chap. ii. 3.
[d] Lightfoot of the temple, c. 15. § 4.
[e] Vide Buxtorfii Synagogam, c. 14.

whole service of the great day of expiation was performed in the second temple, not before any ark, but before ª the stone on which the ark stood in the first temple. But since, on their building of the second temple, they found it necessary, for the carrying on of their worship in it, to make a new altar of incense, a new shew-bread table, and a new candlestick, instead of those which the Babylonians had destroyed, though none of them could be consecrated as in the first temple, there is no reason to believe, but that they made a new ark also; there being as much need of it, for the carrying on of their worship, as there was of the others. And since the holy of holies, and the vail that was drawn before it, were wholly for the sake of the ark, what need had there been of these in the second temple, if there had not been the other also? Were it clear, that it is the figure of the ark that is on the triumphal arch of Titus, still remaining at Rome, this would be an undeniable demonstration for what I here say: for therein his triumph for the taking of Jerusalem being set forth in sculpture, there is to be seen, even to this day, carried before him in that triumph, the golden candlestick, and another figure, which Adrichomius and some others say is the ark: but Villalpandus, Cornelius a Lapide, Ribara, and the generality of learned men, who have viewed that triumphal arch, tell us, that is the table of shewbread. The obscurity of the figures, now almost worn out by length of time, makes the difficulty: but, by the exactest draughts that I have seen of it, it plainly appears to have been the shew-bread table, especially from the two cups on the top of it: for two such cups filled with frankincense were always put upon the shew-bread table, but never upon the ark. Josephus, who was present at the triumph of Titus, and saw the whole of it, ᵇ tells us of three things therein carried before him: 1*st*, The shew-bread table; 2*dly*, The golden candlestick (which he mentions in the same order, as they are on the arch); and, 3*dly*, The law, which is not on the arch. Most likely it was omitted there only for want of room to engrave it: for as there is the figure of a table carried aloft before the shew-bread table, and another before the golden candlestick, to express, by the writings on them, what the things were, which they were carried before; so, after the golden candlestick, there is on the said arch a third table without any thing after it; the arch there ending, without affording room for any other sculpture; where the thing omitted, no doubt, was what Josephus saith was carried

---

ª This the Rabbins call the stone of foundation, and give us a great deal of trash about it. See the Mishna in Yoma; & Buxtor. de Arça, c. 22.
ᵇ Josephus de Bello Judaico, lib. 7. c. 17.

ried in the third place, that is, the law; which is not to be understood of any common volume (of which there were hundreds every where in common use, both in their synagogues and in private hands), but of that which was found in the temple (as the other two particulars were), and laid up there, as the authentic and most sacred copy of it. And it cannot be imagined, it should be carried otherwise, than in that repository in which it was laid, that is, in the ark which was made for it under the second temple. But, to return to the ark under the first temple, which was that I was describing: it was made [a] of wood, excepting only the mercy-seat, but overlaid with gold all over, both in the inside and the outside, and it had a ledge of gold surrounding it on the top, in form of a crown; into which, as into a socket, the cover was let in. The place where it stood was the [b] innermost and most sacred part of the temple, called The holy of holies, and sometimes The most holy place, which was ordained and made of purpose for its reception; the whole end and reason of that most sacred place being none other, but to be a tabernacle for it. This place or room was [c] of an exact cubic form, as being 30 feet square and 30 feet high. In the centre of it the ark was placed upon a stone (say [d] the Rabbins), rising there three fingers breadth above the floor, to be, as it were, a pedestal for it. On the two sides of it stood [e] two cherubims 15 feet high, one on the one side, and the other on the other side, at equal distance between the centre of the ark and each side-wall; where, having their wings expanded, with two of them they touched the said side-walls, and with the other two they did meet, and touch each other exactly over the middle of the ark; so that the ark stood exactly in the middle between these two cherubims. But it is not in respect of these, that God is so often said in scripture to dwell between the cherubims, but in respect of the cherubims only, which were on the mercy-seat, as hath been observed: for most of those places of scripture, wherein this phrase is found, were written before Solomon's temple was built; and till then there were no such cherubims in the most holy place; for they were put there in the temple only, and not in the tabernacle. These cherubims stood not with their faces outward, as they are commonly represented, but with their faces [f] inward; and therefore were in the posture of figures worshipping, and not in the posture of figures to be worshipped, as some fautors of idolatry do assert.

---

[a] Exod. xxv. 10—22.
[b] 1 Kings viii. 16.
[c] 1 Kings vi. 20.
[d] Yoma, c. v. § 2.
[e] 1 Kings vi. 23. 2 Chron. iii. 10.
[f] 2 Chron. iii. 13.

assert. The ark, while it was ambulatory with the tabernacle, was carried [a] by staves on the shoulders of the Levites. These staves were overlaid with gold, and put through golden rings made for them, not on the sides of the ark, as all hitherto have asserted, but on the two ends of it; which plainly appears from this, that, when it was carried into the temple of Solomon, and fixed there in the most holy place, which was ordained and prepared of purpose for it, the scriptures tell us, [b] that the staves being drawn out, reached downward towards the holy place, which was without the most holy place, or holy of holies: for, had they been on the sides of the ark lengthway, they would, on their being drawn out, have reached towards the side-wall, and not downward, unless you suppose the ark to have been there put sideway, with one of its ends downward, and the other upward; which no one will say. And it is a plain argument against it, that the high priest, when he appeared before the ark on the great day of expiation, is said to have gone up to it [c] between the staves; but if these staves had been drawn out from the sides, there would then have been but two feet three inches between them, which would not have afforded the high priest room enough, with all his vestments on, to have passed up between them towards the ark, for the performance of that duty. Neither could the bearers, in so near a position of the staves to each other, go with any convenience in the carrying of the ark from place to place on their shoulders, but they must necessarily have incommoded each other, both before and behind, in going so near together. What became of the old ark, on the destruction of the temple by Nebuchadnezzar, is [d] a dispute among the Rabbins. Had it been carried to Babylon with the other vessels of the temple, it would again have been brought back with them at the end of the captivity. But that it was not so, is agreed on all hands; and therefore it must follow, that it was destroyed with the temple; as were also the altar of incense, the shewbread-table, and the golden candlestick: for all these in the second temple were made a-new after the rebuilding of it. However, the Jews contend, that it was hid and preserved by Jeremiah, say some, out of the [e] second book of Maccabees. But [f] most of them will have it, that King Josiah, being foretold by Huldah the prophetess, that the temple would speedily

---

[a] Exod. xxv. 13. 14. &c. & xxvii. 5. Numb. iv. 4—6. 1 Chron. xv. 15.
[b] 1 Kings viii. 8. 2 Chron. v. 9.
[c] Mishna in Yoma, c. v. Maimonides in Avodhath. Yom Haccipurim.
[d] Vide Buxtorfium de Arca, c. 21. 22.
[e] 2 Maccabees ii.
[f] Vide Buxtorfium, ibid.

speedily after his death, be deſtroyed, cauſed the ark to be put in a vault under ground, which Solomon, foreſeeing this deſtruction, had cauſed of purpoſe to be built, for the preſerving of it. And, for the proof hereof, they produce the text, where Joſiah commands the Levites [a] to put the holy ark in the houſe "which Solomom the ſon of David, king of Iſrael, did build;" interpreting it of his putting of the ark into the ſaid vault, where, they ſay, it hath lain hid ever ſince, even to this day, and from thence ſhall be manifeſted, and brought out again in the days of the Meſſiah; whereas the words import no more, than that Manaſſeh, or Ammon, having removed the ark from whence it ought to have ſtood, Joſiah commanded it again to be reſtored into its proper place. Other dotages of the Rabbins concerning this ark I forbear troubling the reader with.

II. The ſecond thing wanting in the ſecond temple, which was in the firſt, was the *Shechinah*, or the divine preſence, manifeſted by a viſible cloud reſting over the mercy-ſeat, as hath been already ſhewn. This cloud did there firſt appear when Moſes conſecrated the tabernacle, and was afterwards, on the conſecrating of the temple by Solomon, tranſlated thither. And there it did continue in the ſame viſible manner, till that temple was deſtroyed; but, after that, it never appeared more. Its conſtant place was [b] directly over the mercy-ſeat; but it reſted there only, when the ark was in its proper place, in the tabernacle firſt, and afterwards in the temple, and not while it was in movement from place to place, as it often was during the time of the tabernacle.

III. The third thing wanting in the ſecond temple, which was in the firſt, was the *Urim and Thummim*. Concerning this many have written very much; but, by offering their various opinions, have helped rather to perplex than explain the matter. The points to be inquired into concerning it, are theſe two, 1ſt, What it was? and, 2dly, What was the uſe of it?

1ſt, As to what it was, the ſcripture hath no where explained it any farther, than to ſay, that it was [c] ſomething which Moſes did put into the breaſt-plate of the high prieſt. This breaſtplate [d] was a piece of cloth doubled, of a ſpan ſquare, in which were ſet in ſockets of gold, 12 precious ſtones, bearing the names of the 12 tribes of Iſrael engraven on them; which being fixed to the *ephod*, or upper veſtment of the high prieſt's robes, was worn by him on his breaſt on all ſolemn occaſions.

[a] 2 Chron. xxxv. 3.
[b] Levit. xvi. 2.
[c] Exod. xxviii. 30. Levit. viii. 8.
[d] Exod. xxviii. 15—30. & xxix. 8—21.

THE HIGH PRIEST IN HIS ROBES.

In this breaſt-plate the *Urim and Thummim*, ſay [a] the ſcriptures, were put. They who hold them to have been ſome corporeal things there placed beſide the ſtones, will have them to be incloſed within the folding or doubling of the breaſt-plate, which, they ſay, was doubled for this very purpoſe, that it might be made fit, as in a purſe, to contain them in it. [b] Chriſtophorus a Caſtro, and from him [c] Dr Spencer, tells us, that they were two images, which being thus ſhut up in the doubling of the breaſt-plate, did from thence give the oracular anſwer, by a voice. But this is a conceit, which [d] a late very learned man hath ſufficiently ſhewn to be both abſurd and impious, as favouring more of heatheniſm and idolatry, than of the pure inſtitution of a divine law. Some will have them to be [e] the Tetragrammaton, or the ineffable name of God, which being written or engraven, ſay they, in a myſterious manner, and done in two parts, and in two different ways, were the things ſignified by the *Urim and Thummim*, which Moſes is ſaid to have put into the breaſt-plate; and that theſe did give the oracular power to it. And [f] many of the Rabbins go this way; for they have all of them a great opinion of the miraculous power of this name: and therefore, not being able to gainſay the evidence which there is for the miracles of Jeſus Chriſt, their uſual anſwer is, [g] that he ſtole this name out of the temple, from the ſtone of foundation on which it was there written (that is, the ſtone on which the ark formerly ſtood), and keeping it hid always about him, by virtue of that did all his wondrous works. Others, who hold in general for the addition of ſome things corporeal, denoted by the means of *Urim and Thummim*, [h] think not fit to inquire, what they were as to the particular, but are of opinion, that they were things of a myſterious nature, hid and cloſed up in the doubling of the breaſt-plate, which Moſes only knew of, who did put them there, and no one elſe was to pry into; and that theſe were the things that gave the oracular power to the high prieſt, when he had the breaſt-plate on. But this looking too much like a teleſme, or a ſpell,

which

---

[a] Exod. xxviii. 30. Levit. viii. 8.
[b] De Vaticinio.
[c] In Diſſertatione de Urim et Thummim.
[d] Dr Pocock in his comment on Hoſea, c. iii. ver. 4.
[e] Paraphraſis Jonathanis in Exod. xxviii. 30. Liber Zohar, fol. 105 Editionis Gremonenſis.
[f] R. Solomon, R. Moſes Ben Nachman, R. Becai, R. Levi Ben Gerſom, aliique.
[g] Toledoth Jeſu ex editione Wagenſelii, p. 6. 7. Raymundi Pugio Fidei, part 2. c. 8. Buxtorfii Lexicon. Rab. p. 2541.
[h] R. David Kimchi, R. Abraham Seva, Aben Ezra, aliique.

which were of thofe abominations that God abhorred, it will be fafeſt to hold, that the words *Urim and Thummim* meant no fuch things, but only the divine virtue and power, given to the breaſt-plate in its confecration, of obtaining an oraculous anfwer from God, whenever counfel was aſked of him by the high prieſt with it on, in fuch manner as his word did direct; and that the names of *Urim and Thummim* were given hereto only, to denote the clearnefs and perfection which thefe oracular anfwers always carried with them; for *Urim* fignifieth *light*, and *Thummim, perfection:* for thefe anfwers were not, like the heathen oracles, enigmatical and ambiguous; but always clear and manifeſt; not fuch as did ever fall ſhort of perfection, either of fulnefs in the anfwer, or certainty in the truth of it. And hence it is, that the *Septuagint* tranſlate *Urim and Thummim* by the words Δήλωσιν τῇ Ἀληθείαν, *i. e. manifeſtation and truth*, becaufe all thefe oracular anfwers given by *Urim and Thummim*, were always clear and manifeſt, and their truth ever certain and infallible.

2. As to the ufe which was made of the *Urim and Thummim*, it was to aſk counfel of God in difficult and momentous cafes relating to the whole ſtate of lfrael. In order whereto, the high prieſt did put on his robes, and over them his breaſt-plate, in which the *Urim and Thummim* were, and then prefented himfelf before God to aſk counfel of him. But he [a] was not to do this for any private man, but only for the king, for the prefident of the Sanhedrim, for the general of the army, or for fome other great prince or public governor in lfrael, and not for any [b] private affairs, but for fuch only as related to the public intereſt of the nation, either in church or ſtate: for he appeared before God, with the names of the twelve tribes of lfrael upon his breaſt-plate; and therefore, whatever counfel he aſked, was in the name and on the behalf of all the tribes, and confequently it muſt have been concerning matters which related publicly to them all. The place where he prefented himfelf before God, was [c] before the ark of the covenant, not within the vail of the holy of holies (for thither he never entered but once a-year, on the great day of expiation), but without the vail in the holy place: and there ſtanding with his robes and breaſtplate on, and his face turned directly towards the ark and the mercy-feat over it, on which the divine prefence reſted, he propofed the matter concerning which counfel of God was aſked, and

---

[a] Miſhnah in Yoma, c. 7. § 5. The Talmudiſts prove this from Numb. xxvii. 21. See Maimonides in cele Hammikdalh, c. 10. v. 12.

[b] Abarbanel in Exod. xxviii. & in Deut. xxxiii. R. Levi Ben Gerfom. Maimonid. ibid. aliique.

[c] Maimonides, ibid. Yalkut. fol. 248. col. 1.

CONSULTING THE HIGH PRIEST.

and directly behind him, at some distance without the holy place, perchance at the door (for farther no laymen could approach) stood the person in whose behalf the counsel was asked, whether it were the king, or any other public officer of the nation, there, with all humility and devotion expecting the answer that should be given. But how this answer was given is that which is made the great dispute. The [a] most common received opinion among the Jews is, that it was by the shining and protuberating of the letters in the names of the twelve tribes graven on the twelve stones in the breast-plate of the high priest, and that in them he did read the answer. They [b] explain it by the example which we have in the first chapter of the book of Judges. There the children of Israel, either by the president of the Sanhedrim, or some other officer intrusted with the public interest, did ask counsel of God; [c] "Who shall go up for us against the Canaanites first to fight against them?" The answer given by the high priest who did by *Urim and Thummim* then ask counsel of God for them, was, [c] "Judah shall go up:" for having asked the counsel, he did immediately (say they) look into the breast-plate, and saw there those letters shining above the rest, and protuberating beyond them; which being combined into words made up the answer which was given. And this notion was very ancient among them; for both [d] Josephus and [e] Philo Judæus have it; and from them several of the [f] ancient fathers of the Christian church give the same account of this matter. But there are unanswerable objections against it: for, 1*st*, All the letters of the Hebrew alphabet are not to be found in these 12 names, four of them, that is, *Cheth, Teth, Zaddi,* and *Koph,* being wholly wanting in them; and therefore an answer could not be given this way to every thing concerning which counsel might have been asked of God. To solve this, they have added the names of Abraham, Isaac, and Jacob to the breast-plate. But still the letter *Teth* will be wanting; and therefore, farther to botch up the matter, they have added also these words, *Col elleh shilte Israel,* i. e. *All these are the tribes of Israel.* But this is not only without any foundation in scripture, but rather contrary to it; for the description of the breast-plate in scripture being very particular,

---

[a] Maimonides in Cele Hammikdash, c. 10. § 11. Zohar in Exodum. Yalkut ex antiquo libro Siphre. R. Becai in Deut. xxxiii. 8. Ramban, R. Levi Ben Gersom. Abarbanel. R. Azarias in meor Enaiam, R. Abraham Seba, aliique.
[b] Abarbanel in Legem, Ramban in Legem.
[c] Judges i. 1. & i. 2.
[d] Antiq. lib. iii. c. 9.
[e] De Monarchia, lib. 2.
[f] Chrysostom. Hom. 37. adversus Judæos August. lib. 2. Questionum supra Exodum, aliique.

ticular, in the reckoning up of all its parts, seems plainly to exclude whatever is not there named. *2dly*, The assertors of this opinion do not tell us where the words which they would have added were placed in the breast-plate. They could not be written or engraven on the breast-plate itself; for that was only a piece of cloth. They must therefore be engraven, either on some of the twelve stones, or else on others set there on purpose for it. They could not be on any of the twelve stones, because on them were only engraven the names of the twelve tribes of Israel; and they could not be on other stones, because there were none other set there, but these twelve stones only. And in these two particulars the scriptures are sufficiently positive, to exclude all such additions. *3dly*, They that hold this opinion are forced to have recourse to the spirit of prophecy in the high priest, for the right combining of those shining and protuberating letters that were to make up the words of which the answer did consist; which is a difficulty of itself alone sufficient to explode this conceit. *4thly*, There were some answers given of that length (as particularly that in 2d Samuel, ch. v. ver. 23. 24.), that all the letters in the breast-plate, taking in all those also which the assertors of this opinion have added, will not suffice for them.

It would be too tedious to add all else that might be said to shew the absurdity of this opinion. Dr Spencer deservedly saith of it, that it is a talmudical camel, which no one that is in his wits can ever swallow.

There are also other opinions offered by others concerning this matter. But to me it appears plain from scripture, that when the high priest appeared before the vail to ask counsel of God, the answer was given him by an audible voice from the mercy-seat, which was within behind the vail. There it was that [a] Moses went to ask counsel of God in all cases, and from thence he was answered by an audible voice: for from thence God communed with him of all those things which he gave him in commandment unto the children of Israel. And in the same way did God afterwards communicate his will to the governors of Israel, as often as he was consulted by them, only with this difference, that whereas Moses, through the extraordinary favour that was granted unto him, had immediate access to the divine presence, and God did there commune with him, and speak to him, as it were, [b] face to face, as a man speaketh to his friend, none other was admitted thither to ask counsel of him, but through [c] the mediation of the high priest, who, in his

---

[a] Exod. xxv. 22. & xxx. 6. Numb. vii. 89.
[b] Exod. xxxiii. 11.
[c] Numb. xxvii. 21. Judg. xx. 28.

his stead, asked counsel for him by *Urim and Thummim*, that is, by presenting himself with the breast-plate on, over all his other robes, before the vail, exactly over against the mercy-seat, where the divine presence rested. And when he thus presented himself in due manner, according to the prescription of the divine law, God gave him an answer in the same manner as he did unto Moses, that is, by an audible voice from the mercy-seat. For in [a] many instances, which we have in scripture, of God's being consulted this way, the answer in every one of them, [b] except two, is ushered in with, *The Lord said;* and, when the Israelites made peace with the Gibeonites, they are blamed in that they asked not counsel [c] *at the mouth of God:* both which phrases seem plainly to express a vocal answer; and, taking them both together, I think, they can scarce import any thing else. And for this reason it is, that the holy of holies, the place where the ark and the mercy-seat stood, from whence this answer was given, is so often in scripture called [d] the oracle, because from thence the divine oracles of God were uttered forth to those that asked counsel of him.

This, I take to be plain, was the manner of consulting God by *Urim and Thummim* in the tabernacle; but how it was done in the camp raiseth another question: for it appeareth by scripture, that either the high priest, or another deputed in his stead, always went with the armies of Israel to the wars, and carried with him the ephod and breast-plate, therewith to ask counsel of God by *Urim and Thummim* in all difficult emergencies that might happen. Thus [e] Phinehas went to the wars against the *Midianites with the holy instruments,* that is, say the Jewish commentators, [f] with the ephod and the breast-plate, which were, say they, put into an ark or coffer made on purpose for it, and carried by Levites on their shoulders, as the other ark was. And of this ark they understand that place of scripture, where Saul saith to Ahiah the high priest, [g] *Bring hither the ark of God;* for this could not be the ark of the covenant: for that was then at Kirjath-jearim, and never ought to have been removed from its place

[a] Judg. i. 1. 2. xx. 18. 23. 28. 1 Sam. x. 22. xxiii. 2. 4. 11. 12. 2 Sam. ii. 1. & v. 19. 23.
[b] 1 Sam. xxx. 7. 8. 2 Sam. xxi. 1.
[c] Josh. ix. 14.
[d] Psal. xxviii. 2. 1 Kings vi. 5. 16. 19. 20—23. 31. & vii. 49. & viii. 6. 8. 2 Chron. iii. 16. iv. 20. & v. 7. 9.
[e] Numb. xxxi. 6.
[f] Paraphrasis Chaldaica, Jonathanis Ben Uzziel Textum interpretatur his verbis. Et misit eos Moses, et Phineasum, filium Eleazaris Sacerdotum, ad bellum, et Urim et Thummim Sanctitatis ad interrogandum per ea.
[g] 1 Sam. xiv. 18.

place in the tabernacle to be carried to the wars, or any where else from its proper station, and never was so but once against the Philistines; and then God gave the armies of Israel, and also the ark itself, into the hands of the enemy, for the punishment hereof. It must therefore have been no other ark which Saul called to Ahiah for, than that ark, or coffer, in which the ephod and breast-plate were carried; and the end for which he called for it, shews the thing; for it was to ask counsel of God, for which the ephod and breast-plate served. So that the saying of Saul to Ahiah, *Bring hither the ark*, importeth no more, than the saying of David afterwards to Abiathar in the like case, [a] *Bring hither the ephod*. For this ark was the coffer in which the ephod was kept, and with which Abiathar fled to David, when Saul destroyed his father's house. And of the same ark they understand the saying of Uriah the Hittite unto David, when he excused his not going to his house, and lying with his wife. [b] " The ark, and Israel, and Judah, abide in tents, and my lord Joab, and the servants of my lord, are encamped in the open fields; shall I then go into my house to eat, and to drink, and to lie with my wife?" For if this be understood of the ark of the covenant, and the tent or tabernacle in which it was kept, what he said would have been a reason for him never to have lain with his wife; for that was always kept in such a tent or tabernacle, till the temple of Solomon was built. It is most likely, therefore, that the ark which he speaks of was the ark, or coffer, in which the ephod and breast-plate were put, which the priest carried with him who was sent to the war.

The priest that was sent on this occasion, that he might be fully qualified to act in the high priest's stead, whenever there should be occasion for him to ask counsel of God by *Urim and Thummim*, was [c] consecrated to the office by the holy anointing oil, in the same manner as the high priest was; and therefore he was called, *The anointed for the wars*. But how he had the answer is the difficulty: for there was no mercy-seat in the camp to appear before, or from whence to receive the oracle, as there was in the tabernacle. And yet that such oracles were given in the camp is certain, from several instances which we have of it in scripture: for David did, by the ephod and breast-plate only, ask counsel of God [d] three several times, in the case of Keilah; and [e] twice at Ziklag, once on the pursuit of those who had burnt that city, and again on his going from thence for Hebron, there to take possession of
the

---

[a] 1 Sam. xxiii. 9.
[b] 2 Sam. xi. 11.
[c] Maimonides in Cele Hammikdash, c. 1. § 7. and in Melachim, c. 7.
[d] 1 Sam. xxiii.
[e] 1 Sam. xxx. 8. 2 Sam. ii, 1.

the kingdom of Judah, on the death of Saul; and on every one of thefe times he had an anfwer given him, though it is certain the ark of the covenant was not then prefent with him. It is moft likely, fince God allowed that counfel fhould be thus afked of him in the camp without the ark, as well as in the tabernacle where the ark was, that the anfwer was given in the fame manner by an audible voice. It feems moft probable, that the prieft anointed for the wars had a tent in the camp, on purpofe there erected for this ufe, in which a part was feparated by a vail, in the fame manner as the holy of holies was in the tabernacle, and that, when he afked counfel of God in the camp, he appeared there before that vail in the fame manner as the high prieft, on the like occafion, did before that in the tabernacle, and that the anfwer was given from behind it, though no ark or mercy-feat was there. And the words of Uriah above recited plainly refer us to fuch a tent. And it cannot be agreeable to a religion of fo much ceremony and folemnity, to fuppofe them to be without it for fo facred an office.

Although this way of afking counfel of God was frequently ufed during the tabernacle, and no doubt continued afterwards till the deftruction of Jerufalem by the Chaldeans, yet we have no inftance of it in fcripture during the whole time of the firft temple: and it is moft certain, that it was wholly wanting in the fecond temple; for [a] both Ezra and Nehemiah ell us as much. And hence is that faying among the Jews, that the Holy Spirit fpake to the children of Ifrael during the tabernacle by *Urim and Thummim*, and under the firft temple by the prophets, and under the fecond by [b] Bath-kol.

They who would have the *Urim and Thummim* abfolutely to have ceafed under the firft temple, give two reafons for it: 1. [c] That it was an appendant of the theocracy: for as long as God was the immediate governor of Ifrael, it was neceffary, fay they, that a method fhould be eftablifhed, whereby he might at all times be applied to and confulted with by his people; and, for this reafon, they tell us, the oracle by *Urim and Thummim* was appointed. But when the theocracy ceafed (which, they fay, it did, when Solomon the firft hereditary king fat upon the throne) this oracle ceafed with it. And, 2*dly*, they fay, that the *Urim and Thummim* was eftablifhed to afk counfel only about that which belonged to the common intereft of all Ifrael; and therefore,

---

[a] Ezra ii. 63. Neh. vii. 65.
[b] By this the Jews mean a voice from the clouds, fuch as was heard from thence concerning our Saviour, Matth. iii. 7. xviii. 5. 2 Pet. i. 17.
[c] Spencerus De Urim et Thummim, c. 2. § 2.

therefore, whenever the high priest asked counsel of God this way, it was with the names of all the tribes of Israel upon his breast, to denote that what was asked was for the common interest of all of them. But that common interest ceasing upon the division of the kingdom, this way of asking counsel of God must, in the nature of the thing, have then ceased also, as being no longer practicable. But how far these arguments may conclude, is left to every one to consider.

IV. The fourth thing wanting in the second temple, which was in the first, was the *holy fire*, which came down from heaven upon the altar. [a] It descended first upon the altar in the tabernacle at the consecrating of Aaron and his sons to the priesthood, and afterwards it descended a-new [b] upon the altar in the temple of Solomon, at the consecrating of that temple. And there it was constantly fed and maintained by the priests day and night, without suffering it ever to go out, in the same manner as it had been before in the tabernacle, and with this all the offerings were offered that were made by fire. And for using other fire were Nadab and Abihu consumed by fire from the Lord. This, say [c] some of the Jewish writers, was extinguished in the days of Manasseh. But the more general opinion among them is, that it continued till the destruction of the temple by the Chaldeans. After that it was never more restored; but instead of it they had only common fire in the second temple. For what is said of its being [d] hid in a pit by Jeremiah, and again brought thence, and revived upon the altar in the second temple, is a fable that deserves no regard.

V. The fifth thing wanting in the second temple, which was in the first, was the *spirit of prophecy*. But this was not wholly wanting there: for the prophets Haggai, Zachariah, and Malachi, lived after the second temple was built, and prophesied under it. But on their death, which (say the Rabbins) happened all in one year, the prophetic spirit wholly ceased from among them.

Besides these five things, there was wanting also a sixth, that is, *the holy anointing oil*, [e] which was made by Moses for the anointing and consecrating of the king, the high priest, and all the sacred vessels made use of in the house of God. And for this use it was commanded to be kept by the children of Israel throughout their generations. And therefore it was laid up before the Lord in the most holy place. And as the original copy of the the law was placed there on the right side of the ark of the
covenant;

---

[a] Lev. ix. 24.
[b] 2 Chron. vii. 1.
[f] Talmud in Zebachim, cap. 6.

[d] 2 Mac. i. 18. 19.
[e] Exod. xxx. 22—33.

covenant; so perchance the vessel containing this oil was placed on the other side of it, and there kept, till the first temple being destroyed, that also was destroyed with it. Every [a] king was not anointed, but only the first of the family: for he being anointed for himself, and all the successors of his race, they needed no other anointing; only if there arose any difficulty or dispute about the succession, then he that obtained it, though of the same family, was anointed anew to put an end to the controversy, and after that no one was to question the title; and this was the case of Solomon, Joash, and Jehoahaz. But [b] every high priest was anointed at his consecration, or first admission to the office, and so also was [c] the priest that went in his stead to the wars. The vessels and utensils that were anointed were the [d] ark of the covenant, the altar of incense, the shew-bread table, the golden candlestick, the altar of burnt-offerings, the laver, and all the other vessels and utensils belonging to them. And as by this [e] anointing they were first consecrated at the erecting of the tabernacle, by Moses, so in case any of them were afterwards decayed, destroyed, or lost, they could, as long as this anointing oil remained, be again restored, by making and consecrating new ones in their place, of the same virtue and holiness with the former. But this being wanting in the second temple, the want hereof caused a want of sanctity in all things else belonging to it: for although, on the return of the Jews from the Babylonish captivity, and the rebuilding of their temple, they did a-new make an ark, an altar of incense, a shew-bread table, a golden candlestick, an altar of burnt-offerings, and a laver, with the other vessels and utensils belonging to them, and did put them all in their former places, and applied them to their former uses; yet, through want of the holy anointing oil to consecrate them, these all wanted that holiness under the second temple, which they had under the first; and their high priest, who officiated in that temple, was no otherwise consecrated, than [f] by the putting on of his vestments. So that the want of this one thing only in the second temple, caused a great want and defect in all things else that were therein; every thing in it falling short of its former holiness by reason hereof. And therefore this anointing oil might well, under the second temple, have been reckoned among the principal things that were wanting in it. But the Jews superstitiously confine themselves

to

---

[a] Maimonides in Cele Hammikdash, c. 1. § 11.
[b] Exod. xxx. 30.
[c] Maimonides in Cele Hammikdash, c. 1. § 7.
[d] Exod. xxx. 26—29.
[e] Exod. xl.
[f] Maimonides in Cele Hammikdash, c. 1. § 8.

to the number of five particulars in this reckoning. For, in the 8th verse of the first chapter of Haggai, where God saith of the second temple, *I will take pleasure in it, and will be glorified,* the Hebrew word *Aicabedha,* i. e. *I will be glorified,* being written without the letter he at the end of it, which it ought to have been written with, they make a mystery of it, as [a] if this letter (which is the numerical letter for five) were there left out for this purpose, that the want of it might denote the five things of the first temple that were wanting in the second; and therefore will not add a sixth. But, however, there are some among them, who, to make room for it, contract the *Shechinah* and the *spirit of prophecy* under one and the same head, and, instead of them two (which are two of the particulars above mentioned), put *the Holy Spirit,* as reckoning them no other than different manifestations of the same Holy Spirit of God, the one in a place, and the other in a person, and thereby, without altering the number of five in the reckoning up of these defects, have given the holy anointing oil a place among them; and therefore name them [a] as followeth. 1. The ark of the covenant, with the mercy-seat; 2. The holy fire; 3. The *Urim and Thummim;* 4. The holy anointing oil; and, 5. The Holy Spirit. And these, as well as many other particulars of the glory of the first temple, being wanting in the second, there was reason enough for those to weep at the rebuilding of the second temple who remembered the first. But all these wants and defects were abundantly repaired in the second temple, [b] when the desire of all nations, the Lord, whom they sought, came to this his temple, and Christ our Saviour, who was the truest *Shechinah* of the divine majesty, honoured it with his presence: and, in this respect, the glory of the latter house did far exceed the glory of the former house. And herein the prophecies of the prophet Haggai, [c] which foretold it should be so, had a very full and thorough completion.

    The Samaritans, hearing that the Jews had begun to rebuild the temple of Jerusalem, came [d] thither, and,
An. 534. expressing a great desire of being admitted to worship God at the same temple in joint communion
Cyrus 3.
with them, offered to join with them in building of it; telling them, that, ever since the days of Esarhaddon, king of Assyria, they had worshipped the same God that they did. But Zerubbabel and Jeshua, and the rest of the elders of Israel, made answer to them, that they, not being of the seed of Israel, had nothing to do to build a temple to their God with them; that Cyrus's

---

[a] Talmud Hierosol. in Taanith, c. 2.   [c] Hag. ii. 9.
[b] Mal. iii. 1. Hag. ii. 7.   [d] Ezra iv.

rus's commiffion being only to thofe of the houfe of Ifrael, they would keep themfelves exactly to that, and, according to the tenor of it, build the houfe to the Lord their God themfelves, without admitting any other with them into the work. The reafon of this anfwer was, they faw they intended not fincerely what they faid, but came with an infidious defign to get an opportunity, by being admitted among them, of doing them mifchief. And, befides, they were not truly of their religion: for although, from the time that they had been infefted with lions in the days of Efarhaddon, they had worfhipped the God of Ifrael; yet it was only [a] in conjunction with their other gods, whom they worfhipped before, and therefore, notwithstanding their worfhip of the true God, fince they worfhipped falfe gods too at the fame time, they were in this refpect idolaters: and this was reafon enough for the true worfhippers of God to have no communion with them. At which the Samaritans being much incenfed, they did all they could to hinder the work; and although they could not alter Cyrus's decree, yet [b] they prevailed, by bribes and underhand dealings with his minifters, and other officers concerned herein, to put obftructions to the execution of it, fo that for feveral years the building went but very flowly on; which the Jews refenting, according as it deferved, this became the beginning of that bitter rancour which hath ever fince been between them and the Samaritans; which, being improved by other caufes, grew at length to that height, that nothing became more odious to a Jew than a Samaritan; of which we have feveral inftances in the gofpels; and fo it ftill continues. For, even to this day, a *Cuthean* (that is, a Samaritan) in their language, is the moft odious name among them, and that which, in the height of their anger, by way of infamy and reproach, they beftow on thofe they moft hate and abominate. And by this they commonly call us Chriftians, when they would exprefs the bittereft of their hatred againft us.

By thefe underhand and fubdulous dealings, the work of the temple being much retarded, and Cyrus's decree in many particulars defeated of its effect, this feems to have been the caufe, that, in the third year of Cyrus, in the firft month of that year, [c] Daniel did give himfelf up to mourning and fafting for three weeks together. After this, on the 24th day of that month, he faw the vifion concerning the fucceffion of the kings of Perfia, the empire of the Macedonians, and the conqueffs of the Romans; of which the three laft chapters of his prophecies contain an account. And, by what is written in the conclufion of

[a] 2 Kings xvii. 3. [b] Ezra iv. 5. Jofeph. Ant. lib. 11. c. 2. [c] Dan.

the laſt of them, he ſeems to have died ſoon after; and his great age makes it not likely that he could have ſurvived much longer. For the third of Cyrus being the 73d year of his captivity, if he were 18 years old at his carrying to Babylon (as I have ſhewn before, is the leaſt that can be ſuppoſed), he muſt have been in the 91ſt year of his age at this time; which was a length of years given to few in thoſe days. He was a very extraordinary perſon both in wiſdom and piety, and was favoured of God, and honoured of men, beyond any that had lived in his time. His prophecies concerning the coming of the Meſſiah, and other great events of after-times, are the cleareſt and the fulleſt of all that we have in the holy ſcriptures, inſomuch that [a] Porphyry, in his objections againſt them, ſaith, they muſt have been written after the facts were done: for it ſeems they rather appeared to him to be a narration of matters afore tranſacted, than a prediction of things to come; ſo great an agreement was there between the facts, when accompliſhed, and the prophecies which foretold them. But, notwithſtanding all this, [b] the Jews do not reckon him to be a prophet; and therefore place his prophecies only among the Hagiographa: and they ſerve the pſalms of David after the ſame rate. The [c] reaſon which they give for it in reſpect of both is, that they lived not the prophetic manner of life, but the courtly; David in his own palace, as king of Iſrael, and Daniel in the palace of the king of Babylon, as one of his chief counſellors and miniſters in the government of that empire. And, in reſpect of Daniel, they further add,[d] that, although he had divine revelations delivered unto him, yet it was not in the prophetic way, but by dreams and viſions of the night, which they reckon to be the moſt imperfect manner of revelation, and below the prophetic. But [e] Joſephus, who was one of the ancienteſt writers of that nation, reckons him among the greateſt of the prophets; and ſays further of him, that he had familiar converſe with God, and did not only foretell future events, as other prophets did, but alſo determined the time, when they ſhould come to paſs; and that, whereas other prophets only foretold evil things, and thereby drew on them the ill-will both of princes and people, Daniel was a prophet of good things to come, and, by the good report which his

predictions

[a] Hieronymus in Prooemio ad Comment. in Danielem.
[b] Hieronymi Præfatio in Danielem. Maimonides in Moreh Nevochim., part 2. c. 45.
[c] Vide Grotium in Præfatione ad Comment. in Eſaiam, et Huetii demonſtrationem Evangelicum, prop. 4. c. 14. § de propheta Danielis.
[d] Maimonides, ibid. David Kimchi in Præfatione ad Comment. in Pſalmos.
[e] Antiq. lib. 10. c. 12.

BOOK III.   THE OLD AND NEW TESTAMENT.   169

predictions carried with them on this account, reconciled to himself the good will of all men. And the event of such of them as were accomplished, procured to the rest a thorough belief of their truth, and a general opinion that they came from God. But what makes most for this point with us, against all that contradict it, our Saviour Christ acknowledgeth Daniel to be a prophet; for [a] he so styles him in the gospel. And this is a sufficient decision of this matter.

But Daniel's wisdom reached not only to things divine and political, but also to arts and sciences, and particularly to that of architecture. And [b] Josephus tells us of a famous edifice built by him at Susa in the manner of a castle (which he saith was remaining to his time), and finished with such wonderful art, that it then seemed as fresh and beautiful, as if it had been newly built. Within this edifice, he saith, was the place where the Persian and Parthian kings used to be buried; and that, for the sake of the founder, the keeping of it was committed to one of the Jewish nation, even to his time. The copies of Josephus that are now extant, do indeed place this building in Ecbatana in Media; but [c] St Jerome, who gives us the same account of it word for word out of Josephus, and professeth so to do, placeth it in Susa in Persia; which makes it plain, that the copy of Josephus, which he made use of, had it so: and it is most likely to have been the true reading; for Susa being within the Babylonish empire, the scripture tells us, that Daniel had sometimes his residence [d] there; and the common tradition of those parts hath been for many ages past, that [e] Daniel died in that city, which is now called *Tuster*, and there they shew his monument even to this day. And it is to be observed, that Josephus calls this building *Baris*, which is the same name by which Daniel himself calls the castle or palace at Shushan or Susa. For what we translate, [f] at Shushan in the palace, is, in the original, Beshushan Habirah, where, no doubt, the *Birah* of Daniel is the same with the *Baris* of Josephus; and both signify this palace or castle there built by Daniel, while he was governor of that province: for [g] *there he did the king's business*, i. e. was governor for the king of Babylon.

Part of the book of Daniel is originally written in the Chaldee language, that is, from the 4th verse of the 2d chapter to the end of the 7th chapter: for there the holy prophet treating of Babylonish affairs, he wrote of them in the Chaldee or Babylonish language.

[a] Matth. xxiv. 15.
[b] Antiq. lib. 10. c. 12.
[c] Comment. in Dan. viii. 2.
[d] Susa, or Shushan.
[e] Benjaminis Itinirarium.
[f] Dan. viii. 2.
[g] Dan. viii. 27.

language. All the rest is in Hebrew. The [a] Greek translation of this book, used by the Greek churches, through all the eastern countries, was that which was translated by Theodotion. In the vulgar Latin edition of the Bible, there is added in the 3d chapter, after the 23d verse, between that and the 24th verse, the song of the three children; and, at the end of the book, the history of Susanna, and of *Bel and the Dragon;* and the former is made the 13th and the other the 14th chapter of the book in that edition. But these additions [b] were never received into the canon of holy writ by the Jewish church; neither are they extant either in the Hebrew, or the Chaldee language; nor is there any evidence that they ever were so. That there are Hebraisms in them can prove no more, than that they were written by an Hebrew in the Greek tongue, who transferred the idioms of his own tongue into that which he wrote in, as is usual in this case. And that they were thus originally written in the Greek tongue by some hellenistical Jew, without having any higher fountain from whence they are derived, appears from this, that in the history of Susanna, Daniel, in his replies to the elders, alludes [c] to the Greek names of the trees, under which, they said, the adultery, which they charged Susanna with, was committed; which allusions cannot hold good in any other language. However the church of Rome allows them to be of the same authority with the rest of the book of Daniel, and, by their decree [d] at Trent, having given them an equal place with it among the canonical scriptures. But the ancients never did so. Africanus, Eusebius, and Appolinarius, have rejected those pieces, not only as being uncanonical, but also as fabulous; and [e] Jerome gives the history of Bel and the Dragon no better title than that [f] of the fables of Bel and the Dragon. And others who have been content to admit them for instruction of manners, have yet rejected them from being parts of the canonical scripture;

---

[a] Hieronymus in Præfatione ad Danielem et in Prooemio ad Comment. in eundem.

[b] Hieronymus ibid.

[c] In the examination of the elders, when one of them said, *That he saw the adultery committed* ὑπὸ σχῖνον, i. e. *under a mastich tree,* Daniel answers in allusion to σχῖνον, *The angel of God hath received sentence of God* σχίσαι σε μέσον, i. e. *to cut thee in two.* And when the other elder said it was ὑπὸ πρῖνον, i. e. *under an holm tree,* Daniel answers in allusion to the word πρῖνον, *The angel of the Lord waiteth with the sword* πρίσαι σε μέσον, i. e. *to cut thee in two.* Vide Hieron. ibid.

[d] Sessione, 4ta.

[e] Hieronymus, ibid.

[f] Peter Comestor doth also so call them, as doth likewise Erasmus in Scol. super Præf. Hieronymi in Danielem.

ture; whom the Proteftant churches following herein, do give them a place in their Bibles among the apocryphal writings, but allow them not to be canonical.

In the death of Daniel, the Jews having loft a powerful advocate in the Perfian court, this gave their enemies the greater advantage of fucceeding in their defigns againft them. But although they prevailed by underhand dealings to divert thofe encouragements which Cyrus had ordered for the carrying on of the work, yet they could not put an open ftop to it. So that, as far as the Jews of themfelves were able, they ftill carried on the work; in which they were much helped by [a] the Tyrians and the Zidonians, not only in furnifhing them with mafons, and other workmen and artificers, but chiefly in bringing the cedars, which Cyrus had given them, out of the foreft of mount Libanus, from thence to Joppa by fea; from which place they were carried by land to Jerufalem. For the Tyrians and Zidonians, being wholly given to traffic and navigation, did very little addict themfelves to the planting of olive-yards, or vineyards, or the tillage of the ground; neither had they indeed any territory for either: for their gain being very great by fea, they did not fet themfelves to make any enlargements by land, but were in a manner pent up within the narrow precincts of the cities in which they dwelt; and therefore, having very little of corn, wine, or oil of their own, they depended moftly on their neighbours for thefe provifions; from whom they had them either for their money, or by way of barter and exchange for other commodities, which they fupplied them with, and they were moftly furnifhed this [b] way out of the Jews country, and therefore they readily affifted them with their labour and fhipping, to be fupplied with thefe neceffaries in exchange for it. So that as it was by their help that Solomon built the firft temple; fo alfo was it by their help that the Jews were enabled to build the fecond.

In the 7th year after the reftoration of the Jews [c] died Cyrus, their great benefactor, after he had reigned, from his firft taking on him the command of the Perfian and Median armies, [d] 30 years; from his taking of Babylon [e] nine years; and from his being fole monarch of the Eaft, after the death of Cyaxares, or Darius the Median, his uncle, feven [f] years, being at the time of his death [f] 70 years old. There are different accounts of the manner of his death. [g] Herodotus,

An. 530 Cyrus 7.

[a] Ezra iii. 7.
[b] Acts xii. 20.
[c] Cyropedia, lib. 8.
[d] Cicero de Divinatione, lib. 1.
[e] Can. Ptolemæi.
[f] Cyropedia, lib. 8.
[g] Lib. 1.

rodotus [a] Diodorus Siculus, and [b] Juftin, tell us, that, having invaded the Scythians, he was there cut off with all his army, confifting of 200,000 men. But [c] Xenophon makes him die in his bed as fortunately as he lived, amidft his friends, and in his own country: and this is by much the more probable account of the two; for it is by no means likely that fo wife a man as Cyrus, and fo advanced in years as he then was, fhould engage in fo rafh an undertaking, as that Scythian expedition is defcribed to be by thofe who tell us of it. Neither can it be conceived, how, after fuch a blow, his new erected empire could have been upheld, efpecially in the hands of fuch a fucceffor as Cambyfes was, or how it could be poffible, that he fhould fo foon after it be in a condition to wage fuch a war as he did with the Egyptians, and make fuch an abfolute conqueft of that country as he did. That fuch a wild-headed man could fettle himfelf fo eafily in his father's new-erected empire, and hold it in fuch quiet at home, and, fo foon after his coming to it, enlarge it, with fuch conquefts abroad, could certainly be owing to nothing elfe, but that it was founded in the higheft wifdom, and left to him in the higheft tranquillity. Befides, all authors agree, that Cyrus [d] was buried at Pafargada in Perfia; in which country, Xenophon faith, he died, and his monument there continued to the time of Alexander. But if he had been flain in Scythia, and his body there mangled by way of indignity to it, in fuch a manner as Herodotus and Juftin do relate, how can we fuppofe it could ever have been brought thence out of the hands of thofe enraged barbarians to be buried at Pafargada?

This Cambyfes, who fucceeded his father Cyrus, is [e] in fcripture called Ahafuerus. As foon as he was fettled in the throne, the enemies of the Jews knowing him to be of a temper fit to be worked upon for the doing of mifchief, inftead of oppofing the Jews in their building of the temple by fecret machinations, and underhand dealings with the minifters of the court, and other fubordinate officers, as they had hitherto done, they now openly addreffed to the king himfelf to put a ftop to the work. But it feems he had fo much refpect for the memory of his father, that he could not be induced publicly to revoke his decree. However, he otherwife defeated in a great meafure the defign of it, by feveral difcouragements which he put upon it; fo that the work went but heavily all his reign.

Anno 529.
Cambyfes 1.

Cambyfes

---

[a] Lib. 2. p. 90.
[b] Lib. 1. c. 8.
[c] Cyropedia, lib. 8.
[d] Strabo, lib. 15. p. 730. Plutarchus in vita Alexandri, Q. Curtius, Arrianus, aliique.
[e] Ezra iv. 6.

Cambyses had not long been king, ere [a] he re‑
solved upon a war with the Egyptians, by reason Anno 528.
of some offence taken against Amasis their king. Cambyses 2.
Herodotus tells us, it was because Amasis, when he desired of
him one of his daughters to wife, sent him a daughter of Apries,
instead of one of his own. But this could not be true, because
Apries having been dead above 40 years before, no daughter of
his could be young enough at that time to be acceptable to
Cambyses. They speak with more probability, [b] who say, it
was Cyrus, and not Cambyses, to whom this daughter of Apries
was sent. Her name, they say, was Nitetis; and for some time she
concealed her true parentage, and was content to go for the
daughter of Amasis. But, at length, having had several children
by Cyrus, and fully secured herself in his favour and affection,
she discovered to him the whole truth of the matter, and excited
him all she could to revenge upon Amasis her father's wrong;
which he intended to have done, as soon as his other affairs
would have permitted; but, dying before he could execute his
intentions, Cambyses (who they say was her son) undertook the
quarrel on her account, and made this war upon Egypt for no
other reason than to revenge upon Amasis the case of Apries.
But it is most likely, that whereas Amasis had subjected himself
to Cyrus, and become his tributary, he did on his death with‑
draw his obedience from his successor, and that this was the true
cause of the war; for [c] the carrying on whereof Cambyses
made great preparations both by sea and land. For the sea‑
service, he engaged the Cypriots and the Phœnicians to help him
with their fleets; and for the war by land, besides his other for‑
ces, he had a great number of Greeks, Ionians, and Æolians, in
his army, who were the main strength of it. But the greatest
help he had in this war, was from Phanes, an Halicarnassian,
who being a commander of some of the Grecian auxiliaries that
were in the service of Amasis, on some disgust given him, revolt‑
ed to Cambyses, and made those discoveries to him, of the na‑
ture of the country, the strength of the enemy, and the then
state of their affairs, as chiefly conduced to the making of that
expedition successful. And it was by his advice, that Cambyses
contracted with the Arabian king that lay next the borders of
Palestine and Egypt, to supply him with water, while he passed
the deserts that lay between these two countries; where ac‑
cordingly it was brought him on camels backs; without which
he could never have marched his army that way. Being there‑
fore

---

[a] Herodotus, lib. 2. Justin lib. Ægyptii apud Herodotum, lib. 3.
1. c. 9. Athenæus, lib. 13. p. 560. in initio Athenæus, ibid.
[b] Polyænus Stratagem. lib 8. et [c] Herodotus, lib. 3.

fore thus prepared, he invaded Egypt in the fourth year of his
reign. On his arrival on the borders, he found
Amasis was newly dead, and that Psammenitus his
son, being made king in his stead, was drawing together a great army to oppose him. To make his passage open
into the country, it was necessary for him to take Pelusium,
which was as the key of Egypt on that side. But that being a
strong place, it was like to give him much trouble: for the preventing hereof by the counsel, it is supposed of Phanes, he had
recourse to this stratagem. [a] Finding that the garrison were
all Egyptians, in an assault, which he made upon the city, he
placed a great number of cats, dogs, sheep, and other of those
animals, which the Egyptians reckoned sacred, in the front of
the army; and therefore the soldiers, not daring to throw a dart,
or shoot an arrow that way, for fear of killing some of those animals, Cambyses made himself master of the place without any
opposition: for these being the gods which the Egyptians then
adored, [b] it was reckoned the highest impiety to kill any of
them, and, when they died of themselves, they buried them
with the greatest solemnity. By the time that Cambyses had taken this place, [c] Psammenitus came up with his army to oppose his farther progress; whereon ensued a bloody battle between them. At the beginning of it, the Greeks that were in
Psammenitus's army, to be revenged on Phanes for his revolt to
the enemy, brought forth his children (whom he was forced to
leave behind him on his flight), and slew them in the front of
the battle, in the sight of both armies, and drunk their blood.
But this served them not in any stead for the victory: for the
Persians, being exasperated by a spectacle of so horrid a nature,
fell on with such fury and rage to revenge it, that they soon vanquished and overthrew the whole Egyptian army, and cut the
greatest part of them in pieces. The remainder fled to Memphis;
where Cambyses pursuing them, on his arrival thither, sent into the city by the Nile, on which it stood, a ship of Mitylene,
with an herald to summon them to a surrender; but the people
rising on him, in their rage slew the herald, and tore him and
all that were with him to pieces. But Cambyses, after a short
siege, having taken the place, sufficiently revenged their death,
causing ten Egyptians of the first rank to be publicly executed
for every one of those that were thus slain; and the eldest son of
Psammenitus was one of the number. As to Psammenitus himself, Cambyses was inclined to have dealt kindly with him: for
at first he gave him his life, and allowed him wherewith honourably

An. 526. Cambyses 4.

---

[a] Polyænus, lib. 7.
[b] Herodotus, lib. 2. Diodorus Siculus, lib. 1. p. 52.
[c] Herodotus, lib. 3.

nourably to live; but he not being contented herewith, endeavoured to raise new troubles for the recovery of his crown; whereon he was forced to drink bulls blood, and so ended his life. His reign was only six months. For so much time only intervened from the death of his father to the taking of Memphis; when he fell into the hands of the enemy, and all his power ceased; for hereon all Egypt submitted to Cambyses. This happened in the fifth year of his reign; and he reigned three years after. The Libyans, Cyrenians, and Barceans. hearing of this success, sent ambassadors with presents to make their submission to him. From Memphis he went to Sais, where the Egyptian kings, for several descents past, had kept their usual residence; and there, entering into the palace, caused the body of Amasis to be dug up out of his grave, and, after all manner of indignities had been offered thereto in his presence, he ordered it to be cast into the fire and burnt. Which rage against the carcase, sheweth the anger which he had against the man; and, whatsoever it was that provoked it, this seems to be the cause that brought him into Egypt.

Anno 521.
Cambyses 5.

The next year, which was the 6th of his reign, he designed three expeditions, the first against the Carthaginians, the second against the Hammonians, and the third against the Ethiopians. But, the Phœnicians refusing to assist him against the Carthaginians, who were descended from them (they being a colony of the Tyrians), and not being able to carry on that war without them, he was forced to drop this project. But, his heart being intent upon the other two, he sent ambassadors into Ethiopia, who, under that name, were to serve him as spies, to learn and bring him an account of the state and strength of the country. But the Ethiopians, being fully apprised of the end of their coming, treated them with great contempt. And the Ethiopian king, in return for the present they brought him from Cambyses, sent him back only his bow, advising him then to make war upon the Ethiopians, when the Persians could as easily draw that bow as they could; and in the mean time to thank the gods, that they never inspired the Ethiopians with a desire of extending their dominions beyond the limits of their own country. With which answer Cambyses being exceedingly exasperated, immediately on the receipt of it, in a mad irrational humour, commanded his army forthwith to march (without considering, that they were furnished neither with provisions nor any other necessaries for such an expedition), leaving only the Grecian auxiliaries behind, to keep the country in awe during his absence. On his coming to Thebes, in the Upper Egypt, he detached from his army 50,000 men to go

Anno 524.
Cambyses 6.

against

against the Hammonians, with orders to destroy their country, and burn the temple of Jupiter Hammon that stood in it. But, after several days march over the deserts, a strong and impetuous wind beginning to blow from the south, at the time of their dinner, raised the sands to such a degree, and brought them in such a torrent upon them, that the whole army was overwhelmed thereby, and perished. In the interim Cambyses madly marched on with the rest of the army against the Ethiopians, though he wanted all manner of provisions for their subsistence, till at length, they having eaten up all their beasts of burden, they came to feed upon each other, setting out every tenth man by lot for this purpose. By this Cambyses being convinced, that it was time for him to return, marched back his army to Thebes, after having lost a great part of it in this wild expedition; and from thence returned to Memphis; when he came thither, he dismissed all the Greeks to their respective homes; but, on his entry into the city, finding it all in mirth and jollity, because their god Apis had then appeared among them, he fell into a great rage, supposing all this rejoicing to have been for the ill success of his affairs. And, when he called the magistrates, and they gave him a true account of the matter, he would not believe them; but caused them to be put to death, as imposing a lie upon him. And then he sent for the priests, who made him the same answer, telling, him that their god, having manifested himself unto them (which seldom happened), it was always their custom to celebrate his appearance with the greatest demonstrations of joy that they could express. To this he replied, that if their god was so kind and familiar as to appear among them, he would be acquainted with him; and therefore commanded them forthwith to bring him unto him.

The chief god of the Egyptians was [a] *Osiris,* him they worshipped in the shape of a *bull,* and that not only in imagery, but also in reality. For they kept a bull in the temple of *Osiris,* which they worshipped in his stead. At Heliopolis he was called *Mnevis,* at Memphis, *Apis.* The marks of *Apis* [b] were these His body was to be all black, excepting a square spot of white on his forehead. He was also to have the figure of an eagle, say some, of an half moon say others, on his back, a double list of hair on his tail, and a scarabæus or knot under his tongue. When they had found such an one, they brought him with great rejoicing to the temple of *Osiris,* and there kept him, and worshipped him for that god, as long as he lived; and when he was dead,

---

[a] Herodotus, lib. 2. Diodorus Siculus, lib. 1.

[b] Herodotus, lib. 3. Plin. lib. 8. c. 46. Solinus, c. 35. Ammianus Marcellinus, c. 22.

dead, they buried him with great folemnity, and then fought for another with the fame marks, which fometimes it was many years ere they could find; and fuch a one they having found, on Cambyfes's return to Memphis from his Ethiopic expedition, this was the reafon of their great rejoicing at that time. And, in imitation of this idolatry was it, that Aaron made the golden calf in the wildernefs, and Jeroboam thofe in Dan and Bethel, and did fet them up there to be worfhipped by the children of Ifrael, as the gods that had brought them out of the land of Egypt.

This *Apis* being brought to Cambyfes, he fell into a rage, as well he might, at the fight of fuch a god, and drawing out his dagger, run it into the thigh of the beaft; and then, reproaching the priefts for their ftupidity and wretchednefs in worfhipping a brute for a god, ordered them feverely to be whipped, and all the Egyptians in Memphis to be flain that fhould be found any more rejoicing there on this occafion. The *Apis* being carried back to the temple, there languifhed of his wound, and died.

The Egyptians fay, that, after this act (which they reckon to have been the higheft inftance of impiety that was ever found among them), Cambyfes was ftricken with madnefs. But his actions fhewed him to have been mad long before; of which he continued to give divers inftances. They tell us of thefe following.

He had a brother, the only fon of Cyrus befides himfelf, and born of the fame mother; his name, according to Xenophon, was Tanoaxares, but Herodotus calls him Smerdis, and Juftin, Mergis. He accompanied Cambyfes in his Egyptian expedition; but being the only perfon among all the Perfians that could draw the bow which Cambyfes's ambaffadors brought him from the Ethiopian king, Cambyfes from hence contracted fuch an envy againft him, that he could no longer bear him in the army, but fent him back into Perfia. And not long after dreaming, that one came, and told him, that Smerdis fat on the throne, he thereon fufpecting of his brother what was afterwards fulfilled by another of his name, fent after him, into Perfia, Prexafpes, one of his chiefeft confidents, with orders to put him to death; which he accordingly executed. And when one of his fifters, who was with him in the camp, on the hearing of it, lamented his death, he gave her fuch a blow with his foot in the belly, that fhe died of it. She was the youngeft of his fifters, and, being a very beautiful woman, he fell violently in love with her, fo that nothing could fatisfy him, but that he muft have her to wife; whereon he called together all the royal judges of the Perfian nation, to whom the interpretation of their laws did belong, to know of them whether they had any law that would allow it. They being unwilling to authorise any such inceftuous marriage, and at the fame time fearing his violent temper, fhould they contradict him herein, they gave him this crafty anfwer: That they had no law indeed that permitted a brother to marry his fifter; but they had a law which allowed the king of Perfia to do what he pleafed. Which ferving his purpofe as well as a direct approbation of the thing, he folemnly married her; and hereby gave the firft example to that inceft which was afterwards practifed by moft of his fucceffors, and by fome of them carried fo far, as to marry their own daughters. This lady he carried with him in all his expeditions; and her name being Meroe, he from her gave [a] that name to the ifland in the Nile between Egypt and Ethiopia, on the conquering of it, which, in all our maps of the old geography, it ftill bears (for fo far he advanced in his wild march againft the Ethiopians). And fhe being with child by him, when he ftruck her, the blow caufed an abortion; and of this fhe died. And fo vile a marriage deferved no better an end. He caufed alfo feveral of the principal of his followers to be buried alive, without any caufe deferving of it, and daily facrificed fome or other of them to his wild fury. And when Crœfus advised him againft thefe proceedings, and laid before him the ill confequences which they would lead to, he ordered him to be put to death. And when thofe who received his orders, knowing he would repent of it the next day, did therefore defer the execution, he caufed them all to be executed for it, becaufe they had not obeyed his commands; although at the fame time he expreffed great joy that Crœfus was alive. And, out of a mere humour only, to fhow his fkill in archery, he fhot to death a fon of Prexafpes, who was the chief of his favourites. And in fuch wild actions he wore out the 7th year of his reign.

Anno 522.
Cambyfes 8.
In the beginning of the 8th year, he left Egypt, and returned towards Perfia. On his coming into Syria, he there met with an herald, who, being fent from Shufhan, came into the army, and there proclaimed Smerdis, the fon of Cyrus, king, and commanded all men to obey him. The meaning of this was, Cambyfes, when he departed from Shufhan on the Egyptian expedition, placed there in the fupreme government of his affairs, during his abfence, Patizithes, one of the chief of the Magians. This Patizithes had a brother, who did very much refemble Smerdis the fon of Cyrus, and was (for that reafon perchance) called by the fame name. As foon as he had been fully informed of the death of that prince
(which

[a] Strabo, lib. 17. p. 790. Jofeph. Antiq. lib. 2. c. 10.

(which had been concealed from most others), and found that the extravagancies of Cambyses were grown to an height no longer to be borne, he placed this brother of his on the throne, giving out that he was the true Smerdis the son of Cyrus; and forthwith sent out heralds into all parts of the empire to give notice hereof, and command obedience to be paid unto him. Cambyses having seized him that came with this message to the army, on the examining of him, and on the examining of Prexaspes, whom he had sent to kill his brother, found, that the true Smerdis was certainly dead, and that this was none other than Smerdis the Magian, who had invaded the throne; whereon, much lamenting that he had been led by the identity of the name to murder his brother, he gave orders for his army forthwith to set forward to suppress the usurper; but as he mounted his horse for the march, his sword falling out of the scabbard, gave him a wound in the thigh, of which he died in a few days after. The Egyptians remarking, that it was in the same part of the body where he had afore wounded the Apis, reckoned it as an especial judgement from heaven upon him for that fact, and perchance they were not much out in it; for it seldom happened, in an affront given to any particular mode of worship, how erroneous soever it may be, but that religion is in general wounded hereby. There are many instances in history wherein God hath very signally punished the profanations of religion in the worst of times, and under the worst modes of heathen idolatry. While he was in Egypt, having consulted the oracle of Butus in that country, he was told that he should die at Ecbatana; which understanding of Ecbatana in Media, he resolved to preserve his life by never going thither. But what he thought to avoid in Media he found in Syria: for the town where he lay sick of this wound, was of the same name, being also called Ecbatana; [a] of which when he was informed, taking it for certain, that he must there die, he called for all the chief of the Persians together,

and

---

[a] There are many instances of such, who, on their over-curious inquiry into their future fate, have been in the same manner deceived. Thus Henry IV. of England, being foretold that he should die at Jerusalem, was suddenly taken sick in the abbot of Westminster's house, and died there in Jerusalem chamber. And so Ferdinand the Catholic, king of Spain, being foretold, that he should die at Madrigal, carefully avoided going thither. But while he was thus, as he thought, avoiding his death, he found it at Madrigalejo, or Little Madrigal, a poor little village he had never before heard of. For as he was accidentally passing through it, he was suddenly taken ill; and, being carried into a poor cottage, the best reception the place could afford him, he died there, in an hole scarce large enough to receive his bed.

and acquainting them with the true state of the case, that his brother was certainly dead, and that it was Smerdis the Magian that then reigned, earnestly exhorted them not to submit to the cheat, and thereby permit the sovereignty to pass from the Persians again to the Medes, of which nation the Magian was; but to take care to set up a king over them of their own people. But the Persians thinking all this was said by him out of hatred to his brother, had no regard to it; but, on his death, quietly submitted to him whom they found on the throne, supposing him to be the true Smerdis. And it being the usage of the eastern kings in those times, to live retired in their palaces, and there transact all their affairs by the intercourse of their eunuchs, without admitting any else, unless those of their highest confidence, to have access to them, the Magian exactly observed this conduct; and therefore being never seen in public, this made it the harder for them to discover the cheat.

Cambyses reigned [a] seven years and five months: the remaining seven months of the 8th year was the reign of the Magian. Herodotus calls him Smerdis, (as hath been already said), Æschylus, Mardus, Ctesias, Spendadates, and Justin, Orapastes, but in the scripture he is called [b] Artaxerxes. As soon as he was settled in the kingdom, after the death of Cambyses, the Samaritans [c] wrote a letter to him, setting forth, that the Jews were rebuilding their city and temple at Jerusalem; that they having been always a rebellious people, there was reason to suspect, that, as soon as they should have finished that work, they would withdraw their obedience from the king, and pay no more toll nor tribute; which might give an occasion for all Syria and Palestine to revolt also, and the king be excluded from having any more portion on that side the river Euphrates. And, for the truth of what they had informed him of, as to the rebellious temper of that people, they referred him to the records of his predecessors, wherein they desired search might be made concerning this matter. On the receipt of this letter, examination being made, according to the purport of it, into the records of former times concerning the behaviour of the Jews under the Assyrian and Babylonish empires; and it being found in them with what valour they had long defended themselves, and with what difficulty they were at length reduced by Nebuchadnezzar, an order was issued forth to prohibit them from proceeding any further, and sent to the Samaritans to see it put in execution; who immediately, on the receipt hereof, went up to Jerusalem, and having exhibited their order to the Jews made them desist by force

---

[a] Herodotus, lib. 3.   [b] Ezra iv. 7.   [c] Ezra iv. 7—24.

force and power from going on any farther with the work of the house; so it wholly ceased till the second year of Darius king of Persia, for about the space of two years. The king that now reigned having been a chief leader of the sect of the Magians, against whom the Jews were in the utmost opposition in point of religion, the aversion he had to them on this account, no doubt, furthered this decree against them.

That Cambyses was the Ahasuerus, and Smerdis the Artaxerxes, that obstructed the work of the temple, is plain from hence, that they are said [a] in scripture to be the kings of Persia, that reigned between the time of Cyrus, and the time of that Darius by whose decree the temple was finished; but that Darius being Darius Hystaspis (as will be unanswerably demonstrated in its proper place), and none reigning between Cyrus and that Darius in Persia, but Cambyses and Smerdis, it must follow from hence, that none but Cambyses and Smerdis could be the Ahasuerus and Artaxerxes who are said in Ezra to have put a stop to this work.

But though Smerdis was thus unkind to the Jews, [b] he studied to shew grace and favour to all others, that so, gaining their affections, he might the better secure himself in the possession of the throne which he had usurped. And therefore, as soon as he had taken on him the sovereignty, he granted to all his subjects a freedom from taxes, and an immunity from all military services for three years; and also did so many other things for their benefit, as made his death to be very much lamented by a great many of them on the change that after followed. And farther, to secure himself, he took to wife Atossa the daughter of Cyrus, aiming thereby to hold the empire by her title, if in case of a discovery he could not be allowed to have any of his own: She had before been the wife of Cambyses: for, after he had, upon the decision above mentioned, married one of his sisters, he took this other to wife also. And the Magian, while he pretended to be her brother, married her on the same foot.

But these steps which he took for his security, made it the more suspected that he was not the true Smerdis; for if he were, there would have been no need (it was said) of using all these arts and precautions for his establishment in the empire. And the care which he took never to be seen in public augmented the suspicion. To be fully satisfied in this matter, Otanes a noble Persian, brother of Cassandana (who is said by Herodotus to have been mother to Cambyses, and the true Smerdis's brother) having a daughter named Phedyma, that had been one of Cambyses's wives, and was now kept by the Magian in the same quality, sent to her to know, whether it were Smerdis the son of Cyrus that

[a] Ezra iv. 5—7. [b] Herodotus, lib. 3.

that she lay with, or else some other man. The answer which she returned was, that she having never seen Smerdis the son of Cyrus, she could not tell. He then, by a second message, bid her inquire of Atossa (who could not but know her own brother) whether this were he or no? whereon she having informed him, that the present king kept all his wives apart, so that they never conversed with each other, and that therefore she could not come at Atossa to ask this question of her; he sent her a third message, whereby he directed her, that when he should next lie with her, she should take the opportunity, while he slept, to feel whether he had any ears or no: for Cyrus having caused the ears of Smerdis the Magian to be cut off for some crime that deserved it, he told her, that if the person she lay with had ears, she might satisfy herself, that he was Smerdis the son of Cyrus; but that if she found it was otherwise, he was certainly Smerdis the Magian, and therefore unworthy of possessing either the crown or her. Phedyma, having received these instructions, took the next opportunity of making the trial she was directed to; and finding hereon, that the person she lay with had no ears, she sent word to her father of it, and hereby the whole fraud became detected. Whereon Otanes, taking to him six other of the nobility of the Persians, entered into the palace, and there falling on the usurper, and his brother Patizithes, who had been the contriver of the whole plot, slew them both; and then bringing out their heads to the people, declared unto them the whole imposture. Which did set them into such a rage, that they fell on the whole sect which the impostor was of, and slew all of them that they met with that day. For which reason the said day on which this was done, thenceforth became an annual festival among them; and, for a long while after, it was celebrated every year by the Persians in commemoration of the discovery of this imposture, and their deliverance from it. And by reason of the great slaughter of the Magians then made, it was called Magofonia, or the slaughter-day of the Magians. And it was from this time that they first had the name of Magians; which signifying the *Cropt-ear'd*, it was then given unto them by way of nick-name and contempt, because of this impostor, who was thus cropped. For *mige-gush* signified, in the language of the country then in use, one that had his ears cropped; and, [a] from a ringleader of that sect who was thus cropped, the author of the famous Arabic Lexicon, called Camus, tells us, they had all this name given unto them. And what Herodotus, and Justin, and other authors, write of this Smerdis, plainly shews, that he was the man. After this the whole sect of the Magians grew into that

---

[a] Pocockii Specimen Historiæ Arabicæ, p. 146.

that contempt, that they would soon have sunk into an utter extinction, but that a few years after it was, under the name of a reformation, again revived by Zoroastres; of which an account will be hereafter given in its proper place.

In the interim, it may be proper to acquaint the reader, that at this time all the idolatry of the world was divided between two sects, [a] that is, the worshippers of images, who were called the Sabians, and the worshippers of fire, who were called the Magians. The true religion, which Noah taught his posterity, was that which Abraham practised, the worshipping of one God, the supreme Governor and Creator of all things, with hopes in his mercy through a mediator: for the necessity of a mediator between God and man was a general notion, which obtained among all mankind from the beginning; for being conscious of their own meanness, vileness, and impurity, they could not conceive, how it was possible for them, of themselves alone, to have any access to the all-holy, all-glorious, and supreme Governor of all things. They considered him as too high, and too pure, and themselves too low and polluted, for such a converse; and therefore concluded, that there must be a mediator, by whose means only they could make any address unto him, and by whose intercession alone any of their petitions could be accepted of. But no clear revelation being then made of the Mediator whom God had appointed, because as yet he had not been manifested unto the world, they took upon them to address unto him by mediators of their own chusing. And their notion of the sun, moon, and stars, being, that they were the tabernacles or habitations of intelligences, which animated those orbs in the same manner as the soul of man animates his body, and were the causes of all their motions; and that these intelligences were of a middle nature between God and them, they thought these the fittest beings to become the mediators between God and them. And therefore the planets being the nearest to them of all these heavenly bodies, and generally looked on to have the greatest influence on this world, they made choice of them in the first place for their gods-mediators, who were to mediate for them with the supreme God, and procure from him the mercies and favours which they prayed for; and accordingly they directed divine worship unto them as such. And here began all the idolatry that hath been practised in the world. They first worshipped them *per sacella*, that is, by *their tabernacles*, and afterwards by images

---

[a] Vide Pocockii Specimen Historiæ Arabicæ, p. 138. Golii Notas ad Alfraganum, p. 251. Maimonidem in Morch Nevochim. Hotingeri Historiam Orientalem, lib. 4. c. 8. Historiam religionis veterum Persarum per Thomam Hyde.

images also. By these *facella*, or *tabernacles*, they meant the orbs themselves, which they looked on only as the *facella* or *sacred tabernacles*, in which the intelligences had their habitations. And therefore when they paid their devotions to any one of them, they directed their worship towards the planet in which they supposed he dwelt. But these orbs, by their rising and setting, being as much under the horizon as above, they were at a loss how to address to them in their absence. To remedy this, they had recourse to the invention of images; in which, after their consecration, they thought these intelligences, or inferior deities, to be as much present by their influence, as in the planets themselves; and that all addresses to them were made as effectually before the one, as before the other. And this was the beginning of image-worship among them. To these images were given the names of the planets they represented, which were the same they are still called by. And hence it is, that we find Saturn, Jupiter, Mars, Apollo, Mercury, Venus, and Diana, to be first ranked in the polytheism of the ancients; for they were their first gods. After this a notion obtaining, that good men departed had a power with God also to mediate and intercede for them, they deified many of those, whom they thought to be such; and hence the number of their gods increased in the idolatrous times of the world. This religion first began among the Chaldeans; which their knowledge in astronomy helped to lead them to. And from this it was, that Abraham separated himself when he came out of Chaldea. From the Chaldeans it spread itself over all the East, where the professors of it had the name of Sabians. From them it passed into Egypt, and from thence to the Grecians, who propagated it to all the Western nations of the world. And therefore those, who mislike the notion advanced by Maimonides, [a] that many of the Jewish laws were made in opposition to the idolatrous rites of the Sabians, are much mistaken, when they object against it, that the Sabians were an inconsiderable sect, and therefore not likely to have been so far regarded in that matter. They are now indeed, since the growth of Christianity and Mahometism in the world, reduced to an inconsiderable sect; but anciently they were all the nations of the world that worshipped God by images. And that Maimonides understood the name in this latitude, is plain from hence, that he tells us, the Sabians, whom he spoke of, were a sect [b] whose heresy had overspread almost all mankind. The remainder of this sect still subsists in the East, under the same name of Sabians, which they pretend to have received from Sabius a son of Seth's. And among the books wherein the doctrines

[a] In Moreh Nevochim.   [b] Moreh Nevochim, part 1. c. 62.

trines of their sect are contained, they have one, which they call the book of Seth, and say, that it was written by that patriarch. That which hath given them the greatest credit among the people of the east is, that the best of their astronomers have been of this sect, as Thebet Ebn Korrah, Albattani, and others; for the stars being the gods they worshipped, they made them the chief subject of their studies. These Sabians, in the consecrating of their images, used many incantations, to draw down into them from the stars those intelligences for whom they erected them, whose power and influence they held did afterward dwell in them. And from hence the whole foolery of Telesms, which some make so much ado about, had its original.

Directly opposite to these were the Magians, another sect, who had their original in the same eastern countries; for [a] they abominating all images, worshipped God only by fire. They began first in Persia, and there, and in India, were the only places where this sect was propagated; and there they remain even to this day. Their chief doctrine was, that there [b] were two principles, one which was the cause of all good, and the other the cause of all evil, that is to say, God and the devil; that the former is represented by light, and the other by darkness, as their truest symbols; and that, of the composition of these two, all things in the world are made: the good god they name Yazdan, and also Ormuzd, and the evil god, Ahraman: the former is by the Greeks called Oramasdes, and the latter Arimanius. And therefore, when Xerxes prayed for that evil upon his enemies, that it might be put into the minds of all of them to drive their best and bravest men from them, as the Athenians had Themistocles, [c] he addressed his prayer to Arimanius the evil god of the Persians, and not to Oramasdes their good god. And concerning these two gods there was this difference of opinion among them, that whereas some held both of them to have been from all eternity, there were others that contended, that the good god only was eternal, and that the other was created. But they both agreed in this, that there will be a continual opposition between these two till the end of the world; that then the good god shall overcome the evil god, and that from thence forward each of them shall have his world to himself, that is, the good god his world with all good men with him, and the evil god

---

[a] Vide Pocockii specimen historiæ Arabicæ, p. 146, 147, &c et Historiam religionis veterum Persarum per Thomam Hyde.

[b] This opinion Manes, the heretic, received from them, and would have introduced it into the Christian religion, it being the principal point which those of his heresy, called from him Manichees, endeavoured to impose on the world.

[c] Plutarchus in Themistocle.

god his world with all evil men with him; that darkness is the truest symbol of the evil god, and light the truest symbol of the good god. And therefore they always worshipped him before fire, as being the cause of light, and especially before the sun, as being in their opinion the perfectest fire, and causing the perfectest light. And for this reason, in all their temples, they had fire continually burning on altars, erected in them for that purpose. And before these sacred fires they offered up all their public devotions, as likewise they did all their private devotions before their private fires in their own houses. Thus did they pay the highest honour to light, as being in their opinion the truest representative of the good god; but always hated darkness, as being, what they thought, the truest representative of the evil god, whom they ever had in the utmost detestation, as we now have the devil: and, for an instance hereof, whenever they had an occasion in any of their writings to mention his name, they always wrote it backward, and inversed, as thus, Ahrimen. And these were the tenets of this sect, when, on the death of Cambyses, Smerdis and Patizithes, the two chiefest ringleaders of it, made that attempt for the usurping of the sovereignty which I have mentioned.

The [a] seven princes, who had slain these usurpers, entering into consultation among themselves about the settling of the government, on the sixth day after, came to this agreement: That the monarchy should be continued in the same manner as it had been established by Cyrus; and that, for the determining which of them should be the monarch, they should meet on horseback the next morning against the rising of the sun, at a place in the suburbs of the city, which they had appointed for it, and that he whose horse should first neigh, should be the king; for the sun being then the great deity of the Persians, and equally adored by them all, whether of the Sabian or Magian sect, by this method they seemed to refer the election to it. But the groom of Darius, one of the seven princes, being informed of what was agreed on, made use of a device which secured the crown to his master; for the night before having tied a mare to the place where they were the next morning to meet, he brought Darius's horse thither, and put him to cover the mare; and therefore, as soon as the princes came thither at the time appointed, Darius's horse, at the sight of the place, remembering the mare, ran thither and neighed; whereon he was forthwith saluted king by the rest, and accordingly placed on the throne. He was the son of Hystaspes, a noble Persian of the royal family of Achæmenes, who had followed

An. 521.
Darius I.

[a] Herodot. lib. 3. Justin, lib. 1. c. 10.

lowed Cyrus in all his wars. He was at that time governor of the province of Persia, and so continued for many years after his son's advancement to the throne. This Darius, in the writings of the latter Persians, is called Gushtasph, and his father Lorasph; and, under these names, they are much spoken of in that country even to this day.

The empire of Persia being thus restored, and settled by the wisdom and valour of these seven princes, they were afterwards admitted to extraordinary honours and privileges under the new king; for they were to have access to his presence at all times, whenever they should desire, unless only when he was accompanying with any of his wives, and their advice was to be first had in the management of all the public affairs of the empire. And whereas the king only wore his turbant directly upright, and all others till then with its top reversed, or turned backward, these had it by way of special privilege granted unto them from thenceforth, to wear their turbants with the top turned forward. For they having, when they went in to fall upon the Magians, turned the back-part of their turbants forward, that they might by that signal be the better known to each other in the scuffle, in memory of this, as an especial mark of honour, they were permitted to wear their turbants in that manner ever afterward. And from this time the Persian kings of this race had always seven chief counsellors in the same manner privileged, who were their prime assistants in the government, and by whose advice all the public affairs of the empire were transacted; and under this character we find them both in [a] the book of Ezra, and in the [b] book of Esther, made mention of.

As soon as Darius was settled in the throne, [c] to establish him the firmer in it, he took to wife Atossa the daughter of Cyrus, and also another daughter of his, called Artistona. The former had been before wife to Cambyses, her brother, and afterwards to Smerdis the Magian, while he usurped the throne. But Artistona was a virgin, when he married her, and was the most beloved by him of all his wives. Besides these, he took also to wife Parmys, the daughter of the true Smerdis, brother of Cambyses, and Phedyma the daughter of Otanes, by whose means the imposture of the Magian was discovered, and by these had a great many children, both sons and daughters.

Although, by the death of the usurper, his edict which prohibited the building of the temple was now at an end, yet, the Jews neglecting to resume the work, [d] God did for this reason

smite

---

[a] Chap. vii. 14.
[b] Chap. i. 14.
[c] Herodotus, lib. 3.
[d] Haggai i. 6—11. & ii. 17. 19.

smite the land with barrenness, so that both the vintage and the harvest failed them. But in the 2d year of Darius, they being by the prophet Haggai informed of the cause of this judgement upon them, and exhorted to the doing of their duty for the averting of it, they betook themselves again to prepare for the carrying on of the work. It was on [a] the first day of the 6th month (which answers to about the middle of our August) that the word of the Lord, by Haggai the prophet, came to Zerubbabel the son of Salathiel, governor of Judea, and to Jeshua the son of Jozadak the high priest, concerning this matter. And, [b] on the 24th day of the same month, they being excited hereby arose with all the remnant of the people, and obeyed the voice of the Lord, and again applied themselves with all diligence to provide stone and timber, and all other materials, that were necessary for the again carrying on of the work. And, to encourage them to go on vigorously herewith, on the 21st day of the 7th month (i. e. about the beginning of our October), [c] another message from God came to them by the same prophet, which not only assured them of his presence with them herein, to make it prosper in their hands; but also promised them, that [d] the glory of the latter house, when built, should be greater than the glory of the former house; which was accordingly accomplished, when Christ our Lord came to this his temple, and honoured it with his presence. In all other respects this latter temple, the [e] same prophet tells us, at its first building, was as nothing in comparison of the former.

In the [f] 8th month of the same year (which answers to part of our October and part of November), the word of the Lord came by Zechariah the prophet to the people of the Jews, exhorting them to repentance, and promising them mercy and favour on their obedience hereto.

On the [g] 24th day of the 9th month (which fell about the beginning of our December), the Jews, after they had been employed from the 24th day of the 6th month in preparing materials for the temple, went on again with the building of it; [h] whereon the prophet Haggai promised them from God a a deliverance from that barrenness of their land, with which it had been smitten, and plentiful increase of all its fruits for the future; and also [i] delivered unto Zerubbabel a message from God of mercy and favour unto him.

In

[a] Haggai i. 1.
[b] Haggai i. 15.
[c] Haggai ii. 1.
[d] Haggai i. 9.
[e] Haggai ii. 3.
[f] Zech. i. 1.
[g] Haggai ii. 18.
[h] Haggai ii. 10---19.
[i] Haggai ii. 20---23.

In the beginning of the next year (which was the 3d year of Darius according to the [a] Babylonian and Perfian account, but the fecond according to the Jewifh), the Samaritans underftanding, that the building of the temple went on again, notwithftanding the ftop which they had procured to be put to it in the laft reign, they [b] betook themfelves again to their old malicious practices for the obftructing of the work; and therefore applied themfelves to Tatnai, whom Darius had made chief governor, or prefect, of all the provinces of Syria and Paleftine, (which was [c] one of the 20 prefectures into which he had lately divided his whole empire), and made complaint to him againft the Jews as to this matter, fuggefting, that they proceeded herein without authority, and that it would tend to the prejudice of the king; whereon Tatnai, being accompanied by Setharboznai (who feems to have been then governor of Samaria), came to Jerufalem, to take an account of what was there a-doing. But Tatnai, being a man of temper and juftice, after he had made a view of the building, did not proceed roughly and rafhly to put a ftop to it, but firft inquired of the elders of the Jews by what authority they had gone on with it. And they having produced to him Cyrus's decree, he would not take upon him to contradict the fame, or order any thing contrary to it upon his own authority; but firft wrote letters to the king, to know his pleafure concerning it; wherein he fairly ftated the cafe, fetting forth the matter of fact, and alfo the Jews plea of Cyrus's decree, for the juftifying of themfelves herein; and thereon requefted, that fearch might be made among the records of the kingdom, whether there were any fuch decree granted by Cyrus, or no, and that thereon the king would be pleafed to fignify unto him, what he would have done herein. Whereon [d] fearch being made, and the decree being found among the rolls in the royal palace at Ecbatana in Media, where Cyrus was when he granted it, the king refolved to confirm the fame: for having lately married two of the daughters of Cyrus, the better to fortify his title to the crown thereby, he

An. 519.
Darius 3.

thought

---

[a] For the Babylonians and Perfians, at this time, began their year from the beginning of January; but the Jews from Nifan, about 10 or 11 weeks after. And therefore, feeing the eighth month (which anfwers in part to our October) was according to Zechariah (c. i. v. 1.) in the fecond year of Darius, whatfoever was acted from the beginning of January, within a year after, muft be in the 3d year of Darius, according to the Babylonifh account, and alfo according to the exact truth of the matter; for Darius began his reign with the beginning of the Babylonifh year.
[b] Ezra v. 3.—17.
[c] Herodotus, lib. 3.
[d] Ezra vi.

thought it concerned him to do every thing that might tend to support the honour and veneration which was due to the memory of that great prince; and therefore would suffer nothing to be infringed of that, which he had so solemnly granted, but ordered his royal decree to be drawn; wherein recitement being made of the decree of Cyrus, he commanded it in every particular to be observed, and sent it to Tatnai and Setharboznai, to see it fully and effectually put in execution, decreeing, that whosoever should alter the same, or put any obstruction to it, should have his house pulled down, and that, a gallows being made of the timber of it, he should be hanged thereon.

On [a] the 24th day of the 11th month (that is about the beginning of our February), the prophet Zechariah had, in a vision, that revelation made unto him which is contained in the book of his prophecies, from the 7th verse of the 1st chapter to the 9th verse of the 6th chapter. The substance of which is to express the mercy that God would shew unto his people, in the restoration and redemption of Sion, and the vengeance which he would execute upon those that had oppressed them.

About the beginning of the 4th year of Darius, his decree which confirmed that of Cyrus in favour of the Jews, was brought to Jerusalem. It was about the beginning of the former year that Tatnai sent to the king about it, and less than a year's time cannot be well allowed for the dispatch of such an affair; for the king then residing at Shushan in Persia, was at such a distance from Judea, that the journey of the messenger thither to him, could not take up less than three months time, (for [b] Ezra was four months in coming to Judea from Babylon, which was at least one quarter of the way nearer); and, on his arrival, it cannot be supposed that, in a court where the government of so large an empire was managed, he could immediately come at a dispatch. The multiplicity of other affairs there agitated must necessarily detain him some time, before it could come to his turn to be heard for the delivery of his message; and when he had obtained an order to search among the records of the empire for the decree of Cyrus (which we cannot imagine to have been without a farther time of attendance), he or some other messenger first went to Babylon, to make the search there; and, on his failing of finding it in that place, he went from thence to [c] Ecbatana, the capital of Media, where, having found the inrolment of it (for it seems Cyrus was there when he granted it), he returned with it from thence to Shushan. In which three journeys and two searches, considering the distance

An. 518.
Darius 4.

[a] Zechariah i. 7.
[b] Ezra vii. 9.
[c] This is the same that is now called Tauris.

tance of the said three places from each other, and the vast number of records which, in the registers of so large an empire, must be turned over for the finding of that which was searched for, less than five months could not have been expended. And when the record of Cyrus's decree was brought from Ecbatana to Shushan, a month is the least time that can be supposed for the dispatch of the new decree which Darius made in confirmation of it: and then three months more must be allowed for the carrying of it to Tatnai, and from him to Judea. All which put together, make a full year from the time of Tatnai's writing his letter, to the time of the arrival of Darius's decree in answer to it. When Tatnai and Setharboznai, on the perusal of it, found how strictly the king required obedience to be given thereto, they durst not but act in conformity to it; [a] and therefore they did immediately let the Jews know hereof, and forthwith took care to have it fully and effectually put in execution. And from that time, the building of the house went on so successfully, that it was fully finished within three years after: for, by virtue of this decree, the Jews were not only fully authorised to go on with the building, but were also furnished with the expences of it out of the taxes of the province. This had been granted by Cyrus in the former decree, but by the underhand dealings of the Samaritans, and other enemies, in corrupting those, through whose hands the administration of the public affairs and public revenues passed, this part of Cyrus's decree was rendered ineffectual during a great part of his reign, and through the whole reign of Cambyses. And therefore, during all that time, the Jews being left to carry on the work at their own charges only, and they being then very poor, as being newly returned from their captivity, it went very slowly on. But, being now helped again by the king's bounty, they followed it with that diligence, that they soon brought it to a conclusion.

The publishing of this decree at Jerusalem may be reckoned the thorough restoration of the Jewish state: and from the thorough destruction of it, in the burning of the city and temple of Jerusalem by the Chaldeans, to this time, is just 70 years. The time falling so exactly, and the prophet Zechariah confirming it, by expressing, under [b] the 4th year of Darius, that the mourning and fasting of the Jews for the destruction of Jerusalem, and the utter driving of them out of the land on the death of Gedaliah, was then [c] just 70 years: this hath given a plausible handle to some for the placing of the beginning of the 70 years of the Byablonish captivity, spoken of by Jeremiah, at the destruction

---

[a] Ezra vi. 13. And Josephus Antiq. lib. 11. c. 4.
[b] Zech. vii. 1.
[c] Zech. vii. 5.

tion of Jerufalem, and the end of them, at the publication of this decree of Darius. But the fcripture plainly tells us, that thefe 70 years, as prophefied of by the prophet [a] Jeremiah, began from the 4th year of Jehoiakim, and expired [b] on the firſt of Cyrus, on his then granting his decree for the rebuilding of the temple, and the return of the Jews again into their own land. But this matter will admit of a very eafy reconciliation, for both computations may very well ſtand together; for, though the Babylonifh captivity did begin from the 4th of Jehoiakim, when Nebuchadnezzar firſt fubjugated the land, and carried away to Babylon the firſt captives, yet it was not completed till he had abfolutely deſtroyed it in the 11th year of Zedekiah, which was juſt 18 years after. And fo likewife, though the deliverance from this captivity, and the reſtoration of the Jewifh ſtate thereon, was begun by the decree of Cyrus in the firſt year of his reign; yet it was not completed till that decree was put in full vigour of execution by the decree, which Darius granted in the 4th year of his reign for the confirmation of it; which was alfo juſt 18 years after. And therefore, if we reckon from the beginning of the captivity, to the beginning of the reſtoration, we muſt reckon from the 4th year of Jehoiakim to the firſt of Cyrus, which was juſt 70 years; and, if we reckon from the completion of the captivity, to the completion of the reſtoration, we muſt reckon from the 11th of Zedekiah to the 4th of Darius; which was alfo juſt 70 years. So that, whether we reckon from the beginning of the captivity to the beginning of the reſtoration, or from the completing of the captivity to the compleating of the reſtoration, Jeremiah's prophecy of the 70 years captivity will be both ways equally accomplifhed; and therefore, I doubt not, but that both ways were equally intended therein, though the words of the prophecy feem chiefly to refer to the former.

On the publication of this decree of Darius, and the care that was taken to have it fully put in execution, without fuffering any of thofe devices to obſtruct it, which had rendered the former decree ineffectual, the work of the temple went on very fuccefsfully, and the ſtate of the Jews in Judea and Jerufalem feemed fo throughly reſtored, that the Jews who were in Babylon, on their having had an account hereof, thought it might not be any longer proper to keep thofe faſts, which hitherto they had obferved for 70 years paſt, for the deſtruction which Judah and Jerufalem had fuffered from the Chaldeans in the time of Zedekiah, as looking on them now to have obtained a thorough reſtoration from it; and therefore [c] fent meſſengers to Jerufalem, Sharezar, and Regem-melech, to afk advice of the prieſts

and

---

[a] Jer. xxv.   [b] 2 Chron. xxxvi. 20—23.   [c] Zech. vii.

and prophets, that were there concerning this matter. For, from the time of the deſtruction of the city and temple of Jeruſalem, the Jews of the captivity had kept four faſts in commemoration of the calamities which then happened to their nation; the [a] firſt on the 10th day of the 10th month, becauſe then Nebuchadnezzar firſt laid ſiege to Jeruſalem, in the 9th year of Zedekiah; the [b] ſecond on the 9th day of the 4th month, becauſe on that day the city was taken; the third [c] on the 10th day of the 5th month, becauſe then the city and temple were burnt by Nebuzaradan; and the fourth [d] on the 3d day of the 7th month, becauſe on that day Gedaliah was ſlain, and the remainder of the people were thereon diſperſed and driven out of the land, which completed the deſolation of it. Concerning all which faſts, and the queſtion of the Babyloniſh Jews propoſed concerning them, God gave them by the prophet Zechariah that anſwer which we have in the 7th and 8th chapters of his prophecies. Therein [e] the faſts of the 5th and 7th months are ſaid to have been obſerved for 70 years paſt. And, from the 19th year of Nebuchadnezzar according to the Jewiſh account, (which was the 17th according to the Babyloniſh account), [f] when Jeruſalem was deſtroyed, to the 4th year of Darius Hyſtaſpes, when the Jewiſh ſtate was again throughly reſtored, were juſt 70 years, according to the canon of Ptolemy; ſo the ſacred and profane chronology do both exactly agree in this matter. The Jews ſtill obſerve theſe four faſts even to this day, though not exactly on the ſame days in their [g] preſent kalander, as in the former.

In the beginning of the 5th year of Darius, happened [h] the revolt of the Babylonians, which coſt him the trouble of a tedious ſiege again to reduce them, for it laſted 20 months. This city having, for many years during the Babyloniſh empire, been the miſtreſs of the Eaſt, and domineered over all the countries round about them, could not bear the ſubjection which they were fallen under to the Perſians,

An. 517.
Darius 5.

eſpecially

[a] 2 Kings xxv. 1. Jeremiah lii. 4. Zechariah viii. 19.
[b] 2 Kings xxv. 3. Jeremiah xxix. 2. Zechariah viii. 19.
[c] Jeremiah lii. 12. Zechariah vii. 3. 5. & viii. 19.
[d] Jeremiah xli. 1. Zechariah vii. 5. & viii. 19.
[e] Zechariah vii. 1.
[f] 2 Kings xxv. 8. Jeremiah lii. 12.
[g] Their preſent kalendar was made by R. Hillel, about the year of our Lord 360. Their former year was a lunar year, reconciled to a ſolar by intercalations, but in what form is uncertain, only it was always to have its beginning about the time of the vernal equinox, to which ſeaſon, the products of their flocks and their fields, which were required to be uſed at their feaſts of the paſſover, and the Pentecoſt, neceſſarily fixed it.
[h] Herodotus, lib. 3. Juſtin, lib. 1. c. 10. Polyænus, lib. 7.

especially after they had removed the imperial seat of the empire from Babylon to Shushan; for that much diminished the grandeur, pride, and wealth of the place, which they thought they could no other way again retrieve, but by setting themselves up against the Persians, under a king of their own, in the same manner as they had formerly done, under Nabopollasar, against the Assyrians. And therefore, taking the advantage of the revolution which happened in the Persian empire, first on the death of Cambyses, and after on the slaying of the Magians, they began to lay in all manner of provisions for the war; and, after they had covertly done this for four years together, till they had fully stored the city for many years to come, in the 5th year they broke out into an open revolt, which drew Darius upon them, with all his forces, to besiege the city. In the beginning of the 3d year of Darius, we learn from the prophet Zechariah, that [a] the whole empire was then in peace; and therefore the revolt could not then have happened: and the message of Sharezer and Regem-melech from Babylon, [b] in the 4th year of his reign, proves the same for that year also; and therefore it could not be till the 5th year that this war broke out. As soon as [c] the Babylonians saw themselves begirt by such an army, as they could not cope with in the field, they turned their thoughts wholly to the supporting of themselves in the siege: in order whereto, they took a resolution the most desperate and barbarous that ever any nation practised. For, to make their provisions last the longer, they agreed to cut off all unnecessary mouths among them; and therefore, drawing together all the women and children, they strangled them all, whether wives, sisters, daughters, or young children useless for the wars, excepting only, that every man was allowed to save one of his wives which he best loved, and a maid servant to do the work of the house. And hereby was very signally fulfilled the prophecy of Isaiah against them, in which he foretold, "[d] That two things should come to them in a moment, in one day, the loss of children and widowhood; and that these should come upon them in their perfection, for the multitude of their sorceries, and the great abundance of their inchantments." And in what greater perfection could these calamities come upon them, than when they themselves, thus upon themselves, became the executioners of then? And in many other particulars did God then execute his vengeance upon this wicked and abominable city, which was foretold by several of the prophets; and the Jews were as often [e] warned to come out of the place,

before

---

[a] Zechariah i. 11.—15.
[b] Zechariah vii. 1.—3.
[c] Herodotus, lib. 3.
[d] Isaiah xlvii. 9.
[e] Isaiah xlviii. 20. Jeremiah l. 3. and li. 6. 9. 45.

before the time of its approach, that they might not be involved in it. And especially [a] the prophet Zechariah, about two years before, sent them a call from God, that is, "to Zion, that dwelt with the daughter of Babylon, to flee and come forth from that land," that they might be delivered from the plague which God was going to inflict upon it. And when Sharezer and Regem-melech returned to Babylon, no doubt, they carried back with them, from this prophet, a repetition of the same call: and although it be no where said, that they paid obedience to it, and so saved themselves, yet we may take it for certain, that they did, and, by seasonably removing from Babylon before the siege began, avoided partaking of the calamities of it: for almost all the prophecies concerning this heavy judgement upon Babylon speaking of it as the vengeance of God upon them for their cruel dealings with his people, when they were delivered into their hands, and they all at the same time promising peace, mercy, and favour, to all that were of his people, and particularly such a promise having been sent them but the year before [b] by Sharezer and Regem-melech, it is utterly inconsistent with the whole tenor of these sacred predictions, that any of the Jewish nation should be sufferers with the Babylonians in this war; and therefore we may assuredly infer, that they were all gone out of this place before this war begun.

Darius having lain before Babylon a year and eight months, [c] at length, toward the end of the 6th year of his reign, he took it by the stratagem of Zopyrus, one of his chief commanders: for he, having cut off his nose and ears, and mangled his body all over with stripes, fled in this condition to the besieged; where, feigning to have suffered all this by the cruel usage of Darius, he grew thereby so far into their confidence, as at length to be made the chief commander of their forces; which trust he made use of to deliver the city to his master, which could scarce have been any other way taken: for the walls, by reason of their height and strength, made the place impregnable against all storms, batteries, and assaults; and it being furnished with provisions for a great many years, and having also [d] large quantities of void ground within the city, from the cultivation of which it might annually be supplied with much more, it could never have been starved into a surrender; and therefore at length it must have wearied

An. 516.
Darius 6.

and

---

[a] Zechariah ii. 6.—9.
[b] Zechariah viii.
[c] Herodotus, lib. 3. Justin. lib. i. c. 10. Polyænus, lib. 7.
[d] Quintus Curtius, lib. 5. c. 1. Per 90 stadia habitatur, cætera ferunt coluntque, ut si externa vis ingruat, obsessis alimenta ex ipsius urbis solo subministrentur.

and worn out Darius, and all his army, had it not been thus delivered into his hands by this ftratagem of Zopyrus, for which he deſervedly rewarded him with the higheſt honours he could heap on him all his life after. As ſoon as Darius was maſter of the place, he took away [a] all their 100 gates, and beat down [b] their walls from 200 cubits (which was their former height) to 50 cubits; and of theſe walls only [c] Strabo, and other after-writers are to be underſtood, when they deſcribe the walls of Babylon to be no more than 50 cubits high. And as to the inhabitants, after having given them for a ſpoil to his Perſians, who had been before their ſervants, according to the prophecy of Zechariah, chap. ii. 9. and impaled 3000 of the moſt guilty and active of them in the revolt, he pardoned all the reſt. But, by reaſon of the deſtruction they had made of their women in the beginning of the ſiege, he was forced to ſend for 50,000 of that ſex out of the other provinces of the empire, to ſupply them with wives, without which the place muſt ſoon have become depopulated for want of propagation.

And here it is to be obſerved, that the puniſhment of Babylon kept pace with the reſtoration of Judah and Jeruſalem, according to the prophecy of the prophet Jeremiah, chap. xxv. 12. 13. whereby he foretold, that " when the ſeventy years of Judah's captivity ſhould be accompliſhed, God would puniſh the king of Babylon, and that nation for their iniquity, and the land of the Chaldeans, and would make it a perpetual deſolation, and would bring upon that land all the words which he had pronounced againſt it." For accordingly, when the reſtoration of Judah began, in the firſt of Cyrus, after the expiration of the firſt 70 years, that is, from the fourth of Jehoiakim to the firſt of Cyrus, then began Babylon's puniſhment, in being conquered and ſubjected to the Perſians, in the ſame manner as they had conquered and ſubjected the Jews to them in the beginning of the ſaid 70 years. And, after the expiration of the ſecond 70 years, that is, from the 19th of Nebuchadnezzar, when Judah and Jeruſalem were throughly deſolated, to the fourth of Darius, when the reſtoration of both was completed, then the deſolation of Babylon was alſo in a great meaſure completed in the devaſtation which was then brought upon it by Darius. In the firſt part of their puniſhment, their king was ſlain, and their city taken; and thenceforth, from being [d] *the lady of kingdoms*, and miſtreſs of all the Eaſt, it became ſubject to the Perſians. And whereas before it had been the metropolis of a great empire, this honour was now

[a] Jer. li. 58. Herodot. ibid.
[b] Jer. l. 15. & li. 44. 58. Herodot. ibid.
[c] Strabo, lib. 16.
[d] Iſ. xlvii. 5.

now taken from it, and the imperial feat removed from thence to Shushan or Sufa (for this seems to have been done in the first year of Cyrus's reign over the whole empire), and Babylon thenceforth, instead of having a king, had only a deputy residing there, who governed it as a province of the Persian empire. And at the same time that the city was thus brought under, the country was desolated and destroyed by the inundation that was caused, by turning of the river on the taking of the city, which hath been already spoken of, and thereon it became *a possession for the bittern, and pools of water*, as the prophet Isaiah foretold, chap. xiv. 23. " And the sea came up upon Babylon, and she was covered with the multitude of the waves thereof," according as Jeremiah prophesied hereof, chap. li. 42. And, in the second part of their punishment, on Darius's taking the place, all that calamity and devastation was brought upon it, which hath been already spoken of; and from that it did never any more recover itself, but languished a while, and at length ended, according to the words of Jeremiah, *in a perpetual desolation*.

In the 6th year of Darius according to the Jewish account, and on the 3d day of the 12th month, called the month of Adar (which answered to part of the third, and part of the fourth month of the Babylonish year, and consequently was in the 7th year of Darius, according to the Babylonish account), [a] the building of the temple at Jerusalem was finished, and the dedication of it was celebrated by the priests and Levites, and all the rest of the congregation of Israel, with great joy and solemnity. And, among other sacrifices then offered, there was a sin-offering for all Israel of twelve he-goats, according to the number of the tribes of Israel; which is a farther addition of proof to what hath been above said, that, on the return of Judah and Benjamin from the Babylonish captivity, some also of each of the other tribes of Israel returned with them out of Assyria, Babylon, and Media, whither they had been before carried, and, joining with them in the rebuilding of the temple (to which they had originally an equal right), partaked also in the solemnity of this dedication; otherwise there is no reason why any such offering should have been then made in their behalf. But the most of them that returned being of the tribe of Judah, that swallowed up the names of all the rest; for from this time the whole people of Israel, of what tribe soever they were, [b] began to be called Jews; and by that name they have all of them been ever since known all the world over.

An. 515. Darius 7.

This work was 20 years in finishing; for so many years were elapsed

---

[a] Ezra vi. 15—18.
[b] Joseph. Antiq. lib. 14. c. 5. Euseb. Demonst. Evang. lib. 8.

elapsed, from the 2d of Cyrus, when it was first begun, to the
7th of Darius, when it was fully finished. During the latter
part of the reign of Cyrus, and through the whole reign of
Cambyses, it met with such discouragements, through the frau-
dulent devices of the Samaritans, that it went but slowly on for
all that time: and, during the usurpation of the Magians, and
for almost [a] two years after, it was wholly suppressed, that is,
till towards the latter end of the 2d year of the reign of Darius.
But then it being again resumed, on the preaching of the prophets Haggai and Zechariah, and afterwards encouraged and
helped forward by the decree of Darius, it was thenceforth
carried on with that vigour, especially through the exhortations
and prophecies of the two prophets I have mentioned, that, in
the beginning of the 7th year of Darius, it was fully finished,
and dedicated anew to the service of God, in the manner as
hath been said. In this dedication, the 146th, the 147th, and the
148th psalms seem to have been sung: for, in the Septuagint
versions, they are styled *the Psalms of Haggai and Zechariah*,
as if they had been composed by them for this occasion; and
this, no doubt, was from some ancient tradition: but, in the
original Hebrew, these psalms have no such title prefixed to
them, neither have they any other to contradict it.

The decree whereby this temple was finished having been
granted by Darius at his palace in Shushan (or Susa, as the
Greeks call the place), in remembrance hereof [b], the eastern
gate, in the outer wall of the temple, was from this time called
the gate of Shushan, and a picture and draught of that city was
pourtrayed in sculpture over it, and there continued till the last
destruction of that temple by the Romans.

In the next month after the dedication, which was the month
Nisan, the first of the Jewish year, the temple being now made
fit for all parts of the divine service, [c] the passover was observed
in it on the 14th day of that month, according to the law of
God, and solemnised by all the children of Israel that were then
returned from the captivity, with great joy and gladness of
heart, because, saith the book of Ezra, "[d] The Lord hath made
them joyful, and turned the heart of the king of Assyria unto
them, to strengthen their hands in the work of the house of God,
the God of Israel:" from whence [e] Archbishop Usher infers, that
Babylon must necessarily have been reduced by Darius before
this

[a] In the first of Esdras, v. 73. it is said, that the time of the stop
which was put to the building was two years.
[b] See Lightfoot of the Temple, c. 3.
[c] Ezra vi. 19—22.
[d] Ezra v. 22.
[e] Annales Veteris Testamenti, sub A. M. 3480.

this time; for otherwife, he thinks, he could not have been here ftyled king of Affyria, Babylon being then the metropolis of that kingdom.

And if we will add one ftage more to the two above mentioned, of the captivity and reftoration of Judah, and place the full completion of the captivity in the 23d of Nebuchadnezzar according to the Jewifh account (which was the 21ft according to the Babylonifh), [a] when Nebuzaradan carried away the laft remainder of the land; and the full completion of the reftoration at the finifhing of the temple, and the reftoration of the divine worfhip therein; this ftage will have the like diftance of 70 years for the dedication of this temple, and the folemnifing of the firft paffover in it, being in the 7th year of Darius, it will fall in the 70th year from the [b] faid 23d of Nebuchadnezzar, according to Ptolemy's canon. So that taking it which way you will, and at what ftage you pleafe, the prophecy of Jeremiah will be fully and exactly accomplifhed concerning this matter. And, here ending the rebuilding of the fecond temple, I fhall herewith end this book.

[a] Jeremiah lii. 30.
[b] That is, reckoning the 23d year of Nebuchadnezzar, according to the Jewifh account, to be the 21ft according to the Babylonifh account, which Ptolemy went by.

THE

OLD AND NEW TESTAMENT

CONNECTED,

IN

THE HISTORY

OF

THE JEWS AND NEIGHBOURING NATIONS,

FROM

The Declenſion of the Kingdoms of ISRAEL *and* JUDAH, *to the Time of* CHRIST.

BOOK IV.

An. 514.
Darius 8.

THE Samaritans, ſtill carrying on their former ſpite and rancour againſt the Jews, gave them new trouble on this occaſion. The tribute of Samaria had been aſſigned firſt [a] by Cyrus, and afterwards [b] by Darius, for the reparation of the temple at Jeruſalem, and the furniſhing of the Jews with ſacrifices, that [c] oblations and prayers might there daily be offered up for the king, and the royal family, and for the welfare and proſperity of the Perſian empire. This was a matter of great regret and heart-burning to the Samaritans, and was in truth the ſource and the true original reaſon of all the oppoſitions which they made againſt them: for they thought it an indignity upon them to be forced to pay their tribute to the Jews; and therefore they did

[a] Joſeph. Antiq. lib. 11. c. 1.
[b] Joſeph. lib. 11. c. 4.
[c] Ezra vi. 8—10.

BOOK IV.   CONNECTION OF THE HISTORY OF, &c.   201

did, [a] by bribes and other underhand dealings, prevail with the ministers, and other officers, to whose charge this matter belonged, during the latter part of the reign of Cyrus, and all the time of Cambyses, to put a stop to this assignment, and did all else that they could wholly to quash it. But the grant being again [b] renewed by Darius, and the execution of it so strictly enjoined in the manner as hath been before related, the tribute was thenceforth annually paid, to the end for which it was assigned, without any more gainsaying, till this year. But now, on pretence that the temple was finished (though the out-buildings still remained unrepaired, and were not finished till many years after), they [c] refused to let the Jews any longer have the tribute; alledging, that it being assigned them for the repairing of their temple, now the temple was repaired, the end of that assignment was ceased, and that consequently the payment of the said tribute was to cease with it, and for this reason would pay it no longer to them. Whereon the Jews, to right themselves in this matter, sent Zerubbabel the governor, with Mordecai and Ananias, two other principal men among them, with a complaint to Darius of the wrong that was done them, in the detaining of his royal bounty from them, contrary to the purport of the edict which he had in that behalf made. The king, on the hearing of the complaint, and the informing of himself about it, issued out his royal order to his officers at Samaria, strictly requiring and commanding them to take effectual care, that the Samaritans observe his edict, in paying their tribute to the temple of Jerusalem, as formerly, and no more, on any pretence whatsoever, give the Jews any cause for the future to complain of their failure herein. And after this we hear no more of any opposition or contest concerning this matter, till the time of Sanballat; which was many years after.

From the time of the reduction of Babylon, [d] Darius had set himself to make great preparations for a war against the Scythians, that inhabited those countries which lie between the Danube and the Tanais: his pretence for it was to be revenged on them for their having invaded Asia, and held it in subjection to them 28 years, as hath been afore related. This was in the time of Cyaxares, the first of that name, king of Media, about 120 years before. But for want of a better colour for that which his ambition and thirst for conquest only led him to, this was given out for the reason of the war. In order whereto, having

drawn

---

[a] Ezra iv. 5. Joseph. Antiq. lib. 11. c. 2.
[b] Ezra vi.
[c] Joseph. Antiq. lib. 11. c. 4.
[d] Herodotus, lib. 4. Justin, lib. 2. c. 5. Cornelius Nepos in Miltiade.

An. 513.
Darius 9.

drawn together an army of 700,000 men, he marched with them to the Thracian Bosphorus, and having there passed over it on a bridge of boats, he brought all Thrace in subjection to him; and then marched to the Ister or Danube, where he appointed his fleet to come to him (which consisted mostly of Ionians, and other Grecian nations, dwelling in the maritime parts of Asia, and on the Hellespont); he there passed over another bridge of boats into the country of the Scythians, and having there, for three months time, pursued them through several desert and uncultivated countries, where they drew him by their flight of purpose to harass and destroy his army, he was glad at last to return with one half of them, having lost the other half in this unfortunate and ill-projected expedition. And, had not the Ionians, by the persuasion of Hestiæus, prince of Miletus (or tyrant as the Grecians call him), contrary to the opinion of others among them, staid with the fleet to afford him a passage back, he and all the rest must have perished also. Miltiades, prince of the Thracian Chersonesus, which lies at the mouth of the Hellespont, being one of those who attended Darius with his ships, was earnest for their departure, and the first that moved it, telling them, that, by their going away and leaving Darius and his army to perish on the other side of the Danube, they had a fair opportunity of breaking the power of the Persians, and delivering themselves from the yoke of that tyranny which would be to the advantage of every one of their respective countries. This was urged by him in a council of the chief commanders; and would certainly have taken place, but that Hestiæus, in answer hereto, soon made them sensible, what a dangerous risk they were going to run: for he convinced them, that if this were done, the people of each of their cities, being freed from the fear of the Persians, would immediately rise upon them to recover their liberties; and this would end in the ruin of every one of them, who now, with sovereign authority, under the protection of Darius, securely reigned over them. Which being the true state of their case, this argument prevailed with them: so that they all resolved to stay: and this gave Darius the means of again repassing the river into Thrace, where having left Megabyzus, one of his chief commanders, with part of his army, to finish his conquests in those parts, and throughly settle the country in his obedience, he repassed the Bosphorus with the rest, and retired to Sardis, where he staid all the winter, and the most part of the ensuing year, to refresh his broken forces, and resettle his affairs in those parts of his empire, after the shock that had been given them, by the

baffle

baffle and lofs which he had fuftained in this ill-advifed expedition.

Megabyzus, having reduced moft of the nations of Thrace under the Perfian yoke, returned to Sardis to Darius, and [a] from thence accompanied him to Sufa, whither he marched back about the end of the year, after having appointed Artaphernes, one of his brothers, governor of Sardis, and Otanes chief commander of Thrace, and the maritime parts adjoining, in the place of Megabyzus. This Otanes was the fon of Sifamnes, one of the royal judges of Perfia, who having been convicted of bribery and corruption by Cambyfes, there is related this remarkable inftance of that king's juftice towards him, [b] that he caufed him to be flea'd alive, and making with his fkin a covering for the feat of the tribunal, made this his fon, whom he appointed to fucceed him in his office, to fit thereon, that being thus put in mind of his father's punifhment, he might thereby be admonifhed to avoid his crime.

An. 511.
Darius 10.

The Scythians, to be revenged on Darius for his invading their country, [c] paffed over the Danube, and ravaged all thofe parts of Thrace, that had fubmitted to the Perfians, as far as the Hellefpont; whereon Miltiades, to avoid their rage, fled from the Cherfonefus; but, on the retreat of the enemy, he returned, and was again reinftated in his former power by the inhabitants of the country.

An. 510.
Darius 12.

About this time Darius, being defirous to enlarge his dominions eaftward, in order to the conquering of thofe countries, laid a defign of firft making a difcovery of them; [d] for which purpofe having built a fleet of fhips at Cafpatyrus, a city on the river Indus, and as far up upon it as the borders of Scythia, he gave the command of it to Scylax a Grecian of Caryandia, a city in Caria, and one well fkilled in maritime affairs; and fent him down the river, to make the beft difcoveries he could of all the parts which lay on the banks of it on either fide; ordering him, for this end, to fail down the current, till he fhould arrive at the mouth of the river, and that then, paffing through it into the Southern ocean, he fhould fhape his courfe weftward, and that way return home. Which orders he having exactly executed, he returned by the ftraits of Babelmandel and the Red fea, and, on the 30th month after his firft fetting out from Cafpatyrus, landed in Egypt, at the fame place from whence Necho, king of Egypt, formerly fent out his Phœnicians to fail round the coafts of Africa, which

An. 509.
Darius 13.

---

[a] Herodotus, lib. 5.   [b] Herodotus, lib. 5. Valerius Maximus, lib. 6. c. 3. Ammianus Marcellinus, lib. 24.
[c] Herodotus, lib. 6.   [d] Herodotus, lib. 4.

which it is moſt likely was the port where now the town of Suez ſtands, at the hither end of the ſaid Red ſea. And from thence he went to Suſa, and there gave Darius an account of all the diſcoveries which he had made. After this Darius entered India with an army, and brought all that large country under him, and [a] made it the 20th prefecture of his empire; from whence he annually received a tribute of 360 talents of gold, according to the number of the days of the then Perſian year, appointing a talent to be paid him for every day in it. This payment was made him according to the ſtandard of the Euboic talent, which was near the ſame with the Attic; and therefore, according to the loweſt computation, it [b] amounted to the value of 1,095,000 pounds of our money.

A [c] ſedition happening in Naxus, the chief iſland of the Cyclades in the Egean ſea, now called the Archipelago, and the better ſort being therein overpowered by the greater number, many of the wealthieſt of the inhabitants were expelled the iſland, and driven into baniſhment; whereon retiring to Miletus, they there begged the aſſiſtance of Ariſtagoras, for the reſtoring of them again to their country. This Ariſtagoras then governed that city as deputy to Heſtiæus, whoſe nephew and ſon-in-law he was; Heſtiæus being then abſent at Suſa in Perſia: for Darius, on his return to Sardis, after his unfortunate expedition againſt the Scythians, being throughly informed, that he owed the ſafety of himſelf and all his army to Heſtiæus, in that he perſuaded the Ionians not to deſert him at the Danube, ſent for him to come to him, and, having acknowledged his ſervice, bid him aſk his reward. Whereon he deſired of him the Edonian Myrcinus, a territory on the river Strymon in Thrace, in order to build a city there; and, having obtained his requeſt, immediately on his return to Miletus, he equipped a fleet, and ſailed for Thrace, and, having there taken poſſeſſion of the territory granted him, did forthwith ſet himſelf on the enterprife of building his intended city in the place projected. Megabyzus, being then governor of Thrace for Darius, ſoon ſaw what danger this might create to the king's affairs in theſe parts: for he conſidered that the new-built city ſtood upon a navigable river; that the country thereabout afforded abundance of timber for the building of ſhips; that it was inhabited by ſeveral nations both of Greeks and Barbarians, which could furniſh a great multitude of men fit for military ſervice both by ſea and land; that, if theſe ſhould get ſuch a crafty and enterpriſing

An. 504.
Darius 18.

[a] Herodotus, lib. 3.
[b] For, according to the loweſt valuation, an Attic talent of gold amounts to 3000 pounds of our money.
[c] Herodotus, lib. 5.

enterprising a person as Hestiæus at the head of them, they might soon grow to a power both by sea and land, too hard for the king to master; and that especially since, from their silver and gold mines, of which there were many in that country, they might be furnished with means enough to carry on any enterprise they should undertake. All this, on his return to Sardis, he represented unto the king, who being thereby made fully sensible of the error he had committed, for the remedying of it sent a messenger to Myrcinus to call Hestiæus to Sardis to him, under pretence, that having great matters in design, he wanted his counsel and advice concerning them, by which means having gotten him into his power, he carried him with him to Susa, pretending, that he needed such an able counsellor and so faithful a friend to be always about him, to advise with on all occasions that might happen; and that he would make him so far a partaker of his fortunes by his royal bounty to him in Persia, that he should have no reason any more to think either of Myrcinus or Miletus. Hestiæus, hereon seeing himself under a necessity of obeying, accompanied Darius to Susa, and appointed Aristagoras to govern at Miletus in his absence, and to him the banished Naxians applied for relief. As soon as Aristagoras understood from them their case, he entertained a design of improving this opportunity to the making of himself master of Naxus, and therefore readily promised them all the relief and assistance which they desired: but not being strong enough of himself to accomplish what he intended, he went to Sardis, and communicated the matter to Artaphernes, telling him, that this was an opportunity offered for the putting of a rich and fertile island into the king's hands; that, if he had that, all the rest of the Cyclades would of course fall under his power also; and that then Euboea, an island as big as Cyprus, lying next, would be an easy conquest; from whence he would have an open passage into Greece, for the bringing of all that country under his obedience; and that 100 ships would be sufficient to accomplish this enterprise. Artaphernes, on the hearing of the proposal, was so much pleased with it, that, instead of 100 ships, which Aristagoras demanded, he promised him 200, provided the king liked hereof: and accordingly, on his writing to him, having received his answer of approbation, he sent him the next spring, to Miletus, the number of ships which he An. 503. Darius 19. had promised, under the command of Megabates, a noble Persian of the Archæmenian or royal family. But his commission being to obey the orders of Aristagoras, and the haughty Persian not brooking to be under the command of an Ionian, this created a dissension between the two generals, which was carried on so far, that Megabates, to be revenged on Aristagoras, betrayed the design to the Naxians: whereon they provided so fully for their defence, that, after the Persians had, in the siege of the chief city of the island, spent four months, and all their provisions, they were forced to retire, for want wherewith there any longer to subsist, and so the whole plot miscarried; the blame whereof being, by Megabates, all laid upon Aristagoras, and the false accusations of the one being more favourably heard than the just defence of the other, Artaphernes charged on him all the expences of the expedition: and it was given him to understand, that they would be exacted of him to the utmost penny, which being more than he was able to pay, he foresaw that this must end not only in the loss of his government, but also in his utter ruin; and therefore, being driven into extremities by the desperateness of his case, he entertained thoughts of rebelling against the king, as the only way left him for the extricating of himself out of this difficulty; and while he had this under consideration, came a message to him from Hestiæus, which advised the same thing; for Hestiæus after several years continuance at the Persian court, being weary of their manners, and exceeding desirous of being again in his own country, sent this advice unto Aristagoras, as the likeliest means to accomplish his aim herein; for he concluded, that if there were any combustions raised in Ionia, he should easily prevail with Darius to send him thither to appease them, as it accordingly came to pass. Aristagoras therefore finding his own inclinations backed with the order of Hestiæus, communicated the matter to the chief of the Ionians, and finding them all ready to join with him in what he proposed, he fixed his resolutions for a revolt, and immediately set himself to make all manner of preparations to put them in execution.

The Tyrians, after the taking of their city by Nebuchadnezzar, having been reduced to a state of servitude, continued under the pressure of it full 70 years: but these being now expired, they were again, according to the [a] prophecy of Isaiah, restored to their former privileges, and were allowed to have a king again of their own; and accordingly had so till the time of Alexander. This favour seems to have been granted them by Darius in consideration of their usefulness to him in his naval wars, and especially at this time, when he needed them and their shipping so much for the reducing of the Ionians again to their obedience to him. Hereon they soon recovered their former prosperity and, by the means of their traffic, whereby they had made their city the chief mart of all the East, they soon grew to that greatness, both of power and riches, as enabled them, on Alexander's invading

[a] Isaiah xxiii. 15, 17.

vading the East, to make a greater stand against him, than all the Persian empire besides; for they stopped the progress of his whole army full seven months, before they could be reduced, as will be hereafter shewn. This grant was made them by Darius in the 19th year of his reign.

The next year after, Aristogoras, to engage the Ionians the more firmly to stick to him, [a] restored to them all their liberties: for, beginning first with himself at Miletus, he there abolished his own authority, and reinstated the people in the government; and then, going round Ionia, forced all the other tyrants (as the Greeks then called them) in every city to do the same; by which, having united them into one common league, and gotten himself to be made the head of it, he openly declared his revolt from the king, and armed both by sea and land to make war against him. This was done in the 20th year of the reign of Darius.

An. 502. Darius 20.

Aristagoras, to strengthen himself the more against the Persians in this war, which he had begun against them,[b] went in the beginning of the following year to Lacedæmon, to engage that city in his interest, and gain their assistance. But being there rejected, he came to Athens, where he had a much more favourable reception: for he had the good fortune to come thither at a time when he found the Athenians in a thorough disposition to close with any proposal against the Persians that should be offered to them, they being then in the highest degree exasperated against them on this occasion. Hippias the son of Pisistratus, tyrant of Athens, having been expelled thence about 10 years before, after he had in vain tried several other ways for his restoration, at length applied himself to Artaphernes at Sardis; and, having there insinuated himself a great way into his favour, was well heard in all that he had to say against the Athenians, and he spared not to do all that he could to set Artaphernes against them; which the Athenians having advice of, sent an embassy to Sardis, to make friendship with Artaphernes, and to desire him not to give ear to their exiles against them. The answer which Artaphernes gave them was, that they must receive Hippias again, if they would be safe. Which haughty message being brought back to Athens, did set the whole city into a rage against the Persians; and in this juncture Aristagoras coming thither, easily obtained from them all that he desired; and accordingly they ordered a fleet of 20 ships for his assistance.

An. 501. Darius 21.

In the third year of the war, [c] the Ionians having gotten all

---

[a] Herodot. lib. 5.   [b] Ibid.   [c] Herodot. lib. 5.

Anno 500.
Darius 22.

all their forces together, and being affisted with 20 ships from Athens, and five from Eretria, a city in the island of Euboea, they sailed to Ephesus; and, having there laid up their ships, resolved on an attempt upon Sardis; and accordingly marched thither, and took the place. But Sardis being built most of cane, and their houses being therefore very combustible, one of them being accidentally set on fire, did spread the flame to all the rest, and the whole city was burnt down, excepting only the castle; where Artaphernes retired, and defended himself. But, after this accident, the Persians and Lydians gathering together for their defence, and other forces coming in to their assistance from the adjacent parts, the Ionians saw it was time for them to retreat; and therefore marched back to their ships at Ephesus, with all the speed they were able; but, before they could reach the place, they were overtaken, fought with, and overthrown with a great slaughter. Whereon the Athenians going on board their ships, hoisted their sails, and returned home, and would not after this be any farther concerned in this war, notwithstanding all the most earnest intreaties with which they were solicited to it by Aristagoras. However [a] their having engaged thus far, gave rise to that war between the Persians and the Greeks; which, being carried on for several generations after between these two nations, caused infinite calamities to both, and at last ended in the utter destruction of the Persian empire; for Darius, on his hearing of the burning of Sardis, and the part which the Athenians had therein, from that time resolved on a war against Greece; and that he might be sure not to forget it, he caused one of his attendants every day, when he was set at dinner, to say aloud unto him three times, *Sir, remember the Athenians.* In the burning of Sardis, it happened, that the temple of Cybele, the goddess of the country, took fire, and was consumed with the rest of the city; which afterwards served the Persians for a pretence to set on fire all the temples of the Grecians which came in their way, though in truth that proceeded from another cause, which shall be hereafter related.

On the departure of the Athenians, [b] the rest of the confederate fleet sailed to the Hellespont and the Propontis, and reduced the Byzantines, and most of the other Grecian cities in those parts under their power: and then, sailing back again, brought in the Carians to join with them in this war, and also the Cypriots, who all (excepting the Amathusians) entered into the same confederacy against Darius, and revolted from him; which drawing upon them all the forces that the Persians had in

Cilicia,

---

[a] Herodot. ibid. Cornelius Nepos in Miltiade.   [b] Herodot. lib. 5.

Cilicia, and the other neighbouring provinces, and alfo a great fleet from Phœnicia, the Ionians failed thither to their affiftance; and engaging the Phœnician fleet, gave them a great overthrow. But, at the fame time, the Cypriots being vanquifhed in a battle at land, and the head of that confpiracy flain in it, the Ionians loft the whole fruit of their victory at fea, and were forced to return, without having at all benefited either themfelves or their allies by it: for, after this defeat at land, the whole ifland was again reduced; and, within three years after, the fame perfons whom they had now affifted came againft them with their fhips, in conjunction with the reft of the Perfian fleet, to complete their utter deftruction.

The next year after, being the 23d of Darius, [a] Daurifes, Hymees, and Otanes, three Perfian generals, and all fons in law of Darius by the marriage of his daughters, having divided the Perfian forces between them, marched three feveral ways to attack the revolters. Daurifes with his army directed his courfe to the Hellefpont; but, after having there reduced feveral of the revolted cities, on his hearing that the Carians had alfo joined the confederates, he left thofe parts, and marched with all his forces againft them. Whereon Hymees, who was firft fent to the Propontis, after having taken the city of Cyus in Myfia, marched thence to fupply his place on the Hellefpont, where there was much more need of him, and there reduced all the Ilian coaft; but falling fick at Troas, he there died the next year after. Artaphernes and Otanes, with the third army, refolving to ftrike at the very heart of the confederacy, fell into Ionia and Æolia, where the chief of their ftrength lay, and took Clazomenæ in Ionia, and Cyma in Æolia; which was fuch a blow to the whole confederacy, that Ariftagoras hereon, defpairing of his caufe, refolved to leave Miletus, and fhift elfewhere for his fafety; and therefore, getting together all that were willing to accompany him, he went on fhipboard, and fet fail for the river Strymon in Thrace, and there feized on the territory of Myrcinus, which Darius had formerly given to Heftiæus; but the next year after, while he befieged the city, he was there flain by the Thracians, and all his army cut in pieces.

Anno 499. Darius 23.

In the 24th year of Darius, [b] Daurifes having fallen into the country of the Carians, overthrew them in two battles with a very great flaughter; but, in a third battle, being drawn into an ambufh, he was flain, with feveral other eminent Perfians, and his whole army cut off and deftroyed.

Anno 498. Darius 24.

VOL. I. O Artaphernes,

[a] Herodotus, lib. 5. [b] Ibid.

Artaphernes, with Otanes, and the rest of the Persian generals, seeing that Miletus was the head and chief strength of the Ionian confederacy,[a] resolved to bend all their force against it, reckoning, that, if they could make themselves masters of this city, all the rest would fall of course. The Ionians, being informed of this, agreed, in their general council, to bring no army into the field, but provide and strengthen Miletus as well as they could for a siege, and to draw all their forces to fight the Persians by sea; in which sort of fighting they thought themselves, by reason of their skill in maritime affairs, most likely to prevail: in order whereto, they appointed Lada, a small island before Miletus, for their rendezvous; and thither they came, to the number of 353 ships: at the sight of which, the Persians, though their fleet was double the number, fearing the event, came not to a battle with them, till they had, by their emissaries sent among them, corrupted the major part to desert the cause; so that, when they came to engage, the Samians, Lesbians, and several others, hoisting their sails, and departing home, there were not above 100 ships left to bear the whole brunt of the day; who being soon overborne by the number of the enemy, were almost all lost and destroyed. After this Miletus, being besieged both by sea and land, soon fell a prey into the hands of the victors, who absolutely destroyed the place; which happened in the 6th year after the revolt of Aristagoras. From Miletus the Persians marched into Caria, and having there taken some cities by force, and received others by voluntary submission, in a short time reduced all that country again under their former yoke. The Milesians who were saved from the sword in the taking of the city, being sent captives to Darius to Susa, he did them no farther harm, but sent them to inhabit the city of Ampha, which was situated at the mouth of the Tigris, where, in conjunction with the Euphrates, it falls into the Persian gulf, not far from the place where now the city Balsora stands; and there they continued a Grecian colony for many ages after.

After the taking of Miletus, the Persian fleet, which mostly consisted of Phœnicians, Cypriots, and Egyptians, having wintered on the coasts thereabout,[b] the next year took in Samos, Chius, Lesbus, and the rest of the islands; and, while they were thus employed at sea, the armies at land fell on the cities of the continent; and, having brought them all again under their power, they treated them as they had afore threatened, that is, they made all the beautifullest of their youths eunuchs, sent all their virgins into Persia, and

Anno 497.
Darius 25.

Anno 496.
Darius 26.

[a] Herodotus, lib. 6.   [b] Herodotus, lib. 6.

and burnt all their cities, with their temples; into so grievous
a calamity were they brought by this revolt, which the self-
designs of one enterprising busy-headed man, Hestiæus, the Milesian, led them into; and he himself had his share in it; for
this very year, being taken prisoner by the Persians, he was
carried to Sardis, and there crucified, by the order of Artaphernes. He hastened his execution, without consulting Darius about it, lest his kindness for him might extend to the granting him his pardon, and thereby a dangerous enemy to the Persians be again let loose to embarrass their affairs. And that it
would have so happened as they conjectured, did afterwards
appear: for when his head was brought to Darius, he expressed great displeasure against the authors of his death, and caused
his head to be honourably buried, as the remains of a man that
had much merited from him. How he was the cause of the Ionian war, and what was his aim herein, hath been above related.
On the breaking out of that revolt, and the burning of Sardis,
[a] Darius understanding that Aristagoras, the deputy of Hestiæus, was at the head of it, doubted not but that Hestiæus himself was at the bottom of the whole contrivance, and therefore
sent for him, and charged him with it: but he managed the matter so craftily with Darius, as to make him believe, not only
that he was innocent, but that the whole cause of this revolt
was, that he was not there to have hindered it: for he told him,
that the matter appeared plainly to have been long a brewing;
that they had waited only for his absence to put it in execution;
that, if he had continued at Miletus, it could never have happened; and that the only way to restore his affairs in those parts
was to send him thither to appease these combustions; which
he promised not only to do, but to deliver Aristagoras into his
hands, and make the great island of Sardinia to become tributary to him; swearing, that, if he were sent on this voyage, he
would not change his garments till all were effected that he had
said. By which fair speech Darius being deceived, [b] gave him
permission to return into Ionia. On his arrival at Sardis, his
busy head set him at work to contrive a plot against the government there, and he had drawn several of the Persians into
it: but, in some discourse which he had with Artaphernes,
finding that he was no stranger to the part which he had acted
in the Ionian revolt, he thought it not safe for him any longer to tarry at Sardis; and therefore, the next night after getting privately away, he fled to the sea coast, and got over to
the island of Chius. But the Chians, mistrusting that his
coming thither was to act some part for the interest of Darius
among them, seized on his person, and put him in prison; but
afterwards

[a] Herodot. lib. 5.   [b] Herodot. lib. 6.

afterwards, being fatisfied how he was engaged to the contrary, they fet him again at liberty. Hereon he fent one whom he had confidence in, with letters to Sardis, to thofe Perfians whom he had corrupted while he was there; but the perfon whom he trufted deceiving him, delivered the letters to Artaphernes; whereby the plot being difcovered, and all the perfons concerned in it put to death, he failed of this defign. But thinking ftill he could do great matters, were he at the head of the Ionian league, in order to the gaining of this point, he got the Chians to convey him to Miletus. But the Milefians, having had their liberty reftored to them by Ariftagoras, would by no means run the hazard of lofing it again, by receiving him into the city: whereon, endeavouring in the night to enter by force, he was repulfed, and wounded, and thereby forced to return again to Chius. While he was there, being afked the reafon why he fo earneftly preffed Ariftagoras to revolt, and thereby brought fo great a calamity upon Ionia, he told them, it was becaufe the king had refolved to remove the Ionians into Phœnicia, and to bring the Phœnicians into Ionia, and give them that country; which was wholly a fiction of his own devifing; for Darius had never any fuch intention: but it very well ferved his purpofe, firft to excufe himfelf, and next to excite the Ionians with the greater firmnefs and vigour to profecute the war; which accordingly had its effect: for the Ionians hearing that their country was to be taken from them, and given to the Phœnicians, were exceedingly alarmed at it; and therefore refolved, with the utmoft of their power, to ftand to their defence. However, Heftiæus finding the Chians not any way inclined to truft him with any of their naval forces, as he defired of them, he paffed over to the ifle of Lefbus; and, having there gained eight fhips, he failed with them to Byzantium, where, making prize of all the fhips that paffed the Bofphorus, either to or from the Euxine fea, excepting only fuch as belonged to thofe who were confederated with him, he did there, in a fhort time, grow to a great power. But, on his hearing of the taking of Miletus, he left the conduct of his affairs in thofe parts to a deputy, and failed to Chius; and, after fome little oppofition at his firft landing, made himfelf mafter of the ifland, the Chians, by reafon of the lofs they had lately fuftained in the fea fight againft the Perfians at Lada, being too weak at that time to refift him. From thence he failed with a great army of Ionians and Æolians to Thafus, an ifland on the Thracian coaft, and laid fiege to the chief city of that ifland: but hearing that the Phœnician fleet, in the fervice of the Perfians, was failed to take in the iflands on the Afian coaft, he raifed the fiege, and failed back to Lefbus with all his forces, to defend that place;

from

from whence passing over into the continent which was opposite to it, to plunder the country, Harpagus, one of the Persian generals, who happened then to be there with a great army, fell upon him; and, having routed his forces, and taken him prisoner, sent him to Sardis, where he met with the fate which I have mentioned. He was a man of the best head, and the most enterprising genius of any of his age; but he having wholly employed these abilities to lay plots and designs, which produced great mischiefs in the world, for the obtaining of little aims of his own, it happened to him, as most at the end it doth to such refined politicians, who, while they are spinning fine webs of politics for the bringing about of their self designs, often find them to become snares to their own destruction; for the providence of the wisest of men being too short to over-reach the providence of God, he often permits such Ahithophels, for the punishment of their presumption, as well as their malice, to perish by their own devices. And so it happened to Machiavel, the famous master of our modern politicians, who, after all his politics, died in jail for want of bread. And thus may it happen to all else, who make any other maxims than those of truth and justice to be the rules of their politics.

After the Phœnician fleet had subdued all the islands on the Asian coast, Artaphernes [a] sent them to reduce the Hellespont, that is, all its coasts on the European side, for those on the Asian had been already brought under by the armies at land: which Miltiades, prince of the Thracian Cherfonesus, having advice of, and that the fleet was come as far as Tenedos to put these orders in execution, he thought not fit to tarry their arrival, as being too weak to resist so great a power; but immediately carried all that he had on board five ships, and set sail with them for Athens. But, in his passage, one of them, commanded by Metiochus, his eldest son, was taken by the Phœnicians, and Metiochus was carried to Darius to Susa; but, instead of doing him any hurt, he generously gave him an house, and lands also for his maintenance, and married him to a Persian lady, with whom he there lived in an honourable state all his life after, and never more returned into Greece. In the interim Miltiades, with his other four ships, got safe to Athens, and there again settled himself; for he was a citizen of that city, and of one of the most honourable families in it. Miltiades, his father, Cimon's elder brother by the same mother (for they had different fathers), was the first of the Athenians that settled in the Thracian Cherfonesus, being called thither by the Dolonces, the inhabitants of the country, to be their

Anno 495.
Darius 27.

[a] Herodot. lib. 6. Cornelius Nepos in Miltiade.

their prince, who, dying without issue, left his principality to
Stesagoras, his nephew, the eldest son of his brother Cimon: he
dying also without children, the sons of Pisistratus, who then
governed at Athens, sent this Miltiades's brother thither to
succeed him; where he arrived, and settled himself in that
year in which Darius entered on his war against the Scythians,
in which expedition he accompanied him with his ships to the
Danube, as hath been above said. Three years after he was
driven out by the Scythians; but being afterwards brought
back, and restored again by the Dolonces, he continued there
till this time, and then was finally dispossessed by the Phœnicians. While he lived in the Chersonesus, he married, for his
second wife, Hegesipyla, the daughter of Olorus, a Thracian
king in the neighbourhood, by whom [a] he had Cimon, the famous general of the Athenians. After the death of Miltiades,
she had, by a second husband, a son, called also Olorus, by the
name of his grandfather, who was the father of Thucydides,
the historian. She could not have had them both by the same
husband; for Cimon and Thucydides, and consequently Olorus,
were of two different tribes, and therefore they could not be
both descended from Miltiades.

Darius, recalling all his other generals, [b] sent Mardonius,
the son of Gobrias, a young Persian nobleman, who
had lately married one of his daughters, to be the
chief commander in all the maritime parts of Asia,
with orders to invade Greece, and revenge him on the Athenians and Eretrians for the burning of Sardis. On his arrival
at the Hellespont, all his forces being there rendezvoused for
the execution of these orders, he marched with his land forces
through Thrace into Macedonia, ordering his fleet first to take
in Thasus, and then follow after him, and coast it by sea, as
he marched by land, that each might be at hand to act in concert with each other, for the prosecuting of the end proposed
by this war. On his arrival in Macedonia, all that country
dreading so great a power, submitted to him. But the fleet, after they had subdued Thasus, as they were passing farther on
towards the coasts of Macedonia, on their doubling of the cape
of Mount Athos, now called Capo Santo, met there with a terrible storm, which destroyed 300 of their ships, and above
20,000 of their men. And at the same time Mardonius fell
into no less a misfortune by land: for, lying with his army in
an encampment not sufficiently secured, the Thracians took the
advantage of it, and, falling on him in the night, broke into
his camp, and slew a great number of his men, and wounded
Mardonius

Anno 494.
Darius 28.

[a] Plutarchus in Cimone.   [b] Herodotus, lib. 6.

Mardonius himself; by which losses being disabled for any farther action either by sea or land, he was forced to march back again into Asia, without gaining any honour or advantage, either to himself, or the king's affairs, by this expedition.

Darius, before he would make any farther attempt upon the Grecians, [a] to make trial which of them would submit to him, and which would not, sent heralds to all their cities, to demand earth and water; which was the form whereby the Persians used to require the submission of those whom they would have yield to them. On the arrival of these heralds, several of the Grecian cities, dreading the power of the Persians, did as was required of them. But when those who were sent to Athens and Lacedæmon came thither with this commission, they flung them, the one into a well, and the other into a deep pit, and bid them fetch earth and water thence. But this being done in the heat of their rage, they repented of it, when come to a cooler temper: for thus to put heralds to death, was a violation of the law of nations, for which they were afterwards condemned even by themselves, as well as all their neighbours, and would gladly have made any satisfaction for the wrong, that would have been accepted of; and the Lacedæmonians sent a person of purpose to Susa to make an offer hereof.

Anno 493. Darius 29.

Darius, on the hearing of the ill success of Mardonius, suspecting the sufficiency of his conduct, [b] recalled him from his command, and sent two other generals in his stead, to prosecute the war against the Grecians, Datis a Median, and Artaphernes a Persian, the son of that Artaphernes's brother, who was lately governor of Sardis, and gave them particularly in charge not to fail of executing his revenge on the Athenians, and the Eretrians, whom he could never forgive for the part which they had in the burning of Sardis. On their arrival on the coasts of Ionia, they there drew together an army of 300,000 men, and a fleet of 600 ships, and made the best preparations they could for this expedition against the Grecians.

Anno 492. Darius 30.

In the beginning of the next spring, [c] the two Persian generals having shipped their army, rendezvoused their whole fleet at Samos, and from thence sailed to Naxus; and, having there burned the chief city of the island, and all their temples, and taken in all the other islands

Anno 491. Darius 31.

---

[a] Herodotus, lib. 7.

[b] Herodotus, lib. 6. Plutarchus in Aristide. Cornelius Nepos in Miltiade.

[c] Herodotus, lib. 6. Plutarchus in Aristide et Themistocle. Cornelius Nepos in Miltiade.

in those seas, they shaped their course directly for Eretria; and, after a siege of seven days, took the city by the treachery of some of its chief inhabitants, and burnt it to the ground, making all that they found in it captives. And then, passing over into Attica, they were led, by the guidance of Hippias, the late tyrant of Athens, into the plain of Marathon; where being met and fought with by 10,000 Athenians, and 1000 Plateans, under the leading of Miltiades, who was lately prince of the Thracian Chersonesus, they were there overthrown by this small number with a great slaughter, and forced to retreat to their ships, and sail back again into Asia with baffle and disgrace, having lost in this expedition, [a] saith Trogus, by the sword, shipwreck, and other ways, 200,000 men. But [b] Herodotus tells us, they were no more than 6400 that were slain in the field of battle; of which Hippias was one, who was the chief exciter and conductor of this war.

Datis and Artaphernes, on their return into Asia, [c] that they might shew some fruit of this expedition, sent the Eretrians they had taken to Darius to Susa; who, without doing them any farther harm, sent them to dwell in a village of the region of Cissia, which was at the distance of about a day's journey from Susa, [d] where Apollonius Tyaneus found their descendants still remaining a great many ages after.

Darius [e] on his hearing of the unsuccessful return of his forces from Attica, instead of being discouraged by that or the other disasters that had happened unto him in his attempts upon the Grecians, added the defeat of Marathon to the burning of Sardis as a new cause to excite him with the greater vigour to carry on the war against them. And therefore, resolving in person to make an invasion upon them with all his power, he sent orders through all the provinces, to arm the whole empire for it. But, after three years had been spent in making these preparations, a new war broke out in the 4th by the revolt of the Egyptians. But Darius's heart was so earnestly set against the Grecians, that resolving his new rebels should not divert him from executing his wrath upon his old enemies, he determined to make war against them both at the same time; and that, while part of his forces were sent to reduce Egypt, he would in person with the rest fall upon Greece. But he being now an old man, and there being a controversy between two of his sons, to which of them two the succession did belong, it was thought convenient,

Anno 490.
Darius 32.

Anno 487.
Darius 35.

---

[a] Justin, lib. 2. c. 9.
[b] Herodot. lib. 6.
[c] Herodot. lib. 6.
[d] Philostratus, lib. 1. c. 17.
[e] Herodot. lib. 7.

convenient, that the matter should be determined before he did set out on this expedition, lest otherwise, on his death, it might cause a civil war in the empire; for the preventing of which it was an ancient usage among the Persians, that, before their king went out to any dangerous war, his successor should be declared. The matter in dispute ᵃ stood thus. Darius had three sons by his first wife, the daughter of Gobrias, all born before his advancement to the throne, and four others by Atossa, the daughter of Cyrus, who were all born after it. Of the first Artabasanes (who is by some called Artemines, and by others Ariamenes) was the eldest, and of the latter Xerxes. Artabasanes urged that he was the eldest son; and therefore, according to the usage and custom of all nations, he ought to be preferred in the succession before the younger. To this Xerxes replied, that he was the son of Darius by Atossa, the daughter of Cyrus, who was the first founder of the Persian empire; and therefore claimed in her right to succeed his father in it; and that it was much more agreeable to justice, that the crown of Cyrus should come to a descendant of Cyrus, than to one who was not. And he farther added, that it was true, Artabasanes was the eldest son of Darius; but that he was the eldest son of the king: for Artabasanes was born while his father was only a private person, and therefore by that primogeniture could claim no more than to be heir to his private fortunes: but as to him, he was the first-born after his father was king, and therefore had the best right to succeed him in the kingdom. And for this he had an instance from the Lacedæmonians, with whom it was the usage, that the sons of their kings, who were born after their advancement to the throne, should succeed before those who were born before it. And this last argument he was helped to by Damaratus, formerly king of Lacedæmon, who, having been unjustly deposed by his subjects, was then an exile in the Persian court. Hereupon Xerxes was declared the successor, though not so much by the strength of his plea, as by the influence which his mother Atossa had over the inclinations of Darius, who was absolutely governed in this matter by the authority she had with him. That which was most remarkable in this contest, was, the friendly and amicable manner with which it was managed: for, during the whole time that it lasted, all the marks of a most entire fraternal affection passed between the two brothers; and, when it was decided, as the one did not insult, so neither did the other repine, or express any anger or discontent on the judgement given; and although the elder brother lost the cause, yet he cheerfully submitted

---

ᵃ Herodotus, lib 7. Justin, lib. 2. c. 10. Plutarchus in Artaxerxe et in Apophthegm, περὶ φιλαδελφίας.

ted to the determination, wished his brother joy, and, without diminishing his friendship or affection to him, ever after adhered to his interest, and at last died in his service, being slain fighting for him in the Grecian war; which is an example very rarely to be met with, where so great a prize is at stake, as that of a crown; the ambitious desire of which is usually of that force with the most of mankind, as to make them break through all other considerations whatsoever, where there is any the least pretence to it, to reach the attainment.

After the succession was thus settled, and all were ready to set out both for the Egyptian, as well as the Grecian war, Anno 486. [a] Darius fell sick and died, in the second year after the Darius 36. Egyptian revolt, having then reigned [b] 36 years; and Xerxes, according to the late determination, quietly succeeded in the throne. There are writers, [c] who place this determination after the death of Darius, and say, that it was settled by the judgement of Artabanus, uncle to the two contending princes, who was made the arbitrator between them in this contest. But Herodotus, who lived the nearest those times of all that have written of it, positively tells us, that it was decided by Darius himself a little before his death. And his decision being that which was most likely to have the greatest authority in this matter, Herodotus's account of it seemeth the much more probable of the two.

Darius was a prince of wisdom, clemency, and justice, and hath the honour [d] to have his name recorded in holy writ, for a favourer of God's people, a restorer of his temple at Jerusalem, and a promoter of his worship therein: for all which, God was pleased to make him his instrument: and in respect hereof, I doubt not, it was, that he blessed him with a numerous issue, a long reign, and great prosperity; for although he were not altogether so fortunate in his wars against the Scythians and the Grecians, yet every where else he had full success in all his undertakings, and not only restored and throughly settled the empire of Cyrus, after it had been much shaken by Cambyses and the Magian, but also added many large and rich provinces to it, especially those of India, Thrace, Macedon, and the isles of the Ionian sea.

The Jews [e] have a tradition, that in the last year of Darius died the prophets Haggai, Zechariah, and Malachi; that thereon

---

[a] Herodot. lib. 7.
[b] Ptolm. in Canone, Africanus, Euseb. &c.
[c] Justin, lib. 2. c. 10. Plutarchus περὶ φιλαδελφίας.
[d] Ezra v. and in the prophecies of Haggai and Zechariah.
[e] Abraham Zacutus in Juchasin, David Ganz in Zemach David, Sedar Olam Zuta, &c.

on ceased the spirit of prophecy from among the children of Israel; and that this was the obsignation or sealing up of vision and prophecy ᵃ spoken of by the prophet Daniel. And, from the same tradition, they tell us, that the kingdom of the Persians ceased also the same year; for they will have it, that this was the Darius whom Alexander conquered; and that the whole continuance of the Persian empire was only 52 years; which they reckon thus: Darius the Median reigned one year, Cyrus three years, Cambyses (who they say was the Ahasuerus who married Esther) 16 years, and Darius (whom they will have to be the son of Esther) 32 years. And this last Darius, according to them, was the Artaxerxes who sent Ezra and Nehemiah to Jerusalem, to restore the state of the Jews; for they tell us, that Artaxerxes, among the Persians, was the common name of their kings, as that of Pharaoh was among the Egyptians. This shews how ill they have been acquainted with the affairs of the Persian empire. And their countryman Josephus, in the account which he gives of those times, seems to have been but very little better informed concerning them.

In the time of his reign first appeared in Persia the famous prophet of the Magians, whom the Persians call Zerdusht, or Zaratush, and the Greeks, Zoroastres. The Greek and Latin writers much differ about him, some of them ᵇ will have it, that he lived many ages before, and was king of Bactria, and others that there were ᶜ several of the name, who lived in several ages, all famous in the same kind. But the oriental writers, who should best know, ᵈ all unanimously agree, that there was but one Zerdusht or Zoroastres; and that the time in which he flourished, was while Darius Hystaspis was king of Persia. It is certain he was no king, but one born of mean and obscure parentage, who did raise himself wholly by his craft in carrying on that imposture with which he deceived the world. They who place him so high as the time of Ninus, by whom, they say, he was slain in battle, follow the authority of Justin for it. But ᵉ Diodorus Siculus, out of Ctesias, tells us, that the king of Bactria, with whom Ninus had war, was called Oxyartes: and there are some ancient manuscripts of Justin ᶠ in which it is read Oxyartes, and perchance that was the genuine reading, and

Zoroastres

ᵃ Daniel ix. 24.
ᵇ Justin, lib. 1. c. 1. Diog. Laertius in Procemia, Plin. lib. 30. c. 1.
ᶜ Plin. lib. 36. c. 1. See Stanley of the Chaldaic Philosophy, c. 2.
ᵈ Abulfaragius, Ishmael Abulfeda, Sharestani, &c.; vide etiam Agathiam, lib. 2. et Thomman Hyde de Religione veterum Persarum, c. 24.
ᵉ Lib. 2. p. 94.
ᶠ So saith Ligerius.

Zoroaſtres came into the text inſtead of it, by the error of the copier, led thereto perchance by a note in the margin placed there by ſome critic, who, from the character of the perſon, took upon him to alter the name; for he is there ſaid, *Artes Magicas primo inveniſſe*, i. e. *That he was the firſt inventor of Magianiſm;* which Zoroaſtres only was generally taken to be, though in truth he was not the founder of that ſect, but only the reſtorer and reformer of it, as ſhall be hereafter ſhewn.

He was the greateſt impoſtor, except Mahomet, that ever appeared in the world, and had all the craft and enterpriſing boldneſs of that Arab, but much more knowledge; for he was excellently ſkilled in all the learning of the Eaſt that was in his time; whereas the other could neither write nor read; and particularly he was throughly verſed in the Jewiſh religion, and in all the ſacred writings of the Old Teſtament that were then extant, which makes it moſt likely, that he was, as to his origin, a Jew. And it is generally ſaid of him, that he had been a ſervant to one of the prophets of Iſrael, and that it was by this means that he came to be ſo well ſkilled in the holy ſcriptures, and all other Jewiſh knowledge; which is a farther proof, that he was of that people; it not being likely, that a prophet of Iſrael ſhould entertain him as a ſervant, or inſtruct him as a diſciple, if he were not of the ſame ſeed of Iſrael, as well as of the ſame religion with him; and that eſpecially ſince it was the uſage of that people, by principle of religion, as well as by long received cuſtom among them, to ſeparate themſelves from all other nations, as far as they were able. And it is farther to be taken notice of, that moſt of thoſe who ſpeak of his original, [a] ſay, that he was of Paleſtine, within which country the land of Judea was. And all this put together, amounts with me to a convincing proof, that he was firſt a Jew, and that by birth, as well as religion, before he took upon him to be prophet of the Magian ſect.

The prophet of Iſrael, to whom he was a ſervant, ſome [b] ſay, was Elias, and [c] others Ezra: but as the former was too early, ſo the other was too late for the time in which he lived. With this beſt agreeth what is ſaid by a third ſort of writers, [d] that it was one of the diſciples of Jeremiah with whom he ſerved; and, if ſo, it muſt have been either Ezekiel or Daniel; for, beſides theſe two, there was no other prophet of Iſrael in thoſe times, who could have

been

---

[a] Religio veterum Perſarum per Thomam Hyde, c. 24.

[b] Abulfaragius, p. 54.

[c] Abu Mohammed Muſtapha, Hiſtoricus Arab. Religio veterum Perſarum, c. 24. p. 313.

[d] Bundari ex Abu Japhar Tabarita Hiſtorico Arabe. Relig. vet. Perſ. c. 24. p. 314.

been of the disciples of Jeremiah. And as Daniel was of age sufficient at his carrying away to Babylon (he having been then about 18 years old), to have been sometime before under the discipline and tutorage of that prophet; so, having continued till about the end of the reign of Cyrus, he lived long enough to have been contemporary with this impostor; which cannot be said of Ezekiel: for we hear nothing more of him after the 27th year of the captivity of Jehoiachin, which was the year next after the taking of Tyre by Nebuchadnezzar; and therefore it is most likely, that he lived not much beyond that time. It must therefore be Daniel under whom this impostor served; and besides him there was not any other master in those times, under whom he could acquire all that knowledge, both in things sacred and profane, which he was so well furnished with. And, no doubt, his seeing that great, good, and wise man arrive to such an height and dignity in the empire, by being a true prophet of God, was that which did set this crafty wretch upon the design of being a false one; hoping that, by acting this part well, he might obtain the same advancement, and by pretending to that which the other really was, arrive to the like honour and greatness ; and it must be said, that, by his craft and dexterity in managing this pretence, he wonderfully succeeded in what he aimed at. It is said, that, while he served the prophet, under whom he was bred, he did, by some evil action, [a] draw on him his curse, and that thereon he was smitten with leprosy. But they who tell us this, seem to be such, who finding Eliah said to be his master, mistook Elisha for Eliah, and therefore thought Gehazi to have been the person.

He did not found a new religion, as his successor in imposture Mahomet did, but [b] only took upon him to revive and reform an old one, that of the Magians, which had been for many ages past the ancient national religion of the Medes, as well as of the Persians; for it having fallen under disgrace on the death of those ringleaders of that sect, who had usurped the sovereignty after the death of Cambyses, and the slaughter which was then made of all the chief men among them, it sunk so low, that it became almost extinct, and Sabianism every where prevailed against it, Darius and most of his followers on that occasion going over to it. But the affection which the people had for the religion of their forefathers, and which they had been all brought up in, not being easily to be rooted out, Zoroastres saw, that
the

---

[a] Megidi Persa. Buddari. Abu Mohammed Mustapha. Religio vet. Pers. c. 24. p. 113. 114. 115.

[b] Vidi Pocockii Specimen Historiæ Arabicæ, p. 147—149. et Thomam Hyde de Religione veterum Persarum.

the revival of this was the beſt game of impoſture that he could then play; and, having ſo good an old ſtock to graft upon, he did with the greater eaſe make all his new ſcions to grow, which he inſerted into it.

He firſt [a] made his appearance in Media, now called Aderbijan, in the city of Xix, ſay ſome; in that of Ecbatana, now Tauris, ſay others: for Smerdis having been of that province, it is moſt likely that the ſect which he was of had ſtill there its beſt rooting; and therefore the impoſtor thought he might in thoſe parts, with the beſt ſucceſs, attempt the revival of it. And his firſt appearing here is that which I ſuppoſe hath given ſome the handle to aſſert, that this was the country in which he was born.

The chief reformation which he made in the Magian religion was [b] in the firſt principle of it: for whereas before they had held the being of two firſt cauſes, the firſt light, or the good god, who was the author of all good; and the other darkneſs, or the evil god, who was the author of all evil; and that of the mixture of theſe two, as they were in a continual ſtruggle with each other, all things were made; he introduced a principle ſuperior to them both, one ſupreme God, who created both light and darkneſs, and out of theſe two, according to the alone pleaſure of his own will, made all things elſe that are, according to what is ſaid in the 45th chapter of Iſaiah, v. 5. 6. 7. "I am the Lord, and there is none elſe: there is no God beſides me; I girded thee, though thou haſt not known me, that they may know from the riſing of the ſun, and from the weſt, that there is none beſides me. I am the Lord, and there is none elſe. I form the light and create darkneſs, I make peace and create evil, I the Lord do all theſe things." For theſe words being directed to Cyrus, king of Perſia, muſt be underſtood as ſpoken in reference to the Perſian ſect of the Magians, who then held light and darkneſs, or good and evil, to be the ſupreme beings, without acknowledgeing the great God who is ſuperior to both. And I doubt not it was from hence that Zeroaſtres had the hint of mending this great abſurdity in their theology. But to avoid making God the author of evil, his doctrine was, [c] that God originally and directly created only light or good, and that darkneſs or evil followed it by conſequence, as the ſhadow doth the perſon; that light or good had only a real production from God, and the other

---

[a] Bundari. Abu Japhar Tabarita. Religio vet. Perſ. c. 24. Golii Notæ in Alfraganum, p. 207. & 227.
[b] Abul Feda. Ebn Shauna. Pocockii Specimen Hiſtoriæ Arab. p. 147. 148. Religio vet. Perſ. c. 9. p. 163. & c. 22. p. 299.
[c] Shahriſtani. Religio vet. Perſarum, c. 22. p. 299.

other afterwards refulted from it, as the defect thereof. In fum, his doctrine as to this particular was, [a] that there was one fupreme Being independent and felf-exifting from all eternity. That [b] under him there were two angels, one the angel of light, who is the author and director of all good; and the other the angel of darknefs, who is the author and director of all evil; and that thefe two, out of the mixture of light and darknefs, made all things that are; that they are in a perpetual ftruggle with each other; and that where the angel of light prevails, there the moft is good, and where the angel of darknefs prevails, there the moft is evil; that this ftruggle fhall continue to the end of the world; that [c] then there fhall be a general refurrection, and [d] a day of judgement, wherein juft retribution fhall be rendered to all according to their works; after which [e] the angel of darknefs, and his difciples, fhall go into a world of their own, where they fhall fuffer in everlafting darknefs the punifhments of their evil deeds; and the angel of light, and his difciples, fhall alfo go into a world of their own, where they fhall receive in everlafting light the reward due unto their good deeds; and that after this they fhall remain feparated for ever, and light and darknefs be no more mixed together to all eternity. And all [f] this the remainder of that fect, which is now in Perfia and India, do without any variation, after fo many ages, ftill hold even to this day. And how confonant this is to the truth, is plain enough to be underftood without a comment. And whereas he taught, that God originally created the good angel only, and that the other followed only by the defect of good, this plainly fhews, that he was not unacquainted with the revolt of the fallen angels, and the entrance of evil into the world that way, but had been throughly inftructed how that God at firft created all his angels good, as he alfo did man, and that they that are now evil became fuch wholly through their own fault, in falling from that ftate which God firft placed them in. All which plainly fhews the author of this doctrine to have been well verfed in the facred writings of the Jewifh religion, out of which it manifeftly appears to have been all taken; only the crafty impoftor took care to drefs it up in fuch a ftyle and form, as would make

[a] Abulfeda. Shahriftani. Relig. vet. Perf. c. 22.
[b] Religio vet. Perf. c. 9. p. 163. Pocockii Specimen Hiftoriæ Arabicæ, p. 148.
[c] Diogenes Laertius in Proœmio. Plutarchus in Ifide & Ofiride. Shahriftani. Relig. vet. Perf. c. 22. p. 296.
[d] Relig. vet. Perf. c. 33.
[e] Shahriftani. Plutarchus de Ifide & Ofiride. Religio. vet. Perf. p. 299. 395. &c.
[f] Relig. vet. Perf. c. 22. p. 292. 293. Ovington's Travels.

make it best agree with that old religion of the Medes and Persians which he grafted it upon.

Another reformation which he made in the Magian religion, was, [a] that he caused fire-temples to be built wherever he came: for whereas hitherto they had erected their altars, on which their sacred fire was kept, on the tops of hills, and on high places in the open air, and there performed all the offices of their religious worship, where, often by rain, tempests, and storms, the sacred fire was extinguished, and the holy offices of their religion interrupted and disturbed; for the preventing of this he directed, that wherever any of those altars were erected, temples should be built over them, that so the sacred fires might be the better preserved, and the public offices of their religion the better performed before them. For all the parts of their public worship were performed before these public sacred fires, as all their private devotions were before private fires in their own houses; not that they worshipped the fire (for this they always disowned), but God in the fire. For [b] Zoroastres, among other his impostures, having feigned, that he was taken up into heaven, there to be instructed in those doctrines which he was to deliver unto men, he pretended not (as Mahomet after did) there to have seen God, but only to have heard him speaking to him out of the midst of a great and most bright flame of fire; and therefore taught his followers, that fire was the truest *Shechinah* of the divine presence; that the sun being the perfectest fire, God had there [c] the throne of his glory, and the residence of his divine presence, in a more excellent manner than any where else, and, next that, in the elementary fire with us; and for this reason he ordered them still to direct all their worship to God, first towards the sun (which they called Mithra), and next towards their sacred fires, as being the things in which God chiefly dwelt; and their ordinary way of worship was to do so towards both: for when they came before these fires to worship, they always approached them on the west side, that, having their faces towards them, and also toward the rising sun at the same time, they might direct their worship towards both. And in this posture they always performed every act of their worship. But this was not a new institution of his: for thus to worship before fire and the sun, was, as hath been said, the ancient usage of that sect; and according hereto is it, that we are to understand what we find in Ezekiel viii. 16. where it is related, that

the

---

[a] Religio vet. Perf. c. 1. c. 8. & c. 29.
[b] Religio vet. Perf. c. 8. p. 160.
[c] Sanfon in the present State of Persia, p. 185. Religio vet. Perf. c. 4.

the prophet being carried in a vision to Jerusalem, to see the abominations of that place, among other impieties, had there shewn him " about five and twenty men standing between the porch and the altar, with their backs towards the temple of the Lord, and their faces towards the east; and they worshipped the sun." The meaning of which is, that they had turned their backs upon the true worship of God, and had gone over to that of the Magians. For the holy of holies (in which was the *Shechinah* of the divine presence resting over the mercy seat), being on the western end of the temple at Jerusalem, all that entered thither to worship God did it with their faces turned that way: for that was their [a] *Kebla*, or the point towards which they always directed their worship. But the *Kebla* of the Magians being the rising sun, they always worshipped with their faces turned that way, that is, towards the east. And therefore these twenty-five men, by altering their *Kebla*, are shewn to have altered their religion, and, instead of worshipping God according to the Jewish religion, to have gone over to the religion and worship of the Magians.

Zoroastres having thus retained, in his reformation of Magianism, the ancient usage of that sect in worshipping God before fire, to give the sacred fires in the temples which he had erected the greater veneration, he pretended, that, when he was in heaven, and there heard God speaking to him out of the midst of fire, he [b] brought thence some of that fire with him on his return, and placed it on the altar of the first fire temple that he erected (which was that [c] at Xix in Media), from whence they say it was propagated to all the rest. And this is the reason which is given for their so careful keeping of it: [d] for their priests watch it day and night, and never [e] suffer it to go out or be extinguished. And for the same reason also they did treat it with that superstition, that they fed it only with [f] wood stripped of its bark, and of that sort which they thought most clean; and they never [f] did blow it, either with bellows or with their breath, for fear of polluting it: and to do this either of those ways, or to cast any unclean thing into it, was no less than death by the law of the land,

VOL. I.   P   as

---

[a] Kebla, among the eastern nations, signifieth the point of the heavens towards which they directed their worship. The Jews did it towards the temple at Jerusalem, the Mahometans towards Mecca, the Sabians towards the Meridian, and the Magians towards the rising sun.
[b] Religio vet. Perf. c. 8. p. 160.
[c] Golii Notæ ad Alfraganum, p. 227.
[d] Strabo, lib. 15. Ammianus Marcellinus, lib. 23. Agathias, lib. 4
[e] Religio vet. Perf. c. 28. p. 351. and c. 29. p. 355.
[f] Strabo, lib. 15. Religio vet. Perf. ibid.

as long as thofe of that fect reigned in it, which, from the time of Zoroaftres, to the death of Yazdejerd, the laft Perfian king of the Magian religion, was about 1150 years; yea, it went fo far, [a] that the priefts themfelves never approached this fire, but with a cloth over their mouths, that they might not breathe thereon; and this they did, not only when they tended the fire, to lay more wood thereon, or do any other fervice about it, but alfo when they approached it, to read the daily offices of their liturgy before it: fo that they mumbled over their prayers, rather than fpoke them, in the fame manner as the Popifh priefts do their maffes, without letting the people prefent articulately hear one word of what they faid; and, if they fhould hear them, they would now as badly underftand them; for all their public prayers are, even to this day, in the old Perfian language, in which Zoroaftres firft compofed them, above 2200 years fince, of which the common people do not now underftand one word: and in this abfurdity alfo have they the Romanifts partakers with them. When Zoroaftres compofed his liturgy, the old Perfic was then indeed the vulgar language of all thofe countries where this liturgy was ufed: and fo was the Latin throughout all the weftern empire, when the Latin fervice was firft ufed therein. But when the language changed, they would not confider, that the change which was made thereby, in the reafon of the thing, did require that a change fhould be made in their liturgy alfo, but retained it the fame, after it ceafed to be underftood, as it was before. So it was the fuperftitious folly of adhering to old eftablifhments againft reafon that produced this abfurdity in both of them: though it muft be acknowledged, that the Magians have more to fay for themfelves in this matter than the Romanifts; for they are taught, that their liturgy was brought them from heaven, which the others do not believe of theirs, though they ftick to it as if it were. And if that ftiffnefs of humour, which is now among too many of us, againft altering any thing in our liturgy, fhould continue, it muft at laft bring us to the fame pafs: for all languages being *in fluxu*, they do in every age alter from what they were in the former; and therefore, as we do not now underftand the Englifh which was here fpoken by our anceftors 300 or 400 years ago, fo, in all likelihood, will not our pofterity 300 or 400 years hence underftand that which is now fpoken by us. And therefore, fhould our liturgy be ftill continued, without any change or alteration, it will then be as much in an unknown language as now the Roman fervice is to the vulgar of that communion.

But

---

[a] Strabo, lib. 15. p. 732. Religio vet. Perſ. c. 30.

But, to return to the reformations of Zoroaftres; how much he followed the Jewifh platform in the framing of them, doth manifeftly appear from the particulars I have mentioned; for moft of them were taken, either from the facred writings, or the facred ufages of that people. Mofes heard God fpeaking to him out of a flame of fire from the bufh, and all Ifrael heard him fpeaking to them in the fame manner out of the midft of fire from mount Sinai: hence Zoroaftres pretended to have heard God fpeaking to him alfo out of the midft of a flame of fire. The Jews had a vifible *Shechina* of the divine prefence among them refting over the mercy-feat in the holy of holies, both in their tabernacle and temple, toward which they offered up all their prayers; and therefore Zoroaftres taught his Magians to pretend to the like, and to hold the fun, and the facred fires in their fire-temples, to be this *Shechina* in which God efpecially dwelt; and for this reafon they offered up all their prayers to him with their faces turned towards both. The Jews had a facred fire which came down from heaven upon their altar of burnt-offerings, which they did there ever after, till the deftruction of Jerufalem by the Chaldeans, inextinguifhably maintain: and with this fire only were all their facrifices and oblations made, and Nadab and Abihu were punifhed with death for offering incenfe to God with other fire. And in like manner Zoroaftres pretended to have brought his holy fire from heaven; and therefore commanded it to be kept with the fame care. And to kindle fire on the altar of any new erected fire-temple, or to re-kindle it on any fuch altar, where it had been by any unavoidable accident extinguifhed, from any other fire, than from one of the facred fires in fome other temple, or elfe from the fun, was reckoned a crime to be punifhed in the fame manner. And whereas great care was taken among the Jews, [a] that no wood fhould be ufed on their altar in the temple, but that which they reputed clean, and for this reafon they had it all barked and examined before it was laid on; and that when it was laid on, the fire fhould never be blowed up either with bellows or the breath of man for the kindling of it; hence Zoroaftres [b] ordained both thefe particulars to be alfo obferved in refpect of his facred fire among his Magians, commanding them to ufe only barked wood for the maintaining of it, and no other means for the kindling of it up into a flame, but the pouring on of oil and the blafts of the open air. And that he fhould in fo many things write after the Jewifh religion, or have been fo well informed therein,

---

[a] See Lightfoot's Temple-fervice.
[b] Religio Veterum Perfarum, c. 29. & c. 30.

can fcarce feem probable, if he had not been firſt educated and brought up in it.

Zoroaſtres, having thus taken upon him to be a prophet of God, fent to reform the old religion of the Perſians, to gain the better reputation to his pretenſions, [a] he retired into a cave, and there lived a long time as a recluſe, pretending to be abſtracted from all worldly conſiderations, and to be given wholly to prayer and divine meditations; and, the more to amuſe the people who there reforted to him, he dreſſed up his cave with ſeveral myſtical figures, repreſenting Mithra, and other myſteries of their religion; from whence it became for a long while after a uſage among them to chooſe ſuch caves for their devotions, which being dreſſed up in the ſame manner, were called Mithratic caves. While he was in this retirement, he compoſed the book wherein all his pretended revelations are contained, which ſhall be hereafter fpoken of. And Mahomet exactly followed his example herein; for he alfo retired to a cave ſome time before he broached his impoſture, and, by the help of his accomplices, there formed the Alcoran, wherein it is contained. And [b] Pythagoras, on his return from Babylon to Samos, in imitation of his maſter Zoroaſtres (whom [c] Clemens Alexandrinus tells us he emulouſly followed), had there in like manner his cave to which he retired, and wherein he moſtly abode both day and night, and for the ſame end as Zoroaſtres did in his, that is, to get himſelf the greater veneration from the people: for Pythagoras acted a part of impoſture as well as Zoroaſtres, and this perchance he alſo learned from him.

After he had thus acted the part of a prophet in Media, and there ſettled all things according to his intentions, he removed from thence into [d] Bactria, the moſt eaſtern province of Perſia, and there ſettled in the city of Balch, which lies on the river Oxus, in the confines of Perſia, India, and Cowareſmia; where, under the protection of Hyſtaſpes, the father of Darius, he ſoon ſpread his impoſture through all that province with great ſucceſs: for although Darius, after the ſlaughter of the Magians, had, with moſt of his followers, gone over to the ſect of the Sabians; yet Hyſtaſpes ſtill adhered to the religion of his anceſtors, and, having fixed his reſidence at Balch (where it may be ſuppoſed he governed thoſe parts of the empire under his ſon), did there ſupport and promote it to the utmoſt of his power. And, in order

[a] Porphyrius in libro de Nympharum Antro, p. 254. Edit. Cant.
[b] Porphyrius in Vita Pythagoræ, p. 184. Edit. Cantab. Jamblichus in Vita Pythagoræ, c. 5.
[c] Strom. 1. p. 213.
[d] Abu Japhar Tabarita. Bundari. Relig. vet. Perſ. c. 24.

der to give it the greater reputation, [a] he went in perfon into India among the Brachmans, and, having there learned from them all their knowledge in mathematics, aftronomy, and natural philofophy, he brought it back among his Magians, and throughly inftructed them in it. And they continued for many ages after, above all others of thofe times, fkilful in thefe fciences, efpecially after they had been farther inftructed in them by Zoroaftres, who was the greateft mathematician, and the greateft philofopher of the age in which he lived; and therefore took care to improve his fect, not only in their religion, but alfo in all natural knowledge; which fo much advanced their credit in the world, that thenceforth a learned man and a Magian became equivalent terms. And this proceeded fo far, that the vulgar looking on their knowledge to be more than natural, entertained an opinion of them, as if they had been actuated and infpired by fupernatural powers, in the fame manner as, too frequently among us, ignorant people are apt to give great fcholars, and fuch as are learned beyond their comprehenfions (as were Friar Bacon, [b] Dr Fauftus, and [c] Cornelius Agrippa), the name of conjurers. And from hence thofe who really practifed wicked and diabolical arts, or would be thought to do fo, taking the name of Magians, drew on it that ill fignification, which now the word Magician bears among us; whereas the true and ancient Magians [d] were the great mathematicians, philofophers, and divines, of the ages in which they lived, and had no other knowledge but what by their own ftudy, and the inftructions of the ancients of their fect, they had improved themfelves in.

But it is not to be underftood, that all Magians, that is, all of the fect, were thus learned, but only thofe who had this name by way of eminence above the reft, that is, their priefts; for they being all [e] of the fame tribe, as among the Jews (none but

the

---

[a] Ammianus Marcellinus, lib. 23.

[b] John Fauft was the firft inventor of printing at Mentz, and from thence being taken for a conjurer, that ftory is here in England made of him, which goes under the name of Dr Fauftus.

[c] That which contributes moft to the opinion, that Cornelius Agrippa was a Magician, is an impertinent book publifhed under his name, intitled, *De Occulta Philofophia*, which that learned man was never the author of; for it is not to be found in the folio edition of his works, in which only thofe that are genuine and truly his are contained.

[d] Dion Chryfoftomus tells us *(in Oratione Boryfthenica)*, that the Perfians call them Magians who are fkilled in the worfhip of the gods, and not as the Greeks, who being ignorant of the meaning of the word, call them fo who were fkilful in goetic Magic, *i. e.* that which juglers and conjurers pretend to make ufe of.

[e] Religio vet. Perf. c. 30. p. 367. Theodoreti Hift. Ecclef. lib. 5. c. 38.

the son of a priest being capable of being a priest among them), they mostly appropriated their learning to their own families, transmitting it in them from father to son, and seldom communicating it to any other, unless it were to those of the royal family, [a] whom they were bound to instruct, the better to fit them for government; and therefore there were some of them, as tutors as well as chaplains, always residing in the palaces of their kings. And whether it were, that these Magians thought it would bring the greater credit to them, or the kings, that it would add a greater sacredness to their persons, or whether it were from both these causes, the royal family among the Persians, as long as this sect prevailed among them, was always reckoned of the sacerdotal tribe. They were divided into [b] three orders. The lowest were the inferior clergy, who served in all the common offices of their divine worship: next above them were the superintendents, who in their several districts governed the inferior clergy, as the bishops do with us: and above all was the Archimagus, or arch-priest, who, in the same manner as the high priest among the Jews, or the Pope now among the Romanists, was the head of the whole religion. And, according to the number of their orders, the churches or temples in which they officiated were also of three sorts. The lowest sort were the parochial churches, or oratories, which were served by the inferior clergy, as the parochial churches are now with us; and the duties which they there performed were to read the daily offices out of their liturgy, and, at stated and solemn times, to read some part of their sacred writings to the people. In these churches there were no fire altars; but the sacred fire, before which they here worshipped, was maintained only in a lamp. Next above these were their fire temples, in which fire was continually kept burning on a sacred altar. And these were, in the same manner as cathedrals with us, the churches or temples where the superintendents resided. In every one of these were also several of the inferior clergy entertained, who, in the same manner as the choral vicars among us, performed all the divine offices under the superintendent, and also took care of the sacred fire, which they constantly watched day and night by four and four in their turns, that it might always be kept burning, and never go out. 3dly, The highest church above all was the fire temple, where the Archimagus resided, which was had in the same veneration with them as the temple of Mecca among the Mahometans, to which every one

---

[a] Plato in Alcibiade, 1. Stobæus, p. 496. Clemens Alexandrinus in Pædagogo 1. p. 81.
[b] Religio vet. Pers. cap. 28, & cap. 30.

one of that sect thought themselves obliged to make a pilgrimage once in their lives. Zoroastres first settled it at Balch, and there he, as their Archimagus, usually had his residence. But after the Mahometans had over-run Persia, in the 7th century after Christ, the Archimagus was forced to remove from thence into Kerman, which is a province in Persia, lying upon the Southern ocean, towards India, and there it hath continued even to this day. And to the fire temple there erected, at the place of his residency, do they now pay the same veneration as formerly they did to that of Balch. This temple of the Archimagus, as also the other fire temples, were endued with large revenues in lands: but the parochial clergy depended solely on the tithes and offerings of the people; for this usage also had Zoroastres taken from the Jewish church, and made it one of his establishments among his Magians.

The impostor having thus settled his new scheme of Magianism throughout the province of Bactria, with the same success as he had before in Media, he [a] went next to the royal court at Susa, where he managed his pretensions with that craft, address, and insinuation, that he soon got within Darius himself, and made him a proselyte to his new reformed religion; whose example, in a short time, drew after it into the same profession the courtiers, nobility, and all the great men of the kingdom. This happened in the 30th year of Darius; and, although it succeeded not without great opposition from the ringleaders of the Sabians, who were the opposite sect, yet the craft, address, and dexterity of the impostor surmounted them all, and so settled his new device, that thenceforth it became the national religion of all that country, and so continued for many ages after, till this imposture was at last supplanted by that of Mahomet, which was raised almost by the same arts. They who professed this religion [b] in Lucian's time, as reckoned up by him, were the Persians, the Parthians, the Bactrians, the Cowaresmians, the Arians, the Sacans, the Medes, and many other barbarous nations; but, since that, the new imposture hath grown up to the suppressing of the old in all these countries. However, there is a remnant of these Magians still remaining in Persia and India, who even to this day observe the same religion which Zoroastres first taught them; for they still have his book, wherein their religion is contained, which they keep and reverence in the same manner as the Christians do the Bible, and the Mahometans the Alcoran, making it the sole rule both of their faith and manners.

This [c] book the impostor composed while he lived in his retirement

[a] Religio vet. Perf. c. 24.
[b] Lucian de Longævis.
[c] Religio vet. Perf. c. 25. & 26.

retirement in the cave; and therein are contained all his pretended revelations. When he presented it to Darius, it was bound up in twelve volumes, whereof each consisted of 100 skins of vellum; for it ᵃ was the usage of the Persians in those times to write all on skins. This book is called Zendavesta, and, by contraction, Zend; the vulgar pronounce it Zundavestow, and Zund. The word originally signifieth a fire-kindler, such as is a tinder-box with us; which fantastical name the impostor gave it, because, as he pretended, all that would read this book, and meditate thereon, might from thence, as from a fire-kindler, kindle in their hearts the fire of all true love for God and his holy religion. For the better understanding of which, it is to be observed, that, in those eastern countries, their way of kindling fire, is not by a tinder-box, as with us, but by rubbing two pieces of cane one against another, till one of them takes fire: and such a fire-kindler of his religion in the hearts of men the impostor would have his book to be; and therefore called it by that name. The first part of it contains their liturgy, which is still used among them in all their oratories and fire-temples even to this day. The rest treats of all other parts of their religion. And according as their actions do agree or disagree with this book, do they reckon them to be either good or evil. Thence, in their language, they call a righteous action *Zend-aver*, i. e. *what the book Zend allows*, and an evil action *Na-Zend-aver*, i. e. *which the book Zend disallows*. This book Zoroastres feigned to have received from heaven, as Mahomet afterwards (perchance following his pattern) pretended of his Alcoran. It is still preserved among them in the old Persian language and character; and in every oratory and fire-temple, even to this day, there is a copy of it kept (in the same manner as there is with us of the Bible in every parish church), out of which, on certain stated times, the priests read a portion of it to the people. ᵇ Dr Hyde, late professor of the Hebrew and Arabic tongues at Oxford, being well skilled in the old Persic, as well as the modern, offered to have published the whole of it with a Latin translation, could he have been supported in the expences of the edition. But for want of this help and encouragement, the design died with him, to the great damage of the learned world: for a book of that antiquity, no doubt, would be of great use, could it be made public among us, and would unfold and give us light into many things of the times wherein it was written, which we are now ignorant of.

In this book are found a great many things ᶜ taken out of the

---

ᵃ Diodorus Sic. lib. 2. p. 118.
ᵇ Vide eundem De Religione veterum Persarum, cap. 1. p. 25.
ᶜ Pocockii Specimen Hist. Arab. p. 148. Religio veterum Persarum.

the scriptures of the Old Testament, besides those I have already mentioned; which farther proves the author's original to have been what I have said: for therein he inserts a great part of the psalms of David; he makes Adam and Eve to have been the first parents of all mankind, and gives in a manner the same history of the creation and the deluge that Moses doth; only as to the former, whereas Moses tells us, that all things were created in six days, Zoroastres converts those six days into six times, allowing to each of those times several days; so that, putting them all together, the time of the creation, according to his account, amounted to 365 days, that is, a whole year. He speaks therein also of Abraham, Joseph, Moses, and Solomon, in the same manner as the scriptures do. And, out of a particular veneration for Abraham, he called his book *the book of Abraham*, and his religion the *religion of Abraham*: for he pretended, that the reformation which he introduced, was no more, than to bring back the religion of the Persians to that original purity in which Abraham practised it, by purging it of all those defects, abuses, and innovations, which the corruptions of after-times had introduced into it. And to all this Mahomet also (no doubt from this pattern) afterwards pretended for his religion: for the name of Abraham hath for a great many ages past been had in great veneration all over the East, and among all sects; so that every one of them have thought it would give reputation to them, could they entitle themselves to him: for not only the Jews, the Magians, and the Mahometans, but the Sabians, and also the Indians (if the Brahama of the latter be Abraham, as it is with good reason supposed), all challenge him to themselves, as the great patriarch and founder of their several sects; every one of them pretending, that their religion is the same which Abraham professed, and by his reformation established among them: and to restore this reformation was all that Zoroastres, Mahomet, and the author of the Sabian sect, whoever he was, pretended to. This veneration for Abraham in those parts, proceeded from the great fame of his piety, which was (it is supposed) there spread among them by the Israelites in their dispersion all over the East, first on the Assyrian, and after on the Babylonish captivity. And this fame being once fixed, made all parties fond of having him thought their own; and therefore all laid claim to him. And, in this book, Zoroastres commands also the same observances about beasts clean and unclean, as Moses doth; gives the same law of paying tithes to the sacerdotal order; injoins the same care of avoiding all external, as well as all internal pollutions; the same way of cleansing and purifying themselves, by frequent washings; the same keep-

ing

ing of the priesthood always within the same tribe, and the same ordaining of one high priest over all; and several other institutions are also therein contained of the same Jewish extraction. The rest of its contents are an historical account of the life, actions, and prophecies of its author, the several branches and particulars of his new reformed superstition, and rules and exhortations to moral living; in which he is very pressing, and sufficiently exact, saving only in one particular, that is, about incest: for therein he wholly takes this away, and, as if nothing of this nature were unlawful, [a] allows a man to marry, not only his sister or his daughter, but also his mother; and it went so far with that sect in the practice, that, in the sacerdotal tribe, he that was born of this last and worst sort of incest, was looked on as the best qualified for the sacerdotal function; none being esteemed among them more proper for the highest stations in it, than those that were born of mothers who conceived them of their own sons; which was such an abomination, that though all things else had been right therein, this alone is enough to pollute the whole book. The Persian kings being exceedingly given to such incestuous marriages, this seems to have been contrived out of a vile piece of flattery to them, the better to engage and fix them to their sect. But [b] Alexander, when he conquered Persia, did put an end to this abomination; for he did by a law forbid all such incestuous copulations among them.

Zoroastres having obtained this wonderful success, in making his imposture to be thus received by the king, the great men, and the generality of the whole kingdom, [c] he returned back again to Balch; where, according to his own institution, he was obliged to have his residence, as Archimagus, or head of the sect; and there he reigned in spirituals with the same authority over the whole empire, as the king did in temporals; and from hence perchance might proceed the mistake of making him king of Bactria, Balch being in that province. And his being said to have been there slain in battle by Ninus, might also have its original from his suffering this fate in that country, although from another hand: for, after his return to Balch, having enterprised upon Argasp, king of the oriental Scythians (who was a zealous Sabian), to draw him over to his religion, and backed this attempt with the authority of Darius, the more prevalently to induce him to it, the Scythian prince resented it with such indignation to be thus imperiously addressed to concerning this matter, that he invaded

---

[a] Diogenes Laertius in Prœmio. Strabo, lib. 15. Philo Judæus de Specialibus legibus, p. 778. Tertullian in Apologetico. Clemens Alexandrinus in Pædagog. 1. p. 81. et Strom. 3. p. 314.

[b] Plutarchus de Fortuna Alexandri.

[c] Religio vet. Pers. c. 24.

vaded Bactria with an army; and having there defeated the forces of Darius that opposed him, slew Zoroastres, with all the priests of his patriarchal church, which amounted to the number of 80 persons, and demolished all the fire-temples in that province. This happened in the 35th year of the reign of Darius. The Persians tell us, that Lorasp, or Hystaspes, the father of Darius, was slain also in the same war. But, if he lived so long, he must then have been exceeding old; for, allowing him to have been no more than 20 on his first coming with Cyrus out of Persia, he must now have been 93 years old. But this is no strange thing in those parts: for the air being there throughly pure and healthy, the perspiration free and regular, and all the fruits of the earth fully concocted, they who can there avoid the excesses of lust and luxury, usually live to a great age: of which we have lately had two instances, in Aurang-Zeb, king of India, and Rajah-Singah, king of Candia, in the island of Ceylon, the former dying in the year 1708, of the age of near 100, and the other about twenty years before, much older.

But Darius soon revenged the injury upon the Scythian king: for, falling on him before he could make his retreat, he overthrew him with a great slaughter, and drove him out of the province; after which he rebuilt again all the fire-temples that had been demolished by the enemy, and especially that at Balch; which he erected with a grandeur suitable to its dignity, it being the patriarchal temple of the sect; and therefore, from the name of its restorer, it was thenceforth called [a] Azur Gustasp, *i. e.* the fire-temple of Darius Hystaspes. And the care which he took in this matter, shews the zeal which he had for his new religion, which he still continued to propagate after the death of its author with the same ardour as before. And, the better to preserve its credit and reputation after this accident, he thenceforth took it on himself to be their Archimagus: for [b] Porphyry tells us, he ordered, before his death, that, among other his titles, it should be engraven on his monument, that he was *Master of the Magians;* which plainly implies, that he bore this office among them, (for none but the Archimagus was master of the whole sect). But it was not long that he was in it; for he died the next year after. However, from hence it seems to have proceeded, that the kings of Persia were ever after looked on to be of the sacerdotal tribe, and were always [c] initiated into the sacred order of the Magians, before they took on them the crown, or were inaugurated into the kingdom.

The

[a] Religio veterum Persarum, c. 23.
[b] Porphyrius de Abstinentia, lib. 4. p. 165. edit. Cant.
[c] Cicero de Divinatione, lib. 1. Philo Judæus de Specialibus Legibus. Plutarchus in Artaxerxe.

The [a] Greeks had the name of Zoroaſtres in great eſteem, ſpeaking of him as the great maſter of all human and divine knowledge. [b] Plato, [c] Ariſtotle, [d] Plutarch, and [e] Porphyry, mention him with honour, acknowledging his great learning; and ſo do others. [f] Pliny ſaith much of him; and particularly remarks, that he was the only perſon that laughed on the day in which he was born; and that the pulſation of his head did then beat ſo ſtrong, that it heaved up the hand laid upon it; which laſt, he ſaith, was a preſage of his future learning. Solinus tells us the ſame ſtory of his laughing on the day of his birth; and ſaith, that [g] he was *Optimarum artium peritiſſimus, i. e. Moſt ſkilful in the knowledge of the beſt arts.* And Apuleius's character of him is, that he was [h] *Omnis divini arcani antiſtes, i. e. The chief doctor in all divine myſteries.* Cedrenus names him as a famous aſtronomer among the Perſians, and [i] Suidas ſaith of him, that he excelled all others in that ſcience. And this reputation he ſtill hath over all the Eaſt, even among thoſe who are moſt averſe to his ſect to this very day: for they all there, as well Mahometans as Sabians, give him [k] the title of Hakim, that is, of a wiſe and learned philoſopher, and reckon him as the moſt ſkilful and eminent of their ancient aſtronomers. And particularly Ulugh Beigh, that famous and learned Tartarian prince, writing a book of aſtronomy and aſtrology, doth therein [l] prefer Zoroaſtres before all others for his ſkill and knowledge in theſe ſciences. It is to be obſerved alſo, that they who write of Pythagoras, do almoſt all of them tell us, that he was the ſcholar of Zoroaſtres, at Babylon, and learned of him moſt of that knowledge which afterwards rendered him ſo famous in the Weſt. So ſaith [m] Apuleius, and ſo ſay [n] Jamblichus, [o] Porphyry, and [p] Clemens Alexandrinus; (for the Zabratus or Zaratus of Porphyry, and the Na-Zaratus of Clemens, were none other than this Zoroaſtres); and they relate the mat-

ter

---

[a] Diogenes Laertius in Proœmio.
[b] In Alcibiade 1.
[c] In libro de Magia citante Laertio in Proœmio.
[d] De Iſide et Oſiride.
[e] In vita Pythagoræ.
[f] Lib. 30. c. 1. and lib. 7. c. 16.
[g] Cap. 1.
[h] Floridorum ſecunda.
[i] In vocibus Μάγοι & Αςρονομία & Ζωροάςρης.
[k] Religio Vet. Perſ. c. 24. p. 312.
[l] Ibid.
[m] Floridorum ſecundo.
[n] In vita Pythagoræ, c. 4.
[o] In vita Pythagoræ, p. 185. Edit. Cant.
[p] Strom. 1. p. 223.
[q] Jamblichus de vita Pythagoræ, c. 4. Apuleius Floridorum ſecunda.

ter thus: that when Cambyses conquered Egypt, ᵠ he found Pythagoras there on his travels, for the improvement of himself in the learning of that country]; that, having taken him prisoner, he sent him with other captives to Babylon, where Zoroastres (or Zabratus, as Porphyry calls him) then lived; and that there he became his disciple, and learned many things of him of the eastern learning. The words of Porphyry are, ' That by ᵃ Zabratus he was cleansed from the pollutions of his life past and instructed from what things virtuous persons ought to be free, and also learned from him the discourse concerning nature, and what are the principles of the universe.' This story may well enough agree with the time of Zoroastres, but it cannot do so with the time of Pythagoras; what is therein said of his being carried captive to Babylon, it is possible might have happened when Nebuchadnezzar conquered Egypt, but could not be when it was conquered by Cambyses; ᵇ the chronology of the life of Pythagoras may very well admit of the former, but can never of the latter: for, by that time Cambyses had conquered Egypt, Pythagoras had been settled in Italy above 20 years, after all his travels were over, and was then grown an old man, being then about the 63d year of his age. But, however, that Pythagoras was at Babylon, and learned there a great part of that knowledge which he was afterwards so famous for, is agreed by ᶜ all, though there may be some error, as to the time when he is said to have been there, or the manner how he came hither. His stay there, ᵈ Jamblichus tells us, was 12 years; and that, in his converse with the Magians, he learned from them (over and above what hath been afore mentioned out of Porphyry) arithmetic, music, and the knowledge of divine things, and the sacred mysteries pertaining thereto. But the most important doctrine which he brought home from thence, was that of the immortality of the soul: for it is generally agreed among the ancients, ᵉ that he was the first of all the Greeks that taught it. And this I take for certain he had from Zoroastres: for, as I have afore shewn, it was his doctrine, and he is the ancientest whom we have upon record of all the heathen nations that taught it. But Pythagoras did not bring this doctrine into Greece with that purity in which he received it from his master; for having corrupted it with a mixture of the Indian philosophy (for this also he

had

ᵃ In Vita Pythagoræ, p. 285. Edit. Cant.
ᵇ See the bishop of Worcester's tract of the life of Pythagoras.
ᶜ Diogenes Laertius, Porphyrius et Jamblichus in Vita Pythagoræ.
ᵈ Jamblichus in Vita Pythagoræ, lib. 4.
ᵉ Porphyrius in Vita Pythagoræ, p. 188. ct. 201. Edit. Cant. Jamblichus in Vita Pythagoræ, c. 30.

had learned in the East), he made this immortality to [a] consist
in an eternal transmigration of the soul from one body to another; whereas Zoroastres's doctrine was, [b] that there is to be a
resurrection of the dead, and an immortal state after to follow,
in the same manner as [c] Daniel taught, and the people of God
then held, and we now; and there is no doubt but that he had
it from them.

Some of the [d] ancient heretics, especially the followers of
Prodicus, pretended to have the secret books of Zoroastres containing his revelations, and other mysteries of religion, and offered
to make use of them in defence of their heresies. Against these
Plotinus [e] and Porphyry did both write, and fully shewed them
to have been the forgeries of the Gnostic Christians. And others
have gathered together out of Proculus, Simplicius, Damascius
Synesius, Olympiodorus, and other writers, what they call the
oracles of Zoroastres; and several editions have been published of
them in Greek with the scholia or comments of Pletho and Psellus. But all these are mere figments coined by the Platonic philosophers, who lived after the time of Christ, and are condemned
as such by [f] St Chrysostome, who plainly tells us that they
were all figments. If any are desirous to see what unintelligible
and nonsensical stuff these oracles do contain, they may consult
Mr Stanley's book of the Chaldaic philosophy, which is published at the end of his history of philosophy, where they will find
them translated into English from the collection of Francis Patricius.

Abul-Pharagius tells us, that [g] Zerdusht (or Zoroastres) foretold to his Magians the coming of Christ, and that, at the time
of his birth, there should appear a wonderful star, which should
shine by day, as well as by night; and therefore left it in command with them, that when that star should appear, they should
follow the directions of it, and go to the place where he should
be born, and there offer gifts, and pay their adoration unto him;
and that it was by this command, that the three wise men came
from the East, that is, out of Persia, to worship Christ at Bethlehem. And so far [h] Shariastani, though a Mahometan writer, doth
agree with him, as that he tells us, that Zerdusht (or Zoroastres)
foretold

---

[a] Porphyrius in Vita Pythagoræ, p. 17. Edit Cant. et Jamblichus et
Diogenes Laertius in Vita ejusdem.

[b] Diog. Laertius in Procemio.

[c] Chap. xii. 2. 3.

[d] Clemens Alexandrinus. Strom. 1. p. 223.

[e] Vide Lucam Holstenium de vita et scriptis Porphyrii, c. 9. p. 57.
Edit. Cant.

[f] In vita Babylæ Martyris.

[g] Historia Dynastiarum, p. 54.

[h] Religio vet. Pers. c. 31. p. 382, 383.

foretold the coming of a wonderful perſon in the latter times, who ſhould reform the world both in religion and righteouſneſs; and that kings and princes ſhould become obedient to him, and give him their aſſiſtance in promoting the true religion, and all the works thereof. But what theſe attribute to the prophecy of Zoroaſtres,[a] others refer to the prophecy of Balaam; and ſay, that it was by his prediction, that the wiſe men were led by the ſtar to ſeek Chriſt in Judea, and there pay their adoration unto him. But all this ſeems to be taken out of the Legendary writings of the Eaſtern Chriſtians. And Abul-Pharagius, though an Arab writer, being by religion a Chriſtian, it is moſt likely, that what he tells us of this matter was taken from them.

Thoſe who are ſtill remaining of this ſect in Perſia[b] have there the name of Gaurs, which in the Arabic ſignifieth Infidels, and is the uſual appellation which the Mahometans beſtow on all that are not of their religion. But thoſe people have this name in Perſia by way of eminency, as if there were none other ſuch like them; and therefore they are there called by it, as if it were their national name, and are known by none other in that country, and whoſoever ſpeaks of a Gaur there, underſtands none other by it, than one of this ſect. They have a ſuburb at Hiſpahan, the metropolis of Perſia, which is called Gaurabad, or the town of the Gaurs, where they are employed only in the meaneſt and vileſt drudgeries of the town. And ſome of them are ſcattered abroad in other places of that country, where they are made uſe of in the like ſervices. But the bulk of them is in Kerman, which being the barreneſt and worſt province of all Perſia, and where others care not to dwell, the Mahometans have been content to permit them to live there with ſome freedom, and the full exerciſe of their religion. But every where elſe they uſe them as dogs, eſteeming them as to their religion the worſt of all thoſe that differ from them; and it is with a wonderful conſtancy that they bear this oppreſſion. Some ages ſince, for the avoiding of it, ſeveral of them fled into India, and ſettled there in the country about Surat, where their poſterity are ſtill remaining even to this day. And[c] a colony of them is ſettled in Bombay, an iſland in thoſe parts belonging to the Engliſh, where they are allowed, without any moleſtation, the full freedom and exerciſe of their religion. They are a poor, harmleſs ſort of people, zealous in their ſuperſtition, rigorous in their morals, and exact in their dealings, profeſſing the worſhip of one God only, and the belief

[a] Theodorus Tarſenſis.
[b] Thevenot's Travels. Sanſon's preſent ſtate of Perſia. Tavernier Religio vet. Perſ. c. 29.
[c] Qvington's Travels.

belief of a resurrection and a future judgement, and utterly detesting all idolatry, although reckoned by the Mahometans the most guilty of it; for although they perform their worship before fire, and towards the rising sun, yet they utterly deny that they worship either of them. They hold, that more of God is in these his creatures than in any other, and that therefore they worship God toward them, as being in their opinion the truest *Shechinah* of the divine presence among us, as darkness is that of the devils; and as to Zoroastres, they still have him in the same veneration, as the Jews have Moses, looking on him as the great prophet of God, by whom he sent his law, and communicated his will unto them.

Xerxes, having ascended the throne, [a] employed the first year of his reign in carrying on the preparations for the reduction of Egypt, which his father had begun. He [b] confirmed to the Jews at Jerusalem all the privileges granted them by his father, especially that of having the tribute of Samaria for the furnishing them with sacrifices for the carrying on of the divine worship in the temple of God in that place.

Anno 485. Xerxes 1.

In the second year of his reign, he marched against the Egyptians, and, having throughly vanquished and subdued these revolters, he [c] reduced them under an heavier yoke of servitude than they were before; and then, towards the end of the year, after having made Achemenes, one of his brothers, governor of the province, returned again to Susa.

Anno 484. Xerxes 2.

This year Herodotus, the famous historian, [d] was born at Halicarnassus in Caria; for he was 53 years old when the Peloponesian war first began.

Xerxes being puffed up with his success against the Egyptians, upon the advice and instigation of Mardonius, the son of Gobrias, who had married one of his sisters, [e] resolved upon a war with Greece; and, in order thereto, made great preparations for three years together throughout all the provinces of the Persian empire.

Anno 483. Xerxes 3.

Jeshua the high priest of the Jews at Jerusalem, [f] died in the 53d year of his high-priesthood, and [g] Jehoiakim his son succeeded him in that office.

Xerxes, being resolved on the Grecian war, [h] entered into

[a] Herodotus, lib. 7.
[b] Josephus Antiq. lib. 11. c. 5.
[c] Herodotus, lib 7.
[d] Aulus Gellius, lib. 15. c. 23.
[e] Herodotus, lib. 7.
[f] Chronicon Alexandrinum.
[g] Nehemiah xii. 10. Josephus Antiq. lib. 10. c. 5.
[h] Diod. Sic. lib. 11.

a league with the Carthaginians: whereby it was agreed, that, while the Persians invaded Greece, the Carthaginians should fall on all those who were of the Grecian name in Sicily and Italy, that thereby they might be diverted from helping one the other. And the Carthaginians made choice of Hamilcar to be their general in this war, who not only raised what forces he could in Africa, but also with the money sent him by Xerxes hired a great number of mercenaries out of Spain, Gallia, and Italy; so that he got together an army of 300,000 men, and a fleet proportionable hereto, for the prosecuting of the intent of this league.

Anno 482. Xerxes 4.

And thus Xerxes, according as was foretold by the prophet Daniel,[a] having, *by his strength, and through his great riches, stirred up all* the then known habitable world *against the realm of Grecia*, that is, all the West, under the command of Hamilcar, and all the East under his own, he did, [b] in the 5th year of his reign, which was [c] the 10th after the battle of Marathon, set out from Susa to begin the war, and having marched as far as Sardis, wintered there.

Anno 481. Xerxes 5.

Early the next spring [d] Xerxes did set out for the Hellespont; over which two bridges of boats having been laid, the one for his army, and the other for his carriages and beasts of burden, he passed all over in seven days; during all which time they were continually a passing day and night, before all could get over; so great was the number of them that attended him in this expedition. From thence marching through the Thracian Chersonesus, he arrived at Doriscus, a city at the mouth of the river Hebrus, in Thracia; at which place having encamped his army, and ordered his fleet also to attend him on the adjacent shore, he there took an account of both. His land army, upon the muster, was found to be 1,700,000 foot, and 80,000 horse, besides his chariots and his camels, for which, allowing 20,000 more, the whole will amount to 1,800,000 men. His fleet consisted of 1207 ships of the line of battle, besides gallies, transports, victuallers, and other sorts of vessels that attended, which were 3000 more; on board all which were reckoned to be 517,610 men. So that the whole number of forces by sea and land, which Xerxes brought with him out of Asia to invade Greece, amounted to 2,317,610 men. After his passing the Hellespont, the nations on this side, that submitted to him, added to his land army

Anno 480. Xerxes 6.

---

[a] Daniel xi. 2.
[b] Herodot. lib. 7.
[c] Thucydides, lib. 1.
[d] Herodot. lib. 7. Diod. Siculus, lib. 11. Plutarchus in Themistocle & Aristide. Justin. lib. 2. c. 10.

army 300,000 men more, and 220 ships to his fleet, on board of which were 24,000 men. So that, putting all together, his forces by sea and land, by that time he came to the straits of the Thermopylæ, made up the number of 2,641,610 men. And the servants, eunuchs, women, sutlers, and all such other people as followed the camp, were computed to be no less than as many more. So that the whole number of persons of all sorts, that followed Xerxes in this expedition, were at least five millions. This is [a] Herodotus's account of them, and [b] Plutarch and [c] Isocrates agree with him herein. But [d] Diodorus Siculus, [e] Pliny, [f] Ælian, and others, do, in their computations, fall much short of this number, making the army of Xerxes, with which he passed the Hellespont against Greece, to be very little more than that with which Darius his father passed the Bosphorus to make war upon the Scythians. It is probable they might have mistaken the one for the other. The verses engraved on the monument of those Grecians, who were slain at Thermopylæ, best agree with the account of Heredotus; for in them it is said, [g] that they there fought against two millions of men. And he being the ancientest author that hath written of this war, and having lived in the age in which it happened, and treated of it more particularly, and with a greater appearance of exactness than any other, his computation seemeth the most likely to be the truest; and that especially since we find it to be the general opinion of the ancients, both Greeks and Latins, that this was the greatest army that was ever brought into the field.

Josephus tells us, [h] that a band of Jews was also in this army, and brings for proof of it a passage out of the poet Chœrilus, who, in describing the army of Xerxes, as they passed on by their several nations in their march, hath these verses.

> *Then next did march, in habit and in mien,*
> *A people wonderful for to be seen:*
> *Their language is in dialect the same,*
> *Which men do speak of the Phœnician name.*
> *They dwell in the high Solymæan land,*
> *On hills, near which there doth a great lake stand.*

Jerusalem,

---

[a] Herodot. lib. 7.
[b] In Themistocle.
[c] In Panathenaico.
[d] Lib. 11.
[e] Lib. 33. c. 10.
[f] Var. Histor. lib. 13. c. 3.
[g] Herodot. lib. 7. Diod. Siculus, lib. 11. p. 26. This inscription, according to the reading as in Herodotus, saith they were three millions, but as it Diodorus only two millions.
[h] Contra Apionem, lib. 1.

Jerusalem, having also had the name of [a] Solyma, and all the country thereabout being mountainous, and lying near the great lake Asphaltites, commonly called the lake of Sodom, this description seems plainly to suit the Jews, especially since it is also mentioned, that they spake the Phœnician language, the Syriac being then the vulgar language of the Jews. But [b] Scaliger, Cunæus, [c] and [d] Bochartus, understand it of the Solymi in Pisidia. However [e] Salmasius maintains the contrary opinion, and justifies Josephus in it; and it must be said, that it is not at all likely, that when Xerxes called all the other nations of the Persian empire to follow him to this war, the Jews alone should be excused from it. And therefore whether these, whom Chœrilus speaks of, were Jews or not, it must be taken for certain, that they also did bear a part in this expedition.

After Xerxes had taken this account of his fleet and army at Doriscus, [f] he marched from thence with his army through Thrace, Macedon, and Thessaly, towards Attica, and ordered his fleet to attend him on the coast all the way, making the same stations by sea that he did by land. All yielded to him in his march without any opposition, till he came to the straits of Thermopylæ; where Leonidas, king of the Lacedæmonians, with 300 Spartans, and as many other Greeks as made up a body of 4000 men, defended the pass against him. For two days he made it good against all the numerous army of the Persians, repulsing them in every assault with a great slaughter of their men. But on the third day, being ready to be surrounded by the Persians, through the treachery of a certain Greek, who led them by a secret way over the mountains, to fall on them in the rear, all retired, saving Leonidas and his 300 Spartans, and some few others that would not desert them; who, resolutely abiding by the post they had undertaken to defend, were at length all slain upon the spot. But the Persians paid very dear for this victory, having lost in the gaining of it 20,000 of their men, and among them two of the brothers of Xerxes.

After this Xerxes [g] entered through Bœotia into Attica, the country of the Athenians; having spent in his march hither since his passing the Hellespont four months. The Athenians, not able to defend themselves against so great a force, deserted

---

[a] By Abbreviation for Hierosolyma.
[b] In Notis ad Fragmenta.
[c] De Republica Hebræorum, lib. 2. c. 18.
[d] Geographia Sacra, part 2. lib. 1. c. 2.
[e] In Ossilegio Linguæ Hellenisticæ.
[f] Herodot. lib. 7. Diodor. Sic. lib. 11. Plutarchus in Themistocle.
[g] Herodot. lib. 8. Diodor. Siculus, lib. 11. Plutarchus in Aristide & Themistocle.

their city, putting all their men aboard their fleet, and securing their wives and children in Salamis, Ægina, and Trœzene, neighbouring cities, which, by the intervention of the sea, were out of the reach of his army; so that, on his coming thither, he became master of the place without any opposition.

In the interim, the Persian and Grecian [a] fleets lying near each other, the former at Aphetæ, and the other at Artimisium, above Eubœa, had several encounters with each other, in every one of which the Grecians had the advantage; and though it was not great, yet it served them to shew, that the enemy, notwithstanding their great number, were not invincible; which gave them the heart afterwards, with the greater courage and resolution, to fight against them. However, their ships being much shattered by these several encounters, they found it necessary to retire to some safer place to refit; and for this purpose came into the straits of Salamis, where they not only refitted, but were also reinforced and augmented by a great many other ships, which, from several parts of Greece, came thither to them, and there joined them against the common enemy, till at length they there made up a fleet upward of 300 sail. It was while they lay there, that Xerxes entered Athens; and thereon the Persian fleet came hither also, and anchored at Phalerus, a port on that shore. The straits of Salamis, where the Greek fleet lay, was the most advantageous place for them to fight the numerous fleet of the enemy in that they could choose: for the Persians, by reason of the narrowness of that sea, not being able to extend their front in it beyond that of the Greeks, could there have no advantage from their numbers; but although their fleet was four times as great, must in that place fight upon equal terms; which Themistocles the general of the Athenians, having wisely observed, did, by his prudence and dexterity, bring it to pass, that there it came to a battle between them; wherein the Grecians, by the advantage of the place, gained the victory, and gave the enemy such an overthrow, as wholly dashed all the aims and designs of this prodigious expedition, which was one of the greatest, both for expence and number of men, that was ever undertaken; for they having destroyed 200 of their ships, besides those which they took, the rest got away to the Asian coast; and having set in at Cyma, a city in Æolia, they there laid up for the winter, and never came again into Greece; and Xerxes being frighted with an apprehension lest the conquerors should sail to the Hellespont, and there obstruct his return, fled thither with all the haste and precipitation he could, and, having left Mardonius with 300,000 men to carry on the war in Greece, marched

[a] Herodot. lib. 8. Plutarchus in Themistocle. Diod. Siculus, lib. 11.

marched back with the rest to Sardis, and there took up his quarters for the ensuing year. It is remarkable, that, at his coming to the Hellespont, finding the bridge of boats which he had left there broken by storms, he who had passed over that sea but a few months before with such pomp and pride, was forced to repass it in a poor fisher-boat.

About the same time [a] his confederates, the Carthaginians, met with as great, or rather a much greater defeat, in Sicily: for Hamilcar their general, having drawn together his numerous army, of which I have already spoken, and shipped them on board the vast fleet which he had prepared for their transportation, sailed with them for Sicily, and having there landed them at Panormus, a port in that island, laid siege to Himera, a maritime city in the neighbourhood. While he lay there, for his better security, he caused two large camps to be fortified; in the one of which he lodged his land army, and into the other he drew up his ships, placing there all his marines for their defence. At that time Gelo was king of Sicily, a prince of great wisdom, conduct, and valour. As soon as he had an account of this invasion, he drew together an army of 50,000 foot, and 5000 horse, and marched immediately against the enemy, for the defence of the country. On his arrival at Himera, he intercepted a courier carrying letters from the Salinuntines, confederates of the Carthaginians, to Hamilcar; whereby he understood, that the next morning Hamilcar was to celebrate a great sacrifice to Neptune at the camp of the marines, and that he had appointed the Salinuntine horse then to come thither to him. Gelo, taking the advantage of this intelligence, the next morning, at the time appointed, sent thither a party of horse of his own, who being received into the camp for the Salinuntines, first slew Hamilcar, and then set the fleet on fire. As soon as this was done, Gelo having notice of it by a signal given him from the top of an adjacent hill, where he had placed watchmen for this purpose, drew out his army before the other camp of the enemy, and gave them battle. But the flame ascending from the camp of the marines, soon telling the Carthaginians the fate of their fleet, and a messenger at the same time bringing them an account of the death of their general, this so disheartened and confounded them, that, having no longer any courage to stand their ground, they were soon put to the rout, and Gelo slew of them 150,000 on the field of battle, and took all the rest prisoners, which were as many more, and sold them all for slaves; so that all Sicily was filled with them. This defeat was so entire, that of all this prodigious fleet and army the greatest that was ever set forth in those western parts

---

[a] Herodotus, lib. 7. Diodorus Siculus, lib. 11.

parts for any expedition, it is remarked none returned, save only
a few, who escaped in a cock-boat, to bring this dismal news to
Carthage. [a] Herodotus tells us, that this battle was fought on
the same day with that of Salamis; but [b] Diodorus Siculus says
it was at the time when Leonidas was slain at Thermopylæ;
which seems to be the truer account of the two: for, after this
success of Gelo, [c] the Grecians sent to him for his assistance
against Xerxes, which they would not have done afer the battle
of Salamis. For from thenceforth they thought themselves
alone more than sufficient for the enemy, without needing any
other force than that of their own to finish the war.

On Xerxes's departure out of Greece, [d] Mardonius wintered
his army in Thessaly and Macedonia, and early the
next spring marched with it into Bœotia. From
hence he sent Alexander, king of Macedonia, to
Athens, with proposals of accommodation from the king.
Thereby he offered them to rebuild, at the king's charges,
whatsoever had been burnt or demolished in Attica the former
year, to permit them to live according to their own laws, to
reinstate them in all their former possessions, and to add to
them whatsoever other lands they should desire. But the Athenians, not being to be induced to desert the interest of Greece
for any advantage whatsoever, would hearken to none of these
offers: whereon [e] Mardonius, being enraged by the refusal,
marched with all his army into Attica, destroying every thing
wherever he came, and, entering Athens, burnt and demolished whatsoever he there found standing after the former year's
devastation: for the Athenians, not being strong enough to resist such a torrent, had the second time withdrawn to Salamis,
Ægina, and Trœzene, and left the city empty. In the interim, the joint forces of all Greece being drawn together at the
isthmus of Corinth, Mardonius thought fit to march back
again into Bœotia: for that being an open and level country,
was much fitter for him to fight in than Attica, which being
rough and craggy, and full of hills and defiles, could scarce any
where afford him room enough for to draw up his numerous
army in, or a ground proper for his cavalry to do any service
in. On his return, he encamped on the river Æsopus: thither
the Greeks marched after him, under the command of Pausa-
nias, king of Lacedæmon, and Aristides, general of the Athenians. They consisted of 120,000 men, and the Persians of
350,000, saith [f] Herodotus, of 500,000, saith [g] Diodorus
Siculus:

Anno 479.
Xerxes 7.

[a] Lib. 7. [b] Lib. 11. [c] Herodot. lib. 7.
[d] Herodot. lib. 8. Diodor. Sic. lib. 11. Plutarchus in Aristide &
Themistocle. Justin. lib. 2. c. 14.
[e] Herodot. lib. 9. [f] Lib. 9. [g] Lib. 11.

Siculus: and with these forces, near the city of Platæa, it came to a decisive battle between them, in which Mardonius was slain, and all the Persian army cut in pieces. Only Artabazus, who was aware of the event, from the ill conduct which he had observed in Mardonius, made an early escape with 40,000 men, which he commanded, and, by his speed, outmarching the fame of the defeat, got safe to Byzantium, and there passed over into Asia. Besides these, not 4000 of all the rest escaped the carnage of that day, but were all slain and cut in pieces by the Greeks; and this quite delivered them from all farther invasions of that people; for from that time a Persian army was never more seen on this side the Hellespont.

On the same day that the Greeks fought this battle at Platæa, [a] their naval forces got as memorable a victory over the remainder of the Persian fleet in Asia: for at the same time that their land forces rendezvoused at the isthmus of Corinth, their fleet having met together at Ægina, under the command of Leotychides, the other king of the Lacedæmonians, and Xantippus, the Athenian, there came thither to them ambassadors from the Ionians, to invite them into Asia, to deliver the Greek cities there from the slavery of the Barbarians: whereon they sailed for Delos in their way thither; and, while they lay there, other ambassadors came to them from Samos, who having acquainted them, that the Persian fleet which wintered at Cyma, having sailed thence, were then at Samos, and might there be easily vanquished and destroyed by them, earnestly solicited them to come thither and fall upon them; whereon they accordingly set sail forthwith for Samos. But the Persians, hearing of their approach, retired to Mycale, a promontory on the continent of Asia, where their land army lay, consisting of 100,000 men, which were the remainder of those which Xerxes had brought back out of Greece the former year; and there drew up their ships upon the land, and fortified them with a strong rampart drawn round them. But the Greeks following them thither, by the assistance of the Ionians, who revolted to them, vanquished their army at land, took their rampart, and burnt all their ships. And here ended all the great designs of Xerxes in a most miserable disappointment, there being, after these two battles, scarce any of all that prodigious army, with which, the year before, he marched so proudly over the Hellespont, now left, whom either the famine, the pestilence, or the sword, had not absolutely destroyed, excepting those whom Artabazus brought back out of Greece; and of these a great number died, on their return into Asia, by their over-glutting themselves with the plenty of that country, after the hardships they had suffered on the other side

of

[a] Herodot. lib. 9. Diodor. Sic. lib. 11.

of the Hellespont. A greater fleet and army was scarce ever set forth in the West for any expedition, than that of Hamilcar's against Sicily, or ever was there a greater army brought together any where, than that wherewith Xerxes invaded Greece; yet all these numerous forces were baffled, defeated, and destroyed, by those who, in number or power, reckoning all the armies on both sides against each other, could scarce bear the name of an handful of men in comparison of them: and hereby a signal instance was given, that, whatsoever the pride of man may design, or the power of man think to effect, it is still the providence of God that governs the world, and turneth all the affairs thereof which way soever he pleaseth.

The battle of Platæa was fought in the morning, and that of Mycale in the afternoon of the same day; and yet [a] it is commonly said by the Greek writers, that they had an account of the victory of Platæa at Mycale before they begun the battle there, though the whole Ægean sea, which was several days failing, lay between. But Diodorus Siculus clears this matter: for [b] he tells us, that Leotychides, finding the forces that followed him to be in great pain for the Greeks at Platæa, lest they should be overpowered and vanquished by the numerous army of Mardonius, the better to encourage and enhearten his men for the battle, just before he made the first onset, caused it to be given out throughout all the army, that the Persians were defeated, though he then knew nothing of the matter. But what he then feigned happening to be true, and also done the same day, this gave occasion for what is said of that quick intelligence, which was utterly impossible to have come in so short a time from so far distant a place by any human means; and there is no reason to suppose a miracle in this case. And that which is said [c] of the victory of Paulus Æmilius over the Macedonians being known at Rome on the same day on which it was got, at a greater distance than Platæa was from Mycale, no doubt, was from the same cause. That happened to be true which was only feigned when first reported; and afterwards, when it was found to be true, and done on the same day on which the Romans first had the report, it was made a miracle of, as if there had been some supernatural power that brought the intelligence.

Xerxes, on his having received these two great defeats at Platæa and Mycale, [d] left Sardis almost with the same precipitation as he did Athens after the battle of Salamis, making all the haste

---

[a] Diodor. Sic. lib. 11. Herodot. lib. 9. Justin. lib. 2. c. 14.
[b] Lib. 11.
[c] Plutarchus in Paulo Æmilio. Livius, lib. 41.
[d] Herodot. lib. 9. Diodor. Sic. lib. 11.

haſte he could towards Perſia, that thereby he might get as far as he could out of the reach of the conquering enemies. However, he omitted not, before he left thoſe parts, to give [a] order for the burning and demoliſhing of all the temples in the Grecian cities in Aſia; which was accordingly executed upon all of them, excepting only that of Diana at Epheſus, which alone eſcaped this general devaſtation. And this he did, not out of any particular diſpleaſure to the Aſiatic Greeks; for he did the ſame wherever elſe he came, deſtroying all idolatrous temples that came in his way, throughout this whole expedition. The true cauſe of this was his zeal for the Magian religion, in which he had been throughly inſtructed, and made a zealous proſelyte to it by Zoroaſtres: for that ſect expreſſing a [b] great deteſtation againſt worſhipping of God by images, were for deſtroying all idolatrous temples wherever they came. And, to keep Xerxes firm to their party, not only ſeveral of the chief doctors of the Magians, but alſo [c] Oſtanes himſelf, who [d] was then the Archimagus, or great patriarch of the whole ſect, accompanied him as his chaplains through this whole expedition: and by their inſtigation, [e] Tully tells us, it was, that all theſe temples were deſtroyed. This Oſtanes is ſaid to have been [f] grandfather to Zoroaſtres; but it is moſt likely that he was his grandſon, and that it was by miſtake that it hath been ſaid otherwiſe; for Zoroaſtres, it is certain, was [g] a very old man at his death. The name of Oſtanes was very famous among the Greeks; for [h] from him, they ſay, they firſt had the Magian philoſophy; he having communicated it unto them, while he followed Xerxes in this war; and therefore from him they ſometimes call the whole ſect [i] Oſtaneans, inſtead of Magians, as if he had been the chief founder of it.

One of the temples, which by Xerxes's order were thus deſtroyed, was [k] that of Apollo Didumæan, near Miletus, from whence he took an immenſe treaſure. This was diſcovered to the Perſians by the Branchidæ, a family of the Mileſians, that had the keeping of the temple; who thereon finding themſelves, by reaſon of this treachery and ſacrilege, to be become very odious to their countrymen, durſt not, on Xerxes's going away,

ſtay

---

[a] Strabo, lib. 14. p. 634. Cicero de Legibus, lib. 2. Hieronymus in Eſaiæ, c. 37. Æſchylus in Perſis. Herodot. lib. 8.

[b] Clemens Alexand. in protreptico, Laertius in procœmio. Pocockii ſpecimen Hiſt. Arab. p. 148. 149.

[c] Plin. lib. 30. c. 1. 2.

[d] Laertius in procœmio. Suidas in voce Μάγοι.

[e] De Legibus, lib. 2.

[f] Religio vet. Perſ. c. 24.

[g] Ibid.

[h] Plin. lib. 30. c. 1. 2.

[i] Suidas in Ὀστάνει.

[k] Strabo. lib. 14.

stay behind, for fear of their wrath, but followed after him into Persia, and were there planted by him in a small territory, which he gave them, on the river Oxus, in the province of Bactria, where Alexander, on his making himself master of that country, finding their posterity still remaining, [a] caused them all to be put to the sword, thereby cruelly and unreasonably revenging, on the innocent descendants, the crime committed by their ancestors many ages before.

Xerxes, on his return towards Susa, passing through Babylon, [b] made there the same devastation of their temples, as he had in Greece, and the Lesser Asia, and, as it may be supposed, on the same principle, that is, his zeal for the Magian religion, and his aversion to that of the Sabians, who worshipped God by images, [c] of which the Magians had the utmost detestation: for the Babylonians were all Sabians, and indeed were the first founders of the sect; for they first brought in the worship of the planets, and afterwards that of images, and from thence propagated it to all the other nations where it obtained; as hath been already shewn. And for this reason, the Magians, having them in abhorrence, above all other Sabians, prevailed with Xerxes, out of an especial hatred to them, to take Babylon in his way to Susa, of purpose to destroy all the temples they had there; although perchance to recruit himself with the spoils of these temples, after the vast expences which he had been at in his Grecian war, might be the most forcible motive that wrought him into this resolution; for the wealth of their temples was vast and excessive, as having been the collection of a great number of ages. I have already computed how many millions of our money the treasures of the temple of Belus only amounted to, according to the account given us of them by Diodorus Siculus; and if those which he found in the other idol temples in that city were as great, as no doubt they were, they must more than repay him all that he spent in the Grecian war. And without some such recruit, it is scarce possible to imagine, how he could have supported himself at home, after so great a miscarriage and loss. And yet we find, that, after his return, he was supported through all his empire, in the same manner as before, without suffering any great damage either in his authority or power therein, after this so great and so extraordinary a disaster; whereas it usually happens, that princes are ruined at home, as well as abroad, by such misfortunes.

By

---

[a] Strabo, lib. 11. p. 518. Q. Curtius, lib. 7. c. 5.
[b] Arrianus Expeditionis Alexandri, lib. 7. Strabo, lib. 16. Herodotus, lib. 1. Diodorus Siculus, lib. 2.
[c] Pocockii Specimen Historiæ Arabicæ, p. 148. 149.

By the pillaging and deftroying of all thefe heathen temples at Babylon, was fully completed what the prophets Ifaiah and Jeremiah prophefied hereof many years before. [a] "All the graven images of her gods hath he broken unto the ground." [b] "I will punifh Bel in Babylon. I will bring forth out of his mouth that which he hath fwallowed." [c] "And I will do judgement upon all the graven images of Babylon." [d] "Bel is confounded, Merodach is broken in pieces; her idols are confounded, her images are broken in pieces." For when Xerxes deftroyed all thefe temples in Babylon, he took from them all their treafures, which they had been for many ages a-fwallowing; and pulling down all the images that were in them, broke them all to pieces, and converted the gold and filver, of which they were made, to all thofe common ufes for which he had occafion of them

After the battle of Mycale, [e] the Grecian fleet failed to the Hellefpont, to feize the bridges which Xerxes had laid over thofe ftraits, fuppofing that they had been ftill whole. But, on their coming thither, finding that they had been broken by ftorms, Leotychides, with the Peloponnefians, failed home; but Xantippus, with the Athenians and allies of Ionia, ftill ftaying there, made themfelves mafters of Seftus, and the Thracian Cherfonefus; where they took much fpoil, and a great number of prifoners, and then, on the approach of winter, returned to their refpective cities. Xantippus finding all the materials of Xerxes's bridge at Cardia, where the Perfians had caufed them to be brought before his arrival in thofe parts, he carried them with him to Athens, and there laid them up to be a memorial of that total overthrow which they gave their enemy in this war, by the many victories which they had obtained over them. From this time all the Ionian cities in Afia revolted from the Perfians, and, entering into a confederacy with the Grecians, by their help, maintained their liberty for the moft part ever after, during the continuance of that empire.

The Greeks, having fettled their affairs at home, after the great ruffle that was made in them by the late invafion of the Perfians, [f] refolved farther to profecute the war againft them, for the driving of them out of all the cities abroad that were of the Grecian original. For which purpofe, they equipped a ftrong fleet, of which Paufa-

An. 477. Xerxes 9.

nias,

---

[a] Ifaiah xxi. 9.
[b] Jer. li. 44.
[c] Jer. li. 47. 52.
[d] Jer. L 2.

[e] Herodot. lib. 9.
[f] Diodorus Siculus, lib. 11. Plutarchus in Ariftide

nias, king of the Lacedemonians, and Ariftides, the Athenian, having the command, they failed with it to Cyprus; and there having freed a great many Grecian cities from their Perfian garrifons, reftored them again to their own liberty.

About this time, Xerxes at Sufa [a] was acting a very cruel and barbarous tragedy in the houfe of Mafiftes his brother, which had its rife from an inceftuous love firft begun at Sardis: for Xerxes, after his return thither from his flight out of Greece, fell in love with Mafiftes's wife, who was then in that city; but fhe being a very virtuous woman, and very loving and faithful to her hufband, could on no folicitations be prevailed with to defile his bed. But Xerxes, thinking to win her, at laft heaped all manner of favours and obligations upon her, to engage her to yield to him; and particularly he married a daughter which fhe had, named Artaynta, to Darius his eldeft fon, whom he intended for his fucceffor in the throne, and, on his return to Sufa, caufed the marriage to be confummated: which being the greateft favour he could beftow upon the mother, he expected it would engage her to a compliance with his defires. But finding the lady's virtue to be ftill impregnable againft all his attempts, he at length turned the amour from the mother to the daughter, and fell in love with Artaynta; where he foon found a ready compliance to all he defired. While this was a-doing, Hameftris, Xerxes's queen, having wrought a very rich and curious mantle, prefented it to the king; who being very much pleafed with it, wore it when he made his next vifit to his miftrefs, and, on his having enjoyed his luft on her, to exprefs the fatisfaction he had therein, he bade her afk what fhe would of him for her reward, promifing her with an oath, that whatfoever it fhould be, he would give it unto her. Hereon fhe afked of him the mantle which he had then on him. Xerxes, being aware of the mifchief which might follow from his giving of it unto her, did all that he could to divert her from this requeft, offering her whatever elfe was in his power to redeem it from her. But nothing elfe being able to content the lady, and his promife, and the oath being urged for the grant, he was forced to give it unto her, and fhe, out of the vanity and pride of her mind, as foon as fhe had it, put it on, and, as by way of trophy, wore it publicly; whereby Hameftris being throughly confirmed in what fhe was afore only jealous of, became enraged to the utmoft degree; but inftead of turning her wrath againft the daughter, who only was faulty in this matter, refolved to be revenged on the mother, as if all this intrigue had been of her contrivance, who was wholly innocent of it. And therefore waiting the

---

[a] Herodotus, lib. 9.

the great festival that used annually to be celebrated on the king's birth-day, which was then approaching, whereon it was the custom for the king to grant her whatsoever she should then desire, she asked of him the wife of Masistes to be given unto her. The king perceiving the malice of the woman, and what she intended, abhorred it to the utmost, both for the sake of his brother, and also for what he knew of the innocency of the lady, as to that for which Hamestris was exasperated against her; and therefore at first withstood her in this request all that he could. But her importunity not being to be diverted, nor what was said for the custom to be gainsayed, he was forced to yield to her. Whereon the lady being seized by the king's guards, and delivered to her, she caused her breasts, her tongue, nose, ears, and lips, to be cut off, and thrown to the dogs before her face, and then sent her home again thus mangled to her husband's house. In the interim, Xerxes, to mollify the matter as much as he could, sent for Masistes, and told him, that it was his desire that he must part with his wife, and that, instead of her, he would give him one of his daughters in marriage. But Masistes, having an entire affection for his wife, could not be induced to consent hereto: whereon Xerxes told him, in an angry manner, that, since he refused to accept of his daughter, when offered to him, he should neither have her nor his wife either; and so dismissed him in displeasure. Whereon Masistes, suspecting some mischief was done him, made haste home to see how matters there stood; where finding his wife in that mangled condition as hath been mentioned, and being thereby exasperated to the utmost, as the case deserved, he immediately got together all his family, servants, and dependents, and made all the haste he could towards Bactria, the province of which he was governor; purposing, as soon as he should arrive thither, to raise an army, and make war upon the king, to be revenged of him for this barbarous usage. But Xerxes, hearing of his sudden retreat, and suspecting from thence what he intended, sent a party of horse after him, who, overtaking him on the road, cut him off, with his wife and children, and all that belonged to him. This Masistes was brother of Xerxes by Atossa the same mother, as well as by the same father, and was a person of great worth and honour, as well as of great fidelity to the king; and he had done him great services in his Grecian war, having been one of his chief generals, who had the leading of his army in that expedition; and he was personally engaged for him in the battle of Mycale, and was in truth the chief honour of his house, and never gave him any just cause to be offended with him. However, all this could not

not protect him from Xerxes's cruelty; which sufficiently shews, that, where there is a vicious prince, with an arbitrary power in the government, there is nothing that can be sufficient to secure any man's safety under him.

And there is [a] another fact related of Hameſtris, equally cruel and impious; that is, that ſhe cauſed fourteen boys of the beſt families in Perſia to be buried alive, as a ſacrifice to the infernal gods. And, in the relating of this, as well as her other cruelties above mentioned, I have been the more particular, becauſe [b] ſeveral having been of opinion, by reaſon of the ſimilitude that is between the names of Hameſtris and Eſther, that Xerxes was the Ahaſuerus, and Hameſtris the Eſther, mentioned in ſcripture, it may from hence appear, how impoſſible it is, that a woman of ſo vile and abominable a character, as Hameſtris was, could have ever been that queen of Perſia, who, by the name of Eſther, is ſo renowed in holy writ, and is there recorded as the inſtrument by whom God was pleaſed, in ſo ſignal a manner, to deliver his people from that utter deſtruction which was deſigned againſt them.

After the death of Maſiſtes, Xerxes appointed [c] Hyſtaſpes, his ſecond ſon, to be governor of Bactria in his ſtead; which obliging him to be abſent from court, gave Artaxerxes, his younger brother, the opportunity of mounting the throne before him, on the death of Xerxes, as will be hereafter related.

The Grecian fleet, having effected at Cyprus what they went thither for, [d] ſailed from thence to the Helleſpont, and took in Byzantium; where ſeveral Perſians of eminent note, and ſome of them of the kindred of Xerxes, being taken priſoners, Pauſanias treacherouſly releaſed them all, pretending they had made their eſcape, and by ſome of them entered into a treaty with Xerxes to betray Greece unto him, upon condition that he would give him one of his daughters in marriage; which being readily agreed to by Xerxes, Pauſanias thenceforth took upon him to live after another rate than formerly, affecting the pomp and grandeur of the Perſians, and carrying himſelf haughtily and tyrannically towards the allies: whereon, they being diſguſted with his conduct, and not being able any longer to bear it, did put themſelves under the Athenians, who thenceforth, by this means, obtained the chief command at ſea in all the Grecian affairs, and held it for many years after. The Lacedæmonians, having received an account of theſe miſcarriages of Pauſanias, depoſed him from his command on

Anno 476.
Xerxes 10.

the

---

[a] Herodot. lib. 7.
[b] Scaliger and his followers.
[c] Diodor. Sic. lib. 11.
[d] Thucydides, lib. 1. Diod. Sic. lib. 11. Plutarchus in Ariſtide.

the Hellefpont, and recalling him home, put him under public cenfure for them.

However, [a] the next year he went again to the Hellefpont, although without the confent of the ftate, or any commiffion from them, failing thither in a private ſhip; which he hired on pretence of fighting againſt the Perfians as a volunteer in that war, but in reality to carry on his treafonable defigns with them, Artabazus being appointed governor on the Propontis of purpofe to be there at hand to treat with him. But while he was at Byzantium, his behaviour was fuch, that the Athenians drove him thence; whereon he went to the country of Troas, and there tarried fome time the better to carry on his correfpondence with Artabazus; of which there being fome fufpicions, the Lacedæmonians fummoned him home by a public officer, and, on his return, put him in prifon; but no evidence appearing of this thing in his trial, he was again difcharged. But fome time after the whole of it being brought to light, and difcovered by one whom he had made ufe of to carry on the correfpondence, they put him to death for it.

Anno 475. Xerxes 11.

Themiftocles, [b] by his wifdom and great application, having much advanced the power and intereſt of the Athenians, hereby drew on him the bitter enmity of the Lacedæmonians: for they, feeing their honour eclipfed, and that authority, whereby they had hitherto borne the chief fway among the Greeks, now rivalled and diminiſhed by the growing up of this flouriſhing ftate, could not with patience bear it; and therefore, to gratify their revenge, refolved on the ruin of him that had been the author of it. In order whereto, they caufed him firft to be accufed at Athens of being a confederate with Paufanias in his treafon againft Greece; but nothing being proved of what was laid to his charge, he was there acquitted.

Anno 472. Xerxes 14.

But [c] the next year after, Themiftocles being baniſhed Athens, they renewed their defign againft him. He was not baniſhed for any crime, but by oftracifm: which was [d] a way among them, whereby, for the better fecuring of their liberty, they ufed to fupprefs thofe that were grown to too great a power and authority among them, by baniſhing them the city for a certain term of years. Themiftocles being thus neceffitated for a time to leave his country, fettled at

Anno 471. Xerxes 15.

---

[a] Thucydides, lib. 1. Plutarchus in Ariftide & Themiftocle. Cornelius Nepos in Paufania.

[b] Herodotus, lib. 7. &c. Thucydides, lib. 1. Plutarchus in Themiftocle. Diodor. Sic. lib. 11.

[c] Thucydides, lib. 1. Plutarchus in Themiftocle. Diod. Sic. lib. 11.

[d] Plutarchus in Ariftide.

at Argos; of which the Lacedemonians taking the advantage, profecuted anew their charge againſt him before the general council of all Greece, then met at Sparta, and fummoned him to appear before them to anfwer to it, accufing him there of treafon againſt the whole community of Greece. Themiſtocles feeing how bitterly the Lacedemonians were fet againſt him, and knowing that they could carry every thing as they pleafed in that aſſembly, durſt not truſt his caufe with them, but fled firſt to Corcyra, and from thence to Admetus king of the Moloſſians, by whofe aſſiſtance being conveyed to the coaſts of the Ægean fea, he took ſhipping at Pydna in Macedonia, and from thence paſſed over to Cyma, a city of Æolia in the Leſſer Aſia. But Xerxes having put a price of 200 talents upon his head, (which amounted to 37,500 pounds of our money), feveral were there upon the hunt after him for the gain of fo great a reward. For the avoiding of this danger, he was forced there to lie hid for fome time; till at length, by the contrivance and aſſiſtance of his friend and hoſt Nicogenes, the richeſt man of that country, he was conveyed fafe to Sufa, in one of thofe clofe chariots, in which the Perſians ufed to carry their women; they that had the conducting of him giving out, that they were carrying a young Greek lady to the court for one of the nobility; by which means he got to the Perſian court without any danger: where being arrived, he addreſſed himfelf to Artabanus, the captain of the guards, to whofe office it belonged to bring thofe to the audience of the king that had any buſineſs with him: by him he was introduced into Xerxes's prefence; and being there aſked who he was? He told him he was Themiſtocles the Athenian; that, though he had done him great hurt in his wars, yet he had in many things much ferved him, particularly in hindering the Greeks from purſuing him after the battle of Salamis, and obſtructing his retreat over the Helleſpont; that, for thefe his fervices to him being driven out of his country, he was now fled to him for refuge, hoping that he would have more regard to what he had done for his intereſt, than to what with the reſt of his countrymen he had in the wars acted againſt it. Xerxes then faid nothing to him; though, as foon as he was withdrawn, he expreſſed a great deal of joy and fatisfaction, that fo conſiderable a perfon was come over to him, wiſhing that God would always put it into the minds of his enemies thus to drive their beſt men from them. But the next morning having aſſembled the chief of the Perſian nobility about him, and ordered him again to be brought into his prefence, he received him with great kindneſs; telling him in the firſt place, that he owed him 200 talents: for he having fet that price upon his head, it was due to him
who

who had brought him his head, by thus rendering himself unto him; and accordingly commanded it to be paid him: and then ordered him to say what he had concerning the affairs of Greece to impart unto him. But Themistocles being then no otherwise able to deliver himself, than by an interpreter, begged leave, that he might be permitted first to learn the Persian language; hoping that then he might be in a capacity to communicate to the king what he had to impart to him in a much more perfect manner, than he could then promise to do by the interpretation of another: which being granted to him, and, having after a year's time made himself thorough master of that tongue, he was again called into the king; to whom having communicated all that he thought proper, he grew very much into his favour, so that when Mandana his sister, who had lost several of her sons in the battle of Salamis, had prosecuted an accusation against Themistocles for their death, and was very importunate and clamorous to have him delivered up to her a sacrifice to her revenge, he not only caused him to be acquitted by the suffrages of all the nobility then attending the court, but conferred many royal bounties upon him; for he gave him a wife of a noble Persian family, with an house, servants, and an equipage in all things suitable hereto, and an annual revenue sufficient to enable him in the best manner to support the same, and, on all occasions, much caressed him as long as he continued in his court. And it is mentioned as one particular instance of his favour to him, that, by his especial command, he was [a] admitted to hear the lectures and discourses of the Magians, and was instructed by them in all the secrets of their philosophy. But at length, it being thought best for the king's interest, that he should reside in some of the maritime towns near Greece, that he might be there ready at hand for such services as the king might have occasion of from him in those parts, he was sent to live at Magnesia, on the river Meander; where he had not only all there venues of that city (which were 50 talents a-year), but also those of Myus and Lampsacus allowed him for his maintenance, amounting altogether to 150 talents a-year, which was little less than 30,000 pounds of our money. And here he lived all the time of Xerxes, and several years after, in the reign of Artaxerxes his son, in a very plentiful and splendid manner, as well he might on so large a revenue, till at length he ended his days in that city in the manner as shall be hereafter related.

But, according to [b] Thucydides, Xerxes was dead, and Artaxerxes had newly succeeded in the throne, when Themistocles fled out of Greece to the Persian court; and therefore he

[a] Plutarchus in Themistocle.   [b] Lib. 1.

tells us that it was Artaxerxes Longimanus, and not Xerxes, by whom Themistocles was received with so much favour; and Thucydides being an historian of great credit, and having wrote this not many years after the death of Artaxerxes, [a] the Lord Primate Usher, moved by so great an authority, follows him in this matter, and, to make it accord with the other transactions of those times, takes nine years from the reign of Xerxes, and adds them [b] to the two following reigns, making Xerxes to end his reign nine years sooner, and Artaxerxes to begin his reign nine years sooner, than any other author says. Hereby the learned primate doth exceedingly help his hypothesis of the computation of the 70 weeks of Daniel's prophecy; and that, no doubt, induced him to prefer the authority of Thucydides before all others in this particular. For if we put the 20th year of Artaxerxes Longimanus (from whence he reckons the beginning of these 70 weeks, nine years higher than others do, the middle of the last week will fall exactly in with the time when Christ was crucified. And therefore, were the authority of Thucydides sufficient to justify him in this matter, the primate's computation would appear much more plausible than now it doth. But [c] the canon of Ptolemy, Diodorus Siculus, Plutarch, Africanus, Eusebius, and all others that write of these times, being against him herein, it is much more probable, that Thucydides was out in this particular; for although he be a very exact historian in the affairs of Greece, of which he professedly writes, yet it is possible he might be mistaken in those of Persia, which he treats of only by the by.

In the interim, the Athenians, having set out a fleet under the command of Cimon, [d] the son of Miltiades, conquered Eione, on the river Strymon, and other parts of Thrace, and then took in the islands of Scyrus and Naxus, which had revolted from them; and, [e] while they were assaulting the last of these, Themistocles passed by them, in his flight into Asia, and difficultly escaped falling into their hands.

The next year after, [f] Cimon, sailing from Athens with a fleet

---

[a] In Annalibus Veteris Testamenti sub anno Julianæ Periodi, 4241.

[b] *i. e.* To the reigns of Artaxerxes and his son Xerxes, whom the primate makes to reign one year after him.

[c] For these authors say, that Xerxes reigned 21 years, and Artaxerxes 41. But according to the primate, Xerxes reigned but 12 years, and Artaxerxes 50.

[d] Diodorus Siculus, lib. 11. Plutarchus in Cimone.

[e] Plutarchus in Themistocle.

[f] Diodorus et Plutarchus, ibid. Thucydides, lib. 1.

fleet of 200 sail, passed over to the coasts of Asia; where, having augmented it with 100 sail more from the allies, he took in all the maritime parts of Caria and Lycia, driving the Persians out of all the cities they were possessed of in those parts; and then hearing that they had a great fleet on the coasts of Pamphylia, and were also drawing down thither as great an army by land for some expedition, he hastened thither with 250 of his best ships in quest of them; and finding their fleet, consisting of 350 sail, at anchor in the mouth of the river Eurymedon, and their land army encamped on the shore by, he first assaulted their fleet; which being soon put to the rout, and having no other way to fly but up the river, were all taken, every ship of them, and 20,000 men in them, the rest having either escaped to land, or been slain in the fight. After this, while his forces were thus flushed with success, he put them ashore, and fell on the land army, and overthrew them also with a great slaughter; whereby he got two great victories in the same day, of which one was equal to that of Salamis, and the other to that of Platæa. And having gotten information, that there were eighty more Phoenician ships coming to join the Persian fleet, he surprised them in the harbour, before they had any notice of the late defeat, and destroyed every ship of them; and all the men on board were either drowned or slain in the fight. After which success, Cimon returned home in great triumph, and very much enriched and adorned Athens with the spoils got in this expedition.

Anno 470. Xerxes 16.

The next year [a] Cimon sailed to the Hellespont; and, falling on the Persians, who had taken possession of the Thracian Chersonesus, drove them out thence, and subjected their country again to the Athenians; though in truth (it having been the [b] principality of his father Miltiades) he had the best right to it himself. After this he subdued the Thasians, who had revolted from the Athenians, and then, landing his army on the opposite shore of Thrace, he seized all the gold mines on those coasts, and brought under him all that country as far as Macedon, and thereby opened a way for the conquering of that realm also, would he have pursued the opportunity: for [c] the omitting of which, he was afterwards, on his return, brought to trial for his life before the Athenians, a if he had been corrupted by the Macedonians to spare them, and hardly escaped being condemned for it.

Anno 469. Xerxes 17.

Xerxes, being at last daunted and wholly discouraged by the continued series of so many losses and defeats, gave over all thoughts

---

[a] Plutarchus in Cimone.
[b] Herodotus, lib. 6.
[c] Plutarchus in Cimone.

thoughts of any longer carrying on the Grecian war; and therefore, from this time, [a] no more of his ships were seen in the Ægean sea, or any of his forces on the coasts adjoining to it, all the remainder of his reign.

Anno 456.
Xerxes 21.
After this, Xerxes giving himself wholly up to luxury and ease, minded nothing but the gratifying of his pleasures and his lusts; whereby growing into contempt with the people, [b] Artabanus, the captain of his guards, and one who had been long in prime favour and authority with him, conspired against him, and having drawn Mithridates, one of his eunuchs that was his chamberlain, into the plot, by his means got into his bed-chamber, and there slew him, while he slept in his bed; and then, going to Artaxerxes, his third son, acquainted him of the murder, and accused Darius his elder brother to be the author of it, telling him, that it was done to make his way to the throne; that it was his design to cut him off next to secure himself in it; and that therefore it behoved him to look to himself. All which Artaxerxes, as being then a very young man, rashly believing, without any farther examination, to be true, and being irritated thereby in such a manner as Artabanus intended, went immediately to his brother's apartment, and there, by the assistance of Artabanus and his guards, slew him also. And this he did, as he thought, by way of just revenge for the death of his father, and for the securing of his own safety, being imposed on and deceived by the craft of the traitor, who excited him hereto. The next heir was Hystaspes the second of Xerxes; but he being absent in Bactria, of which province he was governor, Artabanus took Artaxerxes, as being next at hand, and put him on the throne; but with design to let him sit on it no longer than till he had formed a party strong enough to seize it for himself. He having been long in great authority, had made many creatures, and he had also seven sons all grown up to be men of robust bodies, and advanced to great dignities in the empire; and his confidence in these was that which put his ambition on this design: but while he was hastening it to a conclusion, Artaxerxes, having got a full discovery of the whole plot, by the means of Megabyzus, who had married one of his sisters, was before hand with him in a counterplot, and cut him off before his treason was fully ripened for execution; whereby having secured himself in thorough possession of the kingdom, he held it 41 years.

He is said to have been [c] the handsomest person of the age

in

---

[a] Plutarchus in Cimone.
[b] Ctesias. Diodorus Siculus, lib. 11. Justin. lib. 3. c. 1.
[c] Strabo, lib. 15. p. 735.

in which he lived, and to have been a prince [a] of a very mild and generous difpofition; he is called by the Greek hiftorians Μακροχειρ, or Longimanus (*i. e.* the long-handed) [b] by reafon of the more than ordinary length of his hands; for they were fo long, that, on his ftanding upright, he could touch his knees with them. But in fcripture he hath the name of Ahafuerus, as well as that of Artaxerxes, and was the fame who had Efther for his queen. I acknowledge there are two very great men, whofe opinion differ from me herein, Archbifhop Ufher, and Jofeph Scaliger.

The former [c] holdeth that it was Darius Hyftafpes that was the king Ahafuerus who married Efther; and that Atoffa was the Vafhti, and Artyftona the Efther of the holy fcriptures. But all that is faid of thofe perfons by the hiftorians who have written of them is wholly inconfiftent herewith: for Herodotus pofitively tells us, that Artyftona [d] was the daughter of Cyrus, and therefore fhe could not be Efther; and that [e] Atoffa had four fons by Darius, befides daughters, all born to him by her after he was king; and therefore fhe could not be that queen Vafhti, who was divorced from the king her hufband [f] in the third year of his reign, nor he that Ahafuerus that divorced her. Furthermore, Atoffa is faid to have had that predominant intereft with Darius even to the time of his death, that it was by her means that, in the laft act of his life, [g] he was influenced to fettle the fucceffion of his crown on Xerxes her fon, to the difinheriting of all his elder fons, who were born to him by a former wife; whereas the Ahafuerus of the book of Efther had removed Vafhti both from his bed and from his prefence by [h] an unalterable decree: and therefore never could admit her again to either all his life after. That which chiefly induced the learned archbifhop to be of this opinion was, that whereas it is faid of Ahafuerus [i] in the book of Efther, that he laid a tribute upon the land, and upon the ifles, [k] the fame is alfo faid of Darius Hyftafpes by Herodotus; and therefore he thought, that they were both the fame perfon. But Strabo, who is an author of as good, if not better credit, attributeth this to [l] Longimanus. It muft be acknowledged, that in the printed copies which we now have of that author, it is read Darius Longimanus in the place which I refer to. But the title Longimanus, and the defcription of the perfon af-

ter

---

[a] Plutarch. in Artaxerxe Mnemone.
[b] Plutarch. et Strabo, ib.
[c] In Annalibus Veteris Teftamenti, fub anno J. P. 4193.
[d] Herodot. lib. 3. et lib. 7.
[e] Herodot. lib. 7. fub initio.
[f] Efther i. 3.
[g] Herodot. lib. 7.
[h] Efther i. 19.
[i] Chap. x. 1.
[k] Herodot. lib. 3.
[l] Strabo, lib. 15. p. 735.

ter in that place added, can belong to none but to the Artaxerxes whom we now speak of; and therefore it is manifest, that there Darius is put instead of Artaxerxes, by the corruption of the text.

Scaliger's opinion is, [a] that Xerxes was the Ahasuerus, and Hamestris, his queen, the Esther of the holy scriptures. His main reason for it is, the similitude that is between the names of Hamestris and Esther. But how much more the dissimilitude of their characters proves the contrary, hath been already shewn; and what will be hereafter said of her dealing with Inarus and the Greeks taken with him in Egypt, and her frequent adulteries, will be a farther confirmation of it. Furthermore it appears from [b] Herodotus, that Xerxes had a son by Hamestris that was marriageable in the 7th year of his reign; and therefore it is impossible she could be Esther; for Esther was not married to Ahasuerus [c] till the 7th year of his reign, nor could possibly have been taken into his bed sooner than two years before. For, according to the sacred history, [d] it was the 4th year of Ahasuerus, when the choice of virgins was made for him, and a [e] whole year being employed in the purifications, whereby they were prepared for his bed, she could not be called thither till the 5th year of his reign; and therefore the 6th was the soonest that she could have a son by him. Besides Artaxerxes, the third son of Hamestris, [f] being grown up to the state of a man at the death of his father, (which happened in the 21st year of his reign) he must have been born before the 6th year of his reign. All which put together, do sufficiently prove, how much soever the names Esther and Hamestris may be alike, the persons could not be the same.

But there being no such objections as to Artaxerxes Longimanus, it is most probable that he was the person. The ancientest and best evidences that can be had of this matter, are from the Greek version of the sacred text, called the Septuagint, the apocryphal additions to the book of Esther, and Josephus; and all these agree for Artaxerxes Longimanus. For Josephus [g] positively tells us it was he; and the Septuagint, through the whole book of Esther, wherever the Hebrew text hath Ahasuerus, translate Artaxerxes; and the apocryphal additions to that book every where call the husband of Esther, Artaxerxes, who could

be

---

[a] De Emendatione, lib. 6.
[b] Lib. 9.
[c] Esther ii. 16.
[d] Esther ii.
[e] Esther ii. 12.
[f] Diodor. Sic. lib. 11.
[g] Antiq. lib. 11. c. 6.

be none other than Artaxerxes Longimanus; for there are several circumstances related of him, both in the canonical and apocryphal Esther, which can by no means be applicable to the other Artaxerxes, called Mnemon. And Severus Sulpitius, and many other writers, as well of the ancients as the moderns, come also into this opinion. And the extraordinary [a] favour and kindness which Artaxerxes Longimanus shewed the Jews, beyond all the other kings that reigned in Persia, first in sending Ezra, and after, Nehemiah, for the repairing of the broken affairs of that people in Judah and Jerusalem, and the restoring of them again to their ancient prosperity, is what can scarce be accounted for on any other reason, but that they had in his bosom such a powerful advocate as Esther to solicit for them. But these, and the other transactions of this king, will be the subject of the next ensuing book.

[a] There were two other kings of Persia, that shewed kindness to the Jews, Cyrus, and Darius Hystaspes. Each of them granted a decree in favour of the Jews: but Artaxerxes went beyond them both; for he granted two decrees, by virtue of which both the ecclesiastical and political state of the Jews were throughly restored: and therefore, where the scripture names those kings of Persia by whose favour this restoration was made, he is named among them in the order as he reigned; for it is said (Ezra vi. 14.), that this was done by the commandment of Cyrus, Darius, and Artaxerxes, *i. e.* Cyrus, the founder of the Persian empire, Darius Hystaspes, and Artaxerxes Longimanus. For of these, and none other, is that text undoubtedly to be understood; and, no doubt, when the church and state were restored, much was done for the restoration of the temple also.

THE END OF VOLUME FIRST.

www.ingramcontent.com/pod-product-compliance
Lightning Source LLC
Chambersburg PA
CBHW030820230426
43667CB00008B/1309